Who Cares

Who Cares

The Social Safety Net in America

CHRISTOPHER HOWARD

OXFORD
UNIVERSITY PRESS

Oxford University Press is a department of the University of Oxford. It furthers
the University's objective of excellence in research, scholarship, and education
by publishing worldwide. Oxford is a registered trade mark of Oxford University
Press in the UK and certain other countries.

Published in the United States of America by Oxford University Press
198 Madison Avenue, New York, NY 10016, United States of America.

© Oxford University Press 2023

Library of Congress Control Number: 2022030847
ISBN 978–0–19–007446–3 (pbk.)
ISBN 978–0–19–007445–6 (hbk.)

DOI: 10.1093/oso/9780190074456.001.0001

1 3 5 7 9 8 6 4 2

Paperback printed by Lakeside Book Company, United States of America
Hardback printed by Bridgeport National Bindery, Inc., United States of America

To Dee, my partner in caring

Anthropologist Margaret Mead was once asked what she considered the earliest evidence of civilization. She answered that it was a human thigh bone with a healed fracture that had been excavated from a fifteen-thousand-year-old site. For an early human being to have survived a broken femur, living through the months that were required for the bone to heal, the person had to have been cared for—sheltered, protected, brought food and drink. While other animals care for their young and injured, no other species is able to devote as much time and energy to caring for the most frail, ill, and dying of its members.

—Ira Byock, M.D., *The Best Care Possible* (2012)

CONTENTS

ACKNOWLEDGMENTS

Writing a book during a pandemic was a strange experience, with plenty of ups and downs. Having a big project and gradually making progress probably helped my sanity. Finding uninterrupted time in the office was easy. If I felt like working at home in the evening or on the weekend, well, I wasn't planning to go out anyway. However, the usual sources of feedback were harder to tap into. Academic conferences were postponed or held virtually. Colleagues had less time and energy than usual to read draft chapters, and understandably so. For two years it felt like I was trying to assemble a complicated device without any instructions and without much help from customer service.

Fortunately, some people did step up. Political theory is not my strong suit, and Claire McKinney helped me understand the work of care theorists. Bob Greenstein, Sarah Halpern-Meekin, Kevin Howard, and Rob Hudson offered constructive feedback on individual chapters. Dee Holmes and Stephen Howard read the entire manuscript. They are not academics, and happily so. They helped ensure that whatever I wrote would be clear to a general audience. As family members, they also lifted my spirits many times. My parents, Alice Howard and Alan Howard, stayed interested and supportive throughout. Indirectly, my undergraduate students played an important role. I have been teaching US social policy for almost 30 years, and this book is designed to answer many of their questions.

My thanks to the College of William & Mary, which granted me a research leave during the 2019–20 academic year. Without this sort of support, it would be hard for me to teach five courses a year, serve as an academic advisor to students, work on committees, and still find time to research and write. Some scholars may not need funds for lab equipment or international travel, but we do need time.

My editor at Oxford University Press, David McBride, had faith in this project from the beginning, even though my initial proposal was long on ambition and short on theory. The anonymous reviewers were very helpful at the proposal stage, suggesting central themes that might unify the project, and again when the manuscript was complete. They also offered words of encouragement that I needed to hear. Emily Benitez was my project editor at Oxford, and she was organized and responded promptly to my questions and concerns. The whole process felt remarkably normal, which is a testament to how well the Press functioned during the pandemic.

Finally, I want to acknowledge my own shortcomings in creating a comprehensive map of the social safety net. As much as I have tried to eliminate factual errors, describe patterns accurately, and think through the larger implications, some readers will find mistakes. When that happens, perhaps you can find a care-ful way of pointing them out.

Introduction

The original idea for this book was to offer "a bird's-eye view of the social safety net." That was the phrase I repeated to anyone who asked what I was working on; that was basically my sales pitch to Oxford University Press. And why do we need such a book? One reason is that our understanding of poverty in the United States is fragmented and disjointed. Many scholars focus on individual social programs such as Medicaid or "welfare" (Berkowitz and DeWitt 2013; Gilens 1999; King 2000; Levine 2008; Michener 2018; Soss, Fording, and Schram 2011; Weaver 2000). Other scholars offer richly detailed profiles of one or two communities, or a handful of families, living in poverty (Campbell 2014; DeLuca, Clampet-Lundquist, and Edin 2016; Desmond 2016; Halpern-Meekin et al. 2015; Hays 2003; Newman and Chen 2007; Rosen 2020; Venkatesh 2002). Although our knowledge is deep in certain ways, broader patterns are harder to see. Another source of fragmentation in the literature is the public–private divide. Those who study government programs, mentioned above, are not the same people who study the role of churches, secular charities, and other non-profit organizations (Brooks 2006; Cnaan 2002; Reich 2018; Salamon 2012; Wuthnow 1991, 2004).[1] Yet we know that both governments and nonprofits care for millions of disadvantaged people every year.

The puzzle is how these different pieces fit together. As someone who teaches policy courses, I have been grappling with this puzzle for years. I wrote this book partly to give students (and myself) a general map of the social safety net. My aim is not to replace the terrific in-depth research, but to put that work in a larger context. A good map could be useful to a variety of students, teachers, and researchers who want to understand poverty and need.

Ideally, this book will be more than a classroom tool. It is hard to find public officials, policy experts, or media pundits who are satisfied with the social safety net. We are told that the status quo is too generous—no, it is woefully inadequate. Policymakers constantly argue about how to fix this policy, cut that program, or add a new benefit. We hear bold claims about what individuals,

Who Cares. Christopher Howard, Oxford University Press. © Oxford University Press 2023.
DOI: 10.1093/oso/9780190074456.003.0001

families, employers, churches, charities, or governments should do differently. These debates have been going on for generations, and they show no signs of ending. Too often they are based on convenient stereotypes, partial information, or wishful thinking. These debates might be more productive if we had a better picture of the entire safety net. (To extend the map metaphor, it is hard to navigate through a dense forest when all you see are the trees and bushes right around you.)

One book will not settle all these disagreements. We live in a polarized era where opposing sides routinely talk past each other or vilify each other. When it comes to social policy, liberals stress the value of government action. Some of their favorite examples are the New Deal, Great Society, and Affordable Care Act—all spearheaded by Democratic presidents. When conservatives try to limit government's role, liberals view them as indifferent to the plight of others, perhaps even cruel.[2] Naturally, conservatives resent being called heartless. They think of themselves as pro-civil society, not anti-poor. Conservatives often sing the praises of churches, charities, and volunteers. They see liberals as all too willing to spend other people's taxes on programs that foster dependence. Although this book will not magically end polarization, it might help readers, whatever their political beliefs, appreciate how different parts of society try to meet basic human needs.

The Covid-19 pandemic provided a stark reminder of how vulnerable we are. The health care system was stretched to the breaking point in 2020. As millions of people lost their jobs, hunger and homelessness became bigger threats. While the pandemic affected everyone, some groups—low-income, disabled, elderly, Black, Hispanic—were especially vulnerable. I never anticipated such a crisis when starting this project, and most of the evidence in this book comes from the years just before the pandemic. The timing is important: *Who Cares* reveals how the American social safety net operates under conditions that could be considered routine, maybe even favorable. Whatever social problems that emerge in the following pages cannot be blamed on Covid-19. Restoring the social safety net to its pre-pandemic state is an option, but doing so could leave millions of Americans struggling with a wide range of hardships.

Like most big projects, this one started slowly. I gradually realized that my handy catchphrase, bird's-eye view of the social safety net, was too ambiguous. In practice, the concept of "safety net" has multiple meanings. Sometimes it is limited to government programs, but other times it embraces the work of charitable organizations. Often the safety net refers to programs available only to low-income people, but sometimes it extends to programs like Social Security that benefit the poor and non-poor. It would be important to clarify what the "social safety net" includes and excludes. Likewise, I ought to acknowledge that many countries have safety nets, and this book is limited to the United States.[3]

My other problem was figuring out how to view the world with a bird's eyes. Was I promising to show readers the entire safety net while soaring high above the ground? This seemed like a genuinely bad approach; a book about everything would take forever to finish. It would probably be very long and boring. Alternatively, a bird's-eye view might require the equivalent of perching in a tree and scanning a small patch of ground for food. For someone trying to produce a general map, that approach didn't make much sense, either.

Clearly, I needed to think harder about the task at hand. This introductory chapter provides the conceptual and theoretical foundation for the rest of the book.

The Social Safety Net

When policy experts talk about the safety net, the first pieces they mention are government programs aimed at low-income people (Bruch, Meyers, and Gornick 2018; Currie 2006; Greenstein 2016; Minton and Giannarelli 2019; Tach and Edin 2017; Waldfogel 2013). Temporary Assistance for Needy Families (TANF), aka "welfare," is a classic example. So are Medicaid and public housing. All these programs require a means test. Individuals who want to receive benefits must prove that their income, and probably their assets, fall below some dollar threshold. If you have little means of supporting yourself, then you might get help from government. Benefits are not distributed by right; they are based on financial need. These means-tested programs are also known as public assistance.

Although public assistance belongs in any discussion of the safety net, we should not stop there. Social insurance programs such as Medicare and Social Security benefit millions of Americans, regardless of income. Individuals earn these benefits, usually with a history of paid employment.[4] Social insurance is especially important in providing income support and medical care. In fact, Social Security moves more Americans out of poverty than any other social program (Meyer and Wu 2018). If we want to know what government does to help poor people, then we need to consider public assistance *and* social insurance. Whether the benefits are narrowly targeted or widely distributed is largely irrelevant. For someone struggling to make ends meet, a dollar from Social Security buys just as much as a dollar from TANF.

This broader vision of the safety net is entirely consistent with the original understanding of social insurance. When President Franklin Roosevelt signed the historic Social Security Act of 1935 into law, he chose his words carefully. "We can never insure one hundred percent of the population against one hundred percent of the hazards and vicissitudes of life, but we have tried to frame a law which will give some measure of protection to the average citizen and to his family against the loss of a job and against poverty-ridden old age" (Roosevelt 1935). From the beginning, Social Security was portrayed as an anti-poverty program. Three decades later, President Johnson delivered his famous State of the Union message where he declared war on poverty. He urged Congress to create a number of programs, including this one: "We must provide hospital insurance for our older citizens financed by every worker and his employer under Social Security, contributing no more than $1 a month during the employee's working career to protect him in his old age in a dignified manner without cost to the Treasury, against the devastating hardship of prolonged or repeated illness" (Johnson 1964). One of our most important anti-poverty programs, Medicare, was enacted in 1965.[5]

There is another, more subtle reason for expanding our conception of the safety net beyond public assistance. Many people make sharp distinctions between "us" and "them" when discussing poverty. We, hard-working taxpayers, deserve help. We are morally and legally entitled to government benefits because of years of paid employment. Those poor people are just looking for handouts. They would rather ride in the wagon than help pull it. They should be grateful for whatever we give them. This line of thinking conveniently overlooks the working poor—millions of Americans who have low-wage jobs and pay taxes. A poor worker might be receiving food assistance at the same time her Medicare payroll taxes are helping a middle-class retiree pay his hospital bills. Moreover, believing these tiers are truly separate understates how vulnerable we all are. Sociologists Mark Rank and Thomas Hirschl have calculated that almost 60 percent of Americans will live in poverty for at least one year between the ages of 20 and 75. Two-thirds of Americans will receive means-tested assistance at some point during their working years (Rank, Eppard, and Bullock 2021; Rank and Hirschl 2015). Most of us will need help from social insurance and public assistance when coping with material hardship. The lines separating "us" and "them" are fuzzier than we care to admit.

Some studies consider unemployment insurance as part of the safety net (Bitler, Hoynes, and Kuka 2017). Others include Social Security (McGarry 2013). The 2020 Democratic Party platform referred to Social Security as "the most enduring thread in our nation's social safety net."[6] Once you make room for one social insurance program, it is hard, logically, to exclude the others. This book incorporates all the major social insurance programs—Social Security, Medicare, Disability Insurance, Unemployment Insurance, and Workers' Compensation (similar to Loprest and Nightingale 2018). Such programs might not be the most efficient way to reduce poverty. However, this book is not an exercise in cost-benefit analysis. Social insurance programs help many low-income Americans meet their basic needs, and that is what matters.

The safety net does not end with public assistance and social insurance. In the United States, tax expenditures and social regulations are important tools of public policy (Gitterman 2010; Hacker 2002; Howard 1997, 2007; see also Olsen 2019). A few of them, notably the Earned Income Tax Credit (EITC) and minimum wage laws, are explicitly designed to help low-income workers. They certainly belong in this book and have been discussed in prior studies of the safety net (Currie 2006; Loprest and Nightingale 2018; Tach and Edin 2017; Waldfogel 2013). One can find other, more inclusive examples of these tools (e.g., tax expenditures for job-related health insurance and retirement pensions, the Family and Medical Leave Act). Unlike Social Security, they typically do not benefit low-income Americans that much.

Attentive readers might notice that I have mentioned the poor as well as the near poor and people with low incomes. What started out as a book about poverty seems to be expanding in scope. This is true, for reasons that will become apparent in the coming chapters. Like "safety net," "poverty" turns out to be a somewhat elastic concept. We will see that ordinary Americans and leading nonprofits define poverty more broadly than government agencies do (Chapters 1, 3). In addition, many public assistance programs distribute benefits to people above and below the official poverty thresholds (Chapters 5–9).

Every map requires boundaries. In this book, the emphasis is on relief from material hardship. A safety net catches people after they have fallen on hard times and provides them with the resources needed to survive. Income. Food. Housing. Medical care. The daily care that children and people with disabilities require. There are other types of hardship; readers interested in social poverty or spiritual poverty will have to look elsewhere (e.g., Halpern-Meekin 2019; Helminiak 2020). For the most part I also exclude efforts to prevent hardship, such as education, job training, and anti-discrimination laws. Those kinds of initiatives are undoubtedly crucial to reducing poverty in the long run. They might be thought of as ladders to help people move up, after a net has cushioned their fall.[7]

This book does not cover every form of material hardship. Some international organizations think of safety nets as protecting people against economic shocks and natural disasters.[8] Floods, hurricanes/typhoons, and earthquakes can produce just as much misery as economic recessions, and those disasters often prompt massive relief efforts. However, if I count attempts to help individuals rebuild their homes after a major hurricane, then I should probably include efforts to help farmers rebound from an infestation or disease that wiped out their crops. I might have to distinguish between natural and man-made disasters, which is often complicated.[9] The scope of this project is already ambitious. I will follow the scholarly convention and exclude relief from natural disasters as part of the US social safety net.

My understanding of the "social" part of the social safety net is broad. It includes the public safety net of government programs, which is what most studies emphasize (Bitler, Hoynes, and Kuka 2017; Currie 2006; Loprest and Nightingale 2018; Tach and Edin 2017). It includes the "family safety net" (Cherlin and Seltzer 2014), such as when adult relatives help with child care. And it includes nonprofit organizations such as food banks, free and charitable clinics, and homeless shelters that help millions of low-income Americans every year. Many of these organizations operate with minimal support from government; they rely more on volunteers, foundation grants, and charitable donations. In short, the social safety net reflects our collective efforts to take care of those in need.

Teaching college students has nudged me toward this broader understanding of the safety net. For years my courses have focused almost entirely on the public safety net. Periodically, students have asked questions like, "If food stamps run out before the end of the month, can poor people get what they need from a local food pantry?" Or, "What happens to all the people on waiting lists for public housing—can they find shelter somewhere, or will they be homeless?" These are great questions, ones that I usually answer with "it depends" (true, but weak) or "I don't know." Policymakers grapple with the same kinds of questions, arguing whether cuts to the public safety net will produce greater hardship or will be offset by help from other parts of society. This book should help readers understand how much help the poor can get outside of public programs.

A brief warning: anyone expecting the social safety net to be divided neatly into public and private sections will be disappointed. The individual pieces range from largely public (e.g., Social Security) to largely private (e.g., the Pocatello Free Clinic in Idaho), with many combinations in between.[10] The public–private mix is pervasive in the social safety net, as it is throughout American society. Having so many organizations involved, however, is no guarantee of adequacy or coherence.

By the end of this book, some readers might conclude that "social safety net" is a deeply misleading term. If millions of Americans are still poor, still hungry, or still struggling to pay medical bills and rent, then whatever we are doing has not made them safe. A net with so many holes hardly qualifies as a net. We should find a more accurate way of describing what we do to address material hardship. I am very sympathetic to this view, but I do not have a better phrase in mind.[11] In the following pages, I will abide by custom and refer to the social safety net without qualification.

Theoretical Framework

To produce a good map of anything, one must decide which features to highlight and which to ignore. A map of New York City that displayed every single building would not be very useful; the same goes for a map of the Amazon basin showing every tree. Both maps would overwhelm the reader with detail, and they would be out of date as soon as they were published. A good map helps orient users to the general terrain and lets them figure out how to explore in more depth. Because there is no one right way to generate such a map, the best I can do is be transparent about my choices.

By design, this map will not highlight the day-to-day struggles of people living in or near poverty. Many writers, especially journalists and sociologists, have done a remarkable job of conveying these painful realities (Abramsky 2013; Collins and Mayer 2010; DeLuca, Clampet-Lundquist, and Edin 2016; DeParle 2004; Desmond 2016; Ehrenreich 2011; Edin and Shaefer 2015; Hays 2003; Rosen 2020; Sherman 2009; Shipler 2004; Tirado 2014; Venkatesh 2002). These studies follow in the footsteps of classics such as Michael Harrington's *The Other America* and Carol Stack's *All Our Kin*. These books help readers understand, in their head and their heart, what it means to be poor. I challenge anyone to read this literature and conclude that people living in poverty have it easy. The chronic stress of their lives is palpable. As an author, I don't see much opportunity to add value here.[12]

This project devotes more attention to those who help care for millions of Americans facing material hardship. The concept of *care* is central. Readers might be surprised to hear a political scientist talk at length about care, and understandably so. It's not exactly one of our specialties. To better grasp the meanings and manifestations of care, we need to borrow insights from political theory. This book aims to provide a theoretically informed, empirically grounded map of the social safety net.

My approach builds on the work of a well-known theorist, Joan Tronto. She has been thinking and writing about care for most of her professional career. Her best-known books are *Moral Boundaries: A Political Argument for an Ethics of Care* (1993) and *Caring Democracy: Markets, Equality, and Justice* (2013). As of June 2022, *Moral Boundaries* had been cited in more than 8,800 books and articles, a sign of its tremendous scholarly impact. The title of my book is based on a related essay she published in 2015.

Tronto notes that "care" in everyday language has two very different connotations—love and support, or burden. Caring about a favorite sports team captures the more positive meaning. Saying that I don't have a care in the world captures the negative sense of problem or load.[13] The practice of caring often entails both. When parents care for their children, when doctors and nurses care for their patients, or when people care for their gardens, they experience the joys and difficulties of caring. This duality captures an essential feature of the social safety net. Caring for the poor and near poor requires actions that we might wholeheartedly support (e.g., feeding a hungry child), and that we might find burdensome (e.g., paying taxes to buy that food).

Tronto and other scholars (e.g., Barnes 2012; Noddings 2002; Sevenhuijsen 2003; Stone 2008) have argued that needing care is an inescapable feature of the human condition. We spend the first years of our lives depending heavily on the care of others: babies don't change their own diapers; children don't earn enough money to pay the rent. When we are adults, friends help us celebrate our personal victories and cope with our losses. Co-workers pitch in when we have challenging assignments. We periodically depend on a doctor's care when we get sick. Should we need hospitalization, we depend on other people to pay taxes or insurance premiums in order to subsidize our care. Following a layoff or serious injury, we might need help compensating for lost wages. In old age we could require the same kinds of daily care that we received as a child. Those who are seriously disabled require constant care.

The implications of this insight are profound. Americans take pride in seeing themselves as rugged individualists. Granted, we need other people to serve in the military and build our highways. But otherwise, individuals are expected to be autonomous and self-sufficient. Americans express this belief in many ways: we should pull ourselves up by our bootstraps, be the captain of our own ship, the author of our own story. In this culture, dependence is, at best, a sign of temporary failure. It could also indicate deeper character flaws such as laziness, promiscuity, or a failure to save. In general, being dependent means being irresponsible.

Care theorists believe that human beings experience independence and dependence throughout their lives. At any given moment, individuals will likely be providing care to someone and depending on care from someone else. We spend our lives embedded in networks of caring relationships. "The guiding thought of the ethic of care is that people need each other in order to lead a good life and that they can only exist as individuals through and via caring relationships with each other" (Sevenhuijsen 2003: 183). Academics are not alone in holding this view. Former First Lady Rosalynn Carter is well known for saying that the world consists of four types of people: those who have been caregivers, are caregivers, will be caregivers, or will need caregivers.[14]

From the beginning, Tronto has insisted that care goes beyond an individual's emotional state. Care is a practice; it requires action. Care "includes everything we do to maintain, continue, and repair our 'world' so that we can live in it as well as possible" (Fisher and Tronto 1990: 40).[15] Although self-care is included, "care implies a reaching out to something other than the self" (Tronto 1993: 102). Care can be episodic, such as when we donate canned goods one day to a local food drive. More often, acts of caring are embedded in ongoing relationships. Those relationships could involve just two people, such as parent and child, or a much larger number. Caring relationships between a church and local community, or between the national government and a group of needy citizens, affect the lives of many people. Caring is not limited to other humans, either. Efforts to restore a polluted river would count, as would tending a garden. (Not surprisingly, this analysis of the social safety net will focus on caring among people.)

In subsequent work, Tronto (2013) made an important distinction between necessary care and personal service. Necessary care is something that people cannot provide for themselves. The injured cannot repair their own broken bones; the homeless cannot afford shelter. Those who need such care are vulnerable members of society. Their health and safety depend on someone else taking care of them. Personal service reverses this relationship. If I pay people to clean my house, then I am hiring them to do something I could do myself. They will care for my house as long as I am satisfied with their performance. My ability to purchase such a service reflects power, not weakness. The social safety net provides necessary care to low-income people. It is not a personal service.

Given all the possible ways of caring, it would help to have some general categories. In *Moral Boundaries* (1993), Tronto identified four stages of caring, four distinct ways in which care is expressed. Her later writings (2013, 2015) employed the same approach. We can care about something or someone; we can take care of them; we can be caregivers; and we can be care-receivers. Tronto thus sees caring as a process and a practice. Connecting her framework to my prior knowledge of social policy triggered something of an "aha" moment for me. The perspective of care offers a potentially powerful way of organizing that information—one that can be expressed in plain language, makes intuitive sense, and is powerful enough to illuminate many parts of the social safety net.

The first stage, "to care about," means recognizing a need. People who care about are attentive to the needs of others. Those others are part of some general group, and the commitment to them is likewise general (Tronto 1989). We might care about hunger or the homeless without having any specific individual in mind. How much we care can vary. Some of us might care more about the elderly than working-age adults. Others might care more about the homeless than the medically uninsured. Caring about largely reflects an individual's mental or emotional state. It does not require much action. Nevertheless, this phase is supposed to be crucial. Without recognizing a need, Tronto argues, we are unlikely to take concrete action. Social scientists who study agenda setting and issue attention (Baumgartner and Jones 2005; Flavin and Franko 2017; Kingdon 1984; Witko et al. 2021) will be quite familiar with this line of reasoning.

Part I of this book will try to gauge how much Americans care about people in need. Each chapter is devoted to the views of important segments of American society—the general public, business and labor, churches and other charities, and government officials. Because I want to map the contemporary social safety net, any statements made before the year 2000 are usually excluded. Except for the postscript, the last relevant year is usually 2019, before the pandemic hit. To reduce bias and avoid "cherry-picking" my evidence, I rely on written documents that are issued on a regular basis. These include annual reports, party platforms, presidential State of the Union addresses, and responses to questions that have been asked in multiple national polls. For my purposes, the running record is more instructive than the one-off speech. Whenever possible, I triangulate evidence from a variety of sources in order to identify general patterns.

Figuring out how much anyone cares about anything is difficult. No one has devised a precise, valid Caring Thermometer. Sometimes the best we can do is establish a rank ordering. The Gallup organization, for instance, routinely asks Americans to name the top problems facing the country today. Those answers provide one way to gauge what people care about. Where does poverty rank compared to climate change, terrorism, education, or other issues? For interest groups and public officials, we can study how much they talk about certain issues (Miler 2018; Witko et al. 2021). Organizations like the US Chamber of Commerce and the AFL-CIO often state their top priorities for the coming year. Does fighting poverty, hunger, or homelessness ever make their lists? Since 2000, Democrats and Republicans have mentioned poverty, the poor, or low-income Americans in every one of their national platforms. The two parties have mentioned lots of other groups and issues as well. Who or what are their highest priorities?

The second step in the process is "to take care of." Having recognized some need, we take responsibility for addressing it. In *Moral Boundaries*, Tronto argued that "taking care of involves the recognition that one can act to address these unmet needs" (Tronto 1993: 106). That responsibility might be inherent in one's position, such as parents who take care of their children. Or, individuals might feel responsible because they recognize a need and see "no other way that the need will be met except by our meeting it" (Tronto 1993: 132). Either way, the responsibility is personal. If I want to take care of vulnerable people, I must do something. Perhaps I will donate money to a charitable clinic or pay taxes to support Medicaid. I don't necessarily have to provide care directly, but I have to take some tangible action that contributes to care.

Tronto does not insist that we take care of others in rigidly defined ways. Nor does taking care of require the commitment of a parent or a savior. She favors a "flexible notion of responsibility" (Tronto 1993: 133).[16] In *Caring Democracy*, she returned to the distinction between caring about and taking care of—that is, the difference between perceiving needs and meeting them. "To make the move to meeting needs, one must go to the next level and assign responsibility for meeting those needs to concrete people, groups, and institutions" (Tronto 2013: 49). The sense of responsibility can be less personal. I might believe that charities should take the lead in caring for the poor without ever making a donation. I might believe that the national government should spend billions of dollars on public assistance but count on someone else's taxes to pay the bill. In short, taking care of someone could mean assuming personal responsibility for meeting their needs or assigning that responsibility to someone else.

Each chapter in Part I of the book will analyze two questions: how much do key parts of society care about the poor and near poor, and who should be responsible to take care of them. Broadly speaking, that responsibility could be assigned to the individual/family, the market, the nonprofit/voluntary sector, or government (Walzer 1986). These two questions are related but analytically distinct. Some individuals could care a lot about poverty, others could care a little, yet they all might want churches, charities, and other nonprofits to take care of this problem. Likewise, church leaders might care a lot about hunger, but some might want government to take the lead responsibility.

Part I of this book emphasizes what we say, while Part II examines what we do. Part I is thus more attuned to politics—public opinion, interest groups, political parties. Part II leans more to policy. Each chapter in Part II draws attention to actions that meet material needs such as income and medical care. In each chapter, I will describe how the poor and near poor take care of themselves. It is crucial to recognize that people living on low incomes are not passive objects of care. They are constantly searching for ways to take care of themselves and their families. Wanting to be self-sufficient, they take jobs with low wages or limited hours. Not wanting to be a burden on society, they turn to family and friends for help. They might borrow money to buy groceries or ask to stay awhile in a relative's spare bedroom.

For millions of Americans, these options are not enough. Some combination of government and charity is needed to reduce their hardship. In Part II, we will meet the people who take care of the poor, including those who pay the taxes needed to fund government programs. These people are usually overlooked by academics. For years the focus has been on benefits received, not taxes paid.[17] Chapters 5–9 try to rectify that imbalance. Readers should not expect the funders to be the same people in every chapter. Income support programs are financed by a wide range of taxpayers (Chapter 5). When it comes to food and housing assistance (Chapters 6 and 7), affluent Americans are responsible for most of the funding. Put bluntly, while some people volunteer to take care of the needy, many of us are coerced by government into doing so.

The third stage involves caregiving. Whereas caring about and taking care of can be accomplished at some distance, without face-to-face interaction, caregiving "almost always requires care-givers to come in contact with the objects of care" (Tronto 1993: 107). This is the realm of doctors, nurses, home health aides, and child-care providers. This is where we find volunteers serving meals at soup kitchens or adult children caring for their aged parents. This is also where we can find landlords, grocery stores, and other businesses that are paid by government to care for the poor and near poor. Caregiving can be paid or unpaid, provided by professionals or amateurs. According to Tronto (1993, 2013), competence is an essential quality that all caregivers must have. Simply being attentive to others and willing to assign responsibility for their care is not enough. Someone must be able to deliver that care.

That ability, however, could be constrained by others (Tronto 2015). If elected officials do not allocate enough money for child-care subsidies, then providers might have to put some poor families on a waiting list. If restaurants and grocery stores donate too little food, then soup kitchens might be open fewer hours. The social safety net is full of examples where those who take care of are different than those who give care. The potential for conflict, or at least a disconnect, is substantial. Thus, it makes sense to distinguish between those who take care of the poor and those who give care to them in Chapters 5–9.

In this book, I do not investigate why people take care of the poor or act as caregivers. This is one place where I depart from Tronto. She believes that care requires both action and a "caring disposition" (1993: 105). That disposition should be rooted in a sincere concern for the well-being of another person. The political scientist in me is genuinely unsure how one could measure such a disposition. Most individuals are involved in multiple caring relationships, and their motives can vary. A middle-aged woman might be caring for her teenage child out of a sense of parental duty, and because she genuinely wants that child to thrive. In her mind, feeling obliged to care and wanting to care could vary from week to week, maybe even day to day. This same woman might work at a nursing home, partly because it is the best-paying job available, and volunteer at a local food pantry out of a sense of compassion. Does she have a caring disposition? Hard to say. Furthermore, if a caring disposition is not a fixed characteristic of a person, but is instead a variable attached to each relationship, then the problems of identifying and measuring it, even qualitatively, multiply.

Such problems are not limited to individuals. In many public programs, care is financed by government but delivered by a large network of for-profit and nonprofit organizations. It seems implausible that every caregiver in every one of these organizations would have the same disposition. Helping the poor could be motivated by a chance to turn a profit or earn a paycheck. It could be motivated by empathy, compassion, or a sense of solidarity. The experience of any single recipient of care could vary depending on which organization they dealt with and which person in that organization was responsible. Volunteers at a major food bank might have different motives than full-time employees, who see the food bank as a job and a calling. Again, we face huge obstacles in generalizing about a caring disposition.

Given these difficulties, I will focus on the practice of care. Chapters 5–9 highlight which parts of society take care of the poor and near poor by financing it, and which parts actually give care. Motives and dispositions certainly deserve to be studied. A government program motivated largely by social control will not meet the needs of recipients as well as a program driven by humanitarian concerns. However, sorting through these motives would take more time and space than my bird's eye can afford.

The fourth step in the process is care-receiving. Sometimes this step involves a direct response, such as saying "thank you" to the caregiver. But that option may not be available. Patients getting surgery might not meet or remember all the medical professionals who were involved (Tronto 2015). Those of us who have been helped by any large organization, from The Salvation Army to the national government, usually have no clue which people contributed money toward our care.

For Tronto, the more important question for care-receiving is whether "caring needs have actually been met" (1993: 108). Determining the adequacy of care is complicated. It requires some involvement by the recipients, even if they cannot speak. A baby is crying, gets fed, stops crying, and falls asleep, which leads us to believe that his need for food has been met. A patient's blood pressure drops suddenly during surgery, indicating that his medical care should be modified, immediately. In both examples care is given, leading to a response. "Observing that response, and making judgments about it (for example, whether the care given was sufficient, successful, or complete?) requires the moral quality of *responsiveness.... [T]*he response will often involve noting that new needs emerge as the past ones are met, thus the process continues" (Tronto 2013: 35; italics in original). The quality of responsiveness is just as important as attentiveness, responsibility, and competence.

When recipients of care are conscious and verbal, we must decide how much input they should have regarding the adequacy of their care. One week after back surgery, a doctor might ask a patient to rate his pain level on a scale of one to ten. A high score could lead the doctor to prescribe a different pain medication or modify the plan for physical therapy. In other situations, caregivers do not ask such questions. When schools provide subsidized meals to children, they seldom ask what the children might prefer to eat instead. When state governments issue unemployment checks, they do not ask recipients if the amounts are enough to pay for rent and utilities. It is not obvious which recipients we should listen to, and how we should respond. A related question is how much their input matters relative to other evidence that caregivers or funders deem important.

These questions are complex and require the skills of a theorist to answer them. Frankly, that's not me. Instead I will use common policy measures to evaluate the adequacy of care. Admittedly, these measures reveal more about the quantity than the quality of care. They are important, but not the only ones worth considering.[18] The measures differ from one chapter to the next, which makes sense given the importance of context to care theorists. After noting who takes care of income support and who gives that care, we will see how many Americans remain in poverty, near poverty, or deep poverty (Chapter 5). After doing the same for food assistance, we will see how many Americans are classified as food insecure (Chapter 6). With housing, we can find estimates of homelessness, cost burdens, and physical adequacy (Chapter 7). The key metrics in Chapter 8 will be rates of uninsurance, underinsurance, and access to medical care. Chapter 9 describes the daily care given to children and people with disabilities. Here, relevant measures of adequacy are harder to find. One reason is that states vary in how they define and report abuse and neglect. Moreover, episodes of neglect often go unreported.

Two quick points before leaving this section. This book is certainly not the first to connect the concept of care to social policy (Bond-Taylor 2017; Duffy 2011; Glenn 2010; Hankivsky 2004; Kershaw 2005; Levitsky 2014; Milligan 2009; Sevenhuijsen 2003; Williams 2001). What this book adds is breadth, covering much of the social safety net rather than individual pieces. Most of this literature has been written by feminist scholars who are interested in the ways in which women function as caregivers, at home or at work. You are unlikely to find much discussion of low-income housing, unemployment benefits, or retirement pensions in those studies. You will here. This book is also distinctive in its heavy reliance on empirical evidence—not just numbers but a wide variety of documents as well. This evidence will reveal how care is discussed and practiced throughout the United States. This book does not justify the value of care as an ethical principle, nor does it identify additional moral qualities that are consistent with care.[19]

The other point to stress is that the social safety net is one manifestation of care. We could easily apply the care approach to education, the environment, foreign aid, or other policy domains. The ramifications are so wide-ranging that Tronto has proposed to modify Harold Lasswell's classic definition of politics— who gets what, when, how. In her version, politics is the process of deciding "who is responsible for caring for what, when, where, and how" (Tronto 2013: 46).

To be fair, this understanding of politics is not entirely modern. Two hundred years ago, Thomas Jefferson declared that "the care of human life and happiness, and not their destruction, is the first and only legitimate object of good government."[20] What sets Tronto and other theorists apart is their insistence that care is central to the workings of a good society. Making decisions about care is difficult, with numerous conflicts over who should help and be helped. Recognizing and resolving those conflicts, rather than ignoring or avoiding them, is crucial. In a good society, citizens will be continuously involved in a variety of caring relationships that gradually enhance their attentiveness, responsibility, competence, and responsiveness. In the process, they will come to understand that the balance of giving and receiving care will not be equal every single day. Individuals will take care of and give care when they can, trusting that other people will reciprocate in the future. Such a society would represent a fifth and final phase of caring, "caring with" (Tronto 2013, 2015).[21] However ambitious this book might be, it only addresses some of the issues raised by Tronto's work, and by care theorists in general.

Patterns of Care

Maps are drawn with certain audiences in mind. A map of the Caribbean region for sailors looks different from a map for tourists. I have chosen care as the main theme of this book, believing that sustained attention to different facets of care will appeal to many readers. Nevertheless, care is such a broad concept that we could wander somewhat aimlessly through the social safety net, finding some care here and a bit more over there. Before we start, it would help to identify specific patterns of care that we might find.

Based on previous studies, we expect a clear distinction between the deserving and undeserving poor. Scholars have found evidence of this division as far back as colonial times and argue that it has continued to the present (Handler and Hasenfeld 1991; Jensen 2015; Katz 1986, 2013; Patterson 1994; Watkins-Hayes and Kovalsky 2016). Notions of deservingness are supposed to shape how Americans talk about poverty and what they do about it. Everyone, from ordinary citizens to presidents, is supposed to have ideas about which categories of poor people deserve more help than others. If these ideas are truly powerful, then they should influence whom we care about and who receives care.

Claims about deservingness only get us so far. We still need to know who qualifies as deserving. Employment is a common way of distinguishing between the deserving and undeserving poor (Cancian and Haskins 2014; Desmond 2015a, 2018; Edin and Shaefer 2015; Halpern-Meekin et al. 2015; Meyer and Wu 2018; Newman and Jacobs 2010; Tach and Edin 2017). From this perspective, the working poor truly deserve to be helped. By holding down a job, the working poor are trying to take care of themselves. Having a paid job proves that they respect mainstream American values. They understand that individual achievement should be based on individual effort. The plight of the working poor must be due to factors beyond their control. The non-working poor are much less deserving because they are counting on other people to act responsibly and support them. The non-working poor must have made bad choices, which caused their misery. We would therefore expect the working poor to be favored over the non-working poor throughout the social safety net. For similar reasons, we expect to find work requirements attached to benefits.

Some authors believe this distinction is too simple. We might consider some of the non-working poor to be deserving if we do not expect them to be employed. Children would belong in this category. So would seriously disabled adults and senior citizens. We would not demand these groups to work their way out of poverty (though we might expect their families to play a major role in their care). However, if able-bodied, working-age adults do not have a job and end up in poverty, then we would not feel they deserve to be helped much at all (Jensen and Petersen 2017; Katz 1986, 2013; Levitsky 2014; Watkins-Hayes and Kovalsky 2016). In the coming chapters, I will try to highlight the ways in which one's employment status—working, not working, being unable to work—affects who receives care.

Alternatively, notions of deservingness could be based on ascriptive characteristics such as race, ethnicity, and gender. Who you are might matter more than whether you are employed. Hierarchical values that establish a clear pecking order in society might trump classic liberal values of work and self-sufficiency (Smith 1993). Many scholars believe that US social policy has systematically favored Whites over Blacks and Hispanics for a century or more (Fox 2012; Gilens 1999; Katznelson 2005; Lieberman 1998, 2015; Quadagno 1994; Soss, Fording, and Schram 2011; Ward 2005). Because Whites see themselves as inherently more deserving, and wield political power, they receive good care with little stigma. Whites want eligibility rules that are standardized and objective. Those features are more common in social insurance programs, which were designed from the start to protect White workers against the hazards of injury, unemployment, and old age. Public assistance programs are designed to serve people in poverty, who are disproportionately racial minorities. While eligibility rules vary from state to state, local officials everywhere can make subjective judgments when implementing those rules. Their decisions typically disadvantage poor Blacks and poor Hispanics. Benefits are relatively meager in the lower tier, and recipients are commonly viewed as freeloaders or cheats.

A related literature contends that US social policy consistently favors men over women (Abramovitz 1988; Collins and Mayer 2010; Gordon 1994; Mettler 1998; Mink 1995; Reese, D'Auria, and Loughrin 2015; Sapiro 1986). Gender inequalities are similar to racial inequalities: men are treated relatively well by social insurance programs, while women struggle to make ends meet on public assistance. Gendered policies reward men as breadwinners and neglect women as caregivers. The patterns are so similar, many of the scholars cited above combine race and gender when analyzing US social policy. Programs such as welfare (formerly Aid to Families with Dependent Children, now TANF) are doubly disadvantaged when they serve poor women of color. The other end of the spectrum would be Social Security. It might be unusually popular and generous because many White men benefit.

To a lesser extent, this book will pay attention to patterns related to who we are politically. This part of the map will be much more visible in Part I than Part II. We have the data to compare what Democrats and Republicans say about poverty and need, both at the level of ordinary citizens (Chapter 1) and public officials (Chapter 4). Chapter 2 profiles major labor unions and business associations, which occupy different spots on the political spectrum. The same is true for the evangelical Protestants, Catholics, and mainline Protestants featured in Chapter 3. While Democrats might think that Republicans don't care about people in need, many Republicans would disagree. Political differences should be evident when people talk about taking care of the disadvantaged: those on the left will probably expect government to play a major role, while those on the right will place more responsibility on individuals and charities. In contrast, we have little information about the political leanings of doctors, nurses, child-care workers, and volunteers working at food pantries, making it difficult to link partisanship or ideology to caregiving in Part II of this book.

The concluding chapter will summarize the defining features of the US social safety net. As we will see, parts of society that care most about the poor and near poor are not always the parts that take care of them or give them care. Patterns of caregiving turn out to be different for income than for food, housing, or daily care. Patterns of care-receiving are more consistent. That does not mean the care is consistently adequate. Some groups are left behind, over and over.

The resulting map of the social safety net is based on the first two decades of the 21st century. The world changed dramatically in 2020 with the spread of Covid-19. As I write (June 2022), the pandemic had not ended, and a full account of its impact will have to be written later. The postscript will make some initial observations about how the social safety net performed under extreme duress.

So much for laying a foundation. If I've done my job, readers should understand the conceptual boundaries of the social safety net and have a basic idea of how the care framework is supposed to provide analytical coherence to the overall map. We also have a few educated guesses (aka hypotheses) about specific patterns of care that might emerge. Now is the time to start exploring the social safety net, beginning with the views of ordinary Americans.

PART I

WHAT WE SAY

1

General Public

Every language has a phrase equivalent to "cheap talk" or "lip service." People might say what their audience wants to hear rather than what they truly believe. Of course, I plan to exercise more. Of course, society will make meaningful sacrifices to benefit future generations. Likewise, it would not be surprising to hear people say they care about the poor, the hungry, or the homeless. Anyone who failed to express some concern for others could come across as cold-hearted, inhumane. In a 2017 poll, three-quarters of Americans said they felt compassion at least a few times a week for people they did not know. Only ten percent admitted that they seldom or never felt this way.[1]

Given the potential for cheap talk, this chapter will use a couple of strategies to determine how much Americans truly care about poverty-related issues. The main strategy is to analyze a wide variety of questions from national opinion polls. For example, some questions contain explicit references to poverty, need, or poor people, but other questions do not. Asking Americans if fighting poverty should be a top priority leads to very different results than asking what the top priorities should be. Different survey questions deal with responsibility for taking care of people in need. The question wording varies, and so do the answers. A second strategy is to supplement the survey data with experiments, focus groups, and interviews conducted by other researchers. In short, the plan is to triangulate evidence concerning the public's views from multiple sources.

My approach differs from most studies of public opinion. Polling organizations ask people what they think or how they feel about a wide range of topics. Many questions are quite specific, such as whether we believe Vladimir Putin will do the right thing in world affairs, or whether scientists are good communicators. The answers are recorded and tabulated, and we are told that the results shed light on public opinion. But unless we know how much people care about any of these topics, it is hard to make sense of their answers or predict their behavior. If people don't care about Putin or scientists, for example, then their views might not be that significant.

Who Cares. Christopher Howard, Oxford University Press. © Oxford University Press 2023.
DOI: 10.1093/oso/9780190074456.003.0002

This chapter begins by investigating how much ordinary Americans care about poverty-related issues. It then turns to the question of which parts of society should be responsible for dealing with those issues. As we will see, public opinion is ambiguous in some respects, clear in others. One pattern is quite evident, and has been for decades: Americans care more about poverty than welfare, and they want government to take care of poor people more than welfare recipients. We will spend some time in this chapter investigating why "welfare" has such negative connotations. That word might be associated with an unwillingness to work; it might be connected to lower-status groups such as women and racial minorities; or it might tap into negative feelings toward government.

Caring About

Political theorists like Joan Tronto are not the only ones interested in care. Polling firms routinely ask Americans whether their leaders care about them. "Does Donald Trump impress you as someone who cares about people like yourself?" "Do you think the Democrats in Congress care about the needs and problems of people like you?" Other survey questions ask respondents what they care about. For years the Gallup organization has conducted a monthly poll asking Americans what they consider to be the most important problem facing the country. This question has probably been used more than any other to gauge what ordinary citizens care about.[2] The question is open-ended, allowing individuals to reply however they like. A majority seldom name the same problem. In November 2019, for instance, the number one problem was dissatisfaction with government/poor leadership (33%), followed by immigration (11%). The combination of poverty, hunger, and homelessness received four percent of the total vote. The gap between rich and poor, which probably reflects inequality more than poverty, registered two percent. Welfare was mentioned by less than one-half of one percent.

That survey was not unusual. Nine months earlier, 35 percent of Americans singled out the government/poor leadership as the most important problem and 19 percent named immigration. Just four percent said poverty, hunger, or homelessness. Over the last two decades, poverty-related problems have been considered the most important by a tiny fraction of the American public. Perhaps surprisingly, Americans do not seem to care about poverty more when times are hard. The US poverty rate grew steadily in the 2000s, from a little over 11 percent in 2000 to 15 percent by 2011 and 2012. Yet concern about poverty, hunger, or homelessness was higher in 2000 than in 2011–2012. Toward the end of 2008, when the Great Recession was in full force, only one to two percent of Americans named poverty, hunger, or homelessness as the country's most important problem. Poverty rates declined after 2014, and by 2018, 11.8 percent of Americans were officially poor (Semega et al. 2019). That year, depending on the month, anywhere from one to six percent of the public named poverty, hunger, or homelessness as the country's most important problem. Regardless of the year or the economy, Americans do not seem to care much about anything related to poverty.

Before lamenting the public's indifference, we should put these answers in context. Only the problems of poor leadership and immigration managed to register double-digit support in November 2019. Every other issue was mentioned by less than ten percent of the public. Although a scant four percent of Americans considered poverty, hunger, or homelessness to be the most important problem, even fewer mentioned the environment, pollution, or climate change (3%). Poverty, hunger, or homelessness ranked higher than the federal budget deficit or debt (2%), education (2%), taxes (1%), Social Security (1%), and national security (1%). These are all serious issues that garner attention from the media and public officials. Just because few Americans mention something as the single most important problem does not automatically mean that problem is insignificant.

Some pollsters ask people to name the main problems facing the country, rather than the most important one. In 2017, an NBC News survey gave respondents a list of over 20 issues and asked them to rank the top three in importance. Poverty was one option on the list; hunger and homelessness were not. Four percent of Americans named poverty as the most important issue, and seven percent listed it as the second or third most important. Poverty (11%) was named as one of the top three problems more often than Social Security (6%), abortion (5%), or military strength (4%). It was named less often than health care (38%), education (24%), racism (23%), and a few other issues. In a similar poll conducted by the Associated Press, 12 percent of Americans listed poverty as one of the country's top three problems in 2016. These are not big numbers, but they are larger than what we found with Gallup's most important problem question.

Sometimes Americans are asked to choose the country's single most important problem from a short list of options. These surveys do not help us much, because poverty is usually omitted from the list. The same is true for hunger, homelessness, and welfare. About a week before the 2016 national elections, ABC News and the *Washington Post* ran a survey asking Americans about the single most important policy issue in their upcoming choice for president. The only possible responses were the economy and jobs, terrorism and national security, immigration, health care, and corruption in government. The 2016 Election Day exit polls, conducted by a consortium of news organizations, asked voters to name the top issues facing the country. The available options were the economy, terrorism, foreign policy, and immigration.[3] A CNN poll from October 2017 allowed respondents to choose among national security, the economy, health care, civil rights, foreign policy, or immigration as the country's most important issue. A Fox News poll from April of that year listed many of these same issues along with crime and drugs, the federal deficit, and climate change. We simply cannot tell how much Americans care about poverty based on these types of questions. Nor do we know how much poverty-related issues influence their vote choice. (However, we can gauge how little polling organizations care about poverty.)

One virtue of the polls discussed so far is they ask about problems facing the country. This wording leaves open the possibility that different parts of society— for example, government, charities, employers, individuals, families—could be responsible for addressing those problems. Other polls ask Americans specifically about the most important problems facing government. Once a year, the Pew Research Center asks the public to name their top issue priorities for the president and Congress. Typically, this survey includes 15–20 questions about individual issues, and respondents can indicate the importance of each one independently of the others. This format does not force people to choose their top three issues, and that makes a huge difference. In January 2019, 60 percent of Americans said that "dealing with the problems of poor and needy people" should be a top priority for the president and Congress. Thirty-four percent referred to this as an important but lower priority. Very few felt that it was a low priority or should not be done. Now it appears that almost all Americans care a lot about the disadvantaged, which definitely was not the impression left by the Gallup polls.[4]

Americans named many issues as top priorities in the Pew survey, and some were ranked more highly (e.g., strengthening the economy, reducing health care costs). Nonetheless, more people gave top priority to helping poor and needy people than they did to strengthening the military. Helping poor and needy people outranked dealing with immigration and reducing the budget deficit. Relative to other issues, helping the poor now looks fairly important. Moreover, public concern has been growing. The percentage of Americans calling poverty a top priority for the president and Congress increased from 49 to 60 between 2014 and 2019.

Not everyone is equally supportive. Individuals with lower incomes are more likely to view helping the poor and needy as a top priority. In 2018, over three-quarters of respondents earning less than $20,000 felt that it should be a top priority for the president and Congress, compared to about one-half of those making more than $100,000. Other studies, based on survey data from 1995 to 2015, have found that lower-income Americans are more likely to name poverty, inequality, and the minimum wage as the country's most important problems (Flavin and Franko 2017; Witko et al. 2021).

For every poll showing that the public wants government to pay attention to poverty-related issues, another poll indicates much less concern. A survey conducted for the Associated Press in December 2019 asked, "Thinking about the problems facing the United States and the world today, which problems would you like the government to be working on in the year 2020?" Not a priority, just working on. Individuals could name as many problems as they wanted. Only 16 percent of Americans responded poverty, hunger, or homelessness. Three percent mentioned helping vulnerable groups like the elderly and the poor. Two years earlier, ten percent of Americans said they wanted government to work on poverty, hunger, or homelessness. That's not exactly a clarion call.

While the general level of caring is hard to pin down, the number of people being cared about is surprisingly large. The American Enterprise Institute (AEI) and the *Los Angeles Times* conducted a special national survey about poverty in 2016. It offers an unusually detailed portrait of public attitudes toward poverty. One question asked Americans what percentage of people currently live below the poverty line.[5] The typical respondent thought the US poverty rate was 40 percent. The estimates were even higher among the Black and female respondents. One out of five people estimated that the rate was 50 percent or more. At the time, the official poverty rate was "only" 13 percent. Most people also overestimated how much income a family of two adults and two children could have and still be considered poor by the government. A survey by the Pew Research Center found similarly high estimates of poverty rates in 2014. In both surveys, only 15–20 percent of Americans gave close to the correct (i.e., official) answer. In a 2013 poll, the average estimate of the poverty rate was 39 percent. Beforehand, the pollsters convened a few focus groups to test out their questions. "Most respondents . . . were shocked to hear that the official poverty line was as low as it is; many suggested that it represents a disconnect with the reality of rising prices over the past few years" (Half in Ten Education Fund and the Center for American Progress 2014, quote from p. 2).[6]

A cynic might cite this evidence as proof that Americans know precious little about poverty. This would not be an earth-shattering conclusion, given that most Americans score badly on tests of political knowledge (Annenberg Public Policy Center 2017; Delli Carpini and Keeter 1996).[7] A sympathetic interpretation is that Americans define poverty more broadly than the Census Bureau does. They might believe that the official poverty line is set too low, a criticism that policy experts have been making for decades (Blank 2008; Fisher 1992; National Research Council 1995). A recent study by the United Way, which is in the business of caring, found that 43 percent of US households cannot afford necessities like food, housing, and medical care (Luhby 2018).[8] This figure is quite consistent with public opinion. If ordinary Americans see the world as the United Way does, then maybe their poverty estimates aren't so dumb after all.

In light of these findings, caring about the poor takes on greater significance. The standard survey questions are usually interpreted as signs of how much Americans care about the 35–40 million people who are officially poor. However, if 40 percent of the country lives in poverty, then these surveys reveal how Americans feel about 130 million of their fellow citizens. Telling elected officials to make poverty a top priority would signify a high level of attentiveness.

These findings also suggest that it makes sense to treat "poverty" and "the poor" as flexible concepts. The official definitions are important because they affect eligibility for government benefits. But those definitions could be flawed, and broader conceptions might be appropriate. As we'll see in Chapter 3, both the United Way and The Salvation Army believe that the poverty line underestimates the true level of need in the United States. In general, it makes sense to study what political actors say about low-income Americans who are facing serious hardships, even those who are not officially poor.

Taking Care Of

Traditionally, polling organizations have framed the issue of poverty as one of individual versus governmental responsibility. Given these two options, most Americans believe that government should be involved. One standard question, featured in the General Social Survey (GSS), is whether "the government in Washington should do everything possible to improve the standard of living of all poor Americans," or whether "each person should take care of himself."[9] The wording makes the results a little hard to interpret. While someone might not want the national government heavily involved, they could feel differently about state and local governments. In addition, "do everything possible" seems like a tall order. Respondents might want the national government to do a lot, but not everything possible. The GSS allows respondents to place themselves on a 1–5 scale. Anyone answering 1 or 2 will be counted as pro–government responsibility. In 2016, 32 percent of Americans were pro-government, and another 43 percent agreed that government and individuals were both responsible for addressing this problem. These numbers have been fairly stable for the last decade, and they suggest broad support for some type of public safety net (Howard et al. 2017).

In recent decades, 60–70 percent of Americans have agreed that government has a responsibility "to take care of people who can't take care of themselves."[10] This question is one of the few to mention care explicitly. Again, the wording is somewhat ambiguous. An affirmative answer might not apply to everyone in poverty if Americans believe that some of the poor can take care of themselves. Likewise, someone who agreed with this statement might be thinking about those who are young, old, sick, or disabled, but who are not poor. A CBS News poll from 2018 asked a variant of this question, dropping the language about government responsibility and referring instead to "what the American way of life represents." In that context, 80 percent of Americans said that it was "very important" to take care of people who cannot care for themselves. Results from this survey were considerably stronger than answers to questions about government responsibility, suggesting that many Americans expect other parts of society to be involved.

Most survey questions try to measure the public's support for government aid targeted at the poor. Broadly inclusive policies can reduce poverty, too. The American National Election Studies (ANES) routinely asks whether the national government should "see to it that every person has a job and a good standard of living," or should let people fend for themselves. While a guaranteed job or income would benefit a wide range of people, the poor would gain the most. Few Americans support such a guarantee. The ANES allows individuals to place themselves on a seven-point scale, and only 28 percent chose one of the three points on the government side of the scale in 2016. In 2008, during the Great Recession, the corresponding number was higher (35%), yet still far from a majority. Americans are much more likely to say that government has a responsibility to "provide a decent standard of living for the old." In the 2016 GSS, 47 percent of respondents definitely agreed that government had such a responsibility, and another 40 percent said this was probably government's responsibility. We can see why Social Security and Medicare are quite popular.

Broad guarantees of food, shelter, and medical care are viewed more positively than promises of income or employment. Most Americans agree that "the government should guarantee every citizen enough to eat and a place to sleep" (Howard et al. 2017). Because the poor are more likely to be hungry or homeless, they would certainly benefit. The GSS regularly poses a question about helping people pay their medical bills, with government responsibility at one end of a five-point scale and individual responsibility at the other. Such help should be especially important to people with low incomes. Slightly over half of Americans saw this as government's responsibility in 2018. A small minority (18%) believed it was the individual's responsibility, and the rest (29%) said responsibility should be shared. Those numbers have not changed much since 2000. A survey conducted by the Associated Press in 2019 found that two-thirds of Americans felt that the government should have a great deal or a lot of responsibility for ensuring that everyone has access to health care.

A few polls have framed the issue of responsibility more broadly. The 2016 AEI/*Los Angeles Times* survey asked which part of society should take the lead in fighting poverty, and offered respondents several alternatives (interestingly, business/employers was not an option). The most popular answer was government (35%), followed by the poor themselves (18%), family (15%), church (13%), and charity (10%). This picture is more nuanced than we normally get from surveys. A different poll, conducted in 2014, asked Americans about hunger. Respondents were allowed to distinguish between levels of government: 47 percent said the federal government should have a great deal of responsibility for dealing with hunger, compared to 42 percent who said the same for local government. The only other option was local nonprofit organizations, such as churches and food banks. Fewer Americans (26%) thought those organizations should have a great deal of responsibility for combatting hunger. When asked whether helping the hungry was the job of churches and charities but not government, 75 percent disagreed (Hart Research Associates and Chesapeake Beach Consulting 2014).

In both surveys, more people expected government, not the nonprofit/voluntary sector, to take care of the needy. Nevertheless, most Americans do not think that responsibility rests solely with government. In the AEI/*Los Angeles Times* poll, almost as many people said that individuals and families should take the lead as those who said government. Almost one-quarter pointed to churches and charities. Based on other surveys, it appears that many people doubt whether government knows how to fight poverty (Ekins 2019; Lauter 2016). In short, Americans believe that many parts of society should take care of the poor.[11]

Another way to ascertain responsibility is by asking who should do more. Several questions in the GSS ask whether we are spending too much, too little, or the right amount on a variety of issues. The "we" is undefined, meaning that respondents could be thinking about government or about other parts of society. In 2018, 73 percent of Americans replied that we were spending too little on assistance to the poor. Only seven percent thought we were spending too much, and the rest said that current spending was about right. In other words, ten times as many people said we were doing too little for the poor compared to too much. That year was no aberration. Since 2000, large majorities of Americans have consistently agreed that we are spending too little on the poor. The numbers are remarkably similar to those for Social Security, the proverbial "third rail" of American politics (in 2018, 61% of Americans said we were spending too little on Social Security, and only 5% thought we were spending too much). In case readers suspect that Americans want to spend more on everything, only 31 percent agreed that we were spending too little on the military and defense in 2018. Even fewer (23%) thought we were spending too little on space exploration.

The ANES asks a different question—whether federal spending on aid to the poor should be increased, kept the same, or decreased. The results tell us more about the public safety net than the entire social safety net. Typically, those who agree that this spending should be increased far outnumber those who say it should be decreased. In 2016, 44 percent supported an increase while only 16 percent called for cuts.

Those who say "we" should spend more on the poor usually outnumber those who call for more federal spending. In the 2016 GSS, 72 percent of Americans agreed that we were spending too little to assist the poor, well above the 44 percent who supported an increase in federal spending (ANES). Why the gap? One possibility is that some respondents would like state and local governments to spend more on the poor, but not the national government. Another possibility is that Americans think "we" includes churches and other charities.

In general, Americans believe that we should do more to take care of the poor. Left unclear is how much more. I might feel that we should spend a few dollars more, you might think we should spend billions more, and the GSS would consider both of us as favoring increased spending. A special survey from 2013 asked whether people would support "the president and Congress setting a national goal to cut poverty in the United States in half within 10 years." This was an ambitious target, one that the most liberal politicians at the time hesitated to state publicly. Even so, 70 percent of Americans said they would support that goal, and most of that group offered strong support (Half in Ten Education Fund and the Center for American Progress 2014).

Some people are skeptical of spending questions when trade-offs are absent. It is easy to talk about government's responsibility when no costs are mentioned. The GSS tries to address this concern by reminding people that "we are faced with many problems in this country, none of which can be solved easily or inexpensively," and then soliciting their views on spending. That reminder should make the dominant answer—we are spending too little on the poor—more credible. In the survey about cutting poverty in half, respondents were asked two follow-up questions. Would they still support this goal if it meant businesses would have to pay workers higher salaries and benefits? Would they still support this goal if it meant government would have to raise taxes on the wealthy and increase spending? Not surprisingly, support dropped—to 59 and 55 percent, respectively, for the two scenarios (Half in Ten Education Fund and the Center for American Progress 2014). Still, a majority continued to favor a national commitment to cut poverty in half.

Other trade-off questions reveal a mixed picture. A 2017 poll by the Pew Research Center presented two options: the government does more to help the needy, even if it means going deeper into debt; or, the government cannot afford to do much more to help the needy. Fifty percent agreed with the first statement, compared to 43 percent with the second. A similar poll from 2016 found the public split more evenly. Back in 2012, Pew asked the question a little differently, and again the public was divided. Page and Jacobs (2009) asked Americans if they favored using their own tax dollars for specific social programs. Seventy-eight percent favored using their tax dollars for "Food Stamps and other assistance to the poor." But we do not know how many tax dollars they had in mind.

Poverty versus Welfare

Everyday Americans do not care equally about everyone in need. The public's willingness to help the poor has long been greater than its willingness to help welfare recipients (Gilens 1999; Howard et al. 2017; Shaw and Shapiro 2002; Smith 1987; Teles 1996). For example, the GSS regularly asks whether "we" (undefined) are spending too much, too little, or about the right amount on assistance to the poor. The public's net support score represents the difference between those who say spending too little minus those who say spending too much. The possible scores range from + 100 to –100. In 2018, the net support score for assistance to the poor was + 66, a strong indication that we should care more. That same year the net support score for welfare was –16. The ANES includes questions about federal spending. Twenty percent of Americans wanted to increase federal welfare spending in 2016, compared to 46 percent who favored a decrease (with the rest opting to spend the same). The net support score was –26. Americans want to spend more on the poor, but less on welfare.

Americans also feel more warmly toward the poor. Social scientists commonly gauge someone's affect is by using a "feeling thermometer." The values for this thermometer typically range from 0 (very cold/unfavorable) to 100 (very warm/favorable). A score of 50 represents a neutral feeling. The ANES regularly includes feeling thermometer questions in their surveys.[12] The thermometer questions about presidential candidates or political parties receive the most attention, but the ANES usually includes a question about feelings toward poor people. In 2016, the typical answer to this question was close to 70, and hardly anyone gave the poor a score below 50.[13] The results were similar in the 2012 and 2008 ANES, and in a more recent survey sponsored by the conservative Cato Institute (Ekins 2019).[14]

A score of 70 might not sound good, but it is. Americans said they felt more warmly toward the poor than toward liberals, conservatives, the Tea Party, big business, Muslims, and the rich, whose averages all hovered around 50 in 2016.[15] Poor people ranked well above Hillary Clinton, Donald Trump, illegal immigrants, and Congress, whose average scores were in the low 40s. About the only groups scoring higher than the poor were the police, scientists, and Christians. Americans do make distinctions when answering these questions, and clearly they do not feel warmly about everyone.

By contrast, the average thermometer score for welfare recipients has been 50 in recent years. That's not awful. It signifies a neutral feeling, and many other groups receive similar scores. Nonetheless, Americans are much more willing to say they feel negatively about people on welfare than about poor people. It makes sense that we would try to take care of people who generate positive feelings. Those who gave the poor a higher thermometer score in 2016 were more likely to favor increased spending on the poor.

Why do Americans view the poor and welfare recipients so differently? A common survey question asks whether poverty is due more to lack of effort or to circumstances beyond one's control. Academics refer to this as a choice between individual and structural explanations of poverty (Hunt and Bullock 2016). The rest of us might view it as the difference between being lazy or unlucky (Petersen 2012). In the mid-1990s, Americans blamed poverty more on a lack of effort than on difficult circumstances. For at least the last decade, more people have pointed to circumstances, and the gap appears to be widening. In March 2020, 71 percent of Americans said that people were poor because they faced more obstacles in life, while only 26 percent attributed poverty to not working hard enough (Howard et al. 2017; Pew Research Center 2020). Some of those obstacles originate with the job market. In the 2016 AEI/*Los Angeles Times* poll, Americans were more likely to agree that it was "very hard for poor people to find work" than they were to say that plenty of jobs were available. A somewhat older question asked whether most poor people were working but not earning enough money, or were they not working. Large majorities thought the poor were working (Howard et al. 2017). We might feel positively about the poor and want to help them because we believe they are trying to take care of themselves by working.

Americans do not expect every poor person to be employed. Respondents to the AEI/*Los Angeles Times* survey were asked which group of poor people should receive more help from the federal government. The three most popular answers were children, the elderly, and the disabled, in that order. All these individuals would have trouble holding a job, for reasons beyond their control. The least popular answers to this question were poor people without job skills and able-bodied adults who have no children and who cannot find work. Presumably they were not deserving of help because they could be employed (see also Cook and Barrett 1992; Hunt and Bullock 2016).

Many Americans feel that welfare recipients could and should do more to help themselves. Asked whether most people on welfare truly need it, approximately 45 percent of Americans in 2016 and 2017 thought that welfare recipients were "taking advantage of the system" and not "genuinely in need of help." According to the AEI/*Los Angeles Times* survey, Americans believe that welfare benefits are more likely to make people dependent (54%) than self-sufficient (35%). A more recent poll found similar results (Ekins 2019). A separate question from 2016 asked about work requirements for welfare recipients. Overwhelmingly (88%),

Americans embraced these requirements. Only a small fraction supported giving benefits "without asking for any effort in return." If recipients are described as able-bodied adults, support for work requirements climbed even higher (Fender 2017). When researchers talk at length with the working poor, they often hear negative stereotypes of welfare recipients. "Lower-wage workers draw strong divisions between themselves and those whom they perceive to be living the 'welfare lifestyle,' which they characterize as choosing not to work, being on welfare for a long time, and, in general, getting benefits without being truly needy" (Halpern-Meekin et al. 2015: 114).

Susan Fiske, a noted social psychologist, has been studying public attitudes toward poor people and welfare recipients for years. With the help of numerous co-authors, she has developed a general model of stereotyping. This model has two dimensions—how warmly we feel about a group, and the group's perceived competence. The first dimension indicates how much we like members of some group, and the second dimension how much we respect them.[16] In one study, participants were asked about society's perception of various groups, not their own views. They were given a list of character traits, some of which showed feelings of warmth (e.g., likeable, sincere, kind) and others indicated competence (e.g., intelligent, independent). Participants were then asked how well those traits described 17 different groups of people. The one group that was viewed as unusually low in both warmth and competence? Welfare recipients (Fiske et al. 1999). I mention this study because independence and competence have long been associated with employment in the United States, and my strong hunch is that Fiske's work reinforces the poll results mentioned above.

The prevailing image of welfare is not entirely negative. In the AEI/*Los Angeles Times* poll, respondents were asked whether welfare recipients would prefer to earn their own living or stay on welfare. A clear majority (61%) replied, earn their own living (see also Ekins 2019).[17] In addition, most respondents did not believe that welfare benefits were generous: a little over one-third thought that benefits were too low to meet basic expenses, and a similar share thought that benefits were only enough to afford the basics. Only 11 percent thought that welfare benefits allowed recipients to live comfortably. Not surprisingly, those who thought benefits were inadequate were the least likely to say that recipients wanted to stay on welfare.

If we think that being employed separates the deserving poor from the undeserving poor, then people who are employed full-time might have different attitudes about poverty than those who are employed part-time or not at all. Based on the 2016 AEI/*Los Angeles Times* poll, full-time workers are somewhat less likely to believe that "government is responsible for the well-being of all its citizens"; that the poor are hard-working; and that it is very hard for poor people to find work. These differences were statistically significant but substantively

small. For example, 62 percent of full-time workers and 70 percent of the unemployed considered the poor to be hard-working. On the crucial question of responsibility for helping the poor, full-time workers were a little less likely to want
churches in the lead and a little more likely to want the poor themselves in the
lead. Still, the top choice was government responsibility for full-time workers,
part-time workers, and the unemployed. There was no statistically significant
relationship between one's employment status and one's views about recipients
wanting to stay on welfare versus earning a living.

The story from the 2018 GSS is basically the same. Work status was weakly
related to one's views about welfare spending. Full-time workers were a bit
more likely to say that we were spending too much, and the unemployed were
a bit more likely to say we were spending too little. The relationship between
work status and support for the federal government doing everything possible
to help the poor was likewise weak. There was no statistically significant difference in public attitudes toward spending on the poor. Most full-time workers
(73%), part-time workers (79%), and the unemployed (80%) thought we were
spending too little.

Employment may not be the whole story, or even the main story. A number
of scholars argue that welfare has been stigmatized in the public mind because
many recipients are thought to be racial minorities, women, or both (Foster
2008; Gilens 1999; Hancock 2004; Johnson 2003; Soss, Fording, and Schram
2011; Soss and Schram 2007; Winter 2008). Unfortunately, polling organizations over the last decade have seldom asked questions connecting race or
gender to poverty or welfare. We have to piece together what we can find.

In the late 20th century, Americans believed that Blacks comprised one-
half or more of the poverty population, which was far above the true number.
According to Gilens (1999), that misperception led Whites to favor cutbacks
in welfare spending. Though few recent polls have revisited this question, our
views seem to have changed. One 2017 survey asked, "In your own community, would you say the people who are poor are mostly white, mostly black,
mostly Hispanic, or some other combination?" Thirty percent replied White,
28 percent said Black, and 18 percent said Hispanic. Most of the rest said
the poor were some combination of groups that included Whites. A poll
conducted the previous year produced similar results.[18] According to the
Census Bureau, 42 percent of the poor were non-Hispanic Whites in 2017,
while 27 percent were Hispanic and 23 percent were Black (Semega et al.
2019). If we distribute the "combination of groups" responses equally to
Whites, Blacks, and Hispanics, then the public's perception of the poverty
population was much closer to reality in 2017 than it was a few decades ago.
If we choose to ignore the combination of groups, then public opinion is still
more accurate than it used to be.

Conceivably, a more accurate picture of poverty is related to changes in public opinion. In the early 1990s, when most of the poor were thought to be Black, the net support for spending on the poor was + 44, and for spending on welfare was - 49 (Gilens 1999: 28). A quarter-century later, support for the former is + 66 while support for the latter is - 26. We have become more willing to help the poor and less opposed to welfare. Correlation is not causation, and more detailed analysis is needed, but the changing racial image of the poor might lead Whites to care more about them.

Alternatively, we can ask Americans what percentage of different groups are in poverty. When respondents estimated the overall poverty rate at 39 percent, they guessed that the average figures for Whites, Hispanics, and Blacks were 35, 43, and 45 percent, respectively (Half in Ten Education Fund and the Center for American Progress 2014). All these numbers were considerably higher than the official poverty figures. Although the general order was correct, the public badly underestimated the gaps. Poverty rates for Blacks and Hispanics are two to three times higher than for Whites and have been for many years (Semega et al. 2019). Americans might care about poverty more if they believe, incorrectly, that roughly the same share of Whites, Blacks, and Hispanics are affected.

Compared to poverty, welfare could be more closely associated with racial minorities. One recent poll asked Americans about the racial composition of several social programs. Respondents had the option of saying that program recipients are mostly White, mostly Black, or a relatively even mix of the two (mostly Hispanic was not an option). The most common answer for welfare was a mix of Black and White. Only one-quarter of Americans said that most welfare recipients were Black. The overall connections between race and welfare seem to have weakened in the public's mind compared to what Gilens (1999) found in the 1990s. This same survey asked about the racial composition of food stamps and Head Start, and the results were comparable to welfare. The one program that deviated from this pattern was public housing, where the leading answer was mostly Black (Delaney and Edwards-Levy 2018).

The racial hypothesis and the work hypothesis are not mutually exclusive. Opposition to welfare might be rooted in a belief that most recipients are Black, and that most Blacks are lazy. Thus, welfare benefits a lot of freeloaders who do not actually need help (Dyck and Hussey 2008; Gilens 1999; see also Fiske 1998 and Winter 2008). In 2012, almost 40 percent of Americans thought that most Blacks on welfare "could get along without it if they tried" (Howard et al. 2017). The GSS frequently includes questions about group attributes, including work ethic. For at least the last two decades, Whites have been thought of as more hard-working than Blacks.

That gap seems to be narrowing. In 2002, 32 percent of Americans put Blacks on the lazy end of the scale, compared to just 9 percent who felt the same way about Whites (Howard et al. 2017). In 2018, the relevant figures were 25 percent for Blacks and 13 percent for Whites. People who felt that Blacks were usually hard-working were also more likely to say that we were spending too little on welfare, rather than too much. Those who thought Blacks were lazy felt that we were spending too much on welfare. That relationship was statistically significant. It also appears that we view Hispanics as more hard-working and less lazy than we did a generation ago. In fact, Hispanics were labeled as lazy (10%) less often than Whites were in the 2018 GSS. The public's opinion of Hispanics was unrelated to their views about welfare spending. Regardless of how hard-working or lazy Hispanics were perceived to be, more people replied that we were spending too much on welfare instead of too little. These results are a reminder that the public does not always view racial minorities as a single, undifferentiated group.[19]

Some people could be giving socially appropriate answers rather than sincere answers when asked explicitly about Blacks or Hispanics (Kinder and Sanders 1996; Sniderman and Carmines 1997; Tesler 2016). Researchers might need a more clandestine approach to study these attitudes. One option is the survey-based experiment, in which respondents are randomly assigned to different groups, each group is given a slightly different version of a question, and then their answers are compared. For example, a vignette might describe a welfare recipient as White to one group and Black to the other, before asking whether the recipient is likely to get off welfare. Some of these experiments find that linking Blacks to welfare leads to negative judgments and diminished support (Gilens 1999; Wetts and Willer 2018). Others find no such link (Sniderman and Carmines 1997) or mixed results (Harrell, Soroka, and Iyengar 2016; Mendelberg 2001).

In a different type of experiment, participants were shown a pair of faces and asked which one looked more like a welfare recipient. Researchers then digitally manipulated the images, over and over, and participants had to pick one as the likely welfare recipient out of each new pair of faces. The result, generated by computer, was a composite sketch of a welfare recipient, and a second sketch of the face seen as unlikely to be on welfare. These two composite images were then shown to a different set of participants, who were asked to identify the race of the faces. The welfare recipient was usually perceived as Black and the non–welfare recipient as White (Brown-Iannuzzi et al. 2017).

Participants were also asked about certain traits they associated with the composite faces. Along with being Black, the welfare recipient was perceived as lazy, incompetent, unhappy, and unlikeable. The non-welfare recipient was rated higher on virtually every trait. Later, these researchers showed the same composite images to a different group of people and asked questions about cash assistance and food stamps (without mentioning that the faces had been generated based on perceived links to welfare). On average, participants judged the face belonging to the welfare recipient to be more irresponsible and less deserving of government aid (Brown-Iannuzzi et al. 2017). Studies like this one demonstrate that race can influence our attitudes about welfare in ways that standard surveys might not detect.

We have much less evidence about gender, poverty, and welfare. Polling organizations do not ask Americans what share of the poverty population is female, or whether female recipients could get by without welfare. The GSS does not ask how hard-working or lazy we think men and women are. It is difficult to know whether Americans care less about welfare because of gender stereotypes. In the experiment described above, participants judged the composite image of the welfare recipient to be Black and female. The non–welfare recipient was perceived as White and male. The racial identity, however, was stronger than the gender identity (Brown-Iannuzzi et al. 2017). A majority of Americans who took part in the AEI/*Los Angeles Times* poll felt that unmarried adults on welfare choose not to marry in order to keep their benefits. Given the long-standing association between welfare and single mothers (Gordon 1994; Mink 1995), respondents could have been thinking about women when answering that question.

A recent national poll asked people to name the top three causes of poverty from a list that included lack of work ethic, lack of job opportunities, lack of educational opportunities, drugs/alcohol, and discrimination. The leading cause was "poor life choices" (Ekins 2019), a rather ambiguous phrase. Given the other possible answers, it seems plausible to interpret poor life choices as a reference to marriage, sexual behavior, or both. The undeserving "welfare queen" has been a popular stereotype since the 1970s, and ordinary Americans worry that welfare gives poor women an incentive to have more kids (Black and Sprague 2016; Foster 2008; Sparks 2003). For a vivid statement of this view, listen to this White woman from Ohio, who participated in a focus group shortly after the 2016 elections:

> We're having women pop out babies like Pez dispensers with different baby daddies and they get welfare every month. They get their housing paid for, their food. They drive these brand new cars, their nails are done, their hair is done; they've got these name brand clothes and purses. But yet I'm struggling to put food on the table for my four kids (quoted in Lapp and Lapp 2016: 7).

Those attuned to coded language will claim that references to baby daddies, new cars, nails, and hair reveal racial as well as gendered thinking. That seems quite likely to me.

Differences of Opinion

We have more evidence that Americans distinguish among the poor based on race than gender, partly because scholars and polling firms have asked about race more often. Let's see how much public opinion varies depending on the race, ethnicity, and gender of the survey respondents. Compared to non-Hispanic Whites, Blacks and Hispanics might care more about poverty and favor doing more to take care of the poor. And we might expect the same of women compared to men. These differences could be rooted in narrow self-interest, given that racial minorities and women are more likely to be poor.[20] They could reflect the nature and degree of contact with poor people (Hunt and Bullock 2016; Thal 2017; Watkins-Hays and Kovalsky 2016), or perhaps different levels of empathy or compassion (Feldman et al. 2020; Feldman and Steenbergen 2001; Gross and Wronski 2021). This section has a simpler purpose, which is determining whether sizable differences exist at all.

The first column in Table 1.1 displays several survey questions related to "caring about." The remaining columns summarize results based on the race, ethnicity, and gender of the respondents. I am relying on the Pew question about top priorities for the president and Congress rather than Gallup's most important problem question. The Gallup numbers regarding poverty, hunger, and homelessness are so low that meaningful variation across groups will be hard to detect. In 2018, 58 percent of Americans said that helping the poor and needy should be a top priority for the president and Congress. Whites (54%) were a bit below the national average, while Hispanics (62%) and Blacks (66%) were above.[21] As mentioned earlier in the chapter, most Americans think that poverty is pervasive. On average, Blacks estimated the poverty rate to be 54 percent in 2016. When African Americans call poverty a top policy priority, they want elected officials to care about half the country. That does not sound like narrow self-interest.

Compared to Whites, Blacks have more sympathetic attitudes toward poverty and welfare (Table 1.1). They feel more warmly toward poor people; they are more likely to think of the poor as hard-working, and more often believe that the poor have trouble finding work. African Americans also respond more positively to various questions about welfare and welfare recipients. Three-quarters of the Blacks surveyed agree that welfare recipients wanted to earn their own living, compared to three-fifths of Whites. Conversely, Blacks are much less likely to say that recipients prefer to stay on welfare. Blacks are also less likely to view welfare benefits as adequate to meet basic expenses. Few Blacks see themselves as the main group on welfare. Blacks are more likely to see Whites as the primary recipients of welfare. The views of Hispanics, however, do not always mirror those held by Blacks. In general, Hispanics are midway between Whites

Table 1.1 **Caring About**

Survey question	Whites	Hispanics	Blacks	Men	Women
	————————Respondents————————				
Top priority for president and Congress:					
help poor and needy people[a]	54 %	62 %	66 %	54 %	63 %
Feeling thermometer (0–100):					
poor people[b]	70	77	85	70	72
people on welfare[c]	50	50	60	50	50
Most poor people are hard-working (% agree)[d]	63	64	78	63	67
Very hard for poor to find work (% agree)[d]	54	60	68	49	64
Welfare recipients prefer to stay on welfare[d]	37	42	20	39	33
Welfare recipients would rather earn own living[d]	59	55	76	57	64
Welfare allows poor to live quite comfortably[d]	10	14	10	15	8
Welfare not enough to meet basic expenses[d]	33	33	51	30	39
Perceived composition of welfare recipients[e]					
more White	22	7	40	27	17
more Black	28	34	12	27	25
about the same	35	25	33	27	39

Sources:

a – Pew Research Center (January 2018).

b – American National Election Studies (2016); note that median scores are used.

c – American National Election Studies (2012); note that median scores are used.

d – AEI/*Los Angeles Times* (2016); note that some respondents said that welfare meets basic expenses, with a little extra, or that it just meets basic expenses.

e – HuffPost/YouGov poll (January 2018); note that many people replied "not sure" to this question.

and Blacks when asked questions about poverty, and they are closer to Whites when asked about welfare. Compared to Whites, a larger share of Hispanics think that Blacks are the main group receiving welfare.

The gender differences are not as pronounced (Table 1.1). In general, women appear to care more about poverty: 63 percent of women think that helping poor and needy people should be a top priority for national officials, compared to 54 percent of men. There is no meaningful difference between men and women regarding their feelings toward poor people or welfare recipients. For the other questions about work and welfare, the gender differences are either modest in size or statistically insignificant. The opinion gaps between men and women are smaller than those between Whites and Blacks.

Nevertheless, we should not exaggerate these differences. The views of Whites, Hispanics, and Blacks are similar in important ways (Table 1.1). Majorities of all three groups want elected officials to make helping poor and needy people a top priority. All three groups feel more warmly toward poor people than people on welfare. Most Whites, Hispanics, and Blacks consider the poor to be hard-working and believe that poor people have a hard time finding a job. All three groups are likely to say that welfare recipients prefer work over welfare. Few Whites, Hispanics, or Blacks think that welfare benefits allow the poor to live comfortably. The views of men and women are similar in many of the same ways.

With respect to taking care of the poor, I will rely on the more nuanced question asked in the AEI/*Los Angeles Times* survey (Table 1.2). By substantial margins, Blacks (49%) are more likely than Whites (32%) to say that government has the greatest responsibility to help the poor. Twice as many Whites as Blacks place responsibility primarily on the poor themselves (22% vs. 11%). Hispanics' answers tend to fall between those of Blacks and Whites, with one interesting exception: Hispanics are roughly twice as likely as Whites or Blacks to say that charities have the greatest responsibility to help the poor. Although all three groups named government more often than any other answer, their second choice varied—the poor themselves (Whites), charities (Hispanics), or churches (Blacks). Women are more likely than men to see government as responsible, though government is the top pick for both groups.

On the spending questions, the gaps between Blacks and Whites are again larger than those separating men and women (Table 1.2). The racial gaps are obvious when the questions refer to spending by the national government. Whether that spending helps the poor or welfare recipients, Blacks are almost twice as likely as Whites to favor increased spending. Interestingly, the racial gap was somewhat smaller when the question asked about what "we" are spending on the poor. Whites are much more likely to say that we are spending too little than they are to say that federal spending should be increased, suggesting that some Whites are objecting to government's role rather than to the idea of helping

Table 1.2 **Taking Care Of**

Survey question	Whites	Hispanics	Blacks	Men	Women
	—————Respondents—————				
Greatest responsibility to help the poor[a]					
government	32 %	36 %	49 %	31 %	39 %
poor themselves	22	14	11	22	14
family	16	15	10	16	14
churches	14	11	15	11	15
charities	9	17	7	11	9
We are spending ___ on assistance to the poor[b]					
too little	67	76	89	68	77
about right	25	18	9	26	16
too much	8	6	2	7	7
Federal spending, aid to the poor[c]					
increase	37	62	68	42	47
keep the same	44	28	25	40	38
decrease	19	11	7	18	15
Federal spending, welfare programs[c]					
Increase	16	25	33	19	19
keep the same	33	30	42	33	37
Decrease	51	45	26	48	43

Sources:
a – AEI/*Los Angeles Times* (2016).
b – General Social Survey (2016).
c – American National Election Studies (2016).

the poor. Hispanics are almost as willing as Blacks to say that federal spending on the poor should be increased, and they are almost as likely as Whites to say that welfare spending should be cut.[22] Women are more likely than men to believe that "we" are spending too little to help the poor, but no less likely to think "we" are spending too much. Women are a little more likely than men to support greater federal spending on the poor, and a little less likely to favor cuts in welfare spending.

When it comes to caring about the poor and taking care of them, Democrats and Republicans are usually far apart (Table 1.3).[23] The partisan gaps are even larger than the racial gaps. Most Blacks, Hispanics, Whites, men, and women believe that helping poor people should be a top priority for the national government. So do most self-identified Democrats (74%) and Independents (55%). But not most Republicans (42%). Democrats are much more likely than Republicans to see the poor as hard-working (80% vs. 48%), and to say that welfare recipients would rather be employed (78% vs. 41%). In general, Democrats tend to blame poverty on circumstances beyond one's control, while Republicans blame it on lack of individual effort (Dunn 2018).[24] Republicans are much more likely to say that recipients prefer to stay on welfare (58% vs. 20%) and are more likely to view welfare benefits as generous. According to Republicans, welfare is for Blacks first and Whites second. Democrats believe the reverse is true. The views of Independents are roughly midway between the two parties, which makes sense.

Republicans appear to have harsher views toward poverty and welfare than Democrats, Independents, Whites, or men. Are Republicans therefore unusually cold-hearted? Not necessarily. Some of their negative reactions might reflect their feelings toward government. When asked which part of society should take the lead in helping the poor, only one-fifth of Republicans opted for government (Table 1.3). They did not coalesce around another option, such as churches or charities, but most Republicans preferred something besides government. Few Republicans want to increase federal spending on the poor, and a large majority support cuts in welfare spending. Nevertheless, most Republicans agreed that "we" were spending too little on the poor, and very few said that we were spending too much. That question did not mention government, and Republicans voiced more support.[25]

Switching the focus from party to ideology does not change the basic patterns. Liberals are more likely than conservatives to say that the needs of poor and needy people should be a top priority for national officials. In the 2018 Pew poll, that gap was 23 points (72% vs. 49%). Liberals are more than twice as likely as conservatives to want government playing the lead role in fighting poverty. While most liberals favor greater federal spending on the poor, most conservatives do not. The more liberal you are, the more you see the poor as hard-working. The more conservative you are, the more you see welfare benefits as too generous and worry about poor people choosing welfare over work. Conservatives are more likely to favor cuts in federal welfare spending.

In a nutshell, the American public does make distinctions among the poor. We want to take care of the poor more than welfare recipients, but that difference could reflect our attitudes about work, race, or both. Americans are more

Table 1.3 **Partisan Differences**

| | —————Respondents————— | | |
	Democrat	Independent	Republican
Caring about			
Top priority for president and Congress:			
help poor and needy people[a]	74%	55%	42%
Feeling thermometer (0-100):			
poor people[b]	77	71	70
people on welfare[c]	56	47	41
Most poor people are hard-working (% agree)[d]	80	64	48
Very hard for poor to find work (% agree)[d]	68	58	43
Welfare recipients would rather earn own living[d]	78	60	41
Welfare recipients prefer to stay on welfare[d]	20	38	58
Welfare not enough to meet basic expenses[d]	52	33	23
Welfare allows poor to live quite comfortably[d]	5	12	18
Perceived composition of welfare recipients[e]			
more White	31	20	11
more Black	18	26	39
about the same	37	30	32
Taking care of			
Greatest responsibility to help the poor[d]			
government	52	34	21
poor themselves	16	20	20
family	10	17	17
church	9	13	18
charity	5	8	15

Table 1.3 **Continued**

	Respondents		
	Democrat	*Independent*	*Republican*
We are spending ____ on assistance to the poor[f]			
too little	82	73	55
about right	16	20	33
too much	2	7	12
Federal spending, aid to the poor[b]			
increase	63	42	24
keep the same	31	42	46
decrease	6	16	30
Federal spending, welfare programs[b]			
increase	30	18	8
keep the same	45	37	22
decrease	26	45	71

Sources:

a – Pew Research Center (January 2018)

b – American National Election Studies (2016); note that median scores are used.

c – American National Election Studies (2012); note that median scores are used.

d – AEI/*Los Angeles Times* (2016); note that some respondents said that welfare meets basic expenses, with a little extra, or that it just meets basic expenses.

e – HuffPost/YouGov poll (January 2018); note that many people replied "not sure" to this question.

f – General Social Survey (2016).

inclined to help if the recipients are unable to work or are not racial minorities. Some Americans care more than others about the poor. Those same Americans usually want us to do more to take care of the poor. Those differences are connected to who we are rather than what we do. Whether we work full-time, part-time, or not at all is much less important than whether we are Black or White, Democrat or Republican, liberal or conservative.

Discussion

Currently, American politics is highly polarized at the elite level, and perhaps among ordinary citizens as well (Abramowitz 2010; Fiorina with Adams and

Pope 2010; Hetherington and Weiler 2009; Iyengar and Krupenkin 2018; Levendusky 2009; Mann and Ornstein 2012; Mason 2018; McCarty, Poole and Rosenthal 2016; Sides and Hopkins 2015). In such a world, people will often be open to information that reinforces their own worldview but reject whatever runs counter to their beliefs or is closely associated with a rival camp. We can imagine how easy it would be to construct two very different interpretations of public attitudes toward poverty.

Suppose that you do not want government doing more to help the poor. You might even want government to do less. Will you run afoul of public opinion? Not when only five percent of Americans name poverty, hunger, or homelessness as the country's most important problem. Not when polls at election time show zero concern for the poor. Not when most Americans think that some combination of individuals, families, churches, and charities should take the lead in helping the poor. You would argue that people are poor because they aren't trying hard enough. You would refer over and over to "welfare" and "welfare recipients." You would attach work requirements to as many public benefits as possible. And you could count on many Whites, men, Republicans, and conservatives to embrace your positions.

Now suppose that you favor a greater government role. You have read the polls and believe that most Americans want Congress and the president to make poverty a top priority. There could even be substantial support for cutting poverty in half within a decade. Because everyone—regardless of race, ethnicity, gender, or political party—believes that poverty affects many more lives than the official poverty estimates, it should be easy to talk about the enormity of the problem. Americans overwhelmingly agree that we are doing too little to assist the poor. Few people want to decrease federal spending on the poor. You would highlight the millions of children, senior citizens, and disabled individuals who are poor. You could focus on specific needs such as food, shelter, and medical care without saying much about welfare. You could argue that many of the jobs available won't pay enough to lift people above the poverty line. If your audience includes many Democrats, Blacks, Hispanics, and women, then your message will surely resonate.

When poll results are consistent with such a wide range of policies, we should question the impact of public opinion. Polls might be used as ammunition by actors who already know what outcomes they favor and want to claim public support (Weaver 2000). Moreover, some policymakers could be unaware that these polls even exist.[26] We would be smart to continue our tour of the social safety net, listening to what interest groups and political parties say about poverty and need. In the next chapter, we will begin by examining how much business and labor groups care about poverty.

2

Business and Labor

Business and labor are two of the most visible interest groups in American politics. For decades they have publicly taken positions on social and economic issues (Gottschalk 2000; Hacker 2002; Hacker and Pierson 2002; Klein 2003; Quadagno 2005). Compared to ordinary Americans, the views of business and labor should be clear. Unions have always claimed to stick up for the little guy. According to A. Philip Randolph, one of the most important labor leaders of the 20th century, "the essence of trade unionism is social uplift. The labor movement has been the haven for the dispossessed, the despised, the neglected, the downtrodden, the poor."[1] Walter Reuther, head of the United Auto Workers, believed that union members "had a 'special responsibility' to help others 'who have been left behind'" (quoted in Chappell 2010: 26). He was part of the Citizens' Crusade Against Poverty in the 1960s and urged the national government to spend more on the poor (Lichtenstein 1995; Rosenfeld and Laird 2016). No matter what government does, joining a union is supposed to help workers achieve economic security through higher wages and better benefits. When he was president of the Service Employees International Union (SEIU), Andy Stern proudly declared that "unions are the best anti-poverty program that America's ever had."[2]

Of course, labor leaders might be exaggerating how much they care about the poor. It would be helpful to get an outsider's perspective. Consider Reverend Martin Luther King, Jr., who praised unions for a long history of accomplishments:

> [T]he labor movement was the principal force that transformed misery and despair into hope and progress. Out of its bold struggles, economic and social reform gave birth to unemployment insurance, old-age pensions, government relief for the destitute and, above all, new wage levels that meant not mere survival but a tolerable life. The captains

Who Cares. Christopher Howard, Oxford University Press. © Oxford University Press 2023.
DOI: 10.1093/oso/9780190074456.003.0003

of industry did not lead this transformation; they resisted it until they were overcome.[3]

Years later, President Jimmy Carter reached a similar conclusion. "Every advance in this half-century—Social Security, civil rights, Medicare, aid to education, one after another—came with the support and leadership of American labor. You have represented all the people, not just your members. You have been the voice of forgotten people everywhere."[4]

Business and labor are usually depicted as antagonists. While it would be harsh to think of business as anti-poor, indifferent is a real possibility. Milton Friedman, the Nobel Prize-winning economist and well-known defender of free markets, argued that "there is one and only one social responsibility of business—to use its resources and engage in activities designed to increase its profits," as long as it did so legally (Friedman 1962: 133). He viewed corporate charity as a misuse of funds. Historically, employers have resisted being taxed or regulated, no matter what social objective was being promoted. They have opposed income redistribution. As the National Federation of Independent Business (NFIB) stated recently, "the role of government is to stay out of the way so #entrepreneurs can grow the economy."[5] Perhaps during periods of unrest, employers will pay more attention to poverty as part of a larger effort to restore social order. This happened after the urban riots of the late 1960s (Chappell 2010). In the first decades of the 21st century, the United States has been relatively tranquil. All things considered, we do not expect to hear much about poverty from the business community.

The question of who should take care of the poor does not, a priori, have an obvious answer. Polling organizations usually frame this question as a choice between individuals and government; sometimes they mention charities, churches, and families as options (Chapter 1). Rarely do these surveys ask if labor unions or employers should be responsible. Union leaders might say this responsibility belongs to government, just as they supported the War on Poverty in the 1960s (Chappell 2010) and defended food stamps against cuts in the 1970s and 1980s (Rosenfeld and Laird 2016). Or, they could argue that poorly paid workers should join unions and push employers to offer better wages and benefits (Greenhouse 2019; Lichtenstein 2013). Employers might insist that the poor should take more responsibility for their plight, without help from unions or government. Some employers might prefer government action if it could improve their competitive position. Companies that pay higher wages than their rivals, for example, might support minimum wage laws. Business and labor are not monolithic interests, and we could find notable differences of opinion within each group.

Organized Labor

The American Federation of Labor–Congress of Industrial Organizations is the largest organization representing workers in the United States and has been for decades. The AFL-CIO is a federation uniting more than 50 unions, embracing everyone from machinists, electricians, and farmworkers to postal carriers and flight attendants. Collectively these unions have over 12 million members.[6] The large number and variety of members make it difficult for the AFL-CIO to speak with a single voice on some issues. In addition, not every union belongs to the AFL-CIO. After examining the national federation, we will turn our attention to some individual unions.

The first task is determining how much unions care about poverty. In a sense, we are trying to approximate the "most important problem facing the country" and the "top priority for the president and Congress" survey questions discussed in the previous chapter. To ascertain labor's priorities, I will not be relying on congressional testimony, which is commonly done in studies of interest groups. Union officials do not determine the subject matter of legislative hearings, and they cannot appear unless invited. The lack of congressional testimony might not reflect a lack of interest. We need to find a venue that labor unions can control.

Every four years, the AFL-CIO holds a national convention. The executive council issues a report, summarizing the major accomplishments and challenges since the last convention. Delegates to the convention deliberate and vote on a series of resolutions, many of which direct the organization to act on specific problems. Delegates also discuss and vote on amendments to the organization's written constitution. These national conventions are a better place to learn about labor's priorities.

Between 2000 and 2020, the AFL-CIO held five national conventions (2001, 2005, 2009, 2013, 2017).[7] During that time the organization adopted over 30 constitutional amendments. Not one of them dealt directly with poverty or poor people. Instead, these amendments affected the internal operations of the organization, such as the frequency of national conventions, the size of the executive council, and relations with member unions.

Official resolutions offer a better window on the larger issues that labor cares about. The AFL-CIO adopted almost 200 resolutions in the last two decades. Most were relatively short (1–3 pages). The topics ranged widely, dealing with labor practices as well as a variety of domestic and foreign policies. In 2001, for example, the AFL-CIO commended members of the armed forces who were battling terrorism; another resolution that year endorsed contraceptive coverage in health plans. In 2013, the organization called for greater federal action to reduce the debt burdens of college students, and for free and fair elections in

Honduras. The 40 or so resolutions approved at each convention are comparable to the party platforms adopted every four years by Democrats and Republicans, with each resolution representing a distinct plank in labor's platform.

I performed a simple content analysis of these resolutions. Slightly over 20 percent of them mentioned "poverty," "poor," or "low income."[8] (However, a few of these references were to countries besides the United States.) At the 2009 convention, on the heels of a painful economic recession, eight out of 45 resolutions mentioned one of these terms. If we limit our analysis to those resolutions that include at least one of these terms, then we find an average of 2.7 mentions per resolution. That works out to roughly one mention for every two pages of text. In only four resolutions were poverty, poor, or low income mentioned more than once per page. Only one resolution (2001) included any of these terms in the title.

More often, these resolutions mentioned workers, working families, working people, and working men and women.[9] Ninety percent of the resolutions contained at least one mention of these terms. In each of those resolutions, these terms appeared an average of 17.5 times, or six times per page. Several resolutions had titles such as "An American Economy that Works for All Working Families" (2001), "Achieving Retirement Security for Working Families" (2009), and "Organizing to Win Power for Working People" (2017). In most of the resolutions mentioning poverty or the poor, references to workers were at least five times more common. The clear implication is that those who deserve our attention, and our care, are wage workers.

The working poor have been profiled extensively in the media (Desmond 2018; Maharidge 2016; Saslow 2013; Semuels and Burnley 2019) and in academic studies (Collins and Mayer 2010; Gitterman 2010; Halpern-Meekin et al. 2015; Newman 1999). Major foundations and nonprofits have called attention to their plight.[10] We know that millions of Americans qualify as working poor, and their very existence proves that individual effort alone is not enough to rise out of poverty. Nonetheless, the AFL-CIO adopted only three resolutions that mentioned "working poor" between 2000 and 2020. Two of these resolutions mentioned the working poor one time each. In the other resolution (2009), the working poor were mentioned three times, all in conjunction with global poverty and developing countries. Overall, that adds up to five references to "working poor" in over 500 pages of text. The near invisibility of the working poor is striking.[11]

Counting how often certain words or phrases are used is one way to measure importance. Another way is by analyzing which topics are addressed early on. The first resolutions at each convention usually called for efforts to strengthen the labor movement. That pattern makes sense considering the much-noted decline of American unions (Greenhouse 2019; Lichtenstein 2013; Walker 2020).

Currently, only 10 to 11 percent of workers belong to a union (US Bureau of Labor Statistics 2019b). Without more members, the AFL-CIO won't have the power needed to influence employers or government officials, and therefore cannot help workers. For example:

> When our unions grow, we can elect more pro-working family elected officials to help pass policies and laws, including labor law reform, that improve workers' lives; build a bigger, stronger labor movement; and give America's workers a genuine voice in their country (Resolution 1, 2001).

> WHEREAS, working people face every day an economy that doesn't work for them: stagnant wages, cuts to health care, systematic discrimination and eroding public services are the norm for too many; and WHEREAS, union membership and collective bargaining remains the most effective tool for working people to exercise their power on the job and in the public sphere . . . (Resolution 4, 2017).

The AFL-CIO has not made connections between a robust labor movement and poverty in these resolutions. They seldom mentioned efforts to organize specific occupations or industries where poor people often work.

In addition, each AFL-CIO convention features an official report by the executive council. These reports describe the main challenges and accomplishments from the past four years, and then lay out priorities for the coming years. In substance and tone, they resemble presidential State of the Union messages. One important difference is that individual trade and industrial departments sometimes submit individual reports. My content analysis used only those parts of the Executive Council Report that reflect the views of the entire organization.[12]

Rarely did the Executive Council Reports mention "poverty," "poor," or "low income"—less than once per ten pages of text (and not at all in 2017). Instead, these reports were filled with references to workers, working families, and the like. The 2001 report, for instance, mentioned different types of workers almost 100 times more often than it referred to poverty or the poor. The most recent report (2017) mentioned different types of workers more than ten times per page. There were only two references to the "working poor" in these five reports.

This does not sound like the same labor movement built by Randolph and Reuther. In fact, the differences between unions today and 75 years ago are not that stark. Safety nets catch people after they have fallen on hard times. The AFL-CIO has long cared about preventing hardships from happening in the first place. The best way they know how to do that is by focusing on jobs. Too many people are unemployed or underemployed. Many employers hesitate to pay good wages and provide decent health and retirement benefits. Most companies will not do so without pressure from unions, government, or both. Labor leaders want government to create a favorable legal environment—one where they are free to organize, bargain collectively, and seek redress when employers violate labor laws (Resolution 9, 2017; Resolution 1, 2013; Executive Council Report 2009, 2017). With such protections, unions can effectively push employers to offer better wages and benefits for millions of workers. A rising tide of compensation will lift all workers' boats.[13]

Labor knows that it cannot succeed alone.[14] The AFL-CIO has frequently called on the national government to promote full employment (e.g., Resolution 20, 2017; Resolution 9, 2013). "Everyone who wants to work has the right to a good job where we earn a fair return on our work and receive a wage that allows us to support ourselves and our families" (Resolution 1, 2017; see also Resolution 3, 2009 and Resolution 6, 2013).[15] Substantial investment in infrastructure projects would help achieve that larger objective (Resolutions 7, 18, and 20, 2017). Although full employment policies would aid the poor, these resolutions do not mention them as important beneficiaries.

The minimum wage might seem like an exception to labor's focus on broad-based policies. The AFL-CIO has stated, multiple times, that it favors a higher minimum wage. At the 2013 national convention, one resolution called for increasing the minimum wage to $10.10 an hour and then indexing it. The organization endorsed a $15 minimum wage (also indexed) at its 2017 convention. In justifying such a large increase, labor leaders noted that after World War II, when the minimum wage was extended to more occupations and its value increased, poverty among African Americans dropped. The gradual erosion of the minimum wage since the 1980s made it hard to sustain those gains. Yet the AFL-CIO does not consider the minimum wage to be solely an anti-poverty policy. As more women enter the labor force, a higher minimum wage is "crucial to closing the gender pay gap and boosting income for middle-class families."[16]

With respect to government spending, the AFL-CIO prefers social insurance over public assistance. Social insurance is broadly inclusive and based on wage work. The organization favors a single-payer system in health care, modeled after Medicare (Resolution 6, 2017). The first step would be lowering Medicare's eligibility age from 65 to 55. Job-based health benefits would continue, but as a supplement to an expanded version of Medicare. In contrast, the 2013 Executive Council Report hailed the passage of the Affordable Care Act without even mentioning Medicaid's expansion. The 2017 Report discussed efforts to prevent repeal of the ACA without mentioning Medicaid.

In similar fashion, the AFL-CIO cares a lot about Social Security. The Executive Council Reports strongly opposed privatizing Social Security in the 2000s, but did not highlight the negative impact on poor retirees. Labor has opposed cuts to Social Security and supported across-the-board increases in benefits. Given that low-income retirees depend more on Social Security than anyone else, this statement could indicate that labor cares about poverty. Still, that connection was not made explicitly (e.g., Resolution 30, 2005; Resolution 11, 2013).

At these conventions, labor seldom mentioned public assistance programs such as Temporary Assistance for Needy Families (TANF), Supplemental Security Income (SSI), public housing, or rental vouchers. All these programs are targeted at people living below the poverty line. Many beneficiaries of these programs are not employed, which makes them harder for labor unions to see. By the same token, the official statements mentioned above seldom refer to churches or charities, other than an occasional appeal to them as political allies. The AFL-CIO does not think much about programs targeted at the poor, and it does not call for additional soup kitchens or nonprofit homeless shelters. In short, organized labor cares about poverty primarily when the needs of the poor dovetail with those of middle-class workers.

Let's focus for a moment on those documents where references to poor, poverty, and low income appear at least once per page. While this might not seem like a high bar, it eliminates all the executive reports and all but ten resolutions. Of those ten, six were rather specific (and short). One called out Walmart for low wages (2005), and another said something similar about tobacco companies (2009). Of the four remaining resolutions, one was aimed at global poverty (2009). Three resolutions, out of almost 200, focused a little bit on poverty in the United States. Two featured the usual call for government and labor unions to boost wages and employment for many workers (Resolution 7, 2001; Resolution 20, 2017). The other one occurred in 2001 (Resolution 35), when the AFL-CIO called on Congress and the president to reauthorize and expand the food stamps program. Nevertheless, this resolution ended by noting how food stamps benefit "low income and unemployed families." The unemployed would include the non-poor and likely some union members. Once again, the AFL-CIO cares about the poor when they are part of some larger group.

Previously, I explained my hesitation to use legislative hearings for measuring how much organized labor (or any interest group, for that matter) cares about a given topic. In case readers are curious, I searched the ProQuest Congressional database for every congressional hearing in which someone from the AFL-CIO testified between January 2000 and October 2019. The total was 352 hearings. Then I restricted the search to hearings in which poverty was one of the subjects. The total dropped down to 10, an average of one hearing every two years. Three of those hearings focused on poverty in other countries. The remaining seven hearings usually focused on inclusive policies to promote retirement security, health care, and homeownership. Over the last two decades, the AFL-CIO was much more likely to testify about matters relating to international trade (72 hearings), regulation of financial institutions (39 hearings), and occupational health and safety regulation (22 hearings).

Using a similar approach, I identified more than 650 congressional hearings over the last two decades in which poverty was listed as a central topic of the hearing. AFL-CIO officials appeared at just a handful of these hearings. Although this might seem like evidence that the AFL-CIO had plenty of opportunities to weigh in, we do not know how often they were invited to testify. Nothing in these hearings suggests that labor cared about poverty more than what we found in the Executive Reports and convention resolutions.

Anyone familiar with US labor history knows that no single organization speaks for all unionized workers. There have been disputes within the AFL-CIO, and some unions have remained independent. Given the wide range of occupations and industries that have been unionized, some labor unions might care about the poor more than AFL-CIO leaders do.

The American Federation of Teachers (AFT) is one of the biggest unions in the country.[17] The AFT is affiliated with the AFL-CIO, and its members interact daily with low-income children. One out of every six American children lives in poverty, and approximately one-half of all schoolchildren are eligible for free or reduced-price school lunches (Layton 2015; Semega et al. 2019). Teachers know that being poor or hungry makes it harder for their students to learn. One might therefore expect a teachers' union to care a lot about poverty. In some respects, the AFT does care more than the AFL-CIO about poverty. AFT President Randi Weingarten (2018) has spoken out about ending poverty, calling it "a moral imperative." That's a stronger statement than Richard Trumka or John Sweeney, past presidents of the AFL-CIO, ever made. Toward the end of 2019, there were more references to food stamps and public housing on the AFT website than on the AFL-CIO website. I searched the AFL-CIO website for any mention of "war on poverty" and found zero documents. The same search on the AFT website produced 40 hits.

In other respects, the attentiveness to poverty is less impressive. The AFT issues a State of the Union report every two years. The most recent one (2018–20) included just three references to poor people, poverty, or low income in 28 pages of text. The government's free and reduced-price meal program was not mentioned. The phrase "working poor" was likewise absent.[18] Not surprisingly, much of that document was shaped by the 2020 pandemic, which could make it an outlier. The 2016–18 report focused largely on the general needs of teachers, students, and families. It promised to fight for "safe, welcoming, well-funded neighborhood public schools and affordable college," along with "good jobs that pay a living wage" and "affordable healthcare" (page 1).[19] Those were the same kinds of cross-class issues highlighted by the AFL-CIO. Workers and working people were invoked far more often than poor people in the AFT State of the

Union reports. In general, the AFT appears to care about poverty more than the AFL-CIO does, but neither organization would be accused of making poverty one of its top concerns.

The American Federation of State, County and Municipal Employees (AFSCME) has over one million members and is also part of the AFL-CIO.[20] Like the AFT, AFSCME is one of the largest public sector unions. Because many AFSCME members are employed by social welfare agencies, this union should be more likely than others to care about the poor. At its 2018 national convention, AFSCME considered approximately 50 resolutions.[21] Many of them dealt with labor laws and regulations or with increasing the union's political power. Several resolutions focused on programs for low-income people. The organization endorsed an increase in the minimum wage, mentioning the needs of working families in poverty but not middle-class families. AFSCME addressed cuts to low-income housing programs more directly than the AFL-CIO ever did at its conventions. AFSCME expressed support for home care services for the elderly and the disabled, many of whom are low-income. It defended Social Security, Medicare, and Medicaid for their ability to help the working poor and all working people. At least a half dozen resolutions mentioned Medicaid, calling for its expansion or an end to threatened cutbacks.

Nevertheless, we should not exaggerate how much the AFSCME cares about the poor. The wording of one resolution was revealing: "Medicaid provides access to health care services for 74 million individuals in the United States, including families, children, the elderly and the disabled, and is the number one payer of long-term care services in the nation."[22] No mention of poor or low-income beneficiaries. Even when remembering the historic work of Rev. King in fighting poverty, the AFSCME declared, "the revival of a 'Poor People's Campaign' is not an indulgence in nostalgia but an essential activity in the fight for justice for all workers and poor people from diverse backgrounds."[23] Much like the AFL-CIO, the organization has tried to find common ground between the poor and other parts of society.

A few unions specialize in representing low-wage workers. Perhaps the best-known example is the Service Employees International Union (SEIU), which split from the AFL-CIO in 2005. The SEIU is one of the largest unions in the United States, with approximately two million members. About half work in health care, ranging from doctors and nurses to lab technicians and nursing home aides. Many have public sector jobs (e.g., bus drivers). Most of the rest are employed in property services, such as janitors, maintenance workers, and security officers. While its membership is diverse, the sheer size of the SEIU means that it represents hundreds of thousands of low-wage workers. Many are women, racial minorities, or recent immigrants.

Circa 2019, the SEIU website contained multiple references to poverty. One of the organization's main concerns, not surprisingly, is jobs that pay "poverty wages" or "poverty-level wages."[24] This is how the SEIU talks about the working poor. In the words of the organization's president, Mary Kay Henry: "Today working Americans live in an era of uncertainty and anxiety. A growing number of working moms and dads fear that the economy of the future won't provide a stable and secure life for their kids. Far too many jobs pay wages that trap people in poverty."[25] In Henry's view, the poor want good-paying jobs, not charity or handouts (Harty 2018). To help the working poor, the SEIU has been fighting for a $15 minimum wage and fewer restrictions on workers joining unions (see also Greenhouse 2019). When the organization talks about public assistance programs, it is mostly to highlight the plight of low-wage workers who "have to rely on Medicaid and food stamps just to survive."[26] Public assistance programs are viewed as a last resort.

The SEIU holds a national convention every four years, and delegates adopted 19 resolutions in 2016.[27] On the one hand, the language of these resolutions seems entirely consistent with those approved by the AFL-CIO. Poverty, the poor, and low income were mentioned in about 20 percent of the SEIU resolutions, and just briefly—an average of once every ten pages. References to working people, working families, and workers were 50 times more common than references to poverty, poor people, or low-income people. Other than the minimum wage, these resolutions rarely mentioned government programs targeted at the poor and near poor. When the SEIU sees low-income people, it thinks they are paid too little for their labor.

On the other hand, the SEIU has discussed gender and racial inequalities more explicitly than the AFL-CIO. When arguing in favor of a $15 minimum wage, the organization noted that "even with multiple jobs, people are unable to make ends meet no matter how hard they work. Most are people of color. In fact, more than half of working people who are Black or Latino make less than $15 an hour compared to 36 percent of white working people" (Resolution 106A). That same resolution declared that home care providers are "underpaid and undervalued simply because it's work that's been done by people of color and women." The organization has a somewhat different rationale for expanding Social Security. "These benefit increases will help everyone, and focus particularly on low- and moderate-income workers, women, and people who lost wage-earning years because they were caring for family members" (Resolution 112A). The SEIU does not see a sharp distinction between what you do (i.e., work) and who you are (i.e., race, gender). Other resolutions adopted in 2016 highlighted the racial and gender dimensions of climate change (Resolution 108A) and elections (Resolution 110A). It appears that the SEIU is more attuned to race and gender than are traditional unions that belong to the AFL-CIO.

Business Groups

In the United States, labor has a voice but usually a weak one. The vast majority of American workers do not belong to a union. The business community may face a different problem—too many voices, some of them quite strong. Individual corporations, trade associations, and peak associations that cut across industry lines are all active in politics, and they don't always share the same interests or ideals. For example, some companies are more reliant than others on low-wage workers, which could affect their willingness to support measures for the poor and near poor. Some companies and even whole industries depend on government contracts and reimbursements; health care is a prime example. Such companies might tolerate or even welcome a large government role in fighting poverty. Other companies might see the taxes needed to finance the welfare state as a threat to their bottom line.

In keeping with the bird's-eye approach of this book, we will focus primarily on three of the most important peak associations. The National Federation of Independent Business (NFIB) is a leading voice for small business and has a reputation for wielding more influence than its size would indicate.[28] The US Chamber of Commerce is one of the country's oldest and largest business organizations. Its members are mostly small- and medium-sized firms, but larger firms belong as well. The Business Roundtable includes executives from the country's largest corporations such as Bank of America, General Motors, Johnson & Johnson, and Walmart. Each of these peak associations represents a wide range of businesses, and some members might not share the association's viewpoint. We will also hear from specific segments of the business community, much as I profiled a few specific labor unions.

Unlike the AFL-CIO, the NFIB does not have regular conventions where members approve or reject policy resolutions. Nor does the NFIB publish an annual report or executive council report.[29] The organization does, however, survey its members every four years about their problems and priorities. The 2016 survey listed 75 potential problems, each on a seven-point scale from "critical" to "not a problem." Access to high-speed internet, employee turnover, the estate tax, and environmental regulations were a few examples. The long list did not include poverty, hunger, or homelessness. Members were asked about the cost of health insurance but not the uninsured. They were asked about Social Security payroll taxes but not the adequacy of Social Security benefits. It appears that the NFIB, or at least their staff, does not care about poor people. While that could be true, the safer inference is that the NFIB thinks primarily about problems related to running a small business. The survey failed to ask questions about many domestic and foreign policy issues (Wade 2016).[30]

The three most critical problems identified in 2016 were "cost of health insurance," "unreasonable government regulations," and "federal taxes on business income." Health insurance was the only problem that at least half the respondents cited as critical. There was a sizable gap between health insurance and the other top problems. (Interestingly, undocumented workers ranked near the very bottom of the list.) The NFIB also sorted the 75 questions into ten general problem clusters, and the most important cluster was taxes, followed by regulations (Wade 2016).

The questions about taxes give us some insight into where NFIB members stand with respect to taking care of the needy. Federal income taxes on business (#3) and state income taxes on business (#9) were identified as two of the biggest problems. The NFIB inferred that respondents considered taxes to be a problem because they were too high (Wade 2016). Federal and state income taxes, from businesses and individuals, happen to be the main source of revenue for public assistance programs like Medicaid. If small business owners want to reduce those taxes, then they are potentially taking less responsibility for helping the poor. Social Security taxes were less of a concern (#21).

Like the AFL-CIO, the NFIB is more inclined to care about programs for workers. We already know about the importance of health insurance. Workers' Compensation finished relatively high on the NFIB list (#13) in 2016, with 20 percent of respondents calling it a critical problem. Unemployment Insurance was ranked 26th. All of these were ranked higher than the minimum wage/ "living" wage (#36), which was the one issue on the list that could be seen as targeted at the poor. Interestingly, small business owners considered the minimum wage to be slightly more of a problem than credit card processing fees and slightly less than the cost of telephone service (Wade 2016).

In general, small business owners have highlighted the same problems in recent years. The cost of health insurance was the #1 problem in 2004, 2008, 2012, and 2016. Federal income taxes on business have consistently been ranked in the top ten. The same goes for state income taxes on business and unreasonable government regulations. Workers' Compensation, Unemployment Insurance, and Social Security taxes usually appeared among the top 25 problems. The minimum wage usually ranked lower, and the problem of undocumented workers consistently appeared at the very bottom of the list. The overall picture seems clear. The small-business community cares primarily about costs, including taxes, and is more concerned about inclusive than targeted social programs (Phillips and Wade 2008; Wade 2012, 2016).

The results of these surveys call attention to certain problems but do not point to solutions (Wade 2016: 1). That job falls to the organization's leaders. Toward the end of 2019, the Advocacy section of the NFIB website was divided into five sections, and three of them were Taxes, Health Care, and Regulatory Reform.[31]

That seems entirely consistent with members' concerns. Lately the NFIB has paid extra attention to taxes, with special surveys of members regarding the impact of federal tax cuts that were enacted in December 2017. (Note: the NFIB refers to them as "tax relief," not tax cuts.) If you come across some report or testimony about taxes on the NFIB website, you are virtually guaranteed to hear that lower taxes foster economic growth. In particular, lower taxes on business are supposed to generate more employment and higher wages.[32] When you believe this strongly in trickle-down economics, you probably won't give much thought to safety nets.

With respect to health care, the NFIB very much wants to reduce taxes and regulations.[33] Some readers might remember that the NFIB was a vocal critic of the Clinton health plan in the 1990s, as well as the plaintiff in a famous Supreme Court case challenging the constitutionality of the Affordable Care Act. The NFIB continued attacking that Act. It favors repealing several taxes that were packaged together with the ACA and dropping mandated insurance coverage for companies with 50 or more employees. The NFIB's larger objectives are to lower costs and increase flexibility for small business owners. To that end it wants government to create incentives for individuals and employers to purchase health insurance. The organization never says that health care is a right, or that universal coverage should be pursued. In fact, NFIB officials have been supporting efforts to attach work requirements to Medicaid. If Medicaid expansion, enacted as part of the Affordable Care Act, is supposed to help the working poor, then the NFIB thinks it appropriate to condition eligibility on employment.[34]

The opening line of the Labor section of the website warns that "the well-financed and influential labor union agenda often has serious implications for small business owners."[35] The chief threat cannot be unionization: only six percent of workers in the private sector belong to a labor union (US Bureau of Labor Statistics 2019b), and small firms are less likely to be unionized than large firms. A bigger concern is the minimum wage, even though the organization's members do not seem that worried. The NFIB leadership argues that any substantial rise would increase poverty, not reduce it. Higher labor costs would trigger layoffs or keep employers from hiring additional entry-level workers. Because much of the minimum wage debate has been happening at the state level, NFIB state directors have taken the lead in making this argument.[36] The minimum wage is the one issue where NFIB officials refer to poor people or poverty with any frequency. Periodically, officials claim that a higher minimum wage would hurt the working poor.[37] Because this issue offers a good vantage point for understanding divisions within the business community, I will return to it later in the chapter.

The US Chamber of Commerce has been representing business interests since 1912. The organization has a national office in Washington, DC, and state-level affiliates. The Chamber is much bigger than the NFIB, and its membership extends beyond small business. The Chamber also states its policy priorities more explicitly and more regularly. Each January, the CEO gives a speech about the state of American business, which summarizes the Chamber's priorities for the coming year. To figure out how much the Chamber of Commerce cares about poverty, I performed a simple content analysis on ten of these speeches (2010–2019), searching for the same words and phrases that I did with the AFL-CIO's resolutions and executive reports.[38]

These speeches touched on a variety of issues such as international trade, cybersecurity, immigration, taxation, and the environment. Generally speaking, the Chamber of Commerce appears to care about a wider range of issues than the NFIB. However, poverty is not one of them. During these speeches, "poverty," "poor," and "low income" were mentioned only three times in over 100 pages of text. The "working poor" were absent, much as they were from the entire Chamber of Commerce website. References to workers and working people have been more common in these speeches, though they appeared less often than in the labor documents discussed previously. The Chamber's motto is "Standing Up for American Enterprise," not American Workers.

These speeches are supposed to be based on formal reports, but the long-time CEO, Thomas Donohue, was known for speaking his mind (Hacker and Pierson 2010; Stolberg 2013). Perhaps he chose to venture off-script and downplay poverty in his speeches. I searched recent Chamber reports and found no additional mentions of poverty or poor people.[39] So far, the Chamber of Commerce appears to care little about the poor.

The Chamber might think more about preventing poverty than relieving it. Much like the NFIB, the Chamber of Commerce focuses on economic growth and believes that lower taxes and fewer government regulations will lead to widespread prosperity. Both organizations consider labor unions to be an obstacle to achieving that goal. Nevertheless, the Chamber is willing to admit that "economic growth alone cannot solve all of our problems" (2013 speech), and that the benefits of economic growth have not been reaching everyone (2019 speech). Jobs are scarce in parts of the country, and many younger workers with jobs are underemployed. The solution, from the Chamber's perspective, is not a stronger safety net. The solution is better education and training. Schools, from pre-K to college, must do a better job of imparting the kinds of knowledge and skills that will help people land good-paying jobs. And employers must do more to train and retrain their workers. The larger goal, according to the 2019 report, is to "promote high-quality, lifelong learning to ensure that all Americans have the opportunity to reach their potential." In the language of business, better inputs will yield better outputs.

The Chamber does have opinions, mostly negative, about the current state of social programs. One looming problem is entitlement spending, which Donohue has called "runaway" (2011 speech) and "unsustainable" (2018 speech). "There is no greater threat to our country's long-term economic security" (2018 speech). Without meaningful reform, Social Security and Medicare will soon be insolvent. "This is perhaps the most predictable crisis in American history," Donohue declared in 2016. One interesting twist here is the connection between entitlement reform and poverty. According to the Chamber, failure to curb entitlement spending means that "the most vulnerable will be left with a fraying safety net" (2019 speech). Because this was one of the very few references to the safety net in these speeches, it is hard to know whether Donohue was genuinely concerned about the poor or simply hunting for a new way to motivate cuts in entitlements. One clue is that calls to increase spending on public assistance programs were noticeably absent from prior speeches and reports.

The Chamber of Commerce and the NFIB are far more worried about health care costs than coverage. Both organizations are opposed to several taxes embedded in the Affordable Care Act. Both organizations want government to give employers more latitude in the kinds of health insurance they offer (i.e., less coverage at lower cost). Neither wants anything close to a single-payer system; neither thinks of health care as a right. The Chamber is a bit more willing to concede that the US health care system was in poor shape before the ACA, and that repealing parts of the Act will not be enough (e.g., 2017 speech). The Chamber is also more conscious of health care as an industry. It wants policy changes that will enable hospitals, pharmaceutical makers, and insurance companies to remain financially viable (e.g., 2019 speech). For the small businesses that belong to the NFIB, health care is almost exclusively a cost. Members of the Chamber of Commerce might see health care as a cost, a source of revenue and profit, or both.[40]

The Chamber's website tracks multiple issues, from agriculture to travel and tourism. Poverty is not one of them (nor is homelessness, hunger, or inequality).[41] Poverty is occasionally mentioned in connection with other issues the organization cares about. For example, many speeches highlight the positive effects of free enterprise and economic growth, and sometimes those effects include poverty reduction.[42] We hear again that the Affordable Care Act imposes too many taxes and regulations on business.[43] We can also learn a bit more about entitlements. The unchecked growth of entitlement spending is a problem because government will find it harder to afford spending on education and infrastructure, two of the Chamber's higher priorities. Entitlement reform means benefit cuts or tighter eligibility, not higher taxes.[44]

The Business Roundtable is a different kind of organization. Its members are senior executives rather than entire firms, and those executives come from the largest corporations in the country. The organization formed in the early 1970s, partly in response to the rapid expansion of government spending and regulation and partly to neutralize the power of labor unions. The Business Roundtable tried to unite corporate leaders who normally divided along industry lines. As David Vogel has noted, "The Roundtable does not attempt to function as 'one great big trade association,' faithfully reflecting the sum of the particular interests of its 190 corporate members; rather it develops positions on a relatively small group of issues and then encourages its membership to participate actively in their resolution" (1983: 34–35; see also Waterhouse 2014).

Some of these issues are more controversial than others. The Business Roundtable made national headlines in 2019 when it issued an innocuously titled Statement on the Purpose of a Corporation, which was endorsed by nearly 200 CEOs.[45] It declared that companies should care about profits *and* social welfare. Corporate leaders should make decisions that benefit a wide range of stakeholders. In fact, the document mentioned corporate responsibilities to employees and communities before shareholders. To some, the 2019 statement represented a major change in philosophy. The Business Roundtable had declared that the primary responsibility of companies was to serve their stockholders as recently as 1997. Other observers were less impressed, seeing the statement as a public relations move designed to give big business the appearance of a social conscience (Gelles and Yaffe-Bellany 2019; Lazarus 2019; Murray 2019).

The 2019 statement is brief (approximately 300 words) and short on specifics. It recommends "investing in our employees. This means paying them fairly and providing important benefits." The statement does not explain what fair compensation means, nor does it take a position on the minimum wage. The only benefits mentioned are education and training; it says nothing about health insurance, retirement pensions, or parental leave. A second principle, "supporting the communities in which we work," is connected largely to environmental sustainability. Other kinds of support, such as paying taxes or helping to provide affordable housing, are absent. The closest the statement comes to discussing poverty is a general claim that a free-market economy is the best way to generate good jobs and economic opportunity for all. Whatever signals this statement might send about corporate social responsibility, it does not have clear implications for the poor or the social safety net.

Although the Business Roundtable does not publish annual reports or hold regular conventions, it does release official statements throughout the year.[46] This is probably the closest we can get to a running record of the organization's views. If we omit statements related to its own staffing and leadership, the Business Roundtable issued almost 70 statements about economic or political issues in 2019. The most common topic was international trade, especially between the United States and China or Mexico. A few statements touched on infrastructure, immigration reform, and education and training, especially for young adults.

In a clear departure from the NFIB and Chamber of Commerce, the Business Roundtable called on national officials to make paid family and medical leave available to as many workers as possible. Many of these issues were also featured in a general statement to the president and Congress that the organization issued in February.

One common theme running through these statements was jobs. Freer trade with other countries would mean more jobs for Americans. More government spending on highways and bridges would boost employment and economic growth. Immigration reform is needed to boost the supply of workers. The Business Roundtable said next to nothing about Americans who cannot work, whose jobs pay too little to move them out of poverty, or who struggle to pay their monthly bills.

The official statements released in 2018 followed a very similar pattern to 2019. Tax reform was a major theme in 2017, appearing more often than international trade. The Business Roundtable issued fewer statements in 2013–2016, with some greater attention to cybersecurity. Reading these statements, one would have no idea that labor unions have been pushing to increase the minimum wage, or that states have been battling over Medicaid expansion. Big business has more pressing concerns.

One place where the Business Roundtable has discussed poverty openly has been in connection with entitlement reform. The organization does not favor increasing taxes to support entitlement programs. Instead, it wants to raise the normal retirement age to 70 for Social Security and Medicare. It also supports making benefits more progressive. For Social Security, that means "adding a new minimum benefit that ensures that the benefits of a full-career worker would be above the poverty line and means-testing benefits eligibility for individuals with high income." In other words, larger benefits for low-wage workers and smaller benefits for high-wage workers. The Business Roundtable has called for more affluent retirees to pay a larger share of Medicare part B (covering routine medical care such as doctor visits) and part D (prescription drugs). The means-testing here occurs more on the revenue side.

Government support for other Medicare beneficiaries should be sustained in order to "protect the safety net for low-income Americans."[47] These statements are interesting because they indicate some concern for the poor, as well as a recognition that social insurance programs are part of the safety net. But we should not make too much of them given how rarely the Business Roundtable talks about poverty.

The NFIB, Chamber of Commerce, and Business Roundtable represent different segments of the business community, and broad segments at that. It would be unreasonable to expect every single member to agree with positions taken by these peak associations, much as individual unions can differ from the AFL-CIO. During the early stages of the 2020 presidential campaign, for example, unions disagreed with one another about the Medicare for All plans offered by some of the Democratic candidates (Luhby 2019; Ollstein 2019). Recent debates over the minimum wage and Medicaid have revealed similar fissures within the business community.

The federal minimum wage was $7.25 in 2019 and had been stuck there for a decade. Its real value has declined because of inflation and is effectively lower than it was in the 1960s and 1970s. In July 2019, the Democratic-controlled House of Representatives approved a $15 minimum wage, which would be phased in gradually by 2025 and then indexed to wages. Many business organizations howled in protest. According to the president of the NFIB, Juanita Duggan, "The House dealt a devastating blow to small businesses today, risking record growth, job creation, and already increasing wages." A spokesman from the National Restaurant Association said the higher wage "would cripple small- and family-owned businesses." The National Retail Federation and the National Association of Manufacturers likewise opposed the move (Rod 2019). The US Chamber of Commerce took a more moderate stance, promising to work with Congress on some increase to the minimum wage (if packaged with other concessions to small business) but opposing the jump to $15.[48]

Such reactions are not surprising considering that the House bill would have doubled the minimum wage. More surprising are the businesses that did not oppose the bill or that spoke up in favor. The retail giant Amazon announced in 2018 that it would be working with Congress to increase the federal minimum wage and would be raising its own minimum wage to $15 per hour. That same year, Target announced that it would increase its starting wage from $12 to $15 per hour by 2020 (Garcia 2018; Settembre 2018). In March 2019, the McDonald's fast-food chain made headlines by announcing that it would no longer lobby against minimum wage increases. It openly broke with the National Restaurant Association on this issue (Rainey 2019). Around that time a new organization, Business for a Fair Minimum Wage, started testifying before state legislatures and Congress in favor of a $15 wage. Most of its members were small business owners, and they argued that a higher wage would "increase consumer buying power, foster a more stable productive workforce, and strengthen local businesses and communities." The head of the US Women's Chamber of Commerce called the increase "a win-win for businesses and workers."[49] The Business Roundtable has endorsed some increase in the minimum wage without stating an acceptable number.[50] House Democrats must have found it easier to support a $15 minimum wage when so many parts of the business community signaled their openness to an increase.

Members of the Business Roundtable have lots of well-paid, white-collar employees, which makes it easier to support a higher minimum wage. Because several states have already raised their minimum wages above the federal standard, businesses in those states might support a higher wage for all states in order to even up the competitive playing field. Sometimes the divisions are due to deliberate pressure. The SEIU and other groups have been pushing McDonald's to raise wages and allow workers to unionize since 2012. Local family-owned restaurants have not faced similar demands. Before Amazon moved to $15, Senator Bernie Sanders publicly criticized the CEO, Jeff Bezos, for becoming one of the richest people in the world while many of his employees struggled to make ends meet. The Walt Disney Company agreed to phase in a $15 minimum wage at Disneyland and Disney World in the face of union demands (Meyersohn 2019; Wiener-Bronner and Isidore 2018; see also Witko et al. 2021).

Depending on the issue, companies might see themselves more as taxpayers or as service providers. Consider how business reacted to the recent expansion of Medicaid, arguably the most important change benefiting low-income Americans in the last two decades. Thanks to the Affordable Care Act (ACA), states can extend Medicaid coverage to everyone with incomes below 138 percent of the federal poverty line. Within the business community, the NFIB has been one of the most prominent critics of the entire ACA, including Medicaid expansion. The NFIB joined several states in challenging the constitutionality of the Act, and the eventual Supreme Court decision (*National Federation of Independent Business et al. v. Sebelius*, 2012) upheld the individual mandate while declaring Medicaid expansion to be too coercive. States that chose not to expand Medicaid would no longer risk losing all their subsidy from the national government (Rosenbaum and Westmoreland 2012).[51]

After the Court's decision, much of the action moved to the state level, where the NFIB worked hard to block expansion. One of their chief objections was cost. In Virginia, the NFIB argued that "small-business owners realize that there is no such thing as free money from the federal government and any burden that comes as a result of Medicaid expansion will come from their bottom line and their ability to create jobs and grow their businesses." In Maine and Arizona, the organization expressed serious doubts that the national government would cover as much of the cost of expansion as promised, thereby forcing state governments and state taxpayers to shoulder more of the burden. The NFIB also stayed active in states that did approve expansion (e.g., Massachusetts), opposing larger Medicaid budgets and higher taxes.[52]

Throughout this process, the NFIB squared off against organizations that get paid to care for Medicaid patients. These service providers have consistently favored Medicaid expansion. When the ACA was first being challenged in court, the American Hospital Association (AHA) filed an amicus brief defending Medicaid's expansion. The National Association of Public Hospitals and Health Systems, the Catholic Health Association of the United States, the Federation of American Hospitals, and the Association of American Medical Colleges all joined the AHA in sponsoring this brief. Several hospital associations filed a similar brief in 2018, opposing a new effort to declare the ACA unconstitutional.[53]

At the state level, service providers have defended Medicaid expansion. Some of their reasons reflect concern for their patients. The Catholic Health Association believes that "in supporting Medicaid expansion, the Catholic health ministry once again is called to stand up for the least among us. We urge lawmakers and policy officials at the state and federal levels to protect and expand the availability of Medicaid for families who cannot afford access to healthcare without it." The American Hospital Association publicized studies showing that health outcomes for patients improved more in states that expanded Medicaid.[54]

At some level, though, health care is a business. A senior executive with the Alabama Hospital Association noted that "currently, 75% of Alabama's hospitals are operating in the red, meaning the dollars they receive for caring for patients are not enough to cover the cost of that care. Expanding Medicaid would be a significant investment in the state's fragile health care infrastructure and would help maintain access to care for everyone" (Japson 2018). The Virginia Hospital & Healthcare Association reminded state officials that health care is a major employer, not just in larger cities but also in rural counties. "While much discussion has focused on Medicaid expansion costs, far less attention has been paid to how expansion would boost job creation." Compared to other states that had expanded Medicaid, Virginia's recent job growth was lagging, the Association found, particularly in health care and social services. The president of the Iowa Hospital Association made a similar argument, pointing to a study showing that expansion would mean over 2,000 new jobs and $2 billion in additional revenues for the state.[55]

Hospitals are not the only businesses that care deeply about Medicaid. In recent years the nursing home industry has made it very clear that it opposes Republican proposals to cap Medicaid spending.[56] At other points in Medicaid's history, doctors, managed care organizations, and pharmaceutical firms have spoken out against cuts to the program, or called for greater spending (Olson 2010). Medicaid is not unique in this respect. Many government programs rely on third-party providers. We can easily imagine why the food industry would support subsidized meals for the poor, or why for-profit child-care chains might speak up in favor of publicly subsidized child-care programs. We can also imagine why many other businesses would be less enthused, viewing social programs as a cost, not a source of revenue.

Discussion

With few exceptions (e.g., the SEIU), major labor unions and business organizations in the United States have said little about poverty-related needs in recent years. Their official statements make few references to poor people, and that includes the working poor. Based on these statements, it is true that labor cares more about the poor than business does. It is also true that today I can jump higher than Abraham Lincoln can. That's not saying much.

After examining a wide range of official documents, we have a better under-standing of why business and labor seem to care so little about poverty. One reason reflects their shared worldview. These organizations focus heavily on ec-onomic growth and jobs. They promise to make life better for the many, not the few. They think more about preventing distress than relieving it. Business and labor are asking the same basic question: how can we generate widespread pros-perity? Of course, the two sides often disagree about the best ways to achieve this goal. The path usually involves less government if you are the NFIB or the Chamber of Commerce, and more government if you are the AFL-CIO. Few of these organizations spend much time talking about the people left behind.

In addition, labor unions and small businesses are legitimately worried about their own survival, which makes it harder to care about others. The AFL-CIO is acutely aware of the decades-long slide in union membership. At its national conventions, much of the talk is about ways to stem or reverse this decline. Union leaders care intensely about labor laws. They want government to make it easier for workers to organize, and for unions to bargain collectively for better wages and benefits. Do that, the argument goes, and you won't need much of a social safety net. The combined efforts of government and labor will move workers and their families into the middle class. For their part, small businesses lead pre-carious lives. According to the US Small Business Administration, 20 percent of small businesses fail in their first year, and about half fail within five years.[57] Organizations such as the NFIB focus on policies that could lower costs or in-crease revenues for their members, which would help them survive. If you are running a small business, chances are good that programs to help the poor look like an added burden.

When unions talk about social programs, they focus almost exclusively on programs tied to paid work. Unions see themselves as advocates for working people and working families. Union leaders pay attention to Social Security, Medicare, Unemployment Insurance, and the minimum wage. All these programs benefit the poor and non-poor. All of them, according to labor, should be protected from benefit cuts and expanded. By contrast, targeted programs that benefit many of the non-working poor, such as public housing or Supplemental Security Income (SSI), have rarely been mentioned.

When business groups talk about these social programs, the message varies. Many businesses are bothered by the cost of entitlements such as Medicare and Social Security. They favor cutting these programs but not abolishing them. Both the Chamber of Commerce and the Business Roundtable have suggested that heavy spending on entitlements poses a threat to funding for safety net programs. However, some businesses are more supportive of government involvement. They might be able to absorb the costs, such as Amazon's embrace of the $15 minimum wage. Or they might depend on those programs for revenue, as with hospitals and nursing homes that treat millions of Medicaid patients. Ironically, business interests might care about public assistance more than organized labor does, if only because many companies are paid by government to provide food, housing, medical care, and other services for low-income Americans.

3

Churches and Other Charities

If business and labor organizations pay little attention to poverty, surely churches and other charities must pay a lot. The latter can respond to social needs in ways that market actors, so focused on profits and paychecks, cannot (Walzer 1986). Every major world religion recognizes problems associated with poverty, whether those problems are material, spiritual, social, or political. Some religions, including those prevailing in the United States, explicitly encourage their followers to alleviate material poverty (Ammerman 2005; Brackney and Das 2018; Cnaan 1999, 2002). The core mission of many secular charities is to care for those in need. Not all beneficiaries have to be poor; some could be flood victims or cancer patients. But many of the largest charities do assist people with limited incomes. The same is true of smaller, local charities.

This chapter begins by investigating how much churches and charities in the United States care about poverty-related issues. The answer may seem obvious. Nevertheless, contemporary churches are involved with many debates, from abortion and same-sex marriage to racial justice, immigration, and climate change. Like labor unions, churches are worried about declining membership. Secular charities like the United Way want to accomplish multiple objectives and remain financially solvent. Poverty is seldom their sole concern. Organizations might care about so many issues that they cannot care deeply about any one of them. Once we address the question of caring about, we will identify who should be responsible for taking care of needy Americans, according to leading churches and charities.

This is probably the strangest chapter in the book. Many academics examine public opinion, if only because democracies are supposed to represent the will of the people. Interest groups are a defining feature of American politics, with business and labor being two of the most prominent groups. Social scientists pay attention to what public officials say about all kinds of issues, including poverty. In that sense, Chapters 1, 2, and 4 feature familiar voices in American politics. There are studies of religion and politics, with an emphasis on public opinion,

Who Cares. Christopher Howard, Oxford University Press. © Oxford University Press 2023.
DOI: 10.1093/oso/9780190074456.003.0004

parties, and elections, but they seldom intersect with studies of social welfare.[1] The literature on philanthropy and secular charities is not large. This chapter begins to fill in these gaps by documenting what churches and other charities say about helping those in need.

Many studies of poverty feature individuals trying to take care of themselves by working in low-wage jobs and paying market prices for whatever they need. When that approach falls short, they turn to their families or government for help. We don't hear much about food pantries and free medical clinics, many of which are run by charitable organizations. We will learn more about these options in Part II of the book.

Churches

The United States was settled by religious dissidents and has long been known as an unusually religious country. Compared to people in other wealthy democracies, Americans in the 21st century are more likely to identify with a specific religion, feel that religion is important in their daily lives, and regularly attend religious services. In the United Kingdom and Germany, less than ten percent of the adult population pray every day. The average among all European countries is 22 percent. In the United States, 55 percent of adults say they pray daily (Fahmy 2018; Norris and Inglehart 2011).

The Pew Research Center routinely conducts surveys about religious life. A recent poll (2018–19) found that 72 percent of American adults identified with a specific religion. Most of the rest were unaffiliated (26%). A large majority of Americans (65%) currently call themselves Christians, mostly Protestants and Catholics. Only seven percent identify with other faiths such as Judaism (2%), Islam (1%), Buddhism (1%), or Hinduism (1%). The importance of organized religion has been waning lately. In 2007, only 16 percent of Americans said they were religiously unaffiliated. Church attendance has been declining as well.[2]

In keeping with the bird's-eye approach, this section will be devoted to how the largest Christian organizations talk about poverty. I do this with some trepidation, knowing that some readers will feel that their faith has been slighted. Recent trends in immigration and religious affiliation suggest that more Americans will be Muslim, Buddhist, or Hindu in the future. However, Christian adherents now outnumber their non-Christian brethren by almost ten to one.[3] It makes sense to focus heavily, but not exclusively, on the religious majority. Consequently, I will usually refer to churches instead of "faith communities," which implies a broader range of religions than discussed here.[4]

The sacred text of Christianity is the Bible, which includes many references to poverty.[5] One recurring theme is that God truly cares about the poor. According to the Old Testament, God "raises the poor from the dust and lifts the needy from the ash heap" (Psalms 113:7).[6] " 'Because the poor are plundered, because the needy groan, I will now arise,' says the Lord; 'I will place him in the safety for which he longs'" (Psalms 12:5). In his famous Sermon on the Mount, recorded in the New Testament, Jesus declared, "Blessed are you who are poor, for yours is the kingdom of God. Blessed are you who are hungry now, for you shall be satisfied" (Luke 6:20–21).[7] It is no coincidence that Jesus Christ was a poor person and spent much of his adult life ministering to the disadvantaged.

A related lesson is that no one should mistreat the poor. "Whoever oppresses a poor man insults his Maker" (Proverbs 14:31); "whoever mocks the poor insults his Maker" (Proverbs 17:5). As part of a general call for kindness and mercy, God tells his followers, "do not oppress the widow, the fatherless, the sojourner, or the poor, and let none of you devise evil against another in your heart" (Zechariah 7:10). Those who ignore these precepts will be judged harshly. When the Lord asks a question like, "What do you mean by crushing my people, by grinding the face of the poor?" (Isaiah 3:15), somebody is in serious trouble.

On a more positive note, God is supposed to look favorably upon those who care for the poor. "Whoever has a bountiful eye will be blessed, for he shares his bread with the poor" (Proverbs 22:9). "Whoever gives to the poor will not want, but he who hides his eyes will get many a curse" (Proverbs 28:27). Farmers are instructed not to harvest all their grain so the poor can find something to eat (Exodus 23; Leviticus 19). The book of Isaiah distinguishes between true and false fasting. Fasting does not honor the Lord if it means simply doing without; we should share our food with the hungry and provide shelter to the homeless (Isaiah 58). Believers can demonstrate how much they love God by helping the poor. "If anyone has the world's goods and sees his brother in need, yet closes his heart against him, how does God's love abide in him?" (1 John 3:17). "Whoever is kind to the poor lends to the Lord, and he will reward them for what they have done" (Proverbs 19:17).

The rewards are potentially enormous. "When you give a feast, invite the poor, the crippled, the lame, the blind, and you will be blessed because they cannot repay you. For you will be repaid at the resurrection of the just" (Luke 14:13–14). The apostle Paul declared that "God loves a cheerful giver." Anyone who gives freely to the poor will find that "his righteousness endures forever" (2 Corinthians 9:7–9). When a rich young man asked how he could achieve eternal life, Jesus replied, "If you would be perfect, go, sell what you possess and give to the poor, and you will have treasure in heaven" (Matthew 19:21; see also Mark 10:17–21 and Luke 12:32–34).[8]

In one of the best-known passages, Jesus describes the Last Judgment as a sorting of all people into two groups. The righteous will inherit the kingdom of heaven. They are the people who fed the hungry, clothed the naked, and visited the sick. However they treated "the least of these" will be interpreted as how they treated Jesus. Everyone else "will go away into eternal punishment" (Matthew 25:31–46).

Christianity is not alone in calling attention to the poor. Many of the passages cited above come from the Old Testament, which is also known as the Hebrew Bible or the *Tanakh*. Those passages represent shared Judeo-Christian values. Later writings in the Jewish Talmud frequently discuss one's obligation to help the poor (Ellis 2018). The concept of *tzedakah* translates roughly as charity, and it means that good Jews should give to others out of a sense of justice. "According to Jewish thought, just as God answered the Hebrews' cries for help during their oppression in Egypt, God expects the Hebrews to answer the cries of others in need" (Cnaan 1999: 93). Two types of charity, *sadaqah* (voluntary) and *zakat* (obligatory), are discussed often in the Qur'an. *Zakat* is one of the five pillars of Islam,[9] and Muslims who have the means are expected to donate a share of their income to help the poor and needy (Allheedan 2016; Bonner 2005; Rahaman 2018). Caring about the needy has deep roots in all these religions. "Provision of services to the poor, orphans and widows, sick and disabled, prisoners and captives, travelers, and neighbors in times of calamity was both emphasized and fostered in the early Jewish, Christian, and Muslim traditions" (Cnaan 1999: 106–7).

All the evidence so far leads to the same conclusion: good Christians (and Jews, and Muslims) should care about the poor and take care of them. The Bible, however, is a long and complicated document. It contains passages that might qualify or even challenge that conclusion. Consider the famous line, "For you always have the poor with you" (Matthew 26:11; see also Mark 14:7 and John 12:8). When Jesus said this, did he mean that poverty was inevitable, we can never end it, and so we should not try? Did he mean that some of the poor do not want to be helped? That is how some people have interpreted this passage (Loftus 2017). An opposing view is that Jesus was referring back to a part of the Old Testament that declared "there will never cease to be poor in the land," and then commanded the faithful to "open wide your hand to your brother, to the needy and to the poor" (Deuteronomy 15:11). In that case the persistence of poverty demands action, not resignation.[10]

There is some ambiguity in the Bible about which poor people deserve our help. In recent years, some policymakers have justified work requirements for public assistance programs by quoting this line from the New Testament: "If anyone is not willing to work, let him not eat" (2 Thessalonians 3:10; for modern invocations, see Bittman 2013 and Dewey 2017). Others have sharply criticized this interpretation for lacking context, arguing that the edict applied only to those who might stop working because they believed judgment day was near. Similarly, many parts of the Bible attribute poverty to forces beyond one's control, such as famine or wicked oppressors (e.g., Genesis 47, Psalms 10, 1 Samuel 8). But some passages link poverty to individual failures such as laziness or lack of faith. "A slack hand causes poverty, but the hand of the diligent makes rich" (Proverbs 10:4). Pulling together certain strands, one could cite the Bible as favoring the working poor over the non-working poor. Or the Bible could favor the poor, period.

The Bible says many times to love our neighbors as ourselves. This is one of the two great commandments, according to Jesus, along with loving God with all one's heart (Matthew 22:34–40). Should we understand "neighbors" to mean people living near us, to humanity in general, or something in between? That answer would affect our sense of obligation to the poor and whether it applies locally, nationally, or internationally.

Finally, the Bible does not offer clear guidance as to who, specifically, should take care of the poor. That responsibility once belonged exclusively to families and religious communities. Someone who reads the Bible literally will probably not expect government to take the lead, partly because so many rulers depicted in the Bible were cruel tyrants. (And nowhere does Jesus advise us to seek assistance from Congress.) Those who read the Bible more as a general guide might point out that it was written centuries before the English poor laws and the modern welfare state. The world has changed, and we must change with it; telling the poor to swing by the nearest wheat field and see what's left to eat seems anachronistic. In our current era, government programs could be accepted, perhaps even embraced, if they helped many of the poor.

To sum up, we know that Americans are unusually religious, that most Americans are Christian, and that the Christian Bible pays considerable attention to poverty. Caring for the poor is an important tenet of multiple faiths. We also know that the Bible discusses many subjects, and large portions say little or nothing about poverty. Questions remain about which poor people are supposed to be helped and who should take care of them. It is unclear how a document written so long ago is supposed to guide us in responding to modern poverty. To gain some insight into these unresolved questions, we will examine some of the leading religious organizations currently operating in the United States. Although no single organization represents all Christians, a few speak for large segments of the community.

Evangelical Protestants are the largest religious group in the United States. Experts disagree about who qualifies as an evangelical: some studies count those who affiliate with specific denominations such as the Southern Baptist Convention and the Assemblies of God; other studies count people who call themselves evangelical, or who share certain beliefs. In general, evangelicals believe the Bible is infallible. They view the crucifixion of Christ as a pivotal episode that made it possible for future generations to overcome sin. Salvation must be based on personal faith. Good works alone will not earn them a place in Heaven. For many evangelicals, being born again, spiritually, signifies their deep faith. As the name suggests, evangelicals believe in spreading the gospel message to others and often hope to convert them. Depending on which definitions and measures are used, roughly one-quarter to one-third of American adults qualify as evangelical Protestants. Some of these evangelicals would also be classified as fundamentalists. They are more likely to read the Bible literally and less likely to be tolerant of other religions.[11]

The National Association of Evangelicals (NAE) is an umbrella group representing 40 different denominations and over 45,000 local congregations. Established in 1942, the NAE offers a good window into evangelicals' attitudes toward a range of issues. By reputation, evangelicals are thought to care more about personal salvation than social justice, and more about abortion and homosexuality than poverty. The reality is more complicated. Before the pandemic, the NAE's website had two sections devoted to poverty (domestic and international) and one to hunger.[12] The domestic poverty section included a variety of articles, statements, resolutions, and press releases—almost 40 of them published between 2010 and 2019. Some drew attention to the geography of poverty, pointing out that it affects rural and suburban areas as well as big cities. Some focused on the causes of poverty, such as predatory lending. And other entries described what churches have been or should be doing to help the poor. The international poverty section of the website contained about half as many items from the same time period. The hunger section was shorter, with seven entries.[13] Already it seems evident that evangelicals care more about the poor than do the largest business and labor organizations.

That said, the NAE website featured links to over 50 topics. Not surprisingly, abortion and same-sex relationships were on the list. So were issues such as the Middle East, nuclear weapons, and refugees. The organization looks inward as well, paying attention to church leadership and church finances.

To get a sense of the relative importance of poverty, some comparisons would be useful. We can work with the topics mentioned above and compare the number of linked stories for each. Over the last decade, the total numbers for abortion and immigration were quite close to domestic poverty (averaging four stories per year).[14] Somewhat less attention was paid to prison reform, marriage, church finances, and church leadership. Behind them came human trafficking, nuclear weapons, same-sex relationships, and hunger.[15]

Occasionally the NAE Board of Directors issues an official statement or resolution. It did so ten times between 2010 and 2019.[16] In general, the NAE has tried to stay out of politics (Green 2019), and such resolutions are not made lightly. Three resolutions mentioned the poor specifically: one in the context of global poverty and the US foreign aid budget; one concerning the impact of climate change on developing countries; and one regarding the domestic problem of short-term, high-interest loans. Two resolutions focused on issues (paid family leave, educational equity) where the poor could benefit, as could many of the non-poor. Only one resolution dealt with abortion or same-sex marriage. Since 2015, the NAE has been publishing a magazine, *Evangelicals*, three times a year. The cover stories have touched on a wide variety of topics, one of which was domestic poverty and one was abortion.[17] In short, though domestic poverty might not be the NAE's top priority, it has received more attention than many other issues. (And the NAE might not have a number-one issue priority.)

Reading through this material, one cannot detect a clear preference for the working poor. The NAE recognizes many types of poor people—children, the disabled, the hungry, the employed, and the unemployed. The organization has invoked the Bible to justify serving "the least of these," broadly understood. There is no mention of withholding food from those who do not work. Nor is there any evident bias in favor of Whites or men. For every statement drawing attention to rural poverty, which might be interpreted as a coded reference to Whites, one can find explicit mention of poverty among Blacks or Latinos.[18]

Fewer in number than evangelicals, mainline Protestants represent approximately 15 percent of the country. They are also a diverse group, defined sometimes by their denominations and sometimes by their beliefs. They might be Methodists or Episcopalians, Presbyterians or Quakers.[19] Typically, mainline Protestants view the Bible as a historical document, one that offers general guidance and should be interpreted in light of changing times. They consider parts of the Bible to be parables or allegories, and not literally true; for instance, few mainline Protestants believe that Jonah was literally swallowed by a whale. A strong belief in Jesus Christ and a desire to follow his teachings are important. Nevertheless, people can get to Heaven without being "born again," and perhaps without being Christian. Compared to evangelicals, mainline Protestants are thought to give more weight to social justice and less to personal salvation. We therefore expect mainline Protestants to care more about poverty. However, their churches have been experiencing a substantial decline in membership, which might lead them to focus more on their own needs than on the world around them (Hudnut-Beumler and Silk 2018; Lipka 2015; Wilson 1999; Wuthnow and Evans 2002).

The National Council of Churches (NCC) is probably the best-known organization representing mainline Protestants. Established in 1950, it includes 38 different denominations and over 100,000 local congregations.[20] Some studies distinguish between mainline Protestant denominations, which are largely White, and historically Black Protestant denominations, which represent another 6 to 7 percent of the country.[21] The NCC includes both. The African Methodist Episcopal Church, African Methodist Episcopal Zion Church, and

National Baptist Convention all belong to the NCC. Their involvement is more than symbolic. The Right Rev. Darin Moore, an African American bishop in the A.M.E. Zion Church, recently served as chairperson of the NCC's governing board.[22]

Compared to the National Association of Evangelicals, the NCC declares its concern for the poor more openly and explicitly. Coping with poverty looks like a top priority.

> At the core of Christian faith is a commitment to work on behalf of and with those marginalized by our society; the hungry, sick, poor, prisoners, strangers and powerless people (Matt. 25:44). Jesus' life provides the model by which we are to work for justice and peace in our world. Like the Old Testament prophets, we raise our voices with the voiceless and help victims defend themselves from injustice.[23]

In recent years, the NCC has designated two issues for special attention—mass incarceration and interreligious relations. Improving the performance of the criminal justice system is seen as a matter of racial justice. The NCC wants to disrupt "the cradle to prison pipeline" that affects so many people of color. Improving relations with Muslims and Jews, Hindus and Buddhists, is seen as an important step toward peace at home and abroad. Both these objectives are entirely consistent with the quotation cited above. Nonetheless, the NCC could be giving priority to prisoners and strangers over the poor, the sick, or the hungry.[24]

Unlike the NAE, the National Council of Churches comments regularly on contemporary events. In 2019 alone, the NCC released 22 official statements. Between 2015 and 2019, the total surpassed 100. Many of these statements were linked to interreligious relations: lamenting shootings at Jewish synagogues; calling for protection of religious minorities in various countries; criticizing the Trump administration's Muslim travel ban. Multiple statements focused on the death penalty, gun violence, or police shootings of Black citizens, all of which connected to the organization's broader interest in criminal justice reform. Several times the NCC expressed frustration or outrage at the treatment of immigrants and refugees by the US government.

What the organization did not say was also instructive. The NCC has avoided making statements about abortion or same-sex marriage. It has said little about declining membership and the resulting strains on local congregations. And it has issued very few statements about poverty or hunger. The NCC criticized the administration's proposed budget for neglecting the poor in 2017. It made similar points that year regarding tax cuts for the rich. The year before it made a special plea to Wendy's restaurants for better treatment of Florida farmworkers who supplied their tomatoes. And that was about all. In its official statements, the National Council of Churches has addressed poverty about as often as relations between the United States and North Korea.[25]

Given the NCC's general pledge, it is strange to find so few statements calling attention to poverty-related problems or policies. Perhaps we are not searching in the right places. It turns out that the "News" section of the NCC website highlighted the same general themes as the official statements, with considerable attention to race, criminal justice, and relations with other religions. (The main difference was greater attention to job announcements and individual awards among the news stories.) Poverty and hunger have been mentioned, but not often.[26]

Looking back a few years helps to clarify this puzzle. At one time the NCC did sponsor a poverty initiative, similar to its current efforts regarding mass incarceration and interreligious relations. The NCC transferred those activities to a newly formed Ecumenical Poverty Initiative (EPI) in 2013. Several denominations that belong to the NCC also belong to this initiative (e.g., the A.M.E. Zion Church, Episcopal Church, Presbyterian Church USA). The Christian Church (Disciples of Christ) provides the institutional home for the EPI, and they belong to the NCC as well. To understand how mainline Protestants talk about poverty, we should start here.[27]

The organizers of the EPI do not mince words. "The goal of the Ecumenical Poverty Initiative is to empower and mobilize the faith community to speak and act to end the scandal of poverty in the United States."[28] Christians are obliged to act. "Jesus calls us to advocate with and for the marginalized, and we take this calling seriously."[29] Shortly after President Trump was inaugurated, the National Council of Churches and the EPI issued a statement expressing "grave concerns about a proposed policy agenda that, if enacted, would put the most vulnerable among us in jeopardy. Throughout Christian scriptures we are instructed to care for the poor and the most vulnerable."[30] The EPI has spoken out at the national, state, and local levels. It has neither ignored the working poor nor given them special attention. Being Black or White, male or female, young or old has not mattered. Like the National Association of Evangelicals, the EPI interprets biblical references to "the least of these" as covering a wide range of individuals.[31]

Protestants and Catholics are the two main wings of Christianity in the United States.[32] Approximately 20 percent of American adults identify as Catholics.[33] Like Protestants, their share of the population has been declining. Indeed, a noticeable fraction of all adults are former Catholics who now affiliate with a different religion or none at all (Masci and Smith 2018; Pew Research Center 2019b). Protestants and Catholics share many of the same beliefs, and someone worshipping in an Anglican or Episcopalian church could encounter many of the same rituals, hymns, and biblical passages as someone in a Catholic church. Nevertheless, there are important differences. Catholics believe theirs is the one true church, with the pope as the ultimate leader. Protestants reject papal primacy. Catholics do not consider the Bible to be the only source of religious doctrine; the traditions of the Church are also authoritative. Catholics and mainline Protestants generally believe that doing "good works" for others will improve their standing with God and their chances of getting into Heaven, whereas evangelical Protestants believe that personal faith is the only way to achieve eternal salvation. But Catholics share with evangelicals an interest in converting others to their faith (O'Collins 2008; O'Collins and Farrugia 2015; White 2017).

The US Conference of Catholic Bishops (USCCB) is a leading voice for American Catholics. Much like the National Association of Evangelicals, the USCCB pays attention to a remarkably wide range of issues. Important priorities for the Conference include religious education; recruiting new priests; religious freedom at home and abroad; abortion, cloning, and assisted suicide; marriage, parenting, and divorce; domestic violence and sexual abuse; racism; capital punishment; weapons of mass destruction; global climate change; genocide; torture; immigrants and refugees; the Israeli–Palestinian conflict; as well as poverty, hunger, homelessness, health care, and economic justice.[34] While it would be hard to argue that any one of these is the most important priority, caring for the poor appears to rank high.

Every four years, the USCCB generates a strategic plan to highlight its top priorities, and that plan must be approved by the bishops and archbishops. The plan from 2017–20 identified five priorities. Two of them made essentially no mention of the poor: promoting religious freedom around the world, and encouraging more Catholics to join the priesthood or become lay leaders. A third priority called for renewed evangelization, "addressed particularly to the marginalized and those most in need of Christ's merciful love." In theory, those people could include the poor (along with many others). The other two priorities mentioned poverty explicitly. In the context of family and marriage, the USCCB sees "the advancement of healthy family life [as] a central strategy for combatting poverty." To promote human life and dignity, the Catholic Bishops have expressed "special concern for the poor and vulnerable."[35] This last priority covers a lot of territory, and the poor were not the only ones singled out for special attention. Nevertheless, the main groups connected to two or more priorities in this strategic plan were the poor, immigrants, and young people.[36]

Strategic plans are usually written for organizational insiders. The USCCB has also prepared a guide called *Forming Consciences for Faithful Citizenship*, aimed at a wider Catholic audience. References to poverty appear throughout. For instance, it describes some actions as "intrinsically evil," such as "treating the poor as disposable." Much of the document explains how core principles of Catholic social thought—human dignity, the common good, subsidiarity, and solidarity—are supposed to shape action in the public sphere. Protecting human dignity means many things, and working to overcome poverty is one of them. Human dignity and the common good are promoted when everyone has a right to food, housing, health care, and employment. Likewise, employers should pay "decent and just wages" and allow workers to unionize. Generating economic growth is not enough. Catholics should embrace policies that foster a "better distribution of income . . . and an integral promotion of the poor which goes beyond a simple welfare mentality" (United States Conference of Catholic Bishops 2015: 16, 21–23).

To be fair, poverty is not portrayed as the only threat to human dignity or the common good. Parts of the document also identify abortion, euthanasia, same-sex marriage, racism, the death penalty, environmental degradation, and torture as threats. Poverty is more prominent in connection with the solidarity principle. Showing solidarity with others builds directly on biblical lessons about loving thy neighbor. Good Catholics should think of themselves as their "brothers' and sisters' keepers, wherever they may be." In the process, Catholics should respect the Church's preferential option for the poor and vulnerable. "While the common good embraces all, those who are weak, vulnerable, and most in need deserve preferential concern. A basic moral test for any society is how it treats those who are most vulnerable." The bishops refer to the Bible (specifically Matthew 25), where those who care for "the least among us" are rewarded at the Last Judgment. And they quote the official Catechism of the Catholic Church: "Those who are oppressed by poverty are the object of *a preferential love* on the part of the Church" (United States Conference of Catholic Bishops 2015: 24–25, italics in original; see also pages 29–32).

None of the USCCB documents described above stress differences between the working poor and the non-working poor. They do not pay special attention to poverty among Whites, Blacks, Hispanics, men, or women. They do not single out the young or the old. Being poor or vulnerable is all that matters. The Catholic Campaign for Human Development, described as "the domestic anti-poverty program of the U.S. Catholic Bishops,"[37] tracks poverty among many different groups. Its website offers vignettes of a diverse mix of individuals and families. Poverty clearly has many faces. The Campaign encourages Catholics to advocate for many anti-poverty programs in the federal budget.[38] Moreover, Catholic leaders believe the official poverty measure underestimates the true level of need.[39]

Anyone who studies large organizations knows that what is discussed at the top might be different at the ground level. Based on their rhetoric, leaders of major Protestant and Catholic organizations clearly care about the poor.[40] But these leaders could be talking just to each other. It would help to know how much regular churchgoers hear about poverty or hunger when they attend weekly services. The bottom line is, quite a lot. The Pew Research Center has periodically asked Americans what issues their clergy talk about. This question has been posed only to people who say they attend services at least once a month, whether they are Christian or not. In 2012, almost three-quarters of regular attendees said that their clergy had discussed poverty and hunger in recent months. The percentages were somewhat higher for Catholics and slightly lower for evangelical Protestants. Mentions of abortion were less common among Catholics and much less common among Protestants. Poverty and hunger were also discussed in Christian churches considerably more than homosexuality. Similar questions asked in 2010, 2008, and 2006 revealed even greater attention to hunger and poverty. (More recent surveys by Pew have asked about clergy discussing economic inequality or sexual harassment/abuse, but not poverty or hunger.[41])

In short, churches in the United States do care about poverty, and their rhetoric does not make distinctions among the poor. When we shift to the next stage of caring—taking care of—all the Christian organizations discussed so far accept responsibility for helping the poor. They encourage their members to donate time, money, and skills to benefit many types of needy people. That much is expected. At the same time, a wide range of Christian leaders have also expressed support for government involvement.

Consider evangelical Protestants. By reputation, evangelicals are politically conservative. They trust God much more than government. Most evangelicals are White, and that group supplies a crucial bloc of Republican voters (Scott 2018). Yet the website of the National Association of Evangelicals contains a remarkable declaration: "Evangelicals believe that government is a gift from God for the common good."[42] A skeptic might wonder if the government the NAE had in mind was a gift only if it outlawed abortion and same-sex marriage. Before the 2012, 2016, and 2020 presidential elections, the NAE joined other religious organizations in asking the major candidates to submit a short video outlining their plans to fight poverty, and then posted those videos online. As a senior NAE official explained in 2015, "Christians are deeply concerned about the suffering of hungry and poor people. . . . We expect our presidential candidates to move beyond platitudes about the middle class and inspirational rags-to-riches stories. We are looking for well-conceived initiatives that can actually be implemented and that will help millions of people rise out of poverty at home and abroad."[43]

Three core principles of Catholic social thought (human dignity, common good, solidarity) lead to a deep concern for the poor. But the fourth principle, subsidiarity, might lead Catholics away from government. Subsidiarity is normally understood to mean giving responsibility to the smallest or most immediate part of society. To deal with problems like hunger and poverty, Catholics would turn first to their family, then their church. That understanding of subsidiarity is correct, up to a point. What happens if families and churches are not up to the task? Would government action then be justified? Yes, it would. During the welfare reform debates of the 1990s, Catholic leaders made it clear that "private charity could not and should not replace the government's rightful role. Subsidiarity does not mean that government steps out of care for the common good" (Coleman 2003: 257). More recently, Church leaders have declared: "Larger institutions in society should not overwhelm or interfere with smaller or local institutions, yet larger institutions have essential responsibilities when the more local institutions cannot adequately protect human dignity, meet human needs, and advance the common good" (United States Conference of Catholic Bishops 2015: 22).

In practice, local institutions often fall short. Time and time again, Catholic leaders and their Protestant counterparts have declared that government action is essential to deal with poverty-related needs. That message has been conveyed clearly by the Circle of Protection, a coalition that includes the National Association of Evangelicals, National Council of Churches, and Conference of Catholic Bishops. The Circle of Protection emerged almost a decade ago as a way for Christian leaders to make their views known in Washington. In particular, they were concerned that elected officials would try to reduce the deficit by cutting back on aid to the poor.

> As Christian leaders, we are committed to fiscal responsibility and shared sacrifice. We are also committed to resist budget cuts that undermine the lives, dignity, and rights of poor and vulnerable people. Therefore, we join with others to form a Circle of Protection around programs that meet the essential needs of hungry and poor people at home and abroad.[44]

The national budget, they argue, is a moral document. As good Christians, they feel obliged to speak up on behalf of "the least of these" during budget debates. In recent years the Circle of Protection has opposed cuts to SNAP (Supplemental Nutrition Assistance Program) and Medicaid. The organization has also called on members of Congress to increase funding for low-income housing, the Earned Income Tax Credit, and the Child Tax Credit.[45]

Religious leaders routinely acknowledge that their ability to meet social needs is limited. When cuts to SNAP were proposed in 2013, the National Association of Evangelicals sent a letter to every member of Congress, expressing their opposition.

> We know from pastoral experience that many parents face excruciating choices between feeding their families, and paying for housing, transportation and medical care. The role of churches and charities is critical,

but we can't fill all the gaps on our own. We need a public-private partnership in which each sector does its part. The SNAP program provides
a basic floor of food security to children, the elderly, the unemployed,
and those whose employment still leaves them in poverty. Churches
can offer personalized, high-touch assistance that complements what
government provides.[46]

A few years later, the Conference of Catholic Bishops wrote to senators on the
Appropriations Committee, urging them to increase funding for low-income
housing programs.

The Catholic Church, inclusive of all its ministries, is one of the largest
private providers of housing services for the poor and vulnerable in the
country. We serve as many as we can, yet lack the resources to assist
all of our brothers and sisters in need. The reality is that we cannot do
it alone, and in many cases government at every level is an important
partner in our work.[47]

In early 2019, when the national government was experiencing a partial shutdown (as elected officials deadlocked over the budget), the Circle of Protection
told Congress that millions of needy people would soon be missing their benefits.
"Churches and faith-based charities will always respond, as best we can, to spikes
in need and services across the country and abroad, but we do not have the capacity to fill such a sharp increase in demand caused by this partial shutdown.
Congress is encouraged to reopen the government immediately."[48]

Two points are worth mentioning here. First, religious organizations do
not see themselves in a zero-sum relationship with government. In their view,
helping the poor, the hungry, and the homeless is an enormous task, one that
requires substantial efforts by churches and government. The second point
concerns the nature of government involvement. Religious leaders talk much
more often about public assistance programs (e.g., SNAP, Medicaid) than social insurance. They want to protect and expand government programs that are
targeted at low-income people, whether or not those people are employed. This
is quite different from labor unions, which tend to focus on inclusive programs
tied to paid work (e.g., Social Security, Medicare).

Before analyzing secular charities, I want to note one limitation of the
preceding discussion. When you shift from the national level, where organizations like the NAE and NCC operate, to the local level, you will find all sorts
of interfaith organizations working to address poverty. Several of them unite
members of Christian, Jewish, Muslim, and other religions, and that is less
common at the national level. Examples can be found from Portland to Miami,

from San Diego to Providence.[49] Poverty is not always their sole concern, but it is one of the main problems these organizations care about.

Other Charities

Legally, religious organizations are one type of public charity. All such charities are exempt from federal income taxes provided they meet the requirements of section 501(c)(3) of the Internal Revenue Code. For example, all public charities must be nonprofits. They cannot be operated to benefit a specific individual or shareholder. They are typically funded by many different individuals or groups, not just one wealthy family. Their ability to engage in electoral or lobbying campaigns is highly constrained.[50] As a result of these and other requirements, many nonprofits do not qualify as charities.

Organized charities have been an integral part of the US social safety net since at least the 19th century. The role of charities changed, but did not disappear, as the modern welfare state took shape in the 20th century (Katz 1986, 2001; Morris 2009). Generalizing about the present state of public charities and poverty is very difficult. At last count over 300,000 public charities were operating in the United States.[51] For every major charity such as Feeding America, there are thousands of smaller, local charities that few people have heard of. No single charity receives more than one percent of all charitable donations.[52] Thus there is no equivalent to the Catholic Church, which represents a sizable part of the religious landscape. With the numerous Protestant churches, we could rely on the National Association of Evangelicals and the National Council of Churches to reveal some general patterns. That kind of association is rare in other parts of the charitable domain. A few come close (e.g., Independent Sector, National Council of Nonprofits), but they focus largely on the internal affairs of charities such as finances, staffing, and leadership.[53] Further complicating matters is that many public charities do not consider fighting poverty to be one of their main objectives. They exist to promote the arts, the environment, civil liberties, or other causes.

To be consistent with the discussion of churches, I will focus on secular charities that are large and well known. Table 3.1 lists the 15 largest US charities based on their private donations. Several of these organizations are not germane to this study. Some devote most of their efforts to meeting needs in other countries (e.g., Compassion International).[54] The YMCA is primarily concerned with physical fitness and recreation, and the Nature Conservancy cares mostly about the environment. Probably the toughest decision involves Goodwill Industries. Readers probably know Goodwill from their stores, which sell used clothing and household goods. Those revenues help finance Goodwill's many education

Table 3.1 **Largest Charities in the United States (2019)**

Name	Primarily domestic or international	Private donations
United Way Worldwide*	domestic	$3.3 billion
Feeding America*	domestic	2.8
Task Force for Global Health	international	2.6
The Salvation Army USA*	domestic	2.0
St. Jude Children's Research Hospital*	domestic	1.7
American Red Cross*	domestic	1.5
Direct Relief	international	1.4
Habitat for Humanity International*	domestic	1.4
YMCA of the USA	domestic	1.1
Americares Foundation	international	1.0
Boys & Girls Clubs of America*	domestic	1.0
Compassion International	international	0.9
Food for the Poor	international	0.9
Goodwill Industries International	domestic	0.9
Nature Conservancy	domestic	0.8

* significant part of the US social safety net
Note: these are the largest charities, apart from religious organizations like the Catholic Church.

Source: *America's Top Charities 2019* (https://www.forbes.com/lists/top-charities/#4ae7693d5 f50).

and job training programs. Given how the social safety net was defined in the Introduction, education and training are classified more as poverty prevention rather than poverty relief. Goodwill Industries therefore operates just outside the social safety net.[55]

The remaining seven charities (Table 3.1) have close links to the US social safety net and merit further study. Collectively these charities address core needs of income (United Way), food (Feeding America), housing (Habitat for Humanity, The Salvation Army), and medical care (American Red Cross, St. Jude Children's Research Hospital).[56] Though the Boys & Girls Clubs might seem like an odd choice, they "provide a safe, affordable place for kids and teens during critical out-of-school time,"[57] which is an important type of daily care. Some of these charities, especially the United Way and The Salvation Army, address multiple needs. Except for St. Jude Hospital, all these charities have local outposts throughout the country. Some of them target low-income people, while others help the poor as part of some larger mission. Some have religious roots, others do not.[58] A few of these charities do serve people overseas, though most of their monies are spent helping Americans. In short, these seven charities are prominent and varied, and they can shed light on the larger issues of caring about the poor and taking care of them. Nevertheless, the problems of generalizing are much bigger than they are with churches, and these national charities might not reflect attitudes held by local charities.

As with business and labor, I examined several types of official documents, including annual reports, strategic plans, and the charities' websites. In general, charities see the needy as a large group, not just those who are officially poor. Feeding America, for example, is very attentive to the problem of food insecurity.[59] According to the Department of Agriculture, those who are food insecure do not have enough food to lead an active, healthy life. They are forced to cut back on food or cannot afford to eat balanced meals. Americans who are food insecure can be found below and above the federal poverty line (Coleman-Jensen et al. 2019; see also Chapter 6 in this book). Likewise, Habitat for Humanity argues that individuals can be housing poor without being income poor. People above the poverty line might still be living in unsafe conditions or spending too much of their income on housing. Those individuals are considered housing poor. Housing insecurity and instability are related problems that can also affect people on either side of the poverty line.[60]

Some charities have created alternatives to the poverty line. According to the United Way, "traditional measures of poverty do not capture the magnitude of people who are struggling financially. Our mission is to make the invisible visible by shining a light on the true number of families struggling in the U.S." Their measure is known as ALICE—Asset Limited, Income Constrained, Employed. The starting point for ALICE is a "bare-bones household budget" that varies from state to state and even within states. That budget reflects a basic level of spending for food, housing, utilities, health care, child care, transportation, technology (i.e., smartphones), and taxes, as determined by the United Way. Before the pandemic, 42 percent of US households could not afford these basic expenses. Although 13 percent were officially poor, 29 percent were struggling to make ends meet on incomes above the poverty line. The ALICE measure is designed to highlight problems facing the latter group, which included 35 million households.[61]

The Salvation Army has developed a Human Needs Index (HNI) based on monthly demand for services at its local centers. The HNI reflects an individual's judgment that they need help and their willingness to seek help. In that sense it is subjective. The HNI does not always move in tandem with the poverty line. The Census Bureau tells us that the poverty rate was a bit lower in 2017 than it was in 2007, when the Great Recession began. The Salvation Army's Index indicates that human needs were higher in 2017 than a decade earlier. The Salvation Army has also found that official measures of poverty and unemployment underestimate the level of need in rural areas.[62]

Among this group of charities, The Salvation Army is the most likely to refer explicitly to poverty or the poor. It is the only one that lists poverty reduction as a major objective. The Salvation Army is also the most openly religious of these charities, and its annual reports usually include quotations from the Bible.[63] The United Way, in contrast, seldom refers explicitly to the poor. Instead it talks about medically underserved areas, urban food deserts, struggling neighborhoods, historically disadvantaged children, and vulnerable families.[64] The Boys & Girls Clubs refers to "helping those who need us most" without labeling their members as poor or low-income. Nevertheless, the organization does note that most members receive free or reduced-price meals at school, and that a growing number of its clubs are located in public housing communities.[65] St. Jude Hospital promises that no child will be denied treatment because of their family's ability to pay, and reports that over half of their patients are uninsured or underinsured.[66] Their patients might be poor, or they might not.

Even when the poor, the hungry, the disadvantaged, or the vulnerable are singled out, they are not the only ones being served. Charities, like churches, care about many types of people. The United Way promises to fight "for the health, education, and financial stability of every person in every community." The Salvation Army's basic mission is "to meet human need wherever, whenever, and however we can." The American Red Cross pledges "to relieve the suffering of individuals, being guided solely by their needs, and to give priority to the most urgent cases of distress."[67] Those are exceptionally broad commitments. At a minimum, individuals with low incomes must share the spotlight with those who suffer through hurricanes, tornadoes, floods, and fires. All the charities just quoted, as well as Feeding America, offer disaster relief to people from every walk of life. Disaster relief generates lots of good press and has been the lead story in recent annual reports from the Red Cross and The Salvation Army.[68] In similar fashion, medical needs cut across income lines. Middle-class kids with cancer can get treatment at St. Jude Hospital; middle-class addicts can get counseling from The Salvation Army. The Red Cross supplies blood to poor patients, rich patients, and everyone in between.

Although the churches discussed earlier in this chapter do not make distinctions between the working poor and the non-working poor, some charities do. The United Way's ALICE measure is designed to draw attention to millions of Americans who are employed yet constantly forced to make painful trade-offs (e.g., skipping a utility payment in order to buy groceries). When the United Way talks about promoting financial stability, it usually refers to working families. The other building blocks are education and health care. The United

Way sees better education as essential for future employment; greater access to health care is valued in part because it can boost educational achievement.[69]

Habitat for Humanity promises to help individuals or families own their homes. To be eligible for assistance, however, people must be able to pay off a mortgage. Their new home is not free. Even though the mortgage comes with a low interest rate, or no interest at all, it would be almost impossible to pay off over 15–30 years without a steady job. While the home is being built, Habitat officials also expect recipients to contribute "sweat equity." And some local affiliates require applicants to be working. Habitat for Humanity in the greater New Haven, CT area expects a two-year history of stable employment.[70]

The Boys & Girls Clubs and The Salvation Army describe their roles as part safety net for today and part ladder for success tomorrow. At the Boys & Girls Clubs, children are promised physical and emotional safety, a refuge from dangers around them. They are supposed to feel secure, to believe that someone cares about their well-being. With the help of staff and volunteers, the organization also wants club members to become better students and more independent adults in the future.[71] The Salvation Army provides emergency shelter and transitional housing for the homeless, whether they are employed or not. It also offers job placement assistance and career coaching for the unemployed. Its Pathway of Hope program is designed to combat chronic poverty by offering a customized package of services, "moving families from crises and vulnerability to stability and eventually self-sufficiency."[72]

Other large charities do not place much emphasis on work or self-sufficiency. St. Jude Hospital treats very sick children. There is no requirement that their parents be employed. The Red Cross does not send donated blood only to hospital patients who have a job. Nor does the organization boast about healing the working poor. Feeding America tends to highlight the food needs of children, families, and senior citizens. Whether they are employed or unemployed is irrelevant.[73]

Distinctions based on ascriptive characteristics are rare. According to The Salvation Army, "all people are deserving of Christ's love, regardless of race, gender, ethnicity, sexual orientation, or gender identity." The United Way and Habitat for Humanity make similarly broad pledges (minus the reference to Jesus Christ).[74] Admittedly, cheap talk is possible, and we should try to find more evidence to reinforce claims like these. The Boys & Girls Clubs reports that 30 percent of its members are White, 26 percent Black or African American, 23 percent Hispanic or Latino, and 6 percent multiracial. The male-to-female ratio is 55/45.[75] When Feeding America last conducted a national survey, it found that 58 percent of its food bank clients were White, 25 percent were Black or African American, 14 percent were Hispanic or Latino, and 4 percent were multiracial. Two-thirds of the adult clients were women and the rest were men.[76] Given that the entire US population is 60 percent non-Hispanic White and almost one-half male,[77] it is hard to conclude that these charities care about Whites and men more than racial minorities and women.[78]

Race, ethnicity, and gender are not the only social groupings that could matter. Children attract significant attention from some of the largest charities. St. Jude Hospital and the Boys & Girls Clubs direct their aid almost exclusively to children, while Feeding America highlights child hunger in many of its reports.[79] Social spending by the US government is heavily skewed in favor of the elderly, especially Social Security and Medicare. Charities might recognize this pattern and try to compensate by helping children. However, some charities (e.g., The Salvation Army, Feeding America) also single out the elderly for attention.[80] We might be seeing a tendency to care about those who cannot support themselves via paid work.

Caring about someone means giving them your attention. Taking care of them entails some measure of responsibility. Many charities believe it is their job to take care of the needy, but not their job alone. Like churches, these charities often expect government to be involved. Both charities and churches focus first on public assistance programs. The Salvation Army belongs to the Circle of Protection, which regularly opposes cuts to Medicaid and other types of public assistance.[81] According to Feeding America, the SNAP program "is an essential resource that helps millions of Americans meet their basic nutritional needs."[82] The United Way is on record favoring Medicaid expansion, more federal spending for child care (especially for low-income families), more spending for rental vouchers, and broader eligibility for the Earned Income Tax Credit (EITC).[83] Not every major charity, it should be noted, offers such broad support. The Red Cross and St. Jude Hospital have typically said little about public assistance programs.[84]

Partnerships between charities and government are commonplace. Feeding America and the Boys & Girls Clubs distribute food supplied by government programs. Those efforts are particularly important during the summer months when children do not get subsidized meals at school. The United Way and The Salvation Army receive some of their funding from federal grants. The doctors at St. Jude Hospital get grants from the National Institutes of Health to support their research concerning pediatric cancers. And sometimes charities help people apply for government benefits. Feeding America helps tens of thousands of people apply for SNAP every year. The United Way offers free tax preparation services so that low-income people who are eligible for the EITC can get their refund checks.[85]

From the viewpoint of charities, government action is essential to meeting critical needs. Secular charities sound much like churches in this regard. "While our impact locally and collectively as a network is vast, United Way recognizes that government spending in our focus areas of health, education and financial stability far exceeds the capability of the nonprofit sector."[86] Toward the end of 2019, the Department of Agriculture posted revised eligibility rules for SNAP, rules that removed almost 700,000 people from the program. Feeding America warned authorities that charities could not possibly fill the void. "As the largest hunger-relief organization in the United States, we know that private charity cannot compensate for the breadth of the impact of cuts to the program. For each meal that the Feeding America network of food banks and food pantries provides, the Supplemental Nutrition Assistance Program (SNAP) provides nine."[87]

Before concluding this section, I want to point out something that might have been missed in the previous chapter. Based on evidence from national associations, businesses do not care much about the poor. Companies are more concerned with economic growth and believe that a rising tide will lift all boats. They balk at paying taxes, and they worry about the cost of entitlements. The main exceptions were businesses that could profit from government funding (e.g., by treating Medicaid patients). It was not a flattering portrait.

When we bring charities into the picture, businesses seem more willing to take care of those in need. The annual reports of the largest charities recognize a long list of corporate donors. Over the years, for example, the Whirlpool Corporation has donated millions of dollars' worth of appliances to homes built by Habitat for Humanity. Nissan gave that charity $1 million in 2018. H&R Block donated software to the United Way so its volunteers could help low-income people file their tax returns. Companies have given free vision screenings and eyeglasses to members of the Boys & Girls Clubs, and millions of pounds of food to Feeding America.[88] Overall, corporations donated $20 billion to charity in 2018, which included cash and in-kind donations (Giving USA Foundation 2019). Even if businesses do not talk much about the poor and the needy, they still feel some responsibility to take care of them. As we will see later in the book, words and deeds do not always align in the social safety net.

Discussion

Low-income people in the United States are not well organized politically. Employers form associations and workers join labor unions, but "the poor have an interest group problem" (Miler 2018: 183; see also Schlozman 2010; Soss, Fording, and Schram 2011; Strolovitch 2007). Even if we go beyond income poverty, we won't find the food insecure, the medically uninsured, or the housing poor joining together to advance their common interests. The absence of formal organization is understandable given their scarce resources. Just staying afloat is a daily struggle.

Churches and other charities help fill that gap. Based on their rhetoric—reflected in official statements, strategic plans, websites, and weekly sermons—churches care a lot about people living in or near poverty. While it is hard to quantify the level of care, it seems clear that churches are more attentive to poverty than business or labor organizations are. The Bible tells Christians to look after "the least of these," and contemporary churches interpret that message to cover many types of needy individuals. Church leaders do not focus heavily on the working poor, the White poor, the urban or rural poor. Secular charities are harder to pin down because of their sheer number and diversity. Nevertheless, several of the largest ones are devoted to meeting the needs of low-income Americans. Those individuals need not be officially poor. Charities believe that the federal poverty line has serious limitations, and they care about people who live above and below that line. While some charities (e.g., Feeding America) devote their attention to the poor and near poor, other charities (e.g., the United Way) think about those individuals as part of some larger group. Some charities care about specific needs like housing or food, but other charities offer a wide range of services to those in need. Some charities appear to favor the working poor, but most do not. Being young or old, sick or hungry, homeless or unemployed is enough to merit their help.

Nonetheless, it would be wrong to conclude that churches and charities care exclusively or even primarily about the poor. Churches are worried about their own survival as more and more Americans disassociate themselves from organized religion. Churches care deeply about the spiritual needs of their own congregations, and meeting those needs must be a top priority. When church leaders look outward, they see poverty, hunger, and homelessness—as well as abortion, immigration, mass incarceration, same-sex relationships, racism, and many other concerns. Most churches engage with more than one issue. Secular charities operate a bit differently. With a few exceptions (United Way, The Salvation Army), the largest charities tend to specialize, providing food, shelter, medical care, or daily care. If we work down the list of the largest charities, we will find some that are diversified (e.g., Catholic Charities USA) and many that are specialized (e.g., American Cancer Society, Feed the Children).[89] Their efforts might not be directed exclusively at the poor. Charities benefit low-income, middle-income, and high-income clients; this is especially true in the medical field. Charities offering disaster relief also serve a broad cross-section of the country.

One of the clearest messages to come out of this chapter is how much help churches and charities expect from government. Some charities receive government grants, and all churches and charities depend on favorable treatment in the tax code. Apart from financial support, churches and charities count heavily on public programs to address the same social needs they care about but cannot fully meet. Many churches and charities embrace public assistance programs. They reject cuts to SNAP, favor Medicaid expansion, and want government to spend more on low-income housing. They definitely do not want the country to return to some "golden age" of relief, before the welfare state existed. Perhaps they are humble by nature, or perhaps they have learned from years of experience. Either way, the country's largest churches and charities do not believe they alone are the answer. Nor will government be enough; the needs are too great. Churches and charities regularly call on individuals, families, and corporations to donate money and time in order to help care for people with various needs.

These are broad generalizations, and exceptions can surely be found. Evangelical Protestants are a diverse bunch, and the National Association of Evangelicals might not reflect all their views. Some evangelicals have drawn sharp distinctions among the poor and questioned the deservingness of people on welfare (Wilson 1999). Some fundamentalists could believe that helping the poor delays the Second Coming of Christ, because only when the world is in total crisis will He return. They don't want a delay (Cnaan 1999). The minority of Protestants who believe in the "prosperity gospel"—and they are not solely evangelicals—might focus on their own path to riches (Bowler 2013; Burton 2017). By the same token, it would not be surprising to find smaller, local charities that said nothing about the importance of government in helping their clients.

The emphasis in this chapter has been on churches and secular charities as agents of relief. They provide essential goods and services, like food and shelter. There is another way to think about their role—as agents of social justice. From this perspective, relief is important work, necessary work, but it does not address the underlying causes of human misery. Relief might make poverty less painful but no less persistent. Investing in human capital makes sense in the long run if you believe those causes are largely economic.[90] Some charities focus on helping individuals develop their human capital to the point where falling into poverty becomes less likely. These charities support education and job training. Goodwill Industries is one example; Teach for America and the United Negro College Fund belong as well. Many churches sponsor adult literacy programs.

Those who believe that some of those causes are political in nature adopt a different strategy. We have seen hints of this already, such as the National Council of Churches calling attention to racial bias in the criminal justice system. Such bias, they argue, is morally wrong, and it aggravates other social problems. Families struggle to stay out of poverty when one parent is in jail. It is hard to escape poverty when you have a criminal record and cannot get a good job. Finding ways to keep people out of the criminal justice system would have the added benefit of keeping them out of poverty. The Conference of Catholic Bishops reminds the faithful about the Two Feet of Love in Action—one for charitable work and one for social justice. For Catholics, promoting social justice can take many forms, including advocacy for a living wage and universal preschool.[91] A two-pronged approach to poverty, based on direct service and structural change, is also common in Judaism.[92]

In recent years, some religious leaders have launched a Poor People's Campaign, one of the most ambitious efforts yet to address underlying causes of poverty. The co-chairs of this campaign are William Barber and Liz Theoharis, both ordained ministers from mainline Protestant churches. Much like the campaign led by Rev. Martin Luther King, Jr., this one hopes to promote a moral revival in which public officials give higher priority to the needs of the poor. Because moral appeals are seldom enough to prompt such a revival, this new campaign is also conducting voter registration drives across the country. More voters might not be enough, either, given structural problems of representation. The current Poor People's Campaign has pushed to expand the scope of the Voting Rights Act, end racial gerrymandering, and make Election Day a national holiday.[93] After Joe Biden was elected president in 2020, leaders of this campaign argued that his new administration owed much to a diverse coalition of low-income people who had supported him at the polls (Barber and Theoharis 2020).

Whether oriented toward relief, justice, or both, churches and other charities often look to government. Having heard from ordinary citizens in Chapter 1 and from organized groups in Chapters 2 and 3, we will next examine how elected officials talk about poverty-related issues.

4

Public Officials

Anyone visiting the United States in 2014 might have thought the country's political leaders were very concerned about the poor. At a time when Democrats and Republicans seemed to argue about everything, the *New York Times* declared that poverty was "the subject of bipartisan embrace" (Peters 2014). President Barack Obama praised the government's anti-poverty programs in January and called for a redoubling of effort to help those left behind.[1] A few days later, Mitch McConnell (R-KY), the Senate Majority Leader, was asking: "We all know the stock market's been doing great, so the richest among us are doing just fine. But what about the poor?" (quoted in Welna 2014). Democrats in the House of Representatives promised to make 50 speeches about poverty in 50 days. Congressional committees held hearings about poverty in January, March, April, June, and July. During the summer, Republican Paul Ryan, chairman of the House Budget Committee, released a sweeping plan to overhaul the public safety net.[2]

All that attention might reflect a larger pattern—or not. The year 2014 happened to mark the 50th anniversary of President Johnson's War on Poverty, and that milestone could have prompted officials to focus on poverty much more than usual.[3] This chapter will offer systematic evidence from the last two decades in order to ascertain how much officials care about the poor (i.e., are attentive to them). Most of the evidence comes from national party platforms and the president's annual State of the Union addresses. To figure out where poverty ranks among all the issues that officials care about, we need to examine documents that highlight important themes and identify policy priorities. By focusing on party platforms and presidential addresses, we can compare Democrats and Republicans more directly than we did business and labor or churches and charities. Both parties issue platforms on the same schedule, and presidents from both parties have delivered multiple State of the Union addresses since 2000.

In general, we would expect public officials to care about poverty more than business and labor do, if only because the poor represent a potentially large

Who Cares. Christopher Howard, Oxford University Press. © Oxford University Press 2023.
DOI: 10.1093/oso/9780190074456.003.0005

bloc of voters. Helping the poor could matter to some middle-class voters as well (Miler 2018). However, public officials might not be equally concerned. Previous research has found that Democrats usually "own" issues related to poverty and social welfare (Egan 2013, 2014; Petrocik 1996). Ownership means that voters trust one political party to handle an issue significantly more than they trust the other party. Democrats thus might pay more attention to poverty and poor people.

"More" is a relative term. Democrats still might not pay much attention to poverty. In a two-party system, some groups can find themselves essentially captured by one party. Such groups are unlikely to ally with the opposing party, and institutional barriers make it difficult to form a viable third party. Party officials believe they can safely ignore the needs of captured groups. The position of African Americans within the Democratic Party is a commonly-cited example (Frymer 1999). A similar dynamic could be affecting poor people.

For their part, Republicans could challenge Democrats' issue ownership. Republicans might talk about poverty just as often as Democrats, if only to scold the poor for making bad choices or to criticize government programs for perpetuating poverty. Congressional Republicans did exactly that when pushing for welfare reform in the 1990s (Haskins 2006; Weaver 2000). As a result, we should do more than count how many times key words appear in these documents. We should also analyze the substance of official statements.

History tells us that both parties will probably care more about the working poor than the non-working poor. President Franklin D. Roosevelt, chief architect of the New Deal, made his views crystal-clear:

> ... continued dependence upon relief induces a spiritual and moral disintegration fundamentally destructive to the national fibre. To dole out relief in this way is to administer a narcotic, a subtle destroyer of the human spirit. It is inimical to the dictates of sound policy. It is in violation of the traditions of America. Work must be found for able-bodied but destitute workers.[4]

Roosevelt strongly preferred public works projects and social insurance programs, which required employment (Béland 2005; Fox 2012; Kennedy 1999). In the 1960s, President Lyndon Johnson insisted that government should offer the poor a hand up, not a handout (Bertram 2015; Davies 1996). When signing the Economic Opportunity Act into law—the centerpiece of his war on poverty—Johnson claimed it would take millions of unemployed men and women "off the streets, put them into work training programs, to prepare them for productive lives, not wasted lives."[5] Bill Clinton repeatedly promised to move people off welfare and into the workforce during his campaign for the

White House in 1992 (Weaver 2000). Republican officials have long been critical of benefit programs that could foster dependence on government. They insist that Americans should be workers, not dependents—makers rather than
takers (Bertram 2015; Haskins 2006).

Given their coalition of voters, Democrats might be more likely to care about
poverty among women and racial minorities. That consideration did not stop
President Clinton, a Democrat, from signing a welfare reform bill in 1996 that
effectively ended cash assistance for many poor women of color. Indeed, bipartisan agreement about the primacy of work might be funneling more Black and
Hispanic women into low-wage, dead-end jobs (Collins and Mayer 2010; Hays
2003). Hence, our expectations about race and gender are not as clear-cut as they
are for work. It seems safer to predict that Democrats will call on government to
play a large role in taking care of the poor. Republicans will favor less government
involvement and expect more from individuals, families, churches, and charities.

Caring About

Social scientists study party platforms to understand which issues parties care
about and how parties intend to deal with those issues (Appelrouth 2019;
Budge and Hofferbert 1990; Gerring 1998; Jordan, Webb, and Wood 2014;
Miler 2018; Pomper and Lederman 1980). Party platforms do have their
shortcomings. Small groups of activists might insert items into the platform that
the majority did not support. This sort of compromise could be more common
in a two-party system, such as in the United States, where each party tries to
represent a wide range of interests. In addition, divided control of government
can prevent a party from delivering on its promises. Nevertheless, scholars have
found that platforms give us a good general idea of the issues that concern party
officials. How effective political parties are in translating attention to concrete
action is a separate matter.[6]

There is no one right way to analyze party platforms.[7] As a first cut, I searched
for every mention of "poverty" or "poor," as long as the latter referred to a person
or group and not the performance of an agency or program (similar to Miler
2018). Between 2000 and 2016, Democrats and Republicans mentioned these
words about 17 times per platform. If we omit references to other countries, then
the average was 12 mentions per platform.[8] Democrats were twice as likely as
Republicans to use these words. Democrats and Republicans were equally likely
to refer to people or communities as "low income." Democrats thus mentioned
poor, poverty, or low income an average of 23 times per platform, compared to
15 for Republicans. Adjusted for the length of the platforms, the Democrats'
lead was a bit larger.[9]

Charities frequently refer to needy individuals in different ways, not just as poor or low income (Chapter 3). Party platforms seldom do this. Most of them made no reference to hunger or food insecurity in the United States (but did mention hunger overseas a few times). The homeless have received slightly more attention, with three to four mentions per platform. Republicans seldom use the term "safety net." One notable exception was this line from their 2000 platform: "For every American there must be a ladder of opportunity, and for those most in need, a safety net of care." Democrats were as likely to mention a safety net for farmers as for the poor.[10]

Counting the frequency of specific words could overstate their importance if individual mentions are clustered together. In the Democrats' 2016 platform, for example, one-third of the references to domestic poverty appeared in a single paragraph. Half the references to "low income" could be found in a single plank devoted to education. In their 2016 platform, Republicans mentioned US poverty 14 times, with nine of those on a single page. This sort of clustering is evident in other platforms as well, for both parties. One can read large sections of these platforms and never come across any mention of people who have trouble making ends meet.

The Comparative Agendas Project (CAP) is a valuable resource for studying how much attention different issues have received in a variety of countries.[11] The CAP has coded the Democratic and Republican party platforms using a list of 21 topical categories (e.g., agriculture, energy, defense). The topic that fits most closely with this chapter is social welfare, and it includes subtopics such as nutrition assistance and cash assistance to the poor. It also contains statements about social programs that do not refer to poor or needy individuals, making it an imprecise measure. The platforms have been coded at the "quasi-sentence" level, which means that each item could be an entire sentence or a distinct part of a sentence. According to the CAP data, Republicans have been about as attentive to social welfare as Democrats have. On average, each Democratic Party platform between 2000 and 2016 included 34 quasi-sentences related to social welfare. The Republicans' average was 43. In absolute terms, Republicans had the lead; adjusted for length of platform, the two parties were similar.[12]

Whether we examine key words or quasi-sentences, neither party can be accused of obsessing over poverty-related issues. The key words appeared once every few pages in the typical party platform. The quasi-sentences, which touch on all types of social programs, appeared no more than once per page. These results are consistent with Gallup's most important problem question, where poverty, hunger, and homelessness were seldom mentioned (Chapter 1).

Simple counts are not the only way to gauge what parties care about. Another approach is based on how early a subject was mentioned in a platform—the sooner, the more important. Democrats have usually mentioned poverty or poor people earlier in their platforms than Republicans have. Alternatively, we might ask whether parties have dedicated specific planks in their platform to anything closely related to poverty. Such planks have been uncommon for both parties. Democrats had one plank about poverty in 2008 and sub-sections about poverty as part of more general planks in 2012 and 2016. Republicans had one plank titled children at risk in 2000, one about welfare reform in 2004, and one about raising families beyond poverty in 2012.

The concept of caring about cannot be measured solely with numbers. We should also examine the kinds of promises made in party platforms. In 2008, Democrats set a goal of cutting poverty in half within a decade. Their 2012 platform declared, "We must make ending poverty a national priority," and Democrats reiterated that pledge in 2016. Democrats have also declared that no American should go hungry (2016). Those were bold promises, and they suggest that Democrats care more about poverty than simple word counts indicate. Republicans have been less ambitious. Their platforms have called for "removal of structural impediments which progressives throw in the path of poor people" (2016). Republicans have encouraged "efforts to reclaim . . . communities from the culture of poverty" (2016). They have praised the 1996 welfare reforms for reducing dependence on government and called for new initiatives to foster a "culture of hope" among the poor (2012, 2016). Republicans have not promised to end poverty or cut it in half.

For context, we can compare how much attention has been paid to poverty relative to other issues in the platforms. Between 2000 and 2016, both parties paid more attention to domestic poverty than to inflation or interest rates. Both parties talked about poverty less than taxes or education (even though education is largely handled by state and local governments). Democrats have paid more attention to poverty than abortion; Republicans were the opposite. Republicans have also focused more on defense and terrorism than poverty, especially after the 9/11 attacks. For Democrats, these two issues received about as much attention as poverty. On the whole, poverty has ranked somewhat higher on the list of issues for Democrats.

In addition, we can compare how much attention has been paid to poor or low-income people relative to other social groups. The Democratic platforms have referred more often to poor people or low-income people than to farmers or taxpayers. The poor have been mentioned somewhat less often than terrorists. Republican platforms have also mentioned the poor or low-income people more often than farmers, but less often than taxpayers or terrorists. Both parties have made more references to veterans than to poor people. Perhaps surprisingly, several of these platforms mentioned the poor as often or more often than the middle class.[13]

One group that truly stands out is workers, and that includes references to working families, hard-working Americans, working people, working men, and working women. They were invoked almost 90 times in the typical Democratic platform—far more than all references to poor, low-income, needy, hungry, and homeless people combined. Now Democratic officials sound like labor unions. They see people as workers (Chapter 2). Indeed, Democratic platforms have referred to people far more often as workers than as citizens. Different types of workers have been mentioned more than 30 times in the typical Republican platform. That is well below the Democratic figure, but it still surpasses the number of times that Republican platforms have mentioned various types of needy Americans. Republicans have been equally likely to refer to people as workers or as citizens.[14]

Work, meaning employment, is central to key planks in these platforms. Sometimes it appears in the title: Raising Workers' Wages (Dem, 2016); Supporting Working Families (Dem, 2016); Standing Up for Workers (Dem, 2012); Republicans' Tax Policy: Protecting Hardworking Americans (GOP, 2008). At other times the value of work is emphasized in the text. In 2012, the Republican Party platform included a plank, A Twenty-First Century Workforce. The very first line read, "The greatest asset of the American economy is the hard-working American." When Democrats described in 2008 how they would be Renewing the American Dream, they declared, "We need a government that stands up for the hopes, values, and interests of working people." The implication is that one must be employed in order to share in that dream.

Given strong, bipartisan support for workers, it seems logical to expect some references to the working poor in party platforms. In fact, that phrase has been completely absent. Not a single mention in two decades, even though the media and academics were frequently discussing the plight of the working poor. Perhaps that silence isn't too surprising if we imagine ourselves as party officials helping to craft a platform. If we want to stress the importance of work, how can we concede that many Americans who follow our advice will still be poor?

Instead, party leaders have asked what Americans, including the poor, need to improve their lives, and then offered employment as the answer. Because Democrats are more likely to talk about workers and about poverty, it is easier to see this approach in their platforms. For those who are not working, Democrats have called for "a world-class education, from early childhood through college," as well as improved job training (2008; see also 2012, 2016).[15] Building human capital now is the key to good-paying jobs in the future. For those who are working, Democrats have consistently supported workers' right to organize, declaring that "when unions are allowed to do their job of making sure that workers get their fair share, they pull people out of poverty and create a stronger middle class" (2008; see also 2016). They have called for a substantial increase to the minimum wage; their 2016 platform endorsed a $15 per hour minimum for all workers. Democrats have also championed a larger Earned Income Tax Credit to boost the income of low-wage workers. Finally, for people who have a work history, Democrats have promised to protect social insurance programs. They have vowed, for instance, to fight any attempt to cut or privatize Social Security. "Without Social Security, nearly half of America's seniors would be living in poverty" (2016). Not content to play defense, Democrats have promised to expand Social Security "so that every American can retire with dignity and respect" (2016). As readers have probably noticed, some of these policies are aimed squarely at low-wage workers (e.g., the EITC), but several have much wider benefits, such as K–12 education, labor unions, and Social Security.

A closer reading reveals that Democrats have linked work primarily to income poverty. They want to help people earn more money during their working years and receive larger benefits from social programs that are explicitly tied to work. That connection starts to break down when the issue is housing assistance. There, Democrats have promised to help "low-income families, people with disabilities, veterans, and the elderly" (2016 platform) without insisting they be employed. Democrats have defended government food programs that help "struggling families put food on the table," and not just working families (2016). Democrats have pushed for Medicaid expansion at the state level to help the uninsured, not the working uninsured (2004, 2016). Democratic officials seem to expect more of the poor when it comes to income support than food assistance, shelter, or medical care.

Republican officials make different connections between work and poverty. To prepare the next generation of workers, Republicans want low-income parents to have more choice over where to send their children to school (e.g., 2000 and 2016 platforms). More choice means more competition among schools, and that is supposed to produce a higher quality education.[16] Republicans do not consider labor unions or a higher minimum wage to be the answer. Much like business organizations, they believe that lower taxes and fewer regulations will expand the economy to the benefit of all. Republicans worry that income support programs will discourage recipients from getting a job. "We need to build on the results of the 1996 reforms and continue to move welfare recipients into jobs and off the welfare rolls" (2004). In the middle of the Great Recession, with unemployment on the rise, the Republican message did not change. "For the sake of low-income families as well as the taxpayers, the federal government's entire system of public assistance should be reformed to ensure that it promotes work" (2008). To that end, Republicans have embraced "the dynamic compassion of work requirements in a growing economy, where opportunity takes the place of a hand-out" (2016). They want to extend those requirements to public assistance programs such as Medicaid and SNAP. In short, Republicans want the hungry and the sick to earn their benefits.

Considering the long-standing associations between public assistance and single mothers, many of them poor women of color (Chappell 2010; Gordon 1994; Mink 1995), we can imagine how an emphasis on work might overlap with gender and race. At times Republicans have explicitly stated that welfare reform means moving more poor single mothers into the job market (2004 platform). Gender is even more evident when Republicans discuss marriage and family. Republicans have associated single-parent families with all sorts of social problems, from teen pregnancy and high school dropouts to drug use and crime (2000).[17] They equate single-parent families with single-mother families (2000). In their 2016 platform, Republicans lamented the billions and billions of government dollars spent on poor single-parent families. More money was not the answer. "Marriage remains the greatest antidote to child poverty," the party declared. At a minimum, government should eliminate policies that discourage marriage; ideally, government would actively promote marriage (between one man and one woman). Pro-marriage policies, Republicans argue, would make poverty less likely to persist from one generation to the next.

Democrats have not talked much about helping low-income women find a husband.[18] Instead, their platforms have called for women to receive equal pay for equal work (2008, 2012, 2016). They believe that female workers stand to gain the most from increases in the minimum wage (2008). Democrats have acknowledged that poverty rates are higher for women and racial minorities (2008, 2012). They have also noted that some environmental hazards, such as excessive lead in drinking water, affect low-income and minority communities the hardest, leading to educational and health problems (2016). More generally, "race still plays a significant role in determining who gets ahead in America and who gets left behind" (2016). Those kinds of statements, highlighting racial and gender disparities, have been much less common in Republican platforms.[19]

As mentioned earlier, party platforms are the product of compromise. Some passages or entire planks might not be supported by everyone who drafted the platform. Presidential State of the Union (SOTU) addresses largely avoid this problem. They reflect the thinking of the single most important official in the country. Though shorter than party platforms, these speeches still cover a wide range of topics, and they can help us figure out which problems are priorities for the president. "The State of the Union is the single most important policy speech that the president gives to Congress, as well as to the public" (Miler 2018: 22). From 2001 to 2020, Republican presidents delivered 12 of these addresses and Democratic presidents delivered eight. That should be enough to reveal similarities and differences between the two parties when it comes to poverty. (Note: when these patterns reinforce those found in party platforms, I will offer fewer examples or direct quotations.)[20]

For ease of presentation, I will discuss SOTU addresses by presidential administration—Bush I, Bush II, Obama I, Obama II, and Trump—and periodically refer to addresses as SOTU 2009, SOTU 2017, and the like.[21] Because each address is usually 10–11 pages, four of them are close to the length of a party platform. The SOTU follows a standard format. Each president spends some time looking back, reviewing problems inherited from past administrations or celebrating triumphs of the current administration. Most of the address looks ahead, highlighting key issues for the coming year. Those issues usually connect to broader themes of national security, economic prosperity, or values/identity.

There are strong parallels between the ways in which poverty has been discussed in recent SOTU addresses and party platforms. Neither party has paid much attention to poverty or poverty-related issues over the last 20 years. In a typical SOTU address, the key terms mentioned before (poor, poverty, low income, needy, homeless, hunger, etc.) have appeared roughly once every three pages. Only one president mentioned the country's "safety net" in his SOTU address. Nobody has mentioned the working poor by name. Barack Obama made few references to poor people in his SOTU from 2014, despite it being the 50th anniversary of the War on Poverty. Yet presidents have routinely talked about workers, hard-working Americans, working families, and the like—more often than the middle class or the poor.[22] President Obama made more references to workers than citizens in his addresses; Presidents Bush and Trump mentioned these two groups in roughly equal numbers. Every president has paid more attention to taxes than to poverty, and more attention to poverty than inflation or interest rates. Every president has paid more attention to terrorists than poor people, and more attention to poor people than farmers.

Recent presidents have stressed the importance of good-paying jobs, not poor relief. But they have tried to generate those jobs in different ways. Throughout the Bush presidency, the preferred approach included tax cuts for individuals and businesses, higher educational standards, and limits on government spending, especially entitlements. Bush declared that "good jobs must be the aim of welfare reform" (SOTU 2002), one of the few times he ever mentioned welfare. Much more than Obama or Trump, Bush discussed terrorism in his SOTU addresses.

President Obama, facing the deepest recession in a generation, believed that jobs would result from government spending on infrastructure, investments in clean energy, affordable health care, and greater access to preschool and college education. He also emphasized the importance of tax cuts for working families (SOTU 2009, 2010), and international trade. Obama I said relatively little about extended unemployment benefits or greater access to food programs, both of which had been implemented. After the economy had regained its footing, the president asked Congress to help "reignite the true engine of America's economic growth: a rising, thriving middle class" (SOTU 2013).

Obama II paid more attention to workers, and his language took on a bolder tone. "No one who works full-time should have to live in poverty" (SOTU 2013). "Helping hard-working families make ends meet, giving them the tools they need for good-paying jobs in this new economy . . . this is where America needs to go" (SOTU 2015). A year later he declared that "America is about giving everybody willing to work a chance, a hand up" (SOTU 2016). A commitment to workers led Obama to support a higher minimum wage and greater spending on education and job training during his second term.

Like Bush and previous Republican presidents, Trump pushed for tax cuts to boost employment and wages (e.g., SOTU 2017, 2018). Trump called for fewer regulations on business, another Republican staple. However, he departed from the party line when discussing infrastructure, trade, and to some degree immigration. Trump's first address mentioned a trillion-dollar initiative to create jobs by spending on infrastructure (SOTU 2017), and he raised the price tag to $1.5 trillion in his 2018 address. That proposal had more in common with FDR than Reagan. Trump questioned the wisdom of free trade and portrayed existing international agreements as a threat to American workers (SOTU 2017, 2019). Repeatedly, Trump blamed immigrants for a wide range of economic and social problems. By cracking down on illegal immigration and giving priority to immigrants with advanced skills and education, the government would help American workers. According to Trump, "open borders have allowed . . . millions of low-wage workers to compete for jobs and wages against the poorest Americans" (SOTU 2018). The list of problems grew longer the following year. "Working-class Americans are left to pay the price for mass illegal migration: reduced jobs, lower wages, overburdened schools, hospitals that are so crowded you can't get in, increased crime, and a depleted social safety net" (SOTU 2019). Although President Bush also emphasized the importance of border security, he did not portray immigrants as an economic threat. In his last SOTU address, Bush said that "we will never fully secure our border until we create a lawful way for foreign workers to come here and support our economy" (SOTU 2008).

These speeches contain a few surprises. The president who was least likely to pay attention to the poor and needy was a Democrat, Obama I. Despite governing in a time of economic recession, President Obama never mentioned low-income people, and made just one reference to poor people, in his first four SOTU addresses.[23] He referred much more often to working families and hard-working Americans. Obama II paid about as much attention to poverty and the poor as did Bush I, Bush II, and Trump. As a result, Republican SOTUs have paid somewhat more attention to poverty than Democratic SOTUs, which was not the case with party platforms.[24] To be fair, Obama's call to end poverty among full-time workers (SOTU 2013) was stronger than anything uttered by

Bush or Trump. It was also more modest than Democratic Party platforms that
advocated eliminating all poverty and all hunger.

Perhaps the biggest surprise comes when presidents connect race, ethnicity, and poverty. Based on these SOTU addresses, no president made these
connections more often than Donald Trump. Obama rarely talked about Blacks,
African Americans, Hispanics, or Latinos, and never at the same time as poverty or work (see also Haines, Mendelberg, and Butler 2019). Trump bragged
about low unemployment rates among African Americans, Hispanic Americans,
and Asian Americans (2018, 2019, 2020). Those numbers, he declared, showed
how well his economic policies were working.[25] In addition, he claimed that his
criminal sentencing reforms would give African Americans a better chance to
become productive citizens (2019). Sometimes Trump was less explicit, using
racially coded language. For instance, he criticized his predecessors for ignoring
"the fates of children in the inner cities of Chicago, Baltimore, Detroit, and so
many other places throughout our land" (2017).

Some readers might wonder why Donald Trump paid more attention to people
of color than Barack Obama did. Part of the story could be the historic nature of
Obama's time in office. As the first African American president, Obama might
have felt pressure to downplay race. He chose to talk about people as Americans
or as workers. Trump, on the other hand, might have crowed about unemployment in order to attract votes from racial minorities in the next election. At a
more general level, we might question whether a president's speeches should be
interpreted as genuine expressions of concern or as strategic calculations. We
might wonder about the sincerity of party platforms as well.

These are valid concerns, and they are one reason why I devote the second
half of this book to analyzing actions rather than words. What we say might not
mirror what we do. For now, let me point out that all political rhetoric can reflect
strategic calculations. Public officials state their positions partly because they
want other people to support them. Acts of persuasion highlight certain parts
of reality while ignoring others. Obama could have talked about poverty in non-
racial terms, perhaps among children, the elderly, or the disabled. He chose not
to. Instead he focused the country's attention on workers. Whether these were
good choices, morally or politically, is not my concern. My point is that he had
other options. The same goes for Republicans who chose not to put their party
on record as supporting an end to poverty or hunger.

Taking Care Of

By reputation, Democrats embrace government while Republicans bank on the
market. Public sector versus private sector. In a polarized era, these differences

seem obvious. When the discussion turns to who should take care of the poor, this view is partly accurate. Nonetheless, it underestimates the degree of overlap between the two parties. And it tells us nothing about how the parties think about the role of churches and other charities.

Democrats are not simply the party of government. By invoking workers so often, Democratic officials have been reinforcing the importance of individual effort and paid employment. Hard work is a prerequisite for success (e.g., SOTU 2013, 2015; platform 2016), and jobs should be based in the private sector whenever possible. In his first SOTU speech (2009), President Obama offered an economic recovery plan that would "save or create 3.5 million jobs. More than 90 percent of these jobs will be in the private sector." Some of Obama's lines could have easily been uttered by Bush or Trump. "The true engine of job creation in this country will always be America's businesses" (SOTU 2010). "I believe what Republican Abraham Lincoln believed: that Government should do for people only what they cannot do better by themselves" (SOTU 2012). In his final State of the Union (2016), Obama declared that "a thriving private sector is the lifeblood of our economy," and he spoke with obvious pride about the country being "in the middle of the longest streak of private sector job creation in history."

Often, however, the market fails to deliver. Democrats have been critical of a "rigged economy" that favors large corporations and the rich (party platform 2012, 2016). They worry that the American Dream will be "an empty promise, unless we also do more to make sure our economy honors the dignity of work and hard work pays off for every single American" (SOTU 2014). Government must address multiple forms of market failure. In Democrats' view, a higher minimum wage and a larger EITC are needed to compensate for millions of low-paying jobs. Rights to unionize and bargain collectively are needed to level the playing field between powerful employers and their weaker employees; stronger labor unions would lead to better wages and benefits. Laws and vigorous enforcement are needed to ensure that women are paid fairly. The government should also do more to ensure that housing and college are more affordable for working families (platform 2016). The United States should have paid sick leave and paid parental leave for all workers (SOTU 2015; platform 2016). The government should make child care more affordable for working parents (platform 2016). Democrats also believe that the Affordable Care Act was needed in part to address the problem of enormous medical bills driving working families into bankruptcy. Medicaid expansion will help many working families afford medical care (platform 2012).

In short, Democratic officials see government, business, and labor as jointly responsible for helping workers avoid poverty and achieve some measure of economic security. That responsibility extends to helping workers' families as well.

To take care of those who are not working, or no longer working, Democrats believe that government should play the lead role. Democrats talk frequently about helping the young and the old. Young people should have access to high-quality public education, from preschool through college (platform 2004, 2012, 2016; SOTU 2012, 2013, 2014). Democrats have promised to protect and expand Social Security on behalf of retirees (e.g., platform 2004, 2008, 2016; SOTU 2016).

Democrats have said much less about helping working-age adults who are not employed. They have occasionally made references to the disabled, such as helping them find a job and avoid discrimination (e.g., platform 2012, 2016). They have credited food stamps with keeping millions of people out of poverty during the Great Recession (platform 2012) and have promised to protect SNAP from cuts (platform 2016). Democrats have included a sentence or two about spending more on low-income housing (platform 2016). Although unemployed adults are eligible to receive SNAP and subsidized housing, Democrats did not highlight this fact. Moreover, their few references to welfare or welfare reform stressed the importance of helping parents find work (platform 2000, 2004). President Obama's State of the Union speeches said even less about supporting unemployed adults, other than moving more of them into the paid workforce.

Charities often describe themselves as working with government or alongside government to help vulnerable members of society (Chapter 3). These organizations see government as a valuable partner. The attraction is not always mutual. Democratic platforms have made few references to religious organizations in connection with poverty. "Throughout history, communities of faith have brought comfort to the afflicted" (platform 2004). "Faith-based organizations will always be critical allies in meeting the challenges that face our nation and our world—from domestic and global poverty, to climate change and human trafficking" (platform 2012). Those organizations have been portrayed as important complements to government, not as substitutes (platform 2000, 2008, 2012). And that is about all Democrats have said. Obama's SOTU speeches barely mentioned faith-based organizations at all. In their platforms and SOTUs, Democrats have said next to nothing about secular charities and nonprofits. Instead, Democrats place heavy emphasis on work and economic opportunity.

At times, Republicans have criticized government for doing a terrible job of taking care of the poor. They have condemned the War on Poverty for spending hundreds of billions of dollars without lowering the poverty rate. Republicans have argued that public assistance programs foster dependence, creating a "poverty trap" for low-income families (platform 2016; see also platform 2004, 2012). To be more precise, they have criticized government policies that are closely associated with Democrats. Republicans believe that the welfare reforms of the 1990s were a rousing success, and they take credit for moving poor people off welfare and into the workforce (platform 2000, 2004). More recently, President Trump claimed that his economic policies pulled millions of Americans off food stamps and welfare (SOTU 2020).

Like business interests (Chapter 2), Republican officials worry about the cost of entitlement programs—primarily Social Security, Medicare, and Medicaid (e.g., platform 2004, 2012, 2016; SOTU 2000, 2005). Republicans believe that entitlements are a fiscal time bomb; government must act now to prevent future harm. Trump was a notable exception. He basically declared entitlements off-limits during his time in office but signaled that reforms could be considered if he were re-elected (Rappeport and Haberman 2020). When most Republicans discuss entitlement programs, they never mention cutting. Rather, they talk about preserving, saving, modernizing, or even strengthening these programs. Sometimes Republicans claim to be saving entitlements for just about everyone, and sometimes for the poor or needy. President Bush claimed that changes to Social Security "must ensure that lower income Americans get the help they need to have dignity and peace of mind in retirement" (SOTU 2005).

Skeptics might wonder if positive-sounding verbs are supposed to disguise painful changes (spoiler alert: they are). Nevertheless, most Republican officials have accepted government's role in taking care of certain people. For example, the 2004 Republican Party platform stated that "young people deserve to know their Social Security will in fact be there when they retire, just as we have guaranteed it to their grandparents and parents today." The 2016 platform made the claim more forcefully: "saving Social Security is more than a challenge. It is our moral obligation to those who trusted in the government's word." Likewise, President George W. Bush declared that government has an obligation to care for the medical needs of the elderly, the disabled, and poor children (SOTU 2006, 2007). Medicare and Medicaid help meet those needs.

Under Bush, Republicans periodically called for expanding government's role in helping the needy. In these moments, Republicans sounded like Democrats. Shortly after taking office, President Bush proposed adding a new prescription drug benefit to Medicare, specifically to help low-income seniors (SOTU 2001). He kept pushing for this benefit until it became law in 2003. The Republicans' 2004 platform noted that President Bush had requested "record levels of Pell Grant funding" so that more low-income students could afford college. That same platform pointed out that Bush and congressional Republicans were behind "the largest expansion in the history of the community health centers program," which offered medical care to many low-income children. Trump was different. He generally avoided new measures that would target benefits to the poor and near poor. But he did propose spending billions of dollars on infrastructure in order to create millions of jobs (SOTU 2017, 2018), and he called on government to lower the price of prescription drugs (SOTU 2018, 2019). Both those steps could have helped people above and below the poverty line.

Republicans count on churches and charities to take care of the poor more than Democrats do. This pattern was very evident during the George W. Bush administration. He often praised the work of charities and faith-based groups in dealing with a variety of problems, from homelessness and domestic violence to addiction and hunger (SOTU 2001–2004). Sometimes Republicans linked those problems directly to poverty. "The participation of faith-based and community groups will be especially important in dealing with the twin problems of non-marital pregnancy and substance abuse. Reducing those behaviors is the surest way to end the cycle of child poverty" (platform 2000). Republicans feel that these nonprofit groups offered hope and compassion in ways that government cannot. These intangible benefits could have an even greater impact than income support. In one of the more memorable passages, Republicans declared that

> ... the American people have a long and seasoned history of working wonders. Government does have a role to play, but as a partner, not a rival, to the armies of compassion. These forces have roots in the areas they serve, often based in local churches, synagogues, mosques, and temples. Their leaders are people to whom the disadvantaged are not statistics, but neighbors, friends, and moral individuals created in the image of God (platform 2004).

In their view, government should harness these benefits by contracting with religious charities to provide needed services. As long as those organizations do not discriminate against clients based on religion, or use taxpayer monies to promote their religion, government should be eager to enlist their help. Furthermore, government should revise the tax code to create more incentives for individuals to make charitable contributions (platform 2000, 2004; SOTU 2001, 2004, 2008).

Charities and faith-based groups received far less attention during the Trump years. The 2016 Republican platform discussed faith in several places, mostly in the context of religious freedom. In particular, the party declared that faith-based groups doing business with the government should not have to adopt practices that conflict with their religion (e.g., allowing same-sex couples to adopt children). Elsewhere the platform stated that "as we have learned over the last five decades, the loss of faith and family life leads to greater dependence upon government." In his four SOTU speeches, President Trump made a few general references to faith or religion, but not one to faith-based organizations that help the needy. Trump's only explicit reference occurred when he praised the charitable work of Rush Limbaugh, the conservative talk-show host (SOTU

2020). Overall, Trump talked about churches and charities more like Obama than Bush.

Traditionally, Republicans have placed considerable responsibility for taking care of the poor on individuals and families. Their 2000 party platform linked poverty to single-parent families, pointing the finger at fathers who had deserted their children and couples who had divorced. Out-of-wedlock births and drug use were also listed as culprits.[26] The 2004 platform, though focused heavily on terrorism and national security, promised to "extend the benefits of welfare reform by strengthening work requirements and promoting healthy marriages." The 2016 platform, as mentioned earlier, referred to marriage as the best antidote to child poverty. In one of the more scathing passages, Republicans blamed government for supporting single-parent families and discouraging marriage: "nearly three-quarters of the $450 billion government annually spends on welfare goes to single-parent households. This is what it takes for a governmental village to raise a child, and the village is doing a tragically poor job of it."

Instead of being dependent on Uncle Sam, individuals should pursue the dignity that comes with a job. In their State of the Union speeches, Bush and Trump emphasized the importance of reducing the scope of government—lower taxes, fewer regulations—so that companies could create more jobs and hire more workers. Both presidents considered paid work to be the best way for individuals to avoid poverty. On this last point, President Obama would strongly agree.

Discussion

When it comes to poverty, Democratic and Republican officials don't always see eye to eye. On balance—combining measures of frequency with qualitative judgments about intensity—Democratic officials have been paying more attention to poverty-related issues. In their party platforms and SOTU addresses, Democrats have mentioned key words (e.g., poverty, poor, low income, needy) more often, and they have made bolder pronouncements about ending poverty and hunger.[27] In particular, they believe that no one who works full-time should live in poverty. To take care of low-income workers, Democrats want government to increase the minimum wage, expand the EITC, and create more favorable conditions for unions. Republican officials prefer to foster growth by lowering taxes and curbing regulations. Republicans trust the market to create decent-paying jobs. They do not trust government programs to give individuals the right incentives concerning work and marriage. Except for Trump, Republican leaders have called on charities to take care of the poor more often than Democrats have. These are classic differences between the two parties.

Nonetheless, Democrats and Republicans are similar in important respects. Officials from both parties have seldom mentioned poverty-related topics in their platforms and SOTU speeches. They have been much more concerned about national security and economic growth, about terrorists and taxes. All that talk about poverty in 2014, mentioned at the start of this chapter, was highly unusual. The more common pattern for both parties has been to speak optimistically about opportunities for people to move up the economic ladder. Both parties have talked at length about what government can do to help workers and working families. Democratic and Republican officials see employment as the best way to prevent poverty. They have seldom discussed safety nets for those experiencing hard times. Neither party has acknowledged the working poor, whose existence represents a direct challenge to their optimistic narratives. Neither party has said much about poverty among Blacks, Hispanics, or women. Democrats may "own" the poverty issue, based on their rhetoric, but the price of ownership has been remarkably low.

Party platforms and State of the Union addresses are not the only official statements worth studying. From time to time, presidents give speeches that deal directly with poverty. On September 10, 2005, for example, President Bush told the country that he had made it easier for Americans to get food stamps and Medicaid. This was rather surprising, coming from a Republican who worried about welfare dependence. President Obama said relatively little about poverty-related topics in his first four SOTU speeches. Yet in March 2011, he gave a weekly radio address that specifically mentioned higher rates of poverty among women. President Trump spoke openly about faith and charity when delivering a commencement address in 2017. All those speeches, however, should be placed in context. Bush was referring specifically to government benefits for people affected by Hurricane Katrina; Obama was recognizing Women's History Month; and Trump was speaking to an audience of devout evangelicals at Liberty University.[28] Anyone studying these types of speeches should take note of the time and place in which they were delivered (Broockman 2012).[29]

By focusing heavily on presidents and party platforms, I have undoubtedly missed relevant statements by individual legislators and bureaucrats. Some Democrats and Republicans have deviated from the patterns described above. While President Obama said little about race and poverty during his time in office, Rep. Danny Davis (D-IL) called attention to poverty, especially among African Americans and Hispanics, in the *Congressional Record* (December 13, 2010). Davis referred repeatedly to poor people, not to workers or working families.[30] By the same token, some Republican officials undoubtedly connected churches and charities to poverty more often than Trump did. A map like this one cannot reveal every peak or valley. The general contours, though, seem clear. A recent and more comprehensive analysis of congressional speech provides partial confirmation for the conclusions in this chapter. The authors found greater attention to upper-class issues like the deficit than to lower-class issues like the minimum wage between 1995 and 2016 (Witko et al. 2021).

As we shift to Part II of the book, the emphasis will be on concrete examples of care. What we say about poverty might or might not correspond with what we actually do about it. As noted in Chapters 2 and 3, business organizations have said precious little about poverty, but they still donate billions of dollars to charity. By the same token, government officials could be doing more for the poor than a few paragraphs in party platforms would indicate. Without mentioning the working poor by name, they still might design policies that benefitted those individuals.

The reverse is also possible. Those who are attentive to the poor might not try to reduce their hardship. Martin Gilens (1999) found that greater media coverage of welfare often meant more negative stories, especially concerning African Americans. Media attention reinforced damaging racial stereotypes. White Americans have wanted to cut welfare spending partly because they believe it helps lazy Black people. To take a more recent example, President Trump devoted considerable attention to illegal immigrants in his speeches. He described them as gang members, drug dealers, sex traffickers, and murderers (SOTU 2018, 2019). Trump wanted to punish or deport those immigrants. Their well-being did not matter to him at all.

PART II

WHAT WE DO

5

Income

Imagine that one of your main goals in life is, "do not be poor." What would it take to accomplish that goal? In the United States, we typically think of poverty as a lack of income. Every year the US government calculates poverty thresholds for different types of households, based on a formula developed in the 1960s (Fisher 1992; Stone 2001). There is no single poverty line. In 2019, for example, single adults under the age of 65 would have been classified as poor if their annual income was below $13,300. The threshold for a single parent and one child was $17,622. A family with two adults and two children would have needed $25,927 to escape poverty.[1]

The official poverty thresholds have been criticized at various times for being too low, too high, and too crude (Blank 2008; Fisher 1992; National Research Council 1995). These are not hairsplitting arguments; several of the problems are substantial.[2] At this point, hardly anyone in or out of government would offer a strong defense of these thresholds on technical grounds. We keep using them mostly because we have been using them for a long time.

The government has responded to many of these criticisms (though how well is debatable). It publishes statistics about people living near poverty as well as in poverty. Officially, the near poor have incomes between 100 and 125 percent of the standard poverty thresholds. Creating a category for the near poor helps deal with the arbitrary nature of thresholds that are expressed as precise dollar figures. A single person with $14,000 of income is probably facing the same struggles as someone with $13,000. Anyone living near poverty could be just one layoff or one serious illness away from falling into poverty. The government also tracks deep poverty. People whose incomes are less than half the poverty threshold are said to live in deep poverty. A family of four trying to survive on $6,000 a year is in a much more desperate situation than a family of four with $25,000. Calling both families "poor" understates their collective plight.

The US Census Bureau has been calculating a supplemental poverty measure (SPM) since 2011. While the traditional poverty measure is based on pre-tax

Who Cares. Christopher Howard, Oxford University Press. © Oxford University Press 2023.
DOI: 10.1093/oso/9780190074456.003.0006

cash income, a better measure would reflect disposable income. The SPM adds in the value of in-kind government benefits for food and housing, and it accounts for payroll and income taxes as well (including tax refunds). The SPM factors in work-related expenses, such as child care and transportation, and tries to estimate basic expenses more accurately. Whereas the standard poverty measure makes geographic adjustments only for Alaska and Hawaii, the SPM reflects different costs of living in over 300 metropolitan and non-metropolitan areas. The net result of all these changes is a slightly higher estimate of poverty. In 2018, the official poverty rate was 11.8 percent and the supplemental rate was 12.8 percent (Fox 2019).

If your goal is not to be poor or nearly poor, then your target income as a single person in 2019 was somewhere between $13,000 and $17,000. A family of four needed between $26,000 and $32,500. As we saw in Chapter 1, many Americans believe those numbers should be higher. The 2016 AEI/*Los Angeles Times* poverty poll asked what was the most amount of money a family of two adults and two children could have and still be poor. The average response was a little over $32,000; the official poverty threshold at the time was about $24,000 (Fremstad 2016). In a more recent poll, over half of those responding said that an individual making $20,000 a year would be poor. Almost a third put the figure at $30,000.[3] The Federal Reserve surveys Americans about their perceived financial situation. In 2018, 34 percent said they were "living comfortably," while 41 percent were "doing ok." The remaining 25 percent were "just getting by" or "finding it hard to get by." The latter number jumped to 44 percent for those earning less than $40,000 (Board of Governors of the Federal Reserve System 2019). It seems fair to say that the usual poverty measures do not reflect the income needs felt by ordinary citizens.

Moreover, we know that the United Way organization has faulted the official poverty line for being too low (Chapter 3). It has calculated an alternative Household Survival Budget that varies from state to state. These budgets make more adjustments to the official poverty threshold than does the SPM. According to the United Way, a single adult in Illinois, living alone, would have needed $19,000 to afford basic expenses in 2017. That was roughly 150 percent of the official poverty threshold. A family of four with two adults and two young children would have needed $57,000—more than twice the poverty threshold. The survival budget for a similar family in Arkansas, where the cost of living is relatively low, was still almost $47,000. In a high-cost state like New York, basic expenses for that family could reach $70,000 per year (and even more in New York City). A single adult in that state would need over $23,000, and in New York City over $30,000.[4]

To complicate matters, most wealthy democracies use a relative measure of poverty instead of an absolute dollar measure (Iceland 2013). Typically, individuals in those countries are considered poor if they have less than half the median income. From this perspective, poverty means more than a lack of resources. It also reflects a subjective feeling of social distance. When you cannot afford to live half as well as the average person, then you live apart from the mainstream. You could easily feel marginalized, hopeless, bitter. If the United States used a relative measure, the number of people in poverty would go up. For example, the median American worker earned about $40,000 in 2018 (Semega et al. 2019). Relative to that figure, a single adult with less than $20,000 could have been classified as poor, which was well above the official poverty threshold.

In short, it is hard to pinpoint how much money you need to escape poverty. The government's poverty thresholds are well established, and they form the basis for official estimates of the poverty population and poverty rate (Semega et al. 2019). When public officials talk about cutting poverty in half, or eliminating it entirely (see Chapter 4), they have those numbers in mind. Maybe we should stick with the official numbers. On the other hand, we have good reason to believe that those numbers are too low. Government officials could have incentives to underestimate the poverty problem, because doing so lessens the number of people they are expected take care of, which then limits how much officials have to impose taxes or regulations. Even if officials recognized the technical flaws of the current thresholds and agreed that higher numbers were justified, most would hesitate to correct them. They don't want to see headlines declaring that poverty increased during their time in office. On the other hand, charities like the United Way could be exaggerating the poverty problem in order to generate larger donations. And relative poverty measures might tell us more about inequality than need.

Faced with such a wide range of estimates, I will try to navigate a middle path. This path sticks a bit closer to the government's numbers than the United Way's, partly because government plays a much larger role than charities in providing income to the poor.[5] (Charities focus on specific goods and services such as food and medical care.) Nevertheless, I am convinced that the traditional poverty thresholds are inadequate. This chapter will therefore highlight what we do, collectively, to care for people who are poor or near poor. Defining the near poor is tricky: the US government sets the upper limit at 125 percent of the poverty threshold, but some academic studies put it as high as 200 percent (e.g., Edelman 2012; Iceland 2013; Newman and Chen 2007). Rather than trying to resolve these differences, I will aim to be transparent about how near poverty is defined. I also recognize that any nationwide standard of need will conceal regional variations. Being poor in New York City is clearly different from being poor in Arkansas. Paying close attention to these kinds of variations would take more time and space than I can afford. A bird's-eye view in this chapter means searching for national patterns.

As we shall see, the income part of the social safety net is designed primarily for wage workers. We expect people to find a job and try to support themselves and their families. Millions of the poor and near poor do just that. Many jobs do not pay well, and government has several ways to help low-income workers. When individuals are unable to work—due to retirement, disability, layoffs, or some other reason—the government usually links cash benefits to how long people worked and how much they earned. These are social insurance programs, and they help a broad cross-section of citizens, not just the poor. By contrast, income support is scarce for adults who are unemployed and lack much of a work history.

The previous chapters explored how much we care about poverty and which parts of society should take care of the poor. The evidence came from opinion polls, speeches, party platforms, and the like. For the rest of the book, the emphasis is on deeds, not words.

Help Yourself

Taking care of people entails more than talking about who is responsible for their care. It also involves acting to meet their needs (Tronto 1993, 2013). In the context of income support, those actions could be as direct as giving money to a panhandler on the street, or as indirect as paying taxes to fund social programs. The needs could be your own, but are usually someone else's. The practice of caregiving calls attention to the people and organizations that distribute income to the poor and near poor. Sometimes those who take care of the needy are the same ones who give care; oftentimes they are not.

The first point to emphasize is that people living in or near poverty rarely spend all day waiting for someone to give them money. Many are trying hard to take care of themselves and their families. In-depth studies have consistently found that most low-income adults who can work want to work. They prefer paychecks to handouts. They want to see themselves as productive members of society, and to set a good example for their children (Collins and Mayer 2010; Edin and Shaefer 2015; Halpern-Meekin et al. 2015; Hays 2003; Newman and Chen 2007; Shipler 2004). Government statistics make it clear that many low-income people are in fact employed. Eight million Americans who lived below the poverty line in 2018 worked full time or part-time (Semega et al. 2019). Many of those living just above the poverty line are employed as well.[6]

These are the working poor.[7] Logically, their incomes must be inadequate because they are not working enough hours, not earning enough per hour, or both. Numerous studies have documented how the low end of the labor market makes it hard to escape poverty (Collins and Mayer 2010; Desmond 2018; Edin and

Shaefer 2015; Loprest and Nightingale 2018; Morduch and Schneider 2017; Schultz 2019; Semuels and Burnley 2019; Thelen 2019). Here we find people working in restaurants, hotels, and grocery stores. Other workers are cleaning office buildings, mowing lawns, or serving as home health aides. Jobs like these are available all across the country. But many of them are part-time. Of the eight million working poor people cited above, more than two-thirds were employed part-time (Semega et al. 2019).

Part-time jobs have all kinds of drawbacks. Part-time hours can be unpredictable, as employers want flexibility to adjust staffing levels to match business conditions. A waitress will be sent home early if the restaurant is having a slow night. A cashier will be expected to pick up an extra shift if a co-worker calls in sick. The lack of set hours makes it very difficult to combine part-time jobs or arrange for child care, which will be discussed in Chapter 9. Recent research has shown that Black, Hispanic, and female workers are more likely to be assigned fluctuating schedules than are White men. The mismatch between variable paychecks and constant expenses for rent and food creates cash flow problems (C. Miller 2019). Even if the hours are predictable, a part-time worker would need to earn a good wage to avoid poverty. Assuming 20 hours per week, 50 weeks per year, a single part-time worker would need to be paid at least $13 per hour, and probably more like $15 or $16. If that worker were a single parent with one child, the hourly wage would have to be closer to $20. That kind of part-time job is hard to find. Moreover, few part-time jobs come with health or retirement benefits.[8] Not surprisingly, most part-time workers would prefer a full-time job; they are underemployed.

Much has been written about the "gig economy," which relies on temporary jobs for on-call workers and independent contractors. These jobs are more viable for college-educated or highly skilled workers (e.g., computer programmers, accountants). The gig economy can enhance their autonomy without jeopardizing their middle-class or upper-middle-class standard of living. Most low-income workers do not have a college degree or specialized skills. Among poor adults, high school dropouts outnumber college graduates.[9] The gig economy does not offer them good options. Selling items on eBay assumes that one has surplus goods of value. Renting out a spare room on Airbnb is possible when you are a homeowner. Workers who complete tasks online for Amazon's Mechanical Turk average less than $5 an hour. Drivers for Uber or Lyft must have a reliable car, which rules out some of the poor and near poor. Drivers' earnings are hard to estimate, and quite variable, but an hourly rate of $9–$12 seems plausible. Like part-time workers in traditional jobs, gig workers seldom receive health and retirement benefits. The owners of gig companies might be getting rich, but their employees are not (Katz and Krueger 2019; Reed 2020; Thelen 2019).[10]

Traditional full-time jobs offer some hope, if workers can find them. A single person working 2,000 hours a year would need to earn $8–$9 an hour to avoid being counted as poor or near poor by the government. A number of entry-level jobs pay that wage. The math becomes less favorable for families with children. If a family of four has one full-time wage earner, one at-home caregiver, and two children, then the wage-earner would need to be paid at least $13 an hour full time, and probably closer to $16. Anything less and the family would be poor. Before the pandemic, nearly one-third of the US labor force was earning less than $12 an hour, and their wages have been stagnant for decades. Some workers with full-time jobs take on extra part-time jobs to help pay the bills (Appelbaum and Winter 2019; Desmond 2018; Loprest and Nightingale 2018).

Getting hired is just part of the battle. Some full-time workers, such as those who work on commission or depend on tips, do not have steady paychecks. Income fluctuations from month to month make it hard to stay afloat, much less save (Morduch and Schneider 2017). Whether part-time or full time, low-income workers are vulnerable to "wage theft." Employers might not pay for all the hours worked, or at the promised hourly wage; they might withhold tip money. One study found that wage theft cost a typical full-time, low-wage worker over $3,000 per year (Cooper and Kroeger 2017; see also Edin and Shaefer 2015).

Low-income workers are constantly at risk of losing their jobs. Companies can find other people to clean floors, cook hamburgers, or run a cash register, and managers don't have much patience for personality clashes. When workers have health problems that keep them away from work, they might get fired. Those problems could be chronic or acute, physical or mental—and low-income people tend to be in worse health than average (Khullar and Chokshi 2018; Lowrey 2014).[11] New parents might need to spend time at home to care for their babies. Poor children might have their own health problems (e.g., asthma) that require parental care and trips to the emergency room. Cars break down, and low-income workers might not be able to afford the repair bill or find alternative transportation. A sudden eviction might force people to skip work while they scramble to find shelter. Sometimes relatives die or get killed, which can lead to emotional distress and new responsibilities to care for surviving kin. The bottom line is that low-income workers don't have much cushion to deal with problems in other parts of their lives (Collins and Mayer 2010; DeParle 2004; Desmond 2016; Edin and Shaefer 2015; Hays 2003).

Most of the poor, however, are unlikely to have a job. Twelve million are poor children under the age of 18. Five million are age 65 or older. Almost four million are working-age adults with a disability (Semega et al. 2019).[12] I mention these groups because most of us would not expect kids, senior citizens, or the disabled to be fully employed. Teenagers might have a part-time job to earn some spending money. Older Americans might keep working for the social benefits or mental stimulation. But 17-year-olds and 70-year-olds shouldn't need a paying job to survive—not in a country as affluent as the United States.

If we include the near poor, the number of low-income Americans increases substantially. Using the official definition of near poverty (incomes between 100 and 125 percent of the poverty threshold), we would add another four million children and two million senior citizens. Move the upper limit to 150 percent, and the total number of low-income children jumps from 12 to 20 million. The number of low-income elderly doubles from five to ten million (a sign that many senior citizens are not playing golf and eating lobster). By defining the near poor as anyone with income from 100 to 200 percent of the poverty threshold—which is closer to what the United Way and a variety of academic studies employ—we would have 27 million low-income children and 15 million low-income senior citizens (Semega et al. 2019).[13]

When steady work at a decent wage is unavailable, people who are poor or near poor seek other ways of generating income.[14] In theory, they could draw on their savings. Everyone is supposed to have a rainy-day fund, a little nest egg. In fact, many Americans have trouble saving money. According to a recent national survey, 20 percent of working adults said they were not saving any money at all for emergencies or retirement. That figure climbed to over 40 percent for people earning less than $30,000 (Dixon 2019).[15] The Federal Reserve has asked Americans how they would pay for an unexpected $400 bill. Twelve percent felt they had no way to cover that expense in 2018, when the economy was in good shape overall. Another 27 percent said they would have to borrow money or sell something (Board of Governors of the Federal Reserve System 2019). A similar study found that 60 percent of Americans lacked the cash to cover an unexpected $1,000 expense such as a major car repair or trip to the emergency room. Such expenses are common: three-quarters of the people surveyed said they or a close relative had faced a surprise bill of at least $1,000, and more than a third said the bill was over $5,000 (Garcia 2019).

Part of the story here is wealth inequality. As much as income inequality has grown in recent decades, wealth inequality has grown even faster. While some Americans have accumulated substantial assets, valued in the millions (or billions) of dollars, many Americans have few assets or none at all. Individuals and families are thus less able to sustain themselves while unemployed than they were a generation ago. The poor and near poor are especially likely to be vulnerable (Dickens, Triest, and Sederberg 2017; Horowitz, Igielnik, and Kochhar 2020).

A more common strategy for generating income relies on credit cards or short-term loans. Both options involve borrowing money at high interest rates. Though credit cards seem ubiquitous, not everyone who applies for one is accepted. Among adults earning less than $40,000, over one-third were denied in 2018 (Board of Governors of the Federal Reserve System 2019). Credit limits are generally lower for the poor. They can use a credit card to buy groceries, but they won't be able to charge a trip to Paris. Cardholders who fail to pay off their charges each month could easily pay 15–20 percent annual interest on the remaining balance. For those with a poor credit history, the interest rate will be closer to 25 percent. On average, low-income households have about $3,000 in credit card debt at any given time (Dilworth 2020; Maldonado 2019; O'Connell 2019). Few of them can afford to pay off such a large amount, and their interest charges and late fees can mount up in a hurry. Some borrowers will eventually file for personal bankruptcy.

The whole business of credit cards works like Robin Hood in reverse. More affluent individuals can qualify for credit cards that offer no annual fees, high credit limits, cash rebates, discounts on purchases, or frequent flyer miles. Most of these individuals are able to pay off their balances every month. If everyone took advantage of these cards, banks would lose money. Realizing this, banks try hard to persuade less affluent individuals to use a different kind of credit card—one with annual fees, lower credit limits, higher interest rates, and no special rewards. Capital One, for example, has recently offered a credit card with a $300 limit, $39 late fee, and 27 percent interest rate, aimed especially at customers with low incomes. Each year, Capital One collects billions and billions of dollars in interest payments. Other banks operate on a similar model. If cardholders are consistently in debt but making some payments, banks might even raise their credit limit to make deeper debt possible. In the words of one industry insider, "the ugly truth is that subprime credit is all about profiting from other people's misery" (Botella 2019). Historically, the national government has done little to protect these borrowers from being exploited (SoRelle 2020).

The world of payday loans, automotive title loans, consumer installment loans, and pawnshop loans is even less forgiving (Bennett 2019; Getter 2017; Valenti and Schultz 2016). Though the details vary, these tend to be small loans (up to $1000) and must be paid back within a few weeks or months. Compared to credit cards, the cost of borrowing is much, much higher. Someone who takes out a typical payday loan of $375 would have to pay back $430 in two weeks. That works out to an annual interest rate of . . . 382 percent. This is why payday lenders are often referred to as predatory lenders. Most borrowers have to take out loans to pay off their original loan. A small debt that was supposed to be paid off quickly grows into a larger debt that stretches on for months or years. One study found that an initial payday loan of $375 would eventually cost the average borrower almost $900 to pay off. Baradaran (2015) recounts the story of a woman who paid $2,500 in interest to cover an initial $300 loan. Borrowers with title loans or pawnshop loans might have to forfeit whatever collateral they put up, such as their car, if they fall behind on payments.

These are harsh terms, and most people try to steer clear of nontraditional lenders. When short on cash, middle-class Americans might charge more to their credit cards or seek out a loan from their bank or credit union. Many of the poor and near poor have no bank account, or they have a small account but no access to credit at their bank. They are classified as "unbanked" or "underbanked." The local payday lender, title lender, or pawnshop is one of the few options available to them.[16] These lenders deliberately locate in poor areas where traditional banks are scarce. In parts of Mississippi, payday lenders outnumber all the McDonald's, Burger King, and Starbucks franchises combined. There are thousands and thousands of storefront lenders across the country. They do fill a void in the financial system and provide an important service—at a steep price. Small-dollar, short-term lending is a multibillion-dollar industry in the United States, with millions of customers who regularly need money to pay for rent, utilities, and food. No wonder that major Wall Street equity funds have been buying up some of the biggest lending chains. To them, this part of the social safety net looks like a good investment (Baradaran 2015; Bennett 2019; Whoriskey 2018; Zito 2018).

People with low incomes have a few other ways to make money. According to a recent survey, 28 percent of US households earning less than $30,000 were playing the lottery weekly. On average they spent a little over $400 per year (Dixon 2018). A Mega Millions ticket might offer a sliver of hope, but it is not a reliable source of income. Some of the poor earn a little money by collecting bottles and cans for recycling, or a little more if they can sell discarded pieces of metal to scrapyards (Edin and Shaefer 2015). The most desperate might sell their own blood plasma. In their study of extreme poverty, Edin and Shaefer found that the going rate from plasma centers was $30 per session, up to twice a week. Donors must be screened for high blood pressure and low blood-iron levels, and some are rejected. Many of the poor live too far away from a plasma center to even consider this option. Otherwise, some communities still permit panhandling (i.e., begging money from strangers). Panhandlers tend to be poor, single middle-aged men with few family members or friends to help them. Most are unemployed and homeless. Panhandling is not a lucrative occupation (Tillotson and Lein 2017).

Finally, cash-strapped people might break the law. Some of the poor and near poor try to sell their monthly SNAP benefits to family or friends (who are less likely to report them). The going rate varies depending on where you live: it would not be unusual to exchange $100 in SNAP benefits for $50–$60 in cash. Selling SNAP benefits is rational only if you have other ways of obtaining enough food (e.g., from local food pantries), and only if you think the chances of being caught are really low. Selling SNAP benefits is a felony punishable by up to 20 years in prison, which is more than some violent crimes. Other people desperate for income might turn to shoplifting, prostitution, selling drugs, or selling stolen goods. It is hard to know exactly how many poor people engage in these types of nonviolent crimes, and how often. What we do know from previous studies is that the vast majority of low-income people want to find a legal path out of poverty (Edin and Lein 1997; Edin and Shaefer 2015; Newman 1999; Rosen 2020).

Help from Family

Everyone gets financial support from their relatives, if only because everyone was once a child. Middle-class parents often spend tens of thousands of dollars on their children's college expenses. Large inheritances enable some Americans to lead a life of luxury. These kinds of income transfers are important, but not essential for anyone's survival. Low-income Americans routinely tap into a "family safety net" (Cherlin and Seltzer 2014; Park, Wiemers and Seltzer 2019) to meet their basic needs. Most of the poor are unemployed, working part-time, or stuck with low-paying jobs; they need additional money to make ends meet. Their family safety net extends across generations, connecting children, parents, and grandparents. It also includes siblings, spouses, in-laws, and romantic partners. On paper, families look like a much better option than credit cards or payday loans. Relatives do not charge exorbitant interest rates on the money they lend, and they can be flexible about when (and if) you pay them back.

As a general rule, the family safety net is not a large or reliable source of income. It is no substitute for a steady job, and it seldom eliminates the need for government assistance. One reason is that low-income people do not have many rich relatives. In fact, they are often connected to people who are struggling as much as they are.[17] Some relatives will be unemployed; some could be incarcerated or disabled. The ones who are employed might have part-time jobs, irregular hours, or fluctuating incomes, all of which create uncertainty and stress. Many relatives do not have savings to deal with emergencies. Some family members might be coping with health problems. Many couples separate or divorce, and the added cost of maintaining two households takes away income that could have been shared with relatives. In circumstances like these, people ask themselves a very reasonable question: How much money can I give a family member today if I might need money tomorrow? Some people can give, but they have reasons to give carefully. Within an extended family, the few people who have money to spare might get requests from several needy relatives. Spreading that money around means less help for each person. As much as relatives want to help—and numerous ethnographic studies show they do—their resources are limited (Edin and Shaefer 2015; Morduch and Schneider 2017; Park, Wiemers, and Seltzer 2019; Seefeldt and Sandstrom 2015).

The family safety net might be enough for children whose parents work full time. Even if the mother or father earns the federal minimum wage, their job will pay $14,500 a year. That alone is not enough to lift a parent with one or two children out of poverty, but it helps them get close. An added benefit is that the income will be spread out evenly from month to month. However, full-time workers are a small fraction of the poverty population. Many children depend on parents who work part-time. Their income is therefore lower and often unpredictable. It can fluctuate wildly as the parent alternates between periods of employment and unemployment. And some children have parents who are not employed at all.

In addition to resource constraints, some family ties are fragile. Most poor children live in single-parent households, headed by women (Semega et al. 2019). The mother might want nothing to do with the father if he was unfaithful or abusive. Some mothers have been threatened with violence when they pushed for child support. Some mothers worry that asking for more support will cause the father to become distant, physically and emotionally, from their children. Absent fathers who stay involved might drop off diapers or formula for the kids rather than giving their mother cash to spend as she chooses.[18] Fathers who have children with multiple women can feel a stronger obligation to help their current family than past families. Rich or poor, some people grow up in dysfunctional families, and as adults they prefer not to interact with their parents or siblings. Rich or poor, divorce is common in America. Divorce affects not only parents with young children, but also older couples. As various family ties weaken or break, the family safety net is weakened (Cancian and Haskins 2014; Cherlin and Seltzer 2014; Hays 2003; McLanahan 2009; Seefeldt and Sandstrom 2015; Sohn 2019).

This is not a blanket dismissal of the family safety net. Relatives often share what they can, and many will step up in crisis situations. But cash is not typically their strong suit. As we will see in coming chapters, the family safety net plays a bigger role in housing and daily care. Affordable housing is scarce in many parts of the country, and moving in with family members can be a viable option. Relatives often serve as caregivers for young children and aging parents. Providing that kind of care requires time and patience and love. When it comes to income support, however, government has much deeper pockets.

Help from Government

If you hold a narrow view of the public safety net, then you might count only means-tested government programs, where eligibility is limited to the poor and near poor. The list of income programs would be short, featuring Temporary Assistance for Needy Families (TANF) and a few others. A broader view would incorporate programs such as Social Security and Unemployment Insurance. These programs help the middle and upper-middle classes deal with sudden drops in income while providing a crucial safety net for millions of low-income Americans. The narrow view makes it appear that public policy reflects religious teachings about helping "the least of these," especially children, the disabled, and the elderly. The broader view leads to the realization that government takes care of wage workers and their families more than anyone else. Hence, what we do in this part of the social safety net corresponds more closely with how public officials and labor leaders talk.

The most controversial program is, paradoxically, one of the smallest. That program is TANF, commonly known as "welfare." The main beneficiaries are poor children and their parents, who are typically single mothers. TANF is a complicated program to describe because it relies on a mix of income support and services, and because eligibility rules and benefit levels vary from state to state. Nationwide, about 20 percent of the monies spent by TANF go to income support (aka basic assistance). In 2018, that portion was close to $7 billion. Eleven states devoted less than ten percent of their TANF spending to income support. In some states (Arkansas, Illinois, Indiana), the figure was below five percent. A larger share of TANF's $31 billion budget goes to services that help parents find employment, and that includes paying for child care (Burnside and Schott 2020; Center on Budget and Policy Priorities 2020b).[19]

To be eligible for TANF, recipients cannot have much income. In 2018, the typical state excluded three-person families with incomes over $840 per month. The official poverty threshold for that family was about twice that amount, meaning that one has to live in deep poverty to qualify for TANF in many states. The income ceiling varies widely: $268 in Alabama, $815 in Michigan, $1,277 in Rhode Island. To stay on TANF, adults must comply with their state's work requirements and time limits. Adults can have their benefits reduced or terminated if they fail to work as expected. The standard time limit is two years for any single spell on TANF, with a five-year lifetime limit (these restrictions do not apply to children). Many states have approved shorter time limits. Legal immigrants usually must reside in the United States for five years before applying for TANF.[20] Because of rules like these, less than one-quarter of poor families with children are receiving cash assistance from TANF. In several states, the figure is less than one out of ten poor families (Burnside and Schott 2020; Center on Budget and Policy Priorities 2020b; Falk and Landers 2019; Goehring et al. 2019).

Approximately three million people receive income support from TANF. Over two million of them are poor children. Thus, a large majority of poor children in the United States do not benefit from cash welfare. Even the ones who qualify for assistance do not receive much money. The maximum monthly benefit in most states is less than half the poverty threshold. Actual benefits are usually lower than the maximum. Benefit levels in southern states are especially low. All over the country, the value of those benefits has eroded substantially over the last two decades as policymakers failed to increase the original TANF block grant. If families rely heavily on TANF for their income, they will be stuck in poverty (Center on Budget and Policy Priorities 2020b; Falk and Landers 2019).

Historically, welfare has had a bad reputation because of the parents. Many Americans believe that adults on welfare could work if they really wanted to (see Chapter 1). The reforms of 1996 were supposed to make welfare harder to get, harder to live on, and harder to keep (Soss, Fording, and Schram 2011; Weaver 2000). In that sense, they succeeded. Very few poor adults are now on welfare. The program is so small that some of those eligible don't even know that TANF exists; others choose not to apply for fear of being rejected or somehow jeopardizing their status as legal immigrants (Edin and Shaefer 2015; Seefeldt and Sandstrom 2015). By shrinking welfare, policymakers have forced more adults to deal with the low-wage labor market and all the difficulties described earlier in this chapter. In the process, government has cut back on the care of poor children. The share of poor families on welfare dropped from 68 percent in 1996 to 22 percent in 2018. The previous AFDC program lifted ten times more children out of deep poverty than TANF does now (Floyd 2020).

In contrast, the Earned Income Tax Credit (EITC) has led a charmed life. This program has been embraced by both political parties because it rewards employment. The biggest debates have involved its expansion, not retrenchment (Howard 1997, 2007). Eligibility for the EITC extends to poor and near poor workers. Workers with dependent children are heavily favored. As a rough rule of thumb, the EITC benefits childless workers with incomes up to the poverty threshold, and workers with children up to twice the poverty threshold. Unlike TANF, the EITC is run entirely by the national government.[21] Unlike TANF, there are no time limits or restrictions on legal immigrants. Benefits are distributed once a year when the individual or family files their tax returns (thereby eliminating the need to deal with traditional caseworkers). The EITC reduces the amount of income tax they owe and often generates a tax refund. The average yearly benefit was about $3,200 for a family of four in 2017, but only about $300 for a single worker with no children. Depending on one's income and number of children, the benefits can be as high as $6,500 per year (Center on Budget and Policy Priorities 2019b).

The EITC functions like a wage subsidy.[22] Suppose a single parent with one child has a full-time job paying $8 an hour. The EITC would effectively raise that worker's wage to $9.50. (If that worker had no children, however, the subsidy would be zero.) The size of the subsidy varies with income: the EITC increases as the poorest workers earn more, flattens out over a middle range of incomes, then phases out. A married couple with two children, and a combined income of $40,000, would benefit less than a similar couple earning $20,000. But both couples would get an income boost (Center on Budget and Policy Priorities 2019b). Not surprisingly, low-wage industries have supported the EITC for a long time. They much prefer it to a higher minimum wage (Herd and Moynihan 2018; Howard 1997).

It is easier to determine the total cost of the EITC than the total number of beneficiaries. The congressional Joint Committee on Taxation (JCT) estimates that the EITC cost the government $70 billion in 2019. The JCT also estimates that 27.5 million tax filing units benefitted from the program (Joint Committee on Taxation 2019). Some of those tax filers were individuals, but more likely they were families with children, in which case the true number of beneficiaries is much higher. A conservative estimate of two people per EITC household means that the program helps almost as many Americans as Social Security. By design, the EITC touches many more lives than TANF. The EITC has the potential to lift more people out of poverty, both because of its sheer size and because so many recipients live close to the poverty threshold.

The EITC and TANF are designed to promote wage work. Both programs favor low-income families with children. A third program, Supplemental Security Income (SSI), does not fit this pattern. SSI provides income support to poor people who are aged, blind, or severely disabled. It does not matter if they are working or ever worked. Whether they have children is irrelevant. What matters is that they are very poor and have little chance of supporting themselves through employment. Most recipients have little income besides SSI (Center on Budget and Policy Priorities 2020a).[23]

Originally, the main beneficiaries were the elderly poor. Now SSI serves primarily the disabled poor. The definition of disability is a strict one: individuals must have a "medically determinable physical or mental impairment that is expected to last (or has lasted) at least 12 continuous months or to result in death." Being sidelined with a broken back for six months will not be enough. Moreover, that disability must prevent adults "from doing any substantial gainful activity," or produce "marked and severe functional limitations" in children (Social Security Administration 2019b: 2). Those definitions leave room for interpretation and dispute, and many applicants who are denied SSI seek help from the courts (Berkowitz and DeWitt 2013; Erkulwater 2006). In 2018, out of 9 million recipients, 6.5 million were disabled and under the age of 65. The most common diagnoses are intellectual disabilities and mood disorders. A little over one million SSI beneficiaries are children. As soon as disabled SSI recipients turn 65, they are classified as aged, so some of the remaining 2.5 million recipients are both elderly and disabled (Social Security Administration 2019b).

The national government spent $52 billion on SSI benefits in 2018. Many states supplement these payments, but seldom by much. Total payments from national and state governments amounted to $55 billion. The maximum benefit for a single person on SSI was around $750 per month, or $9,000 per year. That's considerably more than what TANF or the EITC can offer. Nevertheless, after the Social Security Administration factors in other sources of income (e.g., child support, Social Security), and accounts for recipients living with family members who have income, the average SSI benefit drops closer to $550 per month. That is a sizable amount of money for people living in deep poverty. It is not enough to lift many of them above the poverty threshold (Center on Budget and Policy Priorities 2020a; Social Security Administration 2019b).

TANF, the EITC, and SSI are the main income support programs targeted at low-income Americans. The beneficiaries range from deeply poor children and disabled adults to near poor families with wage-earners. Government bureaucrats, deciding who is eligible and issuing monthly checks or annual tax refunds, play the role of caregivers.

There is another group whose role is essential but frequently overlooked. Taking care of someone can mean helping to pay for their care, even if you are not giving that care directly. TANF, the EITC, and SSI cost more than $150 billion per year, and somebody has to foot the bill. Almost all that money comes from the national government. These programs are financed out of general revenues, which rely heavily on individual income taxes and secondarily on corporate income taxes. Which Americans pay income taxes? Households with incomes of $200,000 or more accounted for seven percent of federal income tax returns in 2019. Collectively, they paid almost 75 percent of all federal income taxes. Those earning between $100,000 and $200,000 paid most of the rest. This is what happens when income is concentrated among the rich and tax rates are progressive. Middle-income Americans do not owe much in federal income taxes, and low-income Americans usually owe nothing and may receive tax refunds because of the EITC (Joint Committee on Taxation 2019). This part of the social safety net depends on the deep pockets of affluent individuals and corporations. The rich take care of the poor, whether they intend to or not.

A good education is often touted as one of the best ways to prevent poverty, yet public schools are not limited to the poor. Public schools serve everyone. For similar reasons, it makes sense to think broadly about how government provides income to the poor and near poor, even if other people benefit as well. We will start by revisiting some of the ways in which people help themselves. The first is by getting a job. Minimum wage laws are supposed to keep employers from exploiting their employees. Most workers in the United States can count on making at least $7.25 an hour, the federal minimum.[24] Many states have chosen to raise their minimum wage to $9, $10, even $12 an hour.[25] At that rate, a full-time job will keep single workers out of poverty (in most parts of the country). Raising the minimum to $15, a goal of labor unions and many Democrats, would do even more. Minimum wage increases have ripple effects, boosting the income of workers earning the minimum and many more whose pay is pegged to a certain level above the minimum (Cooper 2019). Some middle-class workers benefit from minimum wage laws as well, especially those who are not the primary breadwinners in the family. Labor laws that affect workers' ability to unionize and bargain collectively can benefit a wide range of workers, not just the poor. Employers are unlikely to support labor policies that increase their costs, which is an important reason why they prefer the EITC (see Chapter 2).

Government actions also shape how the poor and near poor generate income outside of employment. State governments decide whether to permit lotteries and other forms of gambling. They also decide what interest rates lenders can charge. One-third of the states either prohibit payday lending or cap the interest rate so low that those lenders cannot afford to operate. At the other end of the spectrum are places like Nevada and Texas, where a typical payday loan carries an interest rate north of 600 percent (Bennett 2019). For their part, local governments can influence whether and where panhandling is permitted. When individuals seek help from their family safety net, they might rely on courts and bureaucracies to ensure that alimony or child support payments are made. All these examples illustrate a more general point: when taking care of ourselves, we are seldom acting alone.

To find examples of broadly available programs that help low-income Americans, we should pay close attention to social insurance. The main income support programs are Social Security, Disability Insurance, Workers' Compensation, and Unemployment Insurance. Though no two are exactly alike, social insurance programs have certain features in common. Eligibility is tied to paid work. Most but not all workers are covered. Payroll taxes are usually the main source of financing. Benefits are supposed to help people cope with big drops in wage income. Benefit levels are tied to one's earnings history; the bigger your paychecks in the past, the bigger your government checks in the future. Social insurance programs form the core of modern welfare states, and their sheer size guarantees that many of the poor and near poor will benefit. Exactly how many and how much remain to be seen.

Social Security is the largest and most important of these programs. It provides retirement income for millions of older Americans. In some cases, it pays cash benefits to surviving spouses and children when an eligible recipient dies.[26] Almost every older American is eligible, either because of their work history or because they are related to someone who worked. Eligibility rules do not vary by state.[27] At the end of 2018, 47 million Americans were collecting monthly retirement benefits. Six million more received survivors benefits. The average retirement benefit was $1,461 per month, and for surviving spouses it was $1,388 (Social Security Administration 2019a). Those figures far exceed what the poor get from TANF, and they surpass what the EITC and SSI offer as well. The average retirement benefit alone could lift a single person above the poverty threshold. Moreover, Social Security benefits are indexed for inflation, which protects their value over time.

Because benefits vary with income, these averages can be misleading. A well-paid doctor or lawyer might receive monthly Social Security checks of $2,300 after retiring. Someone who worked for 35 years full time at minimum-wage jobs could expect a monthly check closer to $800 (Social Security Administration 2019a). This feature of the program is supposed to create a strong work incentive for adults before they retire. It also means that Social Security benefits can perpetuate income inequalities that originated in the labor market. Nevertheless, the program is designed to reduce those inequalities by replacing a larger share of pre-retirement earnings for low-income workers. The replacement rates range from about 25 percent for the highest-income workers to a little over 50 percent for low-income workers (National Academy of Social Insurance 2019). The assumption is that affluent workers will have significant sources of retirement income besides Social Security, but poorer workers will not.

This assumption is quite accurate. Approximately one-quarter of the elderly rely on Social Security for 90 percent or more of their income. Those who are living alone or older than 80 are even more dependent on Social Security. Many older Americans don't have much savings, a company pension, or an Individual Retirement Account. They do not have a large stock portfolio or rental property (M. Miller 2019). By necessity, these older Americans might continue working, but they probably won't earn much. For many, the monthly Social Security check is all that stands between them and deep poverty.[28] Other retirees depend heavily on Social Security as well. Those benefits account for at least half the income of half the elderly population (Dushi, Iams, and Trenkamp 2017; Van de Water and Romig 2020). Any across-the-board cut to Social Security will affect millions of older Americans.

The national government also provides income support to individuals who are disabled during their working years. The largest program, Disability Insurance (DI), has the potential to help many low-income workers, in part because it resembles Social Security. Eligibility rules and the benefit formula are standard throughout the country.[29] Spouses and children of the disabled can benefit. The replacement rate for benefits works just as it does in Social Security. DI benefits are likewise indexed for inflation. Monthly benefits for individuals with disabilities can be almost as large as for retirees. Most DI recipients are between the ages of 50 and 64, when chronic health conditions can make it impossible to keep working. In effect, DI offers workers a way to survive before they start receiving Social Security benefits (Erkulwater 2006; Social Security Administration 2019a).

On the other hand, Disability Insurance uses the same strict definition of disability as SSI.[30] DI is designed to help people with severe, permanent disabilities. Many who apply are denied.[31] In 2018, there were approximately ten million beneficiaries, a much smaller number than Social Security. Those who are approved for DI must wait five months before their first check arrives. While that delay is supposed to prevent benefits from helping people with short-term disabilities, it hurts those with limited financial resources. Because benefits are based on past wages, disabled janitors will receive smaller monthly checks than disabled software engineers (Erkulwater 2006; Social Security Administration 2019a).

Workers' Compensation (aka workers' comp) provides income support to individuals with job-related injuries or illnesses. It also helps pay the relevant medical bills (see Chapter 8). Workers' comp covers a wide range of disabilities, including many that are short-term or partial (e.g., broken foot, loss of a finger). That is one key difference between it and Disability Insurance. Eligibility for workers' comp typically begins on the first day of work and includes part-time workers. Claimants do not have to wait months for the first workers' comp check to arrive. All these features help low-income workers (Boden and Spieler 2015; Weiss, Murphy, and Boden 2019).

However, states' compensation laws do not usually cover independent contractors, farm workers, or domestic workers, many of whom are poorly paid. Employers with fewer than three to five workers are usually exempt as well. Eligible workers who seek compensation must prove that their injury or illness was directly related to their job. Doing so can be difficult for a whole host of conditions—for example, lung cancer, hearing loss, carpal tunnel syndrome—that could have other causes. Employers and insurers have incentives to deny claims, and individuals might have to hire personal injury lawyers to battle on their behalf (Boden and Spieler 2015; Howard 2002; Weiss, Murphy, and Boden 2019).

Workers' comp is run almost entirely by the states, leading to enormous and sometimes bizarre variations. Workers with a temporary total disability in Alabama receive at least $232 a week for the duration of their disability. Those same workers in Florida could receive as little as $20 a week, and benefits would last no more than two years. Permanent partial disability benefits could be paid for up to 225 weeks in Ohio and 600 weeks in New Jersey (Weiss, Murphy, and Boden 2019). Each state has its own schedule for job-related loss of body parts. A thumb is worth three times as much in Oregon as Arizona. An eye is worth twice as much in Oklahoma compared to Texas.[32]

Workers' comp is so decentralized that we can only guess how many people benefit. According to the Census Bureau, 1.6 million Americans received income from workers' comp in 2014. The average payment was $736 per month (Moore, Thompson, and Hisnanick 2018).[33] The total cost of cash benefits did not change much from 2014 to 2017, so 1.6 million people is a reasonable starting point for 2017. The number should be higher, though, because some injured or ill workers are discouraged from applying for compensation. Companies' premiums are based on how many of their workers get hurt and receive benefits, a practice known as experience rating. That practice is supposed to reward employers for maintaining a safe workplace; they will pay less for workers' comp insurance. When the workplace is more dangerous, employers may try to keep their premiums from rising by undermining the claims process. If we count all claims, not just those triggering cash payments, then the total number of people helped by workers' comp would be much higher. Most claims involve medical care only, such as when a worker requires a few stitches and returns to work the next day (Boden and Spieler 2015; Weiss, Murphy, and Boden 2019).

The last example is Unemployment Insurance (UI). This type of income support could be essential for millions of poor adults who are chronically unemployed. It could be just as valuable to millions of the poor and near poor who are employed but have little job security. Could be. In practice, UI is not designed with these people in mind. Although eligibility criteria vary from state to state, applicants typically must work a year before filing a claim.[34] Workers who change jobs every few months, or who just entered the labor force, will be excluded. To qualify for UI, workers must be involuntarily unemployed. Quitting because you do not like your work schedule or cannot find affordable child care will not entitle you to benefits. The unemployed must be actively looking for work; some of the long-term unemployed have become so discouraged that they stopped looking. Regular UI benefits typically end after 26 weeks, which also hurts the long-term unemployed. A handful of states have shorter time limits (Stone and Chen 2014; Whittaker and Isaacs 2019; Woodbury 2015). For these and other reasons, less than one-third of the unemployed have received UI benefits in recent years. The rate is even lower for high school dropouts and part-time workers. During the worst years of the Great Recession, when the US government extended benefits to 99 weeks and helped many more workers, the recipiency rate did not rise above 40 percent.[35]

For the minority who do qualify, benefits vary by place and by previous earnings. As of 2019, weekly UI benefits ranged from $45–$265 in Alabama, $122–$488 in Kansas, and $188–$790 in the state of Washington. Some states (e.g., Illinois, Massachusetts) pay extra to help support unemployed workers' dependents. Most states do not. With such wide variations, it is hard to talk about national averages. Typically, UI benefits replace one-third of workers' past wages. For low-income workers, benefits might replace one-half their wages. One-third, one-half—either way, UI will not prevent workers from suffering a serious drop in income (Center on Budget and Policy Priorities 2020c; O'Leary and Wandner 2020).

Social insurance programs are not cheap. Social Security paid out $850 billion in monthly benefits during 2018, making it the largest single item in the national budget. DI benefits totaled over $140 billion (Social Security and Medicare Boards of Trustees 2019). Already we are way beyond the sums required to fund TANF, the EITC, and SSI. The cost of unemployment benefits fluctuates with the economy. In a good year, the US might spend $30–$35 billion; in a deep recession, the total could easily top $100 billion.[36] Workers' comp payments have been around $60 billion annually, though the total cost of premiums paid by employers has been closer to $90 billion (Weiss, Murphy, and Boden 2019).[37] Together, these social insurance programs require more than $1 trillion per year in revenue.

The responsibility for financing these programs falls on many shoulders. Payroll taxes are the main source of revenue. These taxes are typically paid at a flat rate up to a certain level of earnings, at which point the tax is discontinued. Social Security, for example, did not collect payroll taxes on incomes above $132,900 in 2019 (Social Security Administration 2019a). Payroll taxes are therefore regressive: someone earning $200,000 will pay a smaller share of their income than someone else earning $20,000. From a care perspective, funding income support is an essential way that we take care of each other. Responsibility for taking care of elderly, disabled, and unemployed workers does not belong to the rich. It belongs to tens of millions of wage-earners, throughout their working lives. If the poor and near poor want help from social insurance, they will have to earn it.[38]

Whereas social insurance programs are so inclusive and so large that many low-income workers will benefit, the same cannot be said of tax expenditures, also known as tax breaks. Unless deliberately modified (e.g., the EITC), tax expenditures favor those who pay the most income taxes and those who can afford to engage in whatever behavior the tax code is rewarding. For example, the tax code gives large tax breaks to companies that offer retirement pensions to their employees, and to people who contribute to Individual Retirement Accounts. In 2019, the preferential tax treatment of these pensions cost the national treasury $250 billion in foregone revenue—far more than government spent on TANF, the EITC, and SSI combined. Upper-income workers are much more likely to have such pensions, and to have larger pensions (M. Miller 2019). According to the Tax Policy Center, only 18 percent of all workers earning under $20,000 have an employer pension, compared to 85 percent of workers earning over $100,000.[39] These tax breaks help affluent workers live comfortably in retirement and reduce their dependence on Social Security. They have almost no impact on poverty (Ghilarducci 2015; Howard 1997, 2007; Joint Committee on Taxation 2019). We will see this pattern again when examining housing and medical care.

The one tax expenditure that comes closest to the EITC is the Child Tax Credit (CTC). Both programs benefit wage-earners with dependent children. Unlike the EITC, the Child Tax Credit has been available to middle- and upper-middle class families. Historically, this tax credit was either not refundable or just partly refundable, which made it hard for low-income parents to benefit. The CTC was claimed on an estimated 49 million tax returns in 2019 and cost the national government $118 billion in foregone revenue and tax refunds. Little of that money helped the poor or near poor. Almost $50 billion went to taxpayers with at least $100,000 in income. Their average tax credit was worth $2,800. Taxpayers with under $30,000 of income received much less ($18 billion), and their average benefit was $1,600 (DeParle 2019; Joint Committee on Taxation 2019).[40] TANF is often seen as the government's main income support for needy families. The reality is that the EITC and the Child Tax Credit provide much more help to many more families.

Discussion

Millions of low-income Americans try to take care of themselves by holding down a job. When work pays too little or they are unemployed, family members might give them some money. Few organized charities will do so. The more likely source of income support is government. Means-tested programs like TANF are financed with income taxes; the rich pay most of those taxes and help take care of the poor. Inclusive social insurance programs like Social Security are financed with payroll taxes. Tens of millions of current workers take care of millions of former workers who are retired, disabled, or laid off from their jobs.

Caregiving in this part of the social safety is often impersonal. Eligibility for government assistance is based on standard questions about income, assets, and dependents. Need is measured by a set of numbers plugged into a formula embedded in some computer system. Weekly or monthly checks are issued by government bureaucrats who never actually meet the recipients. Anonymity is not necessarily a bad thing. Some recipients might prefer to remain unseen. Getting the right amount of money deposited in the right bank on the right day of the month could be all the care they want. At other times caregiving is mostly a business, and the poor and near poor represent a source of profit. This is the domain of credit card companies, payday lenders, and employers who rely on an army of part-time workers.

The last phase of caring is care-receiving, which refers to the types of people being cared for and the adequacy of their care (Tronto 1993, 2013). The official poverty rate gives us one way to talk about adequacy. Since the 1970s, the poverty rate has fluctuated within a fairly narrow range. When the economy is weak, 15 percent of Americans will be living in poverty. When the economy is strong, the poverty rate might drop as low as 11 percent. The US economy was generally in good shape in 2018, and the poverty rate was 11.8 percent (Table 5.1). Even with the help of minimum wage laws, social insurance programs, TANF, and SSI, 38 million Americans were officially poor (Semega et al. 2019).

In Chapter 1, we saw that ordinary Americans make distinctions between poverty and welfare. They feel more warmly about poor people than welfare recipients and want to spend more on poverty programs than on welfare. This chapter helps explain why. More than half of the official poverty population consists of children, disabled adults, and the elderly (Table 5.1). We do not expect these individuals to find employment; their dependence on others carries little stigma. In addition, millions of poor adults are employed full time or part-time. They are trying to take care of themselves and their families. Some of the poor are unemployed, able-bodied, working-age adults, but they are a minority. If deservingness is based on how we perform our expected roles, then most people in poverty should qualify as the deserving poor.

Table 5.1 **PEOPLE IN POVERTY (work perspective)**

	Official measure		Supplemental measure	
	Number	Rate	Number	Rate
US (2018)	38,200,000	11.8%	41,420,000	12.8%
Age				
65 and older	5,146,000	9.7	7,174,000	13.6
18–64	21,130,000	10.7	24,151,000	12.2
work full time	2,544,000	2.3	4,847,000	4.3
work part-time	5,237,000	12.7	6,112,000	14.9
no paid work	13,349,000	29.7	13,191,000	29.4
disabled	3,818,000	25.7	3,609,000	24.3
under 18	11,924,000	16.2	10,096,000	13.7

Note: all the disabled adults (age 18–64) are also classified as working full time, part-time, or not at all.

Source: Liana Fox, *The Supplemental Poverty Measure: 2018*, Current Population Reports P60-268 (RV), https://www.census.gov/library/publications/2019/demo/p60-268.html (October 2019).

Poverty in America is not distributed equally. Poverty rates are very high among the chronically unemployed (29.7%) and very low among full-time workers (2.3%). Having a steady job pays off. Nevertheless, poverty varies considerably among the deserving poor. The chances of being poor for adults with disabilities (25.7%) are almost as high as for the chronically unemployed. Given the stringent definition of disability used by DI and SSI, we can understand why poverty among the disabled is well above the national average. Many of these individuals are unable to earn much, yet cannot qualify for government benefits.

The poverty rate is noticeably higher among children (16.2%) than the elderly (9.7%). One plausible reason is that government transfers much more income to older Americans than to families with children. Social Security lifts more Americans out of poverty than any other social program. Nothing else comes close. According to the US Census Bureau, Social Security reduced the poverty rate among the elderly by 34 percentage points in 2018. The program moved 18 million older Americans above the poverty line. TANF, a much smaller program, lifted fewer than 250,000 children out of poverty each year (Fox 2019; Meyer and Wu 2018; Romig 2020).

Poverty also has a geographic dimension. Rates are higher in central cities and rural areas, lower in the suburbs. Poverty is more common in the South than any other region. In the rural South, poverty affects 25 percent of children and almost 20 percent of the total population. The numbers are only slightly better for people living in the major urban centers of the Northeast.[41]

Table 5.1 also displays poverty rates for these same groups based on the government's supplemental poverty measure (SPM). The SPM is a better indicator of economic need because it accounts for a variety of taxes and transfers. The national poverty rate is higher with the SPM, even though noncash benefits for food and housing have been given a dollar value and counted as income. With both the official and supplemental measures, poverty is correlated strongly with paid employment and disability (Fox 2019).

Interestingly, the poverty gap between the young (13.7%) and old (13.6%) disappears when we use the SPM. One reason is that the Earned Income Tax Credit and Child Tax Credit provide income support for millions of children; that money is excluded from the official poverty calculations but included in the SPM. The EITC has done more to lower the poverty rate than any other means-tested income transfer (Fox 2019; Meyer and Wu 2018). Another reason for the shift is that the SPM subtracts out-of-pocket medical expenses from income, which affects many older Americans (Fox 2019). Maybe the social safety net is not as biased in favor of the elderly as we've been led to believe.

Any safety net based heavily on paid work is bound to have racial and gender implications. Employers and government agencies do not say they intend to help men more or Whites more. Nonetheless, in an economy where unemployment is consistently higher for racial minorities; where full-time jobs and part-time jobs are not evenly distributed; and where White men consistently earn more than women or racial minorities, we expect to find unequal outcomes.

Table 5.2 compares poverty rates by race, ethnicity, and gender. The first two columns of numbers reflect the official poverty thresholds. One point to note is that among the poor, women outnumber men, and racial and ethnic minorities outnumber Whites. If we believe that, in a hierarchical society, Whites and men are considered more deserving, then most of the poor would be perceived as undeserving. That is a very different picture from the employment perspective, and one that does not square with the public's warm feelings toward poor people.

Although women are more likely than men to be poor, the gender gap is not as large as the racial/ethnic gap. Poverty rates for Blacks (20.8%) and Hispanics (17.6%) are at least twice those for non-Hispanic Whites (8.1%). Blacks and Hispanics represent about one-third of the total US population, but one-half of the poverty population. Blacks and Hispanics are also less likely than Whites to say they are doing okay financially (Board of Governors of the Federal Reserve System 2019). Inequalities are even more apparent among children (not shown). Black children are three times more likely to be poor as White, non-Hispanic children. Most poor children live in single-parent families, and they are much more likely to be poor if that parent is female. When we switch to the SMP, the racial/ethnic differences are still much larger than the gender differences. The main change is that poverty among Asians and Hispanics jumps a few points (Fox 2019).

There are many reasons for these gaps, including schools and the job market. Here I simply want to dig down a level and reveal where these gaps appear in specific social programs.[42] We already know how important Social Security has been in reducing poverty among the elderly. Yet, Blacks and Hispanics over the age of 65 are at least twice as likely to be poor as their White counterparts. Whites are more likely to receive Social Security retirement benefits, partly because they have a longer life expectancy. The average monthly check is about 10 percent larger for Whites than Blacks, and almost 20 percent larger for Whites than Hispanics.[43] Whites tend to earn more during their working years, and Social Security allows income differences to persist in retirement. The gender patterns are somewhat different. More women receive Social Security than men because women live longer. The monthly pensions for women, however, are 25 percent smaller. Poverty among older women is more prevalent than among older men (Moore, Thompson, and Hisnanick 2018; US Department of Health and Human Services 2015).

Similar gaps can be found in other social insurance programs. Blacks and Hispanics are less likely to apply for unemployment benefits, partly because they don't think they have worked enough to qualify (Gould-Werth and Shaefer

Table 5.2 **PEOPLE IN POVERTY (race, ethnicity, gender)**

	Official measure		Supplemental measure	
	Number	Rate	Number	Rate
US (2018)	38,200,000	11.8%	41,420,000	12.8%
Race/ethnicity				
White (non-Hispanic)	15,742,000	8.1	16,932,000	8.7
Black	8,891,000	20.8	8,727,000	20.4
Asian	2,004,000	10.1	2,749,000	13.9
Hispanic (any race)	10,548,000	17.6	12,216,000	20.3
Gender				
Women	21,380,000	12.9	22,151,000	13.4
Men	16,820,000	10.6	19,269,000	12.1
Families				
Married couple	10,530,000	5.4	15,043,000	7.7
Single-mother	10,506,000	25.3	10,390,000	25.0
Single-father	1,684,000	11.6	2,197,000	15.1

Note: some racial groups and those who reported two or more races are not displayed in this table.

Source: Liana Fox, *The Supplemental Poverty Measure: 2018*, Current Population Reports P60-268 (RV), https://www.census.gov/library/publications/2019/demo/p60-268.html (October 2019).

2012). Disability checks and unemployment checks are 10 to 15 percent larger for Whites and 10 to 20 percent larger for men. On the other hand, Blacks are over-represented among DI recipients. The average benefits for workers' comp are larger for Hispanics than Whites, and larger for women than men (Moore, Thompson, and Hisnanick 2018; US Department of Health and Human Services 2015). This seems like progress, right? Not necessarily. Workers' comp distributes income to employees based on the severity of their illnesses and injuries. Women and racial minorities may be "advantaged" because they are performing more dangerous jobs or more stressful jobs. Taking the lead in disability is not a great way to escape poverty.

The largest parts of the public safety net—Social Security, Disability Insurance, EITC—link cash benefits to earnings. In other parts, eligibility and benefits depend on where you live. TANF is a classic example. As mentioned earlier, TANF helps a small percentage of poor families with children. That fraction varies around the country, and it is less than ten percent in at least a dozen states. Black children are more likely to live in those highly restrictive states. Cash benefits are also smaller in states with a larger Black population (Floyd

2018, 2020; Hahn et al. 2017). Other studies have found that TANF time limits are shorter and sanctions are tougher in states where Blacks make up a larger share of the caseload (Soss, Fording, and Schram 2011). When it comes to income support, the public safety net clearly favors some groups over others.

Table 5.3 gives us a snapshot of individuals living just above the poverty line. Near poverty is defined as income between 100 and 150 percent of the relevant poverty threshold, which is higher than the official measure but lower than ones used by academics and the United Way. By this definition, 20 percent of Americans lived in poverty or near poverty in 2018. Sixty-five million people. If we use the supplemental poverty measure, close to 90 million Americans are considered poor or near poor (Fox 2019).

According to the official measures, near poverty is particularly common among the young, the old, Blacks, and Hispanics. Even though Social Security reduces poverty for millions, many older Americans live on a tight budget. They don't have much income besides Social Security, and their out-of-pocket medical costs can be daunting (see Chapter 8). Over 30 percent of Blacks and Hispanics are low-income, compared to just 14 percent of Whites. With the supplemental poverty measure, the extent of near poverty almost doubles (from 8.3% to 15.0% of the population). While that increase is spread across every group, children,

Table 5.3 **POVERTY AND NEAR POVERTY**

	Official rate (%)			Supplemental rate (%)		
	Poor	Near poor	Total	Poor	Near poor	Total
US (2018)	11.8	8.3	20.1	12.8	15.0	27.8
Age						
65 and older	9.7	9.4	19.1	13.6	15.3	28.9
18–64	10.7	7.0	17.7	12.2	13.3	25.5
under 18	16.2	11.1	27.3	13.7	19.0	32.7
Race/ethnicity						
White (non-Hispanic)	8.1	6.0	14.1	8.7	10.7	19.4
Black	20.8	11.9	32.7	20.4	21.5	41.9
Asian	10.1	6.0	16.1	13.9	13.4	27.3
Hispanic (any race)	17.6	14.0	31.6	20.3	24.8	45.1

Near poor = income between 100 and 150 percent of the poverty threshold.

Source: Liana Fox, *The Supplemental Poverty Measure: 2018*, Current Population Reports P60-268 (RV), https://www.census.gov/library/publications/2019/demo/p60-268.html (October 2019).

Blacks, and Hispanics are impacted heavily. Now it appears that one-third of American children qualify as poor or near poor. The comparable rates for Blacks (41.9%) and Hispanics (45.1%) should be alarming (Fox 2019).

None of these tables reveal the depth of poverty. Officially, over 17 million Americans lived in deep poverty in 2018. That's as many people as Kentucky, Massachusetts, and Minnesota combined. The overall rate was 5.3 percent. Deep poverty was higher among children (6.9%), Hispanics (6.9%), and Blacks (9.4%). The official numbers, of course, exclude noncash benefits such as SNAP and subsidized housing. According to the supplemental poverty measure, "only" 4.2 percent of the country was experiencing deep poverty. The rate for children (3.3%) was actually lower than the national average. The rates for Hispanics (4.8%) and Blacks (5.9%) remained above average (Fox 2019; Semega et al. 2019). Regardless which measure you use, the extent of deep poverty shows that the social safety net has major holes. The fact that 38 million Americans were officially poor despite a strong economy is another clear sign.

In theory, a social safety net could be built entirely out of cash. Those who favor a guaranteed minimum income would like us to move in that direction. That kind of safety net would represent a major departure from the status quo. What we currently have relies on a combination of income, goods, and services. We dedicate resources specifically to food and housing, medical care, and daily care. Those who provide care and those who receive it might vary depending on which part of the net we examine. The next chapter demonstrates that food assistance in the United States operates much differently from income assistance.

6

Food

My aim throughout this book has been to map the social safety net when it was operating under more or less normal conditions. While the impact of Covid-19 will be discussed later in the Postscript, I will briefly describe how the pandemic affected the food safety net. Serious problems became evident right away. Low-income children were no longer going to school, where they normally received free or reduced-price meals. Millions of people lost their jobs and needed food assistance. In parts of the country, lines of cars waiting to pick up donated food were a mile long. Volunteers became reluctant to work side by side with others, forcing local food pantries to limit their hours or shut down. Restaurants that had been giving surplus food to charity closed their doors or scaled back to focus on take-out meals. Farmers who had been supplying food to schools and restaurants lost their biggest customers. Some processing plants were forced to shut down when their workers became infected. The pandemic created a perfect storm of increasing demand for food assistance combined with dwindling supply (Abad-Santos 2020; Ebbs 2020; Kulish 2020; Luhby 2020).

As this chapter demonstrates, the food sector of the social safety net was already under stress. Many Americans did not have enough to eat in the years prior to the pandemic. Although few people were starving to death, millions were officially classified as "food insecure" (Coleman-Jensen et al. 2019). Individuals receiving assistance from the Supplemental Nutrition Assistance Program (SNAP) routinely used up their benefits before the month was over. Low-income children were eating at school, but meals on weekends and during summers were a chronic problem. Older Americans sometimes faced hard choices between paying for food or medical care. When grocery stores had gone out of business, local food charities lost important donors. Many low-income Americans did not live near a food pantry or soup kitchen. Over the last decade, a considerable number of hospitals, colleges, and universities started their own food pantries to plug holes in the food safety net.

Who Cares. Christopher Howard, Oxford University Press. © Oxford University Press 2023.
DOI: 10.1093/oso/9780190074456.003.0007

Although casual observers might be aware of some of these problems, food assistance has so many different pieces that it can be hard to see the big picture. This chapter will highlight a few general patterns. First, most people who receive food assistance do not have to work for it. Eligibility and benefits depend more on need (though many recipients happen to be employed). Second, organized charities play a much larger role in food assistance than income support. The most prominent national organizations are Feeding America and Meals on Wheels. Most communities have at least one charitable food pantry, and many religious congregations around the country operate a pantry or soup kitchen.[1] Third, the lines separating public and private are very fuzzy. Practically every type of food assistance combines public and private actors. Individuals and companies that donate to charity could receive a break on their income taxes. Government helps low-income people buy food, but relies on all sorts of businesses to grow, process, distribute, and sell that food. And finally, despite the caring efforts of so many individuals and organizations, the food safety net has many holes.

The previous chapter showed how individuals try to generate enough income to afford the basics, mostly through employment, social insurance, and means-tested income transfers. Many Americans come up short and must find other ways to put food on the table. Government and organized charity are two of their best options. Tens of millions of Americans are helped each year by government programs; tens of millions of Americans are helped each year by food banks, food pantries, and soup kitchens; and many people rely on a combination of public and private assistance. Whether people turn to government or charity, they will also be receiving assistance from business.

Help from Government

The US government operates several food assistance programs, all of them targeted at low-income groups. There is no inclusive program comparable to Social Security. The largest is SNAP, the Supplemental Nutrition Assistance Program (which was called Food Stamps until 2008). Smaller food programs serve low-income infants, children, new mothers, and senior citizens. The national government takes lead responsibility for all these programs, with some variations from state to state.[2]

SNAP is designed to serve a broad cross-section of people living in or near poverty. Recipients can be young or old, disabled or able-bodied. SNAP serves families with and without children. Benefits are available to some households whose gross income is less than 130 percent of the relevant federal poverty threshold; whose net income (after subtracting a variety of program-specific deductions) is less than 100 percent of the poverty threshold; and whose countable liquid assets are below $2,250.[3] These thresholds are somewhat higher if the household contains a disabled or elderly member, and most states have eliminated the asset test. Many households qualify for SNAP based on their participation in some other means-tested program (e.g., SSI, TANF). Depending on the state of residence, their eligibility for SNAP could extend up to 200 percent of the poverty threshold (Aussenberg 2018; Aussenberg, Billings, and Colello 2019; Center on Budget and Policy Priorities 2019a).

Some low-income Americans are excluded. Many legal immigrants were declared ineligible for Food Stamps, TANF, SSI, and Medicaid as part of the welfare reforms of 1996. (Illegal/undocumented immigrants have never been eligible for Food Stamps or SNAP.) At the time, Senator Phil Gramm (R-TX) argued: "immigrants should come . . . with their sleeves rolled up, ready to work, and not with their hands out, ready to go on welfare" (quoted in Golden 1996). Subsequent legislation restored SNAP benefits for some categories of immigrants. Nevertheless, many legal immigrants must reside in the United States for five years before they are eligible.

SNAP is the only food assistance program with work requirements. They apply to adults between the ages of 18 and 59, who generally need to work at least 30 hours per week or earn the equivalent of 30 times the federal minimum wage per week in order to qualify for benefits. There are exceptions: adults who are caring for a child under the age of six, or an incapacitated adult, do not have to meet this requirement. Nor do adults with disabilities. The rules are stricter, however, for able-bodied adults without any dependents. Unless they are pregnant, working at least 20 hours per week, or participating in a job training program, these individuals can receive SNAP for only three months in a three-year period. SNAP is not designed to help single adults who are chronically unemployed or underemployed.[4] Before the pandemic hit, the Trump administration was prepared to impose tougher SNAP work requirements on adults without dependent children. Had those changes gone into effect, hundreds of thousands of people would have lost their benefits (Fadulu 2020).[5]

Most SNAP recipients are children (44%), senior citizens (14%), or disabled, non-elderly adults (10%).[6] They are not expected to be working for a living. Most SNAP households with children have adults earning income. The parents typically have low-wage service or retail jobs, such as cashier or cook. Only seven percent of recipients are able-bodied, working-age adults without dependents. From this angle, SNAP serves the deserving poor. And their needs are great: 80 percent of SNAP recipients have gross incomes below the poverty threshold; nearly 40 percent live in deep poverty. Almost 20 percent of SNAP households have zero income. Considering that women, Blacks, and Hispanics tend to have lower incomes, they also comprise a disproportionate share of SNAP recipients. While the race of many recipients is unknown, racial and ethnic minorities appear to outnumber Whites (Center on Budget and Policy Priorities 2019c; Cronquist 2019). If you feel that poor women should try harder to find a husband, and that racial and ethnic minorities should work more, then you might see SNAP recipients as undeserving.

Like Unemployment Insurance, SNAP reflects the state of the economy. In the wake of the Great Recession, 47 million Americans received benefits in a typical month. The number dropped closer to 36 million by 2019, but it increased during the pandemic. Because people move on and off the SNAP program, the total number of beneficiaries in any given year will be higher than the monthly figures. The cost of the program also fluctuates, in recent years between $60 billion and $80 billion.[7] SNAP is a budgetary entitlement, not an annual appropriation or block grant, so spending can rise or fall without explicit action by policymakers. The national government pays the full cost of benefits, and it splits the cost of administration with the states. Thus, state officials are less concerned about the overall cost of SNAP than they are with TANF (Aussenberg 2018; Wiseman 2019).

Although SNAP benefits vary with income and household size, they are not generous for anybody. The first letter in SNAP stands for Supplementary, and that is no accident. Before the pandemic, the average benefit was approximately $1.40 per meal. A typical single person on SNAP received about $130 per month (Center on Budget and Policy Priorities 2019c; these amounts did increase in 2021). To put benefit levels in context, the Department of Agriculture estimates the cost of four different food plans—thrifty, low-cost, moderate-cost, and liberal. All these plans assume that meals are prepared at home; nothing extra for restaurants or take-out. The average SNAP benefit for an adult has usually been less than the cost of the thrifty plan, which is a very low standard. Child support, alimony, and foster care payments are based on one of the other food plans. Bankruptcy courts use the low-cost food plan when deciding how much income people can keep, and SNAP pays less than that plan (Food Research & Action Center 2012; U.S. Department of Agriculture 2020). Recipients are expected to combine SNAP with other government benefits, earned income, or charity if they want to eat three decent meals a day.

When President Lyndon Johnson signed the Food Stamp Act into law (1964), he promised that it would combine "the best of the humanitarian instincts of the American people with the best of the free enterprise system."[8] Government would help needy people buy food from the private sector. Initially, the program distributed paper coupons that recipients could use in a variety of retail stores. Now every SNAP household receives an electronic benefit transfer (EBT) card, similar to a bank debit card.[9] Recipients use their Food Stamps or EBT card at stores approved by the US Department of Agriculture. Those stores must stock a variety of healthy foods, and they must ensure that SNAP monies are used to purchase eligible items. SNAP is not supposed to pay for alcohol, tobacco, paper products, household cleaners, toiletries, or over-the-counter medicines, including vitamins. SNAP also excludes hot prepared foods, even if sold in grocery stores (e.g., a roast chicken). Recipients are expected to cook their own meals.[10] SNAP can pay for expensive foods like steaks, but those won't be easy to afford on a budget of $4 a day (Aussenberg 2018; Center on Budget and Policy Priorities 2019c).

At first glance, the Special Supplemental Nutrition Program for Women, Infants, and Children (WIC) looks like a miniature version of SNAP. The WIC program is largely governed and funded by the national government, with the Department of Agriculture as the lead agency.[11] Benefits are similar across all 50 states. WIC helps low-income individuals buy food on the private market, and the subsidies are modest—less than $2 per day for each person. The program served approximately seven million people each month in fiscal year 2018, at a total cost of $6 billion. Over two-thirds of WIC recipients live in poverty and about one-third live in deep poverty. Among recipients, racial and ethnic minorities outnumber non-Hispanic Whites. In addition to subsidizing food purchases, WIC and SNAP help educate recipients about good nutrition.[12]

Nonetheless, important differences remain. The WIC program has a very specific objective—"to counteract the negative effects of poverty on prenatal and child health" (Jacknowitz and Tiehen 2009: 153). Benefits are therefore limited to pregnant, breastfeeding, and postpartum women, and to infants and children up to the age of five. Adult men are excluded, but no one has to be employed. Roughly three-quarters of recipients are infants and children. WIC recipients must also be experiencing a "nutrition risk," which could be related to medical or dietary problems.[13] Need is defined broadly, and many states cover families with incomes between two and three times the federal poverty threshold. Some people who are ineligible for SNAP can thus qualify for WIC (and some receive both SNAP and WIC). Unlike most means-tested programs, WIC is available to all immigrants, legal or otherwise.[14] WIC is funded by annual appropriations and is not a budgetary entitlement (Center on Budget and Policy Priorities 2017; Thorn et al. 2018; see also https://www.fns.usda.gov/wic/about-wic).

The WIC program restricts the kinds of food that families can purchase, more so than SNAP. WIC will pay for whole-grain bread but not white bread. Plain Cheerios yes, frosted or flavored Cheerios no. Other WIC-approved items include milk, eggs, orange juice, baby food, peanut butter, fruits, and vegetables. To promote a balanced diet, the government limits how much of these foods can be bought. If a pregnant woman wants peanut butter, WIC will pay for only one 18-ounce jar per month. Each child is allotted no more than one dozen eggs, 36 ounces of breakfast cereal, and four gallons of milk per month (Center on Budget and Policy Priorities 2017; Thorn et al. 2018; see also https://www.fns.

usda.gov/wic/about-wic). WIC may not have work requirements, but it still has plenty of rules.

As children age out of the WIC program, they can qualify for subsidized school meals. The National School Lunch Program started in 1946, and a similar breakfast program emerged in the 1960s.[15] Both are administered by the Department of Agriculture in conjunction with state agencies and local school systems. These programs are available in public and nonprofit private schools, as well as other institutions that care for children.[16] The national government does not require public schools to participate, though some state governments do. Over 90 percent of public schools in the United States are involved with the school lunch program, and a somewhat smaller share with the breakfast program.[17]

In these programs, every single student who eats the school's food is being subsidized. The meals are free to children whose (pre-tax) family income is below 130 percent of their poverty threshold. Children who receive SNAP or TANF automatically qualify for free school meals. On a typical school day, 20 million children will eat a free lunch and 12 million will eat a free breakfast (many children get both). For families with incomes between 130 and 185 percent of the poverty threshold, the meal price is substantially reduced. Lunch can cost no more than 40 cents, and breakfast is capped at 30 cents. Before the pandemic, almost two million children were eating reduced-price lunches each school day. Millions of more affluent students, who might think they are paying full price at the school cafeteria, receive a subsidy of around 30 cents per meal. This provision might strike readers as odd or wasteful, but the reason for it is also why some public schools stay away. Participating in these meal programs means complying with the government's nutritional guidelines, and healthy foods often cost more (Billings 2020; Billings and Aussenberg 2019; Sifferlin 2013).

On any given day, almost 30 million children benefit from the school lunch program.[18] Three-quarters of them receive free or reduced-price meals. The school breakfast program is roughly half as big (Billings 2020). Although the national government does not track the race or ethnicity of beneficiaries, it is safe to assume that Black and Hispanic children are disproportionately represented because their poverty rates are much higher than White children, and because K–12 public schools serve children regardless of immigrant status. Additional evidence comes from the National Center for Education Statistics, which reports that 45 percent of Black and Hispanic children attend schools where at least three-quarters of the students are eligible for free or reduced-price meals. In contrast, only eight percent of White students and 15 percent of Asian students attend such high-poverty schools.[19]

Subsidized school meal programs cost less than SNAP and more than WIC. The national government spends about $17 billion each year on subsidized lunches and breakfasts. Like SNAP, subsidized school meals are budgetary entitlements. Spending levels vary over time based on the state of the economy, birth rates, and immigration. In recent years, spending has been relatively flat (Billings 2020; Billings and Aussenberg 2019; see also https://www.fns.usda.gov/pd/child-nutrition-tables).

The US government operates a few smaller programs as well. The Child and Adult Care Food Program has an annual budget of $4 billion. It subsidizes meals and snacks for four to five million children, using the same eligibility criteria as the school meals programs. Eligible children may be in child-care centers, daycare homes, or afterschool programs. During the summers, the government distributes food assistance to low-income children via schools, libraries, camps, community centers, and recreation programs—both public and nonprofit. The Summer Food Service Program helps feed two to four million children, at a cost of half a billion dollars. The number of recipients falls far short of the 20 million children who eat free lunches during the school year, a sign that many children might not be getting enough to eat in the summer.[20]

Clearly, the public side of food assistance favors low-income children. They are the main recipients of every government program discussed so far. The US government does offer some help to low-income senior citizens, beyond the SNAP program. A small slice (< 5%) of the Child and Adult Care Food Program helps pay for meals at adult daycare facilities. The Commodity Supplemental Food Program targets people over the age of 60, with incomes below 130 percent of the poverty threshold. This program distributes foods with a long shelf life, such as powdered milk, cereal, rice, dry beans, peanut butter, canned meat, and canned vegetables. A predetermined box of food is allocated once a month and is supposed to provide one-quarter of the calories needed by a typical elderly person. In 2018, this program reached an average of 676,000 older Americans each month. The annual budget is so small that each recipient gets about one dollar's worth of food per day. Another option is The Emergency Food Assistance Program, which is open to low-income individuals regardless of age. It pays for a variety of fresh, canned, and dry foods. That program is also quite small ($400 million in fiscal year 2020). Separately, the US Department of Health and Human Services funds a few nutrition programs authorized by the Older Americans Act; total spending was less than $1 billion in 2018.[21] If you are elderly and struggling, SNAP is still your best option for food assistance.

Collectively, food assistance programs cost the national government about $100 billion each year. Every one of these programs is funded by general revenues. Those revenues come primarily from income taxes, and we know who pays those taxes (see Chapter 5). Government bureaucrats issue SNAP cards, and cafeteria workers prepare school meals. They are important caregivers in this part of the social safety net. But the rich help take care of the poor by funding these programs. In that sense, food assistance programs are highly redistributive.

They are also big business. Billions of tax dollars are not being spent to buy government-raised food from government grocery stores. This money helps stimulate demand in the private sector. Originally, food assistance programs had two main objectives—reduce hunger and generate more demand for food (Finegold 1988; Levine 2008; Wiseman 2019). As government programs have grown, so has the number of companies and industries with a vested interest in their operation. Almost 250,000 retailers have qualified to participate in the SNAP program, mostly grocery stores, convenience stores, and big-box superstores.[22] Walmart does more business with SNAP ($11 billion in 2018) than any other company. Billions of SNAP dollars are spent at Target, Aldi, Kroger, Giant, and Food Lion. Independent grocery stores in less affluent neighborhoods count heavily on SNAP customers. Major food and beverage companies such as Kraft Heinz depend on the program as well (Haddon and Newman 2018; Peterson 2019; Reagan 2017; Saslow 2013).

Having a broad corporate constituency could help SNAP resist cutbacks, and perhaps even expand. The grocery business operates on narrow margins, and even small drops in customer demand are noticed. Republican legislators from farm states have historically been sympathetic to the program. Politically, SNAP has more friends in high places than cash welfare ever had. But companies still have to focus on the bottom line. The National Association of Convenience Stores, for example, has been pushing for more "flexibility" in SNAP's stocking standards, allowing stores to carry more boxed or canned goods relative to perishable items. Maybe a can of spray cheese could count as a dairy staple, or a jar of stuffed olives could count as a vegetable. The rationale is that fresh food spoils faster, and convenience stores cannot stay in business if they keep throwing out their products. Promoting good nutrition is not their top priority (Carman 2019; Gundersen 2015; National Association of Convenience Stores 2020).

In other programs, companies and trade associations work diligently to make sure their food is approved for purchase. WIC allows states to strike exclusive deals with the makers of infant formula. Whichever company offers the best discounts will become the sole provider of formula to WIC infants in that state (Carlson, Greenstein, and Neuberger 2017). One recent skirmish involved white potatoes, whose nutritional value was questionable. White potatoes used to be excluded from WIC but are now included, thanks in part to lobbying from the potato industry (Jalonick 2015; Rampell 2014). Subsidized school meals are a bigger target, and business groups have been trying to influence them for years (Levine 2008; Poppendieck 2010).

The giant food and beverage industry–names like Tyson and Archer Daniels Midland–is also involved. Its various lobbying arms, including food processors, distributors, service management companies, soft drink makers, and agricultural giants, work to ensure that the government buys food products from its members and keeps schools open to vending machines and à la carte offerings in the school cafeteria, a little oasis of choice that represents millions of extra dollars of revenue each year. (Haskins 2005)

Not long ago, the Obama administration raised the nutritional standards for school meals, requiring more whole grains and fruits while limiting sodium and fat. The Trump administration, with industry support, tried to weaken those standards. More pizza, more French fries, fewer apples (Del Valle 2019; Jalonick 2017; Reiley 2020).

Our tour of the food safety net so far has been limited to the national level, with good reason. Compared to the national government, state and local governments play a much smaller role. State and local authorities spend little of their own money and make few of the rules governing the food programs discussed above. There are exceptions. Because many recent immigrants are excluded from SNAP, some states have created their own programs, usually small, to help feed them (Koball 2018; National Immigration Forum 2018). In addition, a number of communities have targeted "food deserts"—areas where residents do not have access to affordable, nutritious food—and "food swamps," where unhealthy food is readily available. Such deserts and swamps are usually located in low-income areas of the country.[23] Federal, state, and local governments have used grants, loans, tax breaks, rent subsidies, and changes to zoning laws to improve access to food. They have, for instance, tried to encourage grocery stores to open in low-income neighborhoods, giving residents an alternative to convenience stores where prices can be higher and healthy options are limited. Or, officials have looked for ways to make fresh produce more available at convenience stores (Block and Subramanian 2015; Morris 2019; Trickey 2020). A lack of income is not the only obstacle to food security; geography matters as well.

Help from Charities

Compared to government programs, the "private" side of food assistance is more complicated. The thousands of food banks, food pantries, and soup kitchens differ on multiple dimensions. Some have formal eligibility criteria and others do not. They could be open almost every day, or just once or twice a month. They might offer groceries, prepared meals, or both. Charitable pantries might hand out a predetermined box of food or allow clients to choose from whatever is available. Many of these organizations are secular, and many more are connected to places of worship. Some operate with multimillion-dollar budgets and professional staff, but most are small outfits run by volunteers. All these variations might seem like a good reason to skip this part of the social safety net. However, millions of Americans rely every month on these organizations for food. Even a partial picture of charitable food assistance is better than none at all.

Two national networks play a crucial role in uniting these diverse efforts. The largest is Feeding America, which includes 200 regional food banks and 60,000 local food pantries, soup kitchens, and shelters across the country. Approximately 90 percent of all the local food charities in the United States belong to this network.[24] The national headquarters has a full-time staff whose main jobs include fundraising, building corporate partnerships, directing donated food to the most appropriate food banks, advocating for public policies, and conducting research. The national office used to sponsor a detailed survey of its members every four years, and the resulting *Hunger in America* reports offered the best single portrait of private food assistance. The last of these reports was published in 2014, and the organization now conducts smaller studies on specific topics. The other food network is Meals on Wheels, which encompasses over 5,000 local organizations. They prepare and deliver nutritious meals to the elderly. These two organizations offer important insights into the workings of private food assistance.

Because Feeding America is so large and decentralized, precise numbers can be hard to come by. The organization says it provided 4.2 billion meals in 2019. That figure is based on the total volume of food distributed (close to 5 billion pounds), divided by 1.2, which is the weight in pounds of a typical meal according to the Department of Agriculture. Feeding America distributed that food to over 40 million Americans (Feeding America 2019). On average, then, each client received enough food to make about 100 meals per year. Charity will feed them for a few days out of every month. Some people will get more than that, and some will get less, but no one will be able to rely on charitable food alone.

The regional banks collect food that has been donated or bought at a steep discount, and then distribute it to other organizations.[25] Food banks are basically large warehouses with truckloads of food coming in and going out every day. The logistical challenges are significant, with food banks operating like airport hubs whose flights are sometimes predictable and sometimes not. Like airports, food banks are less common in rural parts of the country. Montana has one food bank in the Feeding America network, whereas Florida has nine and New York has ten. They also vary in size. The Houston Food Bank, one of the country's largest, might distribute enough food in a year to make 100 million meals. The Food Bank of Lincoln (Nebraska) supplies the equivalent of 10 million meals.[26]

Regional food banks do not have much direct contact with individual clients.[27] That job belongs to local providers, mainly food pantries and soup kitchens. These organizations typically rely on food banks for most of their inventory.[28] In addition, they might receive food from local merchants or local food drives, and they might purchase food with cash donations. Churches, temples, and mosques play a vital role. According to the 2014 Hunger in America survey, almost two-thirds of the local organizations in the Feeding America network were faith-based. This makes perfect sense; feeding the hungry has long occupied a special place in many of the world's religions. Secular nonprofits represented about one-quarter of the local organizations in the network. Most of the rest were in the public sector, such as Community Action Agencies or school-based pantries—more evidence of the public–private mix (Weinfield et al. 2014).

At one end of the spectrum are places like the Holy Apostles Soup Kitchen in New York City, which offers free hot lunches to 1,000 or more people every weekday (as well as free Sunday dinners).[29] Anyone waiting in line can talk with a social services specialist who will try to help them find housing, medical care, or employment. To serve that many people, the kitchen must be staffed from six in the morning until five in the afternoon to allow enough time for cooking and clean-up. The Lakeview Pantry provides food six days a week in the Chicago area. It operates three sites and leases a 10,000-square-foot warehouse, and distributed the equivalent of 1.6 million meals in 2019.[30] More common, however, are smaller organizations like the Westminster Presbyterian Church (Spokane, Washington), whose food pantry is open only on Wednesdays and Fridays from 11 a.m. to 1:45 p.m. Or the Dilworth Soup Kitchen in Charlotte, North Carolina, which serves lunch for one hour every Monday.[31]

Soup kitchens usually serve whoever walks through the door, no questions asked. In practice, they care for people in their local area; not many folks drive 100 miles for a free meal. If soup kitchens turn someone away, it's usually because they ran out of food. Food pantries work differently. Clients will be asked to give their name, because most pantries limit visits to once (maybe twice) a month. Each visit will generate enough food to last three days, maybe more. The types of food available are limited and can vary from month to month. As a result, some individuals will visit multiple pantries each month. Most clients will be asked the size of their household, which affects how much food they are allotted. Because pantries intend to serve the poor and near poor, they often ask people about their income. A verbal declaration could suffice, but clients might have to bring documentation. Finally, clients will have to offer proof of residence because pantries restrict eligibility to those living nearby. Food pantries will turn people away if they live outside the service area. In this part of the social safety net, geography definitely matters.[32]

Traditional food pantries and grocery stores occupy fixed locations, and not everyone can access them easily. The nearest one could be more than an hour's drive away in rural parts of the country. Some urban areas are not well-served by public transportation, making access to food pantries and grocery stores more difficult. And no matter where they live, older Americans and disabled adults often have trouble getting around. As a result, some food banks and pantries deliver food by truck to specific places on a regular schedule. That food might be available once a week, once a month, or every two months, depending on the organization. On the eastern shore of Virginia, a mobile pantry drops food once a month at two different churches. The Community Action Agency in Cincinnati sends a mobile food pantry to two or three different locations each month. In Montana, the food bank network can mail 30-pound boxes of nonperishable food to low-income individuals who live too far from a regular pantry or mobile drop site.[33] These efforts represent another kind of remedy to the problem of food deserts and food swamps.

Like the Holy Apostles Soup Kitchen, many of these charitable organizations do more than distribute and prepare food. They also help clients apply for government benefits. In a recent annual report, Feeding America proudly claimed that their network members helped clients receive over 200 million meals from SNAP in 2018. As we saw in Chapter 3, leaders of charitable organizations believe that government benefits are essential to the well-being of the clients they serve. Representatives from Feeding America point out that SNAP provides many more meals than they do. In their view SNAP, not charity, represents "the nation's first line of defense against hunger."[34] The organization's 2014 survey found that 40 percent of local food charities were helping clients qualify for SNAP. Between 20 and 30 percent of them were helping clients qualify for WIC, SSI, TANF, Medicaid, or low-income housing. Some of the larger operations even offer culinary training programs to help people land a job.[35]

Because food charities do not keep consistent, detailed records, we know less about their clients than those who receive public benefits. According to the 2014 Hunger in America survey, at least 29 percent of the people benefitting from food pantries or soup kitchens are children. I say "at least" because the survey did not ask about child-specific programs designed to help during the summers and weekends. Those are not large programs, so it seems reasonable to estimate that children constitute roughly one-third of all people who receive charitable food assistance. Compared to their share of the total US population, children are overrepresented—even though they receive sizable benefits from SNAP, school meals, and WIC.[36]

According to that same survey, 11 percent of clients are elderly and the rest are working-age adults. Senior citizens are slightly underrepresented relative to their share of the US population. Still, with all the monies spent on Social

Security and SNAP, readers might be surprised to discover that millions of older Americans seek out free food. Working-age adults receive a larger share of charitable food assistance than government food assistance. Charities do not insist that adults be employed or have a long work history, which makes their food easier to access. For adults who have little connection to the workforce, and thus little income from a job or the government, food pantries and soup kitchens are a crucial part of the social safety net (Weinfield et al. 2014).

In terms of race and ethnicity, those who receive charitable food assistance resemble those who receive government benefits. They are disproportionately Black (26%) and Hispanic (20%). Millions of Whites use food pantries and soup kitchens as well. They represented 43 percent of all clients in 2014. That figure was considerably less than their share of the total population (Weinfield et al. 2014).

Just as public programs require tax dollars, charitable programs require donors. In 2019, a small portion (6%) of Feeding America's revenue came from cash donations.[37] Far more important are the goods donated to regional food banks. One of the biggest donors is the national government. The Commodity Supplemental Food Program and The Emergency Food Assistance Program distribute tons of commodities to charitable food banks. Most of the food, however, comes from the private sector. The largest donors, whom Feeding America refers to as Visionary Partners, give at least $4 million, 40 million pounds of food, or a combination of $2 million and 20 million pounds of food. These donors include major grocery store chains—Albertson's, Costco, Food Lion, Kroger, Publix, Sam's Club—as well as Target and Walmart. They include major food companies such as Conagra, General Mills, and Kraft Heinz. Other companies, known as Leadership Partners, donated tons of food as well (Feeding America 2019). In other words, corporate America is helping charities take care of people who are hungry. And companies are doing so more intentionally than rich individuals whose income taxes happen to fund SNAP, WIC, and school meals.

Companies have different reasons for donating food. Farmers and agribusiness firms sometimes donate produce that is fresh and edible, but not the right size or shape for grocery stores. They donate surplus items as well. Companies donate foods whose packaging has cosmetic flaws. Grocery stores and restaurants donate prepared foods that did not sell. In 2019, Feeding America claims to have rescued 3.6 billion pounds of food from different parts of the supply chain.[38] A cynic might argue that such donations aren't exactly praiseworthy if companies were going to throw out the food anyway, and if government rewards their charitable acts with tax deductions. Perhaps. Those concerns should also apply to middle-class families who donate to charity clothes that no longer fit or are no longer wanted.

While large corporations help take care of the hungry, a huge number of volunteers and a smaller number of paid staff act as caregivers. According to government statistics, 77 million Americans volunteered in their community in 2018. Collectively they gave almost 7 billion hours of their time.[39] Religious organizations are the most common conduit for volunteers. Collecting, distributing, preparing, or serving food is the second most common volunteer activity. Put these two facts together and you can imagine how important volunteers are to pantries and soup kitchens run by churches, temples, and mosques. The 2014 Hunger in America survey found that two million people volunteered at food banks, pantries, or soup kitchens in a typical month.[40] The Bureau of Labor Statistics estimated that seven million Americans volunteered to collect, prepare, distribute, or serve food at some point in 2015. On average, food pantries received a total of 60 hours of volunteers' time each month, while soup kitchens received 80 hours. If these numbers seem modest, remember that many of these organizations are open for just a few hours or few days each week. Half the local organizations in the Feeding America network rely entirely on volunteers (US Bureau of Labor Statistics 2016; Weinfeld et al. 2014; https://www.nationalservice.gov/serve/via).

Meals on Wheels is a much smaller operation. Before the pandemic, the organization was delivering 220 million meals a year to 2.4 million senior citizens. Clients don't have to be low income, but many are. Over one-third of them live in poverty. Many others are essentially house-bound or have difficulties preparing their own meals. More than three-quarters of recipients are age 75 or older; most are taking three or more medications daily; and most live alone. All of them are vulnerable in some way. Given the age profile, women (69%) far outnumber men. The racial/ethnic profile of recipients is unusual for this part of the social safety net. Only 28 percent are identified as Black, Hispanic, or members of any other minority group. Because Meals on Wheels serves people from a wide range of incomes, and because Whites live longer, Whites are more prevalent here than in SNAP or the Feeding America network. The typical Meals on Wheels client is an older White woman.[41]

Food is not the only benefit. Meals on Wheels also wants to lessen the social isolation experienced by many senior citizens. Meals are hand-delivered by volunteers who are encouraged to talk with recipients and ask about their well-being, performing what the organization calls friendly visits and safety checks. In that sense, Meals and Wheels offers food and daily care. In fact, the organization sees good nutrition and compassion as essential to good health among the elderly, a reminder that parts of the social safety net have multiple functions.[42]

While local volunteers act as caregivers, it is less obvious who is taking care of Meals on Wheels in the sense of funding. Many pockets are required. The national office, known as Meals on Wheels America, operated on a budget of

$37 million in 2018, which was far too small to support 220 million meals. Most of their revenues came from donated public service announcements, not donated food. The national office does negotiate discounts with food companies that local affiliates can take advantage of. Those affiliates also seek food donations from local restaurants and grocery stores, and cash donations from local businesses, foundations, and individuals. In addition, the US government helps fund Meals on Wheels. Through the Older Americans Act, the Department of Health and Human Services provides roughly one-third of the monies spent by local affiliates. State governments might contribute a small amount. Meals on Wheels also charges seniors for their services. Depending on where you live, a typical meal might cost $5–$10, and clients are expected to pay based on a sliding scale. (SNAP cards can be used as payment.) The organization insists that no one will be turned away because they cannot afford to pay. Nonetheless, many local affiliates do have waiting lists because the need exceeds their capacity. Given the number of meals served and cost of each meal, the total budget for Meals on Wheels nationwide is probably around $2 billion.[43]

Both Feeding America and Meals on Wheels rely heavily on volunteers. They are a diverse group racially and religiously. They are young, middle-aged, and old, college graduates and high school dropouts. They live in big cities, suburbs, and small towns. There is, however, a gender imbalance. Women are much more likely than men to volunteer with a food charity (US Bureau of Labor Statistics 2016; Weinfield et al. 2014).

In several parts of the country, Feeding America and Meals on Wheels work together. The Feed More organization in Richmond, Virginia combines the Central Virginia Food Bank and Meals on Wheels under one roof. Their food bank also includes a mobile pantry that serves urban and rural residents in central Virginia. In Pennsylvania, the Chester County Food Bank provides not only hot meals for the local Meals on Wheels affiliate, but also emergency food boxes that clients can use in case heavy snow prevents volunteers from delivering their meal. The Brazos Valley Food Bank (Texas) uses Meals on Wheels to distribute bags of food that senior citizens can eat or cook during the weekend, when Meals on Wheels does not deliver.[44] While these efforts might look like charity, once you start asking how that food made its way to those in need, you discover that government and business played supporting roles.

Other Coping Strategies

The combination of earned income, government benefits, and organized charity is not enough to feed everyone. To fill in the gaps, many Americans rely on their family safety net. Several studies have found that adults use up their SNAP benefits in the first two to three weeks of the month, and then turn to family, friends, or organized charity. As the old saying goes, "there's a lot of month left at the end of the money." Family and friends might loan them money for groceries. More often, they might give them food or invite them over to share a meal. We don't have good estimates of how many people get how many meals from extended family and friends, but we know that it happens with some regularity. It is not always a reliable source of food, because family and friends could be facing their own challenges. This is especially true among the poorest of the poor. And some individuals may feel too ashamed to ask family for help putting food on the table (Edin and Lein 1997; Edin et al. 2013; Kalil and Ryan 2010; Schenck-Fontaine, Gassman-Pines, and Hill 2017; Stack 1983).

Even with help from family and friends, many Americans are forced to make difficult trade-offs. The 2014 Hunger in America survey revealed that almost two-thirds of Feeding America's clients had to choose between paying their medical bills and paying for food. Thirty percent faced this choice every month. A similar share had to decide whether to pay their utility bills or pay for food. Over half made trade-offs between housing and food (Gundersen, Engelhard, and Hake 2017; Weinfield et al. 2014). In short, for millions of Americans, getting enough to eat means risking their well-being in other ways. They have to rob Peter to pay Paul.

Discussion

Millions of ordinary Americans act as caregivers in the food safety net. While some are paid, many others are unpaid. They volunteer at local food pantries, soup kitchens, and Meals on Wheels; they are employed by school cafeterias; they process applications and issue SNAP cards; they share food with family members and friends who are struggling. Almost all of them come face-to-face with the people they are trying to help. Behind these caregivers are a very different set of actors who are responsible for growing, processing, distributing, and paying for this food. This group includes affluent Americans whose taxes finance government food programs. Companies, large and small, sell food to SNAP and WIC clients, and they make sizable donations to food banks. In this part of the social safety net, those who take care of others are quite different than those who give care. Rarely is it accurate to call food assistance strictly public or strictly private.

In most respects, recipients are a diverse group. They are overwhelmingly low income. With a few exceptions, government programs and charitable organizations are designed to feed the poor and near poor. This part of the social safety net is focused on serving "the least of these" (see Chapter 3). Besides their economic similarities, recipients cut across age, gender, racial, and ethnic lines. They might be employed, underemployed, or unemployed. They can be found in every part of the country, whether urban, rural, or suburban. They might need food for a few days or the entire year. Low-income children, many of them racial minorities, are one of the main beneficiaries of government programs. Working-age adults find it easier to qualify for charity than SNAP because of the latter's work requirements. Whether those adults (or anyone) actually benefit from food pantries and soup kitchens depends partly on geography.

To understand how adequate all this care is, we need to revisit the concept of food insecurity that was mentioned at the start of this chapter. Just as poverty thresholds are used to measure a lack of income, indicators of food insecurity are used to measure a lack of food. According to the US government, food security means "access by all people at all times to enough food for an active, healthy life" (Coleman-Jensen 2019: 2). Those who lack such access are food insecure. Although we commonly talk about fighting hunger, food insecurity is different. Food insecurity is supposed to be a more objective measure based on specific behaviors. Hunger is more of a feeling. Some people with plenty of food might report being hungry, and some people with little food but a high pain threshold might not say they feel hungry.[45]

The extent of food security or insecurity is determined by a series of survey questions. The official version consists of 18 questions, which are asked as part of the Food Security Supplement to the Current Population Survey, conducted by the Census Bureau. Each question pertains to the household, not to each individual. If households do not have any children under the age of 18, then they answer only ten of these questions. Some questions ask whether respondents agree with statements such as, "The food that we bought just didn't last and we didn't have money to get more," and "We couldn't feed our children a balanced meal because we couldn't afford that." Other questions are designed to reveal whether any adults in the house went without food for a whole day because they didn't have enough money, and whether any children in the house had to skip a meal because there wasn't enough money. Some organizations use a subset of these questions to make their surveys easier to administer and less expensive (Coleman-Jensen et al. 2019; Gundersen, Engelhard, and Hake 2017).

Answers to these questions are then combined into an index. For households without children, indicating a problem on at least three out of ten questions will classify them as low food security, or food insecure. Those who indicate a problem on six or more questions are considered to have very low food security (akin to deep poverty). The scoring for households with children is a bit more complicated. For the entire household, low food security means indicating at least three problems on the 18-item survey, and very low food security means eight or more problems. Eight questions apply specifically to children, and two or more problems from that list mean that the children are food insecure. Five or more problems indicate very low food security (Coleman-Jensen et al. 2019).

Much like the official poverty thresholds, these numbers could overstate or understate the true problem. The category of food insecure includes people who have trouble "sometimes," which could mean a day or two each year. That might sound more like a nuisance than a pressing social problem. The way questions are phrased, food insecurity could affect only one person and not the entire household. Being food insecure, even for an extended period, does not necessarily mean that one is starving or malnourished. On the other hand, someone who experiences one or two of the problems highlighted on the survey will not be classified as food insecure. An adult who lost weight because they could not afford to buy food will not be classified as having a problem (Coleman-Jensen et al. 2019). Some of us would disagree. Furthermore, some households could qualify as food secure only because they are already receiving help from Food Stamps or a local food pantry. They cannot afford to buy enough food on their own. And "not starving" is an awfully low standard in a country as prosperous as the United States. All things considered, this measure of food insecurity should be treated as a ballpark estimate.

In 2018, 14.3 million households were food insecure, meaning one out of every nine (Table 6.1). Over five million households (4.3%) were experiencing very low food security. Some readers might notice that these percentages were quite close to the rates of poverty and deep poverty at the time. This is true, but the income poor and the food insecure are not the same people. A little more than one-third of food-insecure households live in poverty. Most live above the poverty line. One-quarter have incomes between 100 and 185 percent of poverty, and one-quarter have higher incomes (the rest are unknown). Remarkably, those with very low food security have a similar income profile. Food insecurity affects the poor and near poor, as well as many working-class and middle-class people. The wide scope of food insecurity adds credibility to claims by policy experts, United Way, and The Salvation Army that the official poverty thresholds are too low (see Chapter 5). And it helps explain why many food-insecure households (44%) do not participate in SNAP, WIC, or free- and reduced-price school lunches. They earn too much to get help from government (Coleman-Jensen et al. 2019).

Households with children present a mixed picture. Almost 14 percent were classified as food insecure in 2018 (Table 6.1). In half of these households, just the adults were food insecure; in the other half, both the adults and the children were. The numbers were worse if the children are living in a single-parent household, especially if that parent is a single mother. Seldom, however, do children have to deal with very low food security. When money is tight, parents will usually feed their children as best they can and make do with less themselves. The

Table 6.1 **Food Insecurity in the United States (2018)**

Households	Food insecure		Very low food security	
	Number	*Rate*	*Number*	*Rate*
Total	14,311,000	11.1 %	5,581,000	4.3 %
With no children	9,068,000	9.9	4,088,000	4.5
With children				
under age 18	5,243,000	13.9	1,493,000	4.0
under age 6	2,339,000	14.3	619,000	3.8
and single mother	2,596,000	27.8	881,000	9.4
and single father	516,000	15.9	170,000	5.3
With elderly	2,934,000	7.5	1,016,000	2.6
Income-to-poverty ratio				
below 1.0	4,285,000	35.3	1,929,000	15.9
1.0–1.85	3,518,000	23.9	1,290,000	8.8
above 1.85	3,831,000	5.4	1,314,000	1.9
White, non-Hispanic	6,869,000	8.1	2,760,000	3.2
Black, non-Hispanic	3,526,000	21.2	1,505,000	9.1
Hispanic, any race	2,937,000	16.2	919,000	5.1

Notes: rate = percent of households, not percent of food-insecure households; income, and thus the income-to-poverty ratio was unknown for 2.7 million of these households.

Source: Coleman-Jensen et al. 2019, Table 2.

WIC program and subsidized school meals will also help feed their kids. Elderly households, in contrast, fare better than average when it comes to food security (Coleman-Jensen et al. 2019).

Blacks and Hispanics have a much greater risk of food insecurity than non-Hispanic Whites. (Table 6.1) Among Blacks, the rates of food insecurity (21.2%) and very low food security (9.1%) are almost twice the national average. Blacks are more likely to experience very low food security than Whites experience *any* type of food insecurity (8.1%). Nonetheless, given the sheer number of Whites in the general population, they account for about one-half of all households dealing with food insecurity. The situation for Hispanics (16.2% food insecure) is closer to Blacks than Whites.

When it comes to food, geography matters. Many people in rural areas live in food deserts, far from a grocery store. Charitable pantries and soup kitchens might not be close, either. Many people in big cities live in food deserts or food swamps. Food insecurity is more prevalent in urban areas (13.2%) than the suburbs (8.9%). Outside metropolitan areas, which includes small towns and farms, we find more food-insecure households (12.7%) than average. The highest rates are in states like Mississippi, New Mexico, Oklahoma, and West Virginia. The same patterns hold true for people with very low food security (Coleman-Jensen et al. 2019).

Why should we care if kids miss a meal now and then? Does it really matter if their families can't always afford to eat a balanced meal? Numerous studies have found that people who experience food insecurity run a greater risk of health problems such as anemia, asthma, and depression. The 2014 Hunger in America survey found that one-third of Feeding America's clients had diabetes, and over half had high blood pressure. Individuals in poor health might need special diets and more expensive food. They might be unable to shop around for the best deals, or to wait in line for an hour before the local food pantry opens. Without a reliable supply of nutritious food, they might one day need expensive medical care. Children who are food insecure have trouble meeting developmental milestones and succeeding in school. It is really hard to concentrate when you are hungry. Food-insecure children are also more likely to have behavioral problems (Carlson and Keith-Jennings 2018; Gundersen, Engelhard, and Hake 2017; Gundersen and Ziliac 2015; Hartline-Grafton 2017; Johnson and Markowitz 2018; Jyoti, Frongillo, and Jones 2005; Peltz and Garg 2019).[46] Later in life they could have more difficulty getting into college and finding a decent-paying job. There is an old saying, "an army marches on its stomach." Soldiers perform better when they are well-fed, and so does everyone else.

7

Housing

Building a safety net for housing is more difficult than it is for food. Housing is expensive—the single-largest item in the typical household budget. Americans spend twice as much on housing (including utilities) as they do on food.[1] Moreover, housing costs are "lumpy." If you are short on money, you cannot skip a rent or mortgage payment as easily as you can skip a meal. Nor can you move to a cheaper place for a few days the way you might temporarily buy cheaper food. For charities, running a shelter is a much bigger undertaking than a food pantry.

A few numbers can show what individuals living in or near poverty are up against. For homeowners with a mortgage, the median monthly cost of housing in 2018 was $1,566. The typical renter paid "only" $1,058 each month. Financial experts and the government have long advised Americans to keep housing costs below 30 percent of their gross income so they have enough money left to buy food, medical care, transportation, and clothes.[2] Anyone who follows this advice would need to earn at least $42,000 to afford a typical apartment. That group excludes everyone living in poverty and most of the near poor as well. A single person in poverty would have to spend all their money on rent. The numbers look even worse for would-be homeowners.[3]

Granted, averages can be deceiving. A single person can get by with a smaller-than-average apartment. Housing costs vary around the country, and rents will be lower in states like Mississippi and South Dakota, or in cities like Toledo, Ohio. Nationally, fifteen million apartments rented for $500–$1,000 per month in 2018. The cheapest of these would have been within reach of the near poor and some of the poor. Four million units rented for less than $500, which were obviously too few to house all 38 million Americans living in poverty.

Large segments of the population must deal with above-average housing costs. A typical apartment contains 2.5 people, and most families with children are larger than that. They need more room, which costs extra. Many Americans live in expensive parts of the country. It is hard to find a $500-a-month apartment in most big cities. Even $1,000 a month can be a challenge. In Boston and

Who Cares. Christopher Howard, Oxford University Press. © Oxford University Press 2023.
DOI: 10.1093/oso/9780190074456.003.0008

Washington, DC, a typical two-bedroom apartment rents for $2,500 per month. The average is more than $3,000 in New York City and San Francisco (Temple 2019). Paying those prices will be a major challenge for the middle class, much less the poor and near poor.

The high cost of housing creates difficult trade-offs. Many low-income Americans go on the market and pay the going rate. Millions of them end up spending at least half of their income on housing, forcing them to cut back on other essentials. Some accept a smaller place than they need, perhaps squeezing four people into a one-bedroom apartment. Or they might have to put up with landlords who neglect their properties. Some people have such poor credit histories that landlords refuse to rent to them. They could end up living in an extended-stay hotel or motel, which can cost more than an apartment (Frazier 2021). Other people will rely on family members or friends to shelter them. Nevertheless, doubling up has its drawbacks: not everyone wants to spend their twenties living with their parents; few people look forward to sleeping on the couch in their cousin's apartment.

Not much help is available elsewhere. Low-income housing has never been a high priority in Washington. The budget for all rental assistance programs is less than the budget for SNAP. A small fraction of the poor reside in public housing developments. A slightly larger fraction receive vouchers to rent apartments from private landlords. State and local governments run a variety of affordable housing programs to increase supply and subsidize demand. For example, some governments pay local motels to shelter people temporarily (Walker and Graham 2018). Most of these programs are quite small, and their definition of "affordable" covers a broad group of people. Few low-income people benefit. In contrast, government has done much more to help middle-income and upper-income Americans become homeowners.

Those who seek housing from nonprofit organizations are often desperate. A variety of nonprofits offer temporary shelter to battered women and children, the chronically homeless, or to victims of floods, fires, and other disasters. These individuals are highly vulnerable, but not always poor. In some cases, charities help turn renters into homeowners. Their impact is limited: these charities touch thousands of lives in this country, not millions.

There is no single yardstick for housing comparable to poverty rates or food insecurity.[4] Some organizations keep track of homelessness. For those who have housing, we can document its physical adequacy (e.g., indoor plumbing, reliable heat). We can also determine how heavy a cost burden is borne by each household.[5] No matter which indicator is used, all reveal serious flaws in the housing safety net.

Buying

Owning a home has long been part of the American Dream (Dreier and Schwartz 2015). Homeownership indicates a certain level of independence and security.[6] Moving from renter to owner is one of the most visible signs of joining the middle class. For millions of Americans, the home is their most valuable asset. Since World War II, over half of American households have owned their home outright or were paying off a mortgage. Almost two-thirds of households currently are homeowners.[7]

The chances of owning a home increase with age and income. It takes time to save for a down payment, and it takes a good-paying job to afford a mortgage, property taxes, and insurance. According to the National Association of Realtors, the median price of homes sold in the United States was $285,000 in May 2020. The most expensive homes were in the West, averaging over $400,000. In the Midwest region, where prices were lowest, the typical home sold for $227,000. Depending on where they live, buyers would need $20,000–$40,000 to afford a ten percent down payment. Even though interest rates are low, the monthly payments for a typical home would be far too large for low-income Americans to afford. Without help, they would need homes priced below $100,000, yet very few (7% in May 2020) are selling in that range.[8]

The national government helps homeowners in a couple of ways. The most expensive is through the tax code. Homeowners can deduct their mortgage interest, as well as the property taxes on their residence, from their taxable income. These two provisions used to cost the national government $100 billion in revenue each year. At their peak, they were claimed by over 30 million households. Since the tax laws were changed in 2017, the cost has been cut in half. A separate tax break, applied to capital gains from selling a home, is worth $35 billion per year. These provisions, however, do practically nothing for low-income Americans. In 2019, tax filers with less than $40,000 of income received less than one percent of the mortgage interest deduction. Almost all the benefits went to people with incomes over $100,000—people who could afford to buy a home without a government subsidy. Decades of special treatment in the tax code have helped affluent Americans pay for expensive homes and add to their wealth. The beneficiaries have been disproportionately White (Desmond 2017; Howard 1997; Joint Committee on Taxation 2015, 2019).

For those who are not so well-off, the government can help them secure a loan. The Federal Housing Administration (FHA) serves people whose income, debts, or credit history makes it difficult to obtain a traditional home loan. The agency is particularly interested in assisting first-time homebuyers.[9] The government does not make the loans directly but insures private lenders against the risk of default. With an FHA loan guarantee, homebuyers do not need a large down payment (3%–5% is common), and their loan comes with a competitive interest rate (Jones 2019; US Department of Housing and Urban Development 2019).[10]

Since it began in 1934, the FHA has helped millions of Americans become homeowners. The rapid growth of the middle class after World War II was fueled in part by FHA-backed loans (Schwartz 2014). The program continues to touch many lives. In 2018, the FHA insured 20 percent of all new home loans. For Black and Hispanic borrowers, FHA's share was closer to 40 percent. Over 80 percent of all first-time homebuyers relied on the FHA to back their loans. Yet the cost to taxpayers is close to zero. The FHA charges all borrowers a small fee to compensate lenders for any losses related to mortgage defaults. In effect, the FHA requires borrowers to take care of each other (Jones 2019; US Department of Housing and Urban Development 2019).

We should not overstate the positive impact of this program. The FHA discriminated against racial minorities for many years, and the middle class it built was predominantly White (Rothstein 2017; Taylor 2019; Thurston 2018). Although lending practices have changed and the FHA now serves more minority homebuyers, the numbers are modest—roughly 125,000 Black and 175,000 Hispanic borrowers in 2019. (FHA's total that year was close to a million.) Regardless of one's race or ethnicity, homes are expensive. The typical loan insured by the FHA is currently in the range of $180,000 to $200,000.[11] Assuming a small down payment, those homes would sell for less than the national average, but for much more than the poor could afford. Some of the near poor could qualify, as long as interest rates were low and the loan amount was below the FHA average. Otherwise, borrowers would run afoul of FHA's requirement that housing costs are below 31 percent of their gross income at the time of the loan (US Department of Housing and Urban Development 2019). To pay off their loan, the near poor would need a good, steady income for the next 15 or 30 years, and that can be hard to achieve (Chapter 5). In short, the FHA's most likely beneficiaries are working-class or middle-class Americans, not people who live in or near poverty.[12]

The national government and state governments operate a few other programs to boost homeownership, but they are much smaller than those described above (Schwartz 2014).[13] Another avenue, which is also limited, involves nonprofits and charities. Habitat for Humanity is the largest example. This organization has been building or renovating affordable homes since 1976. It relies heavily on volunteer labor, cash gifts, corporate donations (e.g., building supplies, appliances), and proceeds from the sale of items donated to their ReStores. Habitat for Humanity is a charity, but it does not give away homes the way soup kitchens offer free meals. Recipients must contribute "sweat equity," usually between 250 and 500 hours, during the construction phase for new homes. Recipients are also responsible for paying off low-interest or no-interest loans, and Habitat has been known to foreclose on delinquent mortgages. The organization believes in giving people a hand up, not a handout.[14]

Keep in mind that Habitat for Humanity performs much of its charitable work in other countries. In fiscal year 2019, it built approximately 4,000 new homes and repaired 8,000 existing homes in the United States and Canada. That same year it built 7,000 homes in Central and South America, and almost 8,000 homes in Asia and the Pacific. In addition, Habitat assisted in the construction of over 80,000 homes overseas (e.g., by ensuring access to clean water), and served as a consultant or facilitator for close to one million homes (Habitat for Humanity 2019). One can be impressed by Habitat's global efforts while still recognizing that it cares for a tiny fraction of the poor and near poor in the United States.[15]

Against long odds, some low-income individuals have become homeowners. They might have bought decades ago when homes were less expensive or their incomes were higher. That would help explain why the elderly poor are more likely than the non-elderly poor to own a house.[16] Others could live in parts of the country where homes routinely sell for under $100,000. Or, they might have bought a manufactured/mobile home. In any of these scenarios, the FHA might have helped them.

These individuals are fortunate, because owning a home has a profound effect on economic security. Consider two households, both over the age of 65 and both in the lowest income quartile. One is a homeowner and the other is a renter. On average, the owner will have built up $80,000 in home equity and a net worth of $105,000. This individual is not wealthy but has developed a financial cushion. The average renter, in contrast, will have a net worth of only $1,000 (Joint Center for Housing Studies 2019a).

Renting

The lower your income, the more likely you are to rent a place to live. Most renters would like to be homeowners, but do not believe they can afford a mortgage (Joint Center for Housing Studies 2019b). Renting can be challenging, especially for people who live in or near poverty. These individuals are competing not only with each other for affordable housing; they must also contend with people possessing higher incomes who want to save money by renting for less than they can afford. According to a recent study, of the eight million units that were affordable for people with extremely low incomes (i.e., incomes less than 30% of the area median), over three million were being rented by people in a higher income category. Renters with incomes between 30 and 50 percent of the area median faced the same problem. In addition, young professionals in their 20s and 30s often room together, occupying some of the 3- and 4-bedroom rental units that could hold families with children. Many undergraduate and graduate students want to live off campus, and that can drive up rental prices as well. Adding to these difficulties, rent and utility costs have been rising faster than incomes across the country (Airgood-Obrycki and Molinsky 2019; Desmond 2015b; US Department of Housing and Urban Development 2020c).

Since the Great Recession, the situation has deteriorated. Millions of Americans lost their homes when the housing bubble burst, leading to greater demand for rental units. Higher demand, higher rents. Increasingly, developers have focused on building studio and one-bedroom apartments for affluent renters, especially in major metro areas. In 2010, there were more renters with incomes below $15,000 than above $75,000. By 2018, the reverse was true (Airgood-Obrycki and Molinsky 2019; Edin and Shaefer 2015; Joint Center for Housing Studies 2019b).

As a result, the supply of low-rent housing falls far short of demand.[17] For every 100 households with extremely low incomes, only 38 rental units are available and affordable (i.e., they cost no more than 30 percent of the renter's income). Only 33 of those 38 units are available, affordable, and physically adequate. Although the ratio varies from state to state, the gap is always substantial. The smallest gap is in West Virginia, which has 62 affordable and available units per 100 households with extremely low incomes. The shortage is much worse in California (23 per 100), Florida (26), New Jersey (29), and Texas (29)—some of the most populous states.[18] No matter where they live, poor families with children will struggle. One study estimated that just 22 units were available and affordable for every 100 extremely low-income families with children (Airgood-Obrycki and Molinsky 2019; Joint Center for Housing Studies 2019b).

Landlords in low-income neighborhoods enjoy a remarkable amount of leverage. They can charge rents that are not much below those found in more affluent neighborhoods. They can profit from the acute shortage of affordable housing. In one study of Milwaukee, the monthly rent for a two-bedroom apartment was only ten percent less for a poor household than a non-poor household. The landlords' profit was much greater—both in percentage terms and absolute dollars—when the tenants were poor. National data reveal similar patterns. Put simply, low-income renters run a high risk of being exploited (Desmond 2016; Desmond and Wilmers 2019; Rosen 2020).

Unless they get outside help, most of the poor will have to devote 40 percent, 50 percent, or more of their income to housing. The national government operates several programs to assist low-income renters, but the cumulative impact is modest. These programs help approximately five million households, which translates to a little more than ten million people.[19] A large majority of those who are eligible for housing assistance do not receive any help because the government does not appropriate enough money. In parts of the country, it can take years or even decades to move off the waiting list and into a subsidized apartment (Desmond 2016; Fischer 2019; Rosen 2020; Schwartz 2014).

Before discussing individual programs, let's focus on what they have in common. In this part of the social safety net, responsibilities for caring are shared widely. Depending on the program, the national government works with state governments or local Public Housing Authorities (PHAs). They, in turn, often work with private landlords. Sometimes governments pay companies in the private sector to supply more low-income units. Rental assistance programs are financed largely by income taxes, meaning the affluent are paying to take care of the poor and near poor. In the largest programs (public housing and rental vouchers), recipients are expected to pay 30 to 40 percent of their income on rent.[20] They must help take care of themselves.

Public housing is the oldest and best-known of these programs. Since the New Deal, the national government and local PHAs have been responsible for housing some of the poorest Americans (McCarty, Perl, and Jones 2019; Schwartz 2014; Venkatesh 2002). Unlike most means-tested programs, eligibility for public housing varies across and within states. Individuals must have incomes that are less than 80 percent of their area median. This group includes the poor, the near poor, and people who might be considered working class or middle class. In practice, most residents in public housing have incomes well below that threshold. Over 80 percent of them have less than half the median income in their area, which is a good proxy for the poor and near poor. Most residents have less than one-third the area median income. The typical public housing apartment has two people living on $15,000.[21] Officially, they are poor.

This pattern is no accident. Public housing has always been designed to serve people who cannot afford to pay market prices for an apartment. That way, government will not compete with the private sector (Schwartz 2014). The typical resident of public housing spends less than $400 a month on rent. The poorest spend less than $100 a month.[22] Few landlords are willing to rent at that price.

Although public housing residents are obligated to pay rent, few are required to be employed.[23] Many do work, without being required; roughly one-third of these households have wage income. The rest rely on cash benefits such as Social Security, SSI, and TANF. This is a clear sign that public housing serves people who are not expected to hold a job. Over two-thirds of recipients are children, disabled, or elderly. Their need for housing assistance could last for years. As a result, public housing has no time limits (though residents can be evicted for a variety of reasons). The typical resident has been there for five to ten years.[24]

Public housing used to be the primary way of helping low-income renters. The stock has been gradually shrinking since the 1990s, in large part because officials have spent too little on maintenance and nothing on new construction.

The United States currently has about one million public housing units with two million residents. Annual spending is $7 billion. Compared to the income and food assistance programs discussed in previous chapters, or to tax breaks for wealthy homeowners, public housing is quite small (McCarty, Perl, and Jones 2019; Schwartz 2014; US Department of Housing and Urban Development 2020a).

The national government relies more on vouchers and tax credits to help low-income renters. The basic idea is to steer them away from public housing and toward the private market. Housing choice vouchers (aka Section 8 vouchers) are the centerpiece; they are administered by the Department of Housing and Urban Development (HUD) and local PHAs. Public housing projects are often located in low-income neighborhoods. Rental vouchers are supposed to give tenants more options. They might be able to move into middle-class or working-class neighborhoods, if landlords there agree to participate in the program. Tenants must pay 30 percent (in some places, up to 40 percent) of their income toward rent. The voucher covers the difference between that amount and the fair market rent for a given area, which is usually between the 40th and 50th percentile of local rental prices. These vouchers will not support tenants living in upscale apartments. By the same token, landlords will not participate if they can find other tenants to pay higher rents, or if they feel that the program's requirements are too burdensome. Most landlords do not take part, and many voucher holders cannot find a place to rent in their area (Collinson, Ellen, and Ludwig 2021; McCarty, Perl, and Jones 2019; Schwartz 2014; Thrush 2018).

The US government funds approximately two million of these vouchers, and they help five million people pay rent. In terms of total income and sources of income, voucher holders look much like those in public housing. Most of their households have an elderly person, a disabled adult, or a child. Assistance is based on need, not employment, and there are no time limits. The typical voucher holder pays about $350 per month in rent. Some tenants can afford to pay only $50–$100 each month.[25] Given the high cost of housing, the government usually pays more than half the rent. The total cost of these vouchers has been around $20–25 billion. That sum represents over half of HUD's spending on rental assistance (US Department of Housing and Urban Development 2020a).

Whereas tenant vouchers are held by individuals, project vouchers are tied to a specific place. The owners sign contracts with local PHAs to rent to qualified tenants for a fixed period, typically from 10 to 40 years. When tenants leave, the voucher remains. PHAs cover the difference between what tenants can pay and the fair market rent. Compared to public housing and tenant vouchers, project-based vouchers serve people who are less likely to be employed, more likely to be elderly, and more likely to be poor.[26] Project-based vouchers cost the government half as much as tenant-based vouchers (McCarty, Perl, and Jones 2019; Rosen 2020; Schwartz 2014; US Department of Housing and Urban Development 2020a).

HUD's basic approach to rental assistance is to boost demand. The Low-Income Housing Tax Credit (LIHTC), administered by the Internal Revenue Service, uses a different tactic. This program creates an incentive for developers to build or rehabilitate affordable rental housing, which is in short supply. The total cost is roughly $10 billion per year. Each state is allocated a certain portion of the tax credits, based on population. State housing agencies then solicit proposals from developers and decide which projects will benefit. Those tax credits can be used for ten years after the project is completed. Because developers need money up front, they often sell their credits to private investors (Joint Committee on Taxation 2019; McCarty, Perl, and Jones 2019; Tax Policy Center 2020).

The LIHTC plays a relatively modest role in the housing safety net. The tax credit has been generating about 100,000 units each year. At that rate, it will take decades to make a meaningful dent in the supply shortage. Just as importantly, "Low-Income" does not mean poor. The income thresholds for the LIHTC are somewhat higher than for public housing or rental vouchers. Most tenants can have incomes between 50 percent and 80 percent of the area median. Furthermore, rents are based on the area median income, not tenants' actual income. In short, the LIHTC is designed to help moderate-income renters as much or more than the poor and near poor (McCarty, Perl, and Jones 2019; Schwartz 2014; Tax Policy Center 2020).

The remaining rental assistance programs are small. HUD spends a few billion dollars annually on permanent supportive housing and rapid re-housing for the homeless. Many of these recipients are poor and disabled. Besides housing, they might receive help dealing with mental illness or substance abuse. States and localities receive about $1 billion annually from the federal HOME block grant. Eligibility extends up to 80 percent of the area median income, helping people with low and modest incomes.[27] The Community Development Block Grant has a broader set of objectives and somewhat bigger budget. The share for affordable housing is also about $1 billion, and spread thinly among many communities. Overall, housing and community development represents less than one percent of state governments' budgets (McCarty, Perl, and Jones 2019; Theodos, Stacy, and Ho 2017; US Department of Housing and Urban Development 2020a).

Distributing money isn't the only way governments help renters. To manage costs, a few states (e.g., California) and some localities (e.g., New York City) have rent control laws.[28] Typically, these laws limit the size of rent increases; sometimes they establish a dollar ceiling for rent, or specify how often landlords can raise the rent.[29] In any form, rent control is rare. Some states explicitly prohibit it.

According to the Census Bureau's American Housing Survey, only two percent of all rental units were covered by rent control in 2017. Less than half of those units were occupied by people making less than $40,000 per year. Rent control aided more people with incomes above $100,000 than under $10,000. Clearly, the benefits are not being distributed according to need.[30]

A more common approach relies on zoning laws. The practice of "inclusionary zoning" started in the suburbs and spread to big cities and smaller towns. While inclusionary zoning can take many forms, the overriding objective is to increase supply. If a developer wants to build 50 apartments, local authorities might insist that five of those units be set aside for people with below-average incomes. Or, developers might be allowed to build more units on a given parcel of land if they add some affordable housing (Schwartz 2014).

The working definition of "affordable," however, varies from place to place. Some communities are less interested in promoting low-income housing than workforce housing.[31] Being affordable or inclusionary means helping teachers, police officers, and hospital staff live in the same communities where they work. Many of these individuals earn too much to qualify for public housing or rental vouchers, yet they find local housing prices to be daunting (Ford and Schuetz 2019; Parlow 2013; Schwartz 2014).[32] A family of four, with a combined income of $90,000, could be covered by inclusionary zoning in Washington, DC. That family is far from poor.[33] Alternatively, some communities are rezoning areas that were exclusively for single-family houses and are now permitting multi-family homes. By allowing more townhomes, duplexes, and triplexes, communities can create more units of affordable housing, and perhaps even genuinely mixed-income neighborhoods (Badger and Bui 2019; Kahlenberg 2019). Just how affordable that housing is remains to be seen. With zoning laws, the details matter a great deal in determining how much help reaches the poor and near poor.

Finally, eviction laws can mean the difference between having a roof over your head and being homeless. Thanks largely to the work of Matthew Desmond and his colleagues, we know that millions of Americans are being evicted each year. Non-payment of rent is the leading cause; low-income individuals are especially vulnerable. Many of those evicted will become homeless. They will have trouble holding down a job and struggle with their mental health. Being evicted makes it much harder to qualify later for public housing or rental vouchers (Desmond 2016). The practice of eviction differs from state to state. The rate of court-ordered evictions in 2016 was nine percent of all renters in South Carolina, four percent in Indiana, and two percent in New York. Despite its smaller size and cheaper rents, South Carolina managed to evict more people than did New York.[34] In addition, we know that laws governing the landlord–tenant relationship vary around the country. Examples include how many days tenants have to pay the monthly rent without incurring a late fee, or without triggering the eviction process.[35]

Through a combination of direct spending, vouchers, tax credits, laws, and regulations, governments try to help some low-income renters cope with high housing costs. Rental units are provided primarily by the private sector. Though it may sound strange, landlords and developers function as caregivers in this part of the social safety net. As we saw earlier (Chapter 2), the attitude of business depends on how much government action helps or hurts their bottom line. Landlords can be counted on to oppose rent control (e.g., Barbanel and Parker 2019). On the other hand, property management companies are deeply involved with government rental vouchers. The top ten companies manage almost 350,000 subsidized units across the country. When the pandemic hit in 2020, their trade association repeatedly called on Congress to increase funding for vouchers and other rental assistance programs. Tenants were having trouble paying their share of the rent, which was not good for them or their corporate landlords.[36] This episode reminds us that housing assistance, like food assistance, is partly a business.

Shared Households/Doubling Up

Plan A for most Americans is owning a home. Plan B is renting a place of their own. When neither option is feasible, the next step usually involves moving in with family or friends. This practice is known informally as doubling up and more formally as creating shared households. According to the Census Bureau, such households must "include at least one 'additional' adult, a person aged 18 or older, who is not the householder, spouse, or cohabiting partner of the householder. Adults aged 18 to 24 who are enrolled in school are not counted as additional adults" (Semega et al. 2019: 18). Most of the additional adults are related to someone else in the household. The family safety net thus plays a crucial role in housing.

The number of shared households in the United States is large and growing.[37] In 2017, 79 million adults lived in a shared household—almost one-third of the entire adult population. Forty million of them were the additional adults. Of that group, 82 percent were living with a relative. The most common pattern involved adult children living in their parents' home. They were typically in their 20s and early 30s and lacked a college degree. Others shared a household with adult siblings or grandparents. Young adults were not the only ones seeking help. Over five million elderly individuals had moved in with one of their adult children, a marked increase since the 1990s (Fry 2018; Mykyta and Macartney 2012).

Shared households are so prevalent, they must cut across income lines. The cost of housing makes it hard for many people to live on their own. Some adult children are staying with their parents in order to save up money for a down payment on a house. Others are living in expensive urban areas and not earning enough to pay market rents. Besides cost, some shared households form because of issues with daily care. As disabled children become adults, some remain with their parents. When senior citizens have trouble living independently, due to physical or mental decline, they might move in with family members who will care for them. Not every shared household indicates distress, either. Some consist of friends who have good-paying jobs and enjoy each other's company.

Nevertheless, many low-income Americans are in shared households because they cannot afford their own place. Almost seven million households with multigenerational families lived in poverty in 2017. Another five million of these households had incomes between 100 and 150 percent of the poverty threshold. Two million households featured poor or near poor adults living with unrelated adults.[38] Shared households like these are not distributed evenly across the country. California, Florida, New York, and Texas are especially likely to have people living in poverty and doubling up. The numbers in Florida have been growing rapidly. In other states (e.g., Maine, Montana), the problem has been declining in size and affecting few people.[39]

In-depth studies reveal what life is like in poor, shared households. While the experience varies a great deal, some aspects can be quite positive. Families typically charge relatives little or no rent and can be flexible about when rent is paid. Those with little income might work out barter arrangements involving child care, housekeeping, or SNAP cards. Combining the incomes of two or three adults could help all of them afford a better place to live. Living together might generate some emotional support during hard times. For those who have been evicted, or suffered a serious injury/illness, extended family might be the only ones who can save them from homelessness (Desmond 2012, 2016; Edin and Lein 1997; Edin and Shaefer 2015; Newman 1999; Rosen 2020).

Sharing a household can also be difficult, even dangerous. Moving in with relatives who live far away means leaving one's job, social network, or both. Doubling up often leads to overcrowded rooms and a lack of privacy. Relatives who move in may end up sleeping on couches or the floor. Late-night arguments between a few people can keep everyone else awake. Poor sleep makes it harder for children to learn at school. Landlords might object to overcrowded apartments and threaten to evict everyone; some of those threats will be carried out. The host family may tire of the daily strain and ask their relatives to leave. At their worst, shared households create opportunities for domestic violence and sexual abuse, affecting adults and children (Desmond 2012, 2016; Edin and Lein 1997; Edin and Shaefer 2015; Goldstone 2019).

Moreover, some people cannot or will not move in with family members. Many low-income Americans have family members who are too poor or troubled to lend a hand. Some relatives could refuse to offer shelter, feeling that the individual has done too little to help themselves, or has asked for help too many times. Those in need might feel ashamed of their situation and refrain from asking kin for assistance (Desmond 2012, 2016). History matters: hard feelings between members of any extended family can last for decades. Though vital to many, the family safety net can do only so much when it comes to housing.

Temporary Shelter

Every year, hundreds of thousands of Americans end up in temporary shelters (aka emergency shelters). Some of these individuals can no longer afford housing because of job loss, major medical bills, or divorce. Some are fleeing abusive relationships. Others have chronic problems with mental illness or substance abuse. As mentioned earlier, government spends some money on permanent housing for the homeless. The number of permanent beds has increased in recent years, and experts believe this is a more effective way to help the homeless (Schwartz 2014).[40] Nevertheless, demand for these beds routinely exceeds the supply, and many people must find housing some other way. Almost 400,000 temporary shelter beds were available year-round in 2019. Roughly half were reserved for adults and the other half for families with children. During the winter months, an additional 22,000 beds became available (National Alliance to End Homelessness 2020; US Department of Housing and Urban Development 2020b).

There is no nationwide network of shelters comparable to Feeding America. While systematic data are lacking, temporary shelters are highly diverse. Many of the caregivers are secular or religious charities. They could be as large as The Salvation Army, which operates approximately 600 shelters across the country and provided almost ten million nights of lodging in 2018 (The Salvation Army 2019). They could be as small as local churches that open their doors on cold winter nights to a handful of homeless people. In my community, the main shelter for abused women and children can house about 50 people at any one time.[41] Other shelters are operated by nonprofit organizations that do not qualify as charities. Temporary shelters piece together funding from governments, foundations, corporations, and individuals. Volunteers donate their time.[42] In that sense, many parts of society help take care of the homeless.

Homeless shelters cannot care for everyone. They simply lack the money and the space. Like food pantries, many shelters will serve people from the local area only. Shelters dedicated to homeless families might insist that children be under a certain age. Shelters serving individuals might target those with mental illness or addiction. Other places will exclude people who appear to be drunk or on drugs. During the screening process, applicants could be asked a series of questions concerning the nature and depth of their problems, only to learn later that shelter space is reserved for the most vulnerable. Some shelters will conduct criminal background checks before accepting new residents (Edin and Shaefer 2015; Goldstone 2019; Perez 2014; Raphelson 2018).

For those who get in, shelter life is never easy. In some communities, the homeless have to move weekly or even daily from one church to the next. Shelter residents might be allowed to stay overnight, but not during the day. They often sleep on the floor or share a large room with strangers. A lucky few will have their own room with a bed and a door. Shelters do not allow people to bring much with them, and some residents have to pay to store their possessions elsewhere. These shelters are temporary, with time limits generally between a week and a few months. Consequently, residents are racing against the clock to find more permanent housing. At any moment, their stay could be shortened: shelters have rules about appropriate behavior, and they will kick out people who break those rules. Some of the other residents (and perhaps some staff) will make it hard to remain calm and collected. Compared to sleeping on the sidewalk or under a bridge, temporary shelters are a step up. But very few people would choose to live there. "Family homeless shelters take a collection of hurting, desperate families with nothing in common except destitution and a history of bad breaks and abuse, and mix them together over meals and in programs. As a result, sometimes these shelters can be damaging places in their own right" (Edin and Shaefer 2015: 103; see also Desmond 2016; Goldstone 2019; Perez 2014).

Discussion

At first glance, housing assistance looks like food assistance. Individuals seldom have to be employed in order to qualify for public housing, rental vouchers, SNAP, WIC, or subsidized school meals. Instead, they must demonstrate financial need. Many recipients will have paying jobs and are trying hard to work their way out of poverty, but eligibility is not tied to wage work. The Trump administration tried but failed to increase work requirements for food and housing in order to cut spending (Fadulu 2020; Fischer 2018; Wogan 2018). Certain groups of low-income people—children, the elderly, the disabled—are more likely to receive food and housing assistance. These means-tested programs are funded by income taxes; in that sense, the rich are taking care of the poor by paying for some of their food and rent. For-profit companies (e.g., grocery stores, landlords) are the primary caregivers in both parts of the social safety net. Although charities and other nonprofits are more important with food and housing than income, these organizations consistently play a secondary role to government.

Nevertheless, housing assistance and food assistance differ in important ways. Governments help more low-income people obtain food than shelter. That gap is obvious if you compare direct spending programs, and it remains true even if you include FHA-backed loans and rent control. Housing assistance, however, is not limited to the poor and near poor. Tax breaks for homeowners have been the centerpiece of US housing policy for decades, with the benefits flowing chiefly to people in higher income brackets. The government helps them pay off mortgages and build wealth. Taking care of low-income renters has been, and still is, a lesser concern.[43] Another difference is that charities and nonprofits play a much larger role in food assistance. Food banks, food pantries, and soup kitchens help millions more Americans than do temporary shelters and Habitat for Humanity.

Care is far from adequate in the housing safety net. The most extreme form of hardship is homelessness. The homeless are difficult to count, and HUD estimates their number at one point in time each January. More than 560,000 Americans were considered homeless in 2019.[44] Over 200,000 of them were unsheltered, that is, living on the streets. The rest were in temporary shelters. In some states (e.g., California, Oregon), most of the homeless are unsheltered. In other states (e.g., Massachusetts, Nebraska, New York), less than ten percent of the homeless are unsheltered (US Department of Housing and Urban Development 2020b).

HUD's approach underestimates the true size of the homeless population. Some of the unsheltered homeless will not be counted because they are too hard to find, living in cars or abandoned buildings. People are constantly moving in and out of temporary shelters, and many who were not there in January will be later that year. One could argue that individuals who are involuntarily doubling up with family/friends or living in motels are also homeless (Goldstone 2019).

Whether the correct number is closer to 700,000, one million, or more, the presence of so many homeless people indicates serious gaps in the social safety net. As we would expect, many of the homeless live in large states where low-cost housing is scarce. Over a quarter of the homeless live in California. Over half live in California, New York, Florida, or Texas. One-quarter of the homeless population can be found in the New York City and Los Angeles metro areas. The gender patterns might be a little more surprising. Sixty percent of the homeless, and almost 70 percent of the unsheltered homeless, are men (Table 7.1). Many are single and jobless. They may have chronic problems with mental health or substance abuse. The availability of temporary shelter beds for these individuals, as well as treatment and counseling, is far from

Table 7.1 **HOMELESS IN AMERICA (2019)**

	Unsheltered		Sheltered		Total	
	Individuals	%	Individuals	%	Individuals	%
Total	211,293	100	356,422	100	567,715	100
Men	145,509	68.9	197,678	55.5	343,187	60.5
Women	62,700	29.7	157,211	44.1	219,911	38.7
Whites	119,487	56.6	151,120	42.4	270,607	47.7
African Americans	56,381	26.7	169,354	47.5	225,735	39.8
Hispanics/Latinos (any race)	48,133	22.8	76,482	21.5	124,615	22.0
Under age 18	9,916	4.7	97,153	27.3	107,069	18.9

Source: U.S. Department of Housing and Urban Development, *The 2019 Annual Homeless Assessment Report (AHAR) to Congress* (2020).

adequate. Families with children are more likely than single men to find temporary shelter.[45]

The racial and ethnic patterns are striking (Table 7.1). Hispanics and especially Blacks run a higher risk of being homeless. In 2019, Hispanics/Latinos made up 18.5 percent of the total US population and 22 percent of the homeless. Blacks/African Americans were 13 percent of the population and 40 percent of the homeless (US Department of Housing and Urban Development 2020b).[46] That is a huge disparity. At the same time, Blacks and Hispanics are more likely to benefit from public housing and vouchers. Roughly 45 percent of rental assistance recipients are Black, while 20 to 25 percent are Hispanic.[47] This seems like a sizable advantage. Depending on whether we care about spending or outcomes, the housing safety net could be favoring racial minorities, or failing them.

Not everyone with permanent housing has adequate housing. HUD classifies dwellings into one of three categories—severely inadequate, moderately inadequate, or adequate. Severely inadequate places could lack running water, electricity, or reliable heat. Moderately inadequate places could have water leaks, holes in the floor, and signs of rats (just one of those problems would not be enough). Adequate housing refers to every dwelling that is not inadequate.[48] The American Housing Survey (2017) found that five percent of all dwellings were inadequate to some degree. Over one million units were severely inadequate. The residents were disproportionately poor and near poor. Being Black, Hispanic, or disabled was also associated with severely inadequate housing. Whites and the elderly were less likely to be affected. HUD classified almost five million housing units as moderately inadequate. The demographics of those residents were quite similar to those in severely inadequate places.[49] When affordable housing is so scarce, people are forced to live in substandard dwellings.

Adequate housing is not always affordable. One commonly used measure is cost burden. Anyone spending more than 30 percent of their income on housing is said to be cost burdened. Anyone spending more than 50 percent is severely cost burdened. The poor and near poor are not alone in dealing with the high price of housing. Almost one-third of American households are cost burdened (Joint Center for Housing Studies 2019b).

This problem, however, is more common among renters than homeowners, and much more common among low-income renters. Consider the plight of renter households with incomes under $15,000. Seventy percent of them are severely cost burdened. Most of their money goes to rent and utilities, and they find it practically impossible to save for emergencies or retirement. Much like the homeless, many of these individuals live in California, Florida, New York, or Texas. Among renters with incomes between $15,000 and $30,000, 70 percent are cost burdened, and 40 percent are severely cost burdened (Joint Center for Housing Studies 2019b; National Alliance to End Homelessness 2020). The high cost of housing affects their lives month after month after month. No wonder that landing a spot in public housing or receiving a rental voucher can be such a life-changing event. People could be able to cut their housing expenses in half, freeing up money for other essentials. When that happens, studies show that low-income children eat better, their health improves, and they perform better in school. The impact on adults' health is positive as well (Airgood-Obrycki and Molinsky 2019; Desmond 2015a; Kimberlin, Tach, and Wimer 2018). High housing costs lead to food insecurity much more often than food costs create housing problems.

Housing costs weigh more heavily on Blacks and Hispanics. Roughly 30 percent of minority homeowners are cost burdened, compared to 20 percent of White homeowners. Among renters, slightly over half of Blacks and Hispanics are cost burdened. The rate for Whites is ten points lower. These differences are not simply due to Whites having, on average, more money. "Black and Hispanic households earning less than $15,000 are still more likely to be cost burdened than whites at that income level" (Joint Center for Housing Studies 2019b: 32).[50] At their current levels, public housing and rental vouchers are not big enough to eliminate these inequalities.

Every two years, HUD reports to Congress about the country's "worst case housing needs." Homeowners and the homeless are excluded. The focus is on the most vulnerable renters. "Renter households with worst case housing needs are those with very low incomes that do not receive government housing assistance and pay more than one-half of their incomes toward rent, those that live in severely inadequate conditions, or both" (US Department of Housing and Urban Development 2020c: iii). Very low income means less than half the area median. Over seven million households had worst case housing needs in 2017. Almost all of them were severely cost burdened, and a small fraction had inadequate housing. Essentially, worst case needs are measuring cost burdens among the most vulnerable Americans.

The worst case needs measure is based on the average income in a given locale, not a single national standard. This is helpful given the vast differences in incomes and housing prices around the country. As Table 7.2 shows, most of the households with worst case needs are extremely low income (<30% of area median). They have a high chance of spending 60 or even 70 percent of their incomes on rent (Desmond 2015b). One might wonder how many poor people could avoid being cost burdened. The answer is, not many. A total of 7.5 million extremely low-income households were renting without government assistance in 2017. Over five million of them were severely cost burdened. Another 800,000 were spending between 30 and 50 percent of their incomes on rent, making them cost burdened. If we move up a notch in income and focus on households with 30 to 50 percent of the area median, the vast majority are also cost burdened (US Department of Housing and Urban Development 2020c).

Table 7.2 **WORST CASE HOUSING NEEDS (2017)**

	Very low income		Extremely low income	
Social group	*Households*	*%*	*Households*	*%*
Total	7,716,000	100	5,555,000	100
Non-Hispanic Whites	3,634,000	47.1	2,559,000	46.1
Non-Hispanic Blacks	1,578,000	20.5	1,161,000	20.9
Hispanics	1,884,000	24.4	1,369,000	24.6
Families with children	2,571,000	33.3	1,985,000	35.7
Elderly, no children	1,932,000	25.0	1,341,000	24.1
Non-elderly with disability	1,304,000	16.9	na	na

Worst case housing needs = very low-income renter households that are severely cost burdened, have inadequate housing, or both.

Very low income = between 0 and 50% of area median income.

Extremely low income = between 0 and 30% of area median income.

Severely cost burdened = spending at least 50% of income on housing.

Source: U.S. Department of Housing and Urban Development, *Worst Case Housing Needs: 2019 Report to Congress* (2020).

Many types of poor households devote more than half their money to rent (Table 7.2). These households include children, the elderly, and the disabled. If they rely heavily on the SSI program for income (Chapter 5), they will be hard pressed to afford rent in much of the country. Although every region is affected, worst case housing needs are more evident in the South and West. Once again, Blacks and Hispanics are highly vulnerable. They represent a disproportionate share of the worst case needs population. That fact also increases their chances of being evicted and suffering the problems that eviction can trigger (Desmond 2016; US Department of Housing and Urban Development 2020c). Whether we examine problems that are acute (homelessness) or chronic (cost burdens), racial minorities are more likely to fall through the gaps in the housing safety net.

In Chapters 5–7, we have surveyed parts of the social safety net that distribute care based on wage work (income) or need (food, housing). The next chapter, medical care, represents a hybrid of these two principles. It also puts the business side of care on full display.

‖ 8 ‖

Medical Care

Everybody needs medical care at some point. Certain types of care are routine and not terribly expensive. Doctors charge $100–$200 for an annual check-up. A basic dental exam and cleaning costs about the same.[1] Over-the-counter medications for headache or heartburn sell for less than $10. Medical care can also be unpredictable, high-priced, or both. Hospitals routinely charge at least $10,000 for an uncomplicated childbirth, and more for a cesarean delivery. Slipping on ice and breaking an ankle might lead to a bill of $20,000 if surgery is required. Chemotherapy for cancer patients can total thousands of dollars every month. The price of recovering from a stroke or heart attack could easily top $100,000. Intensive care for premature babies can be just as expensive (Dallas 2019; Sanger-Katz 2019).[2]

Some individuals will enjoy good health throughout life. Others will face a few large medical bills, but nothing that threatens them financially. Many people are less fortunate: they will develop a chronic medical condition or experience a serious illness or injury. Some will have to cope with multiple health problems. Most Americans have not saved $50,000 or $100,000 in case of medical emergencies. Most have not saved $50,000, period (Chapter 5).

Medical care is a classic case where insurance is essential. Although individuals do not know how much medical care they will require, or when, they know the cost is potentially enormous. Without good insurance, people might have to forgo needed treatment or face bankruptcy (Gilligan et al. 2018; Hamel et al. 2016). Lack of insurance could lead to deteriorating health, making it harder to hold down a full-time job and thus harder to pay for food and housing. As a general rule, insurance works best when the relevant risks (e.g., sickness, unemployment, auto accident) are shared broadly. We should not be surprised if many of the poor and near poor receive medical care as part of larger insurance programs that benefit a wide range of people.[3]

In some respects, the safety net for medical care resembles that for income (Chapter 5). Employment is key. Millions of retired workers count on Medicare

Who Cares. Christopher Howard, Oxford University Press. © Oxford University Press 2023.
DOI: 10.1093/oso/9780190074456.003.0009

and Social Security, the two biggest social insurance programs. Millions of current workers and their families rely on employers to provide health insurance. But, many jobs do not come with health benefits, and health insurance is not designed to cover all expenses. Individuals will often need extra money to pay their medical bills. The same is true of social insurance programs that provide income support.

In other respects, this part of the social safety net is similar to food, where public assistance and charity play important roles (Chapter 6). The government provides health insurance for millions of low-income Americans via Medicaid. Some of them are employed and some are not. All across the country, free and charitable clinics treat patients with limited means. Hospitals provide care for which they are not compensated. Finally, medical care is big business, much like food. Doctors, nurses, hospitals, drug makers, and many others are paid hundreds of billions of dollars to be caregivers for the sick and injured.

The combination of private insurance, social insurance, out-of-pocket spending, public assistance, charity, and corporate caregivers could make this part of the social safety net strong and secure. One way or another, virtually all Americans would have access to the medical care they need (Badger and Hall 2019). It is also possible that we will encounter familiar holes and weak spots. To determine which verdict is closer to the truth, we must examine an unusually large number of programs and efforts.

Before we start, a note of clarification. There is no bright line separating this chapter, medical care, from the next chapter about daily care. The basic distinction is that medical care is designed to prevent or treat illnesses and injuries. The main caregivers are trained medical professionals such as doctors, nurses, pharmacists, and x-ray technicians. In contrast, daily care helps people who have trouble living independently (Colello 2019). Daily care could involve dressing, bathing, or feeding someone. It might mean helping people walk or preparing their meals. Daily care can be provided by trained professionals, but it does not have to be. Family members provide substantial amounts of daily care.

In deciding what goes where in these two chapters, I recognize that medical care and daily care can be given in the same place. People admitted to a hospital will be have their meals prepared by a cook, not a doctor. Kids who scrape their knee at daycare will get a Band-Aid, but probably not from a registered nurse. The question is which form of care predominates. In most cases, the choice of whether something qualifies as medical care or daily care is straightforward. Probably the trickiest one to classify is long-term care for the disabled. It will be discussed in the next chapter, partly because that care is often provided by people without specialized medical training. Further, many people reside in long-term care facilities because they cannot take care of themselves. While they might require medical attention now and then, their primary needs are to be kept safe, clean, and fed.

Taking Care of Yourself

Those who take care of our medical needs are usually different from the actual caregivers. The first group includes those who help pay for medical care—workers, employers, taxpayers, and charitable donors. The second group refers to trained medical professionals and the companies that make medical equipment and pharmaceuticals. Individuals might be able to take care of themselves by paying for health insurance and out-of-pocket medical expenses. But they cannot produce vaccines, operate an x-ray machine, or perform surgery on themselves. Everybody depends on somebody else for their medical care. Self-sufficiency is not an option.

Let's start with who pays for medical care. Before the pandemic, 91 percent of Americans had health insurance for part or all of the year. That was a higher rate of coverage than almost any year since the government began keeping records. Roughly 180 million Americans were insured through an employer, either as workers or members of their immediate family. To take care of one's medical needs, the smart move is to get a job. These insurance plans rarely cover every medical expense. Individuals are still responsible for deductibles and co-payments, and for over-the-counter medicines. Out-of-pocket expenses can run to hundreds or thousands of dollars per year.[4] The smarter move for individuals is to get a job and save some money. Many employers, however, do not offer health benefits. One-third of private firms failed to provide these benefits at the turn of the century. By 2019, the figure was up to 43 percent. Job-based health insurance has been declining even in years when the economy seemed healthy (Claxton et al. 2019; Keisler-Starkey and Bunch 2020).

Health insurance is not available equally to all workers. Coverage is more common in the public sector, both civilian and military (Craig 2015; Kleykamp and Hipes 2015). For workers in the private sector, large companies and unionized occupations or industries are the best bets. In contrast, only about one-third of retail companies offer health benefits. Regardless of the industry, coverage of part-time workers is the exception, not the rule (<20% of all firms). Temporary workers are rarely covered. Even among companies that offer health insurance, certain employees could be ineligible. This is especially true among lower-wage workers and recent hires (Claxton et al. 2019). Considering the kinds of jobs held by the poor and near poor (Chapter 5), these patterns spell trouble.

When employers offer health insurance, some workers will decline it. They might be covered already by a spouse's plan. The more common reason is the expense. In 2019, the typical health insurance policy for a family cost $20,576 (equivalent to a new Honda Civic or Toyota Corolla). The employee's share was approximately $6,000; the employer paid the rest. An individual policy cost roughly $7,000, with employees responsible for paying about $1,250.[5] At these prices, no wonder many employers do not provide health insurance. For a typical family, signing up for health insurance means giving up $500 of income every month. Many cannot afford that and still pay for rent, utilities, and food. Imagine a company where at least one-third of the workers earn less than $25,000 per year. If that company offers health benefits—and that's a big if—typically half the eligible workers will say no (Claxton et al. 2019; Keisler-Starkey and Bunch 2020).

The cost of health insurance is a huge obstacle. Some employers have responded by offering insurance with lower monthly premiums but higher deductibles. Covered workers might be responsible for the first $2,500 (individual) or $5,000 (family) of their medical bills in a given year, before their insurance kicks in. In effect, this sort of policy guards against serious illnesses or injuries only. To cover the more routine forms of medical care, many employers permit workers to set up individual health savings accounts. (Doing so costs employers nothing because employees provide all the funding.) Although high-deductible plans have become more popular in recent years, the typical policy is only about 10 to 15 percent cheaper than traditional versions of health insurance (Claxton et al. 2019). Low-income workers still find it difficult to afford high-deductible plans, as do many employers. Alternatively, insurance companies might sell individual policies, aimed at workers whose employers do not offer group coverage. Individual rates are higher than group rates, making this option highly unattractive to the poor and near poor.[6] The more likely customers are self-employed workers with above-average incomes.

The government has taken several steps to make private health insurance more affordable, and in that sense "private" is a misnomer. For example, employers have been able to deduct the cost of health insurance premiums from their taxable income since at least the 1950s (Howard 1997). This tax expenditure has become one of the largest in the entire tax code, costing the national government more than $150 billion in 2019. It also ranks as one of the most expensive social programs in the United States, comparable to Disability Insurance and much larger than SNAP/Food Stamps. The congressional Joint Committee on Taxation estimates that the revenue loss from this one provision will exceed $200 billion in 2022. Smaller tax expenditures for health savings accounts and for insurance purchased by the self-employed each cost the US government $6–$7 billion (Joint Committee on Taxation 2019).

The Affordable Care Act (ACA) includes a number of provisions to boost private health insurance. The ACA tries to remedy the cost problem by creating health insurance exchanges (aka marketplaces). Depending on where you live, these exchanges are run by the national government, state governments, or both. The objective is to help individuals and small businesses band together and buy private health insurance at a better price. The ACA subsidizes individual buyers through the tax code. The health premium tax credit cost the national government more than $50 billion in revenue in 2019. While some of these subsidies benefit the near poor, much of the money helps middle-income workers and their families (Garfield, Orgera, and Damico 2019; Joint Committee on Taxation 2019; Kaiser Family Foundation 2013).

In addition, the ACA has made health insurance more available by regulating the behavior of insurers and employers. No longer can individuals with pre-existing medical conditions be denied coverage. This is one of those inclusive policies that benefits low-income Americans, who are more likely to have high blood pressure, diabetes, depression, and other chronic ailments (Khullar and Chokshi 2018; Michener 2018; Thorpe et al. 2017).[7] The ACA also allows adult children to remain on their family policy until the age of 26. For young adults working in part-time or temporary jobs, or in sectors like retail where health benefits are uncommon, this provision can be highly beneficial. Finally, companies with the equivalent of 50 or more full-time employees must make health insurance available to 95 percent of their workforce (and their families). Failure to do so can trigger a financial penalty.[8] Changes like these only matter, though, if individuals and families can afford to buy health insurance in the first place.

Altogether, two-thirds of Americans have private health insurance through employment, the ACA exchanges, or individual purchase. Workers and employers paid more than $1 trillion for this coverage in 2019 (Martin et al. 2021). Coverage rates vary dramatically by income. A large majority (88%) of Americans with incomes at least four times the poverty line have private health insurance. This group includes individuals earning at least $50,000 a year and families of four with more than $100,000. By contrast, one-quarter of those living below the poverty line have private health insurance. Less than half of Americans with incomes between 1x and 2x the poverty line are similarly insured, and many of them only with help from the Affordable Care Act (Keisler-Starkey and Bunch 2020). Because of the high costs and close links to employment, private health insurance in the United States is not a viable option for most of the poor and near poor.[9] They must rely on government or charity to take care of their medical needs.

With private health insurance, the differences by race/ethnicity are considerable. Seventy-five percent of non-Hispanic Whites and of Asians have private health insurance coverage, compared to 56 percent of Blacks and 50 percent of Hispanics (Keisler-Starkey and Bunch 2020). Whites are doubly advantaged: they are more likely to have health insurance at their place of work, and better able to purchase insurance on their own. Gender differences are much smaller. Men are slightly more likely than women to have private health insurance.[10]

Help from Government

The United States does not have national health insurance, but government still spends hundreds of billions of dollars on medical care every year. Its primary role is to take care of payments; the caregivers usually come from the private sector. To receive government's help, many Americans must demonstrate financial need. The biggest and best-known example is Medicaid. Other Americans have to work for their benefits. They can become eligible after years of employment (Medicare) or after experiencing a job-related injury or illness (Workers' Compensation). Eligibility for these social insurance programs is not means-tested.

Like Social Security, Medicare aids a wide range of workers and their spouses. Approximately 60 million Americans benefit from one or more parts of Medicare. The vast majority are age 65 or older; some are working-age adults with long-term disabilities.[11] Most recipients are not poor, and Medicare is often labeled a middle-class entitlement. Nevertheless, seven million Medicare recipients live below the poverty line. That's more people than TANF or public housing serve. An additional 11 million Medicare recipients live between 1x and 2x the poverty line. Medicare is definitely part of the social safety net. Because most recipients are elderly and life expectancy varies, men, Blacks, and Hispanics are underrepresented among beneficiaries. The modal recipient is White and female.[12]

Medicare has three distinct parts, and the people who take care of financing them are not always the same. Part A of Medicare covers "big ticket" expenses that are hard to predict such as hospital care, surgery, and some nursing home stays.[13] This is the one part of Medicare that most closely follows social insurance principles. Participation is compulsory among wage workers, which spreads the risk of high medical costs. Eligibility rules and benefits are uniform across the country. Most of the financing comes from payroll taxes levied on employers and employees ($285 billion in 2019).[14] They are taking care of millions of elderly and disabled Americans who rely on Medicare, many of whom are low-income.

Part A of Medicare is unusual among social insurance programs, and some of those differences benefit low-income Americans. For one thing, the level of medical care is not tied to past wages. Everyone who qualifies for part A is supposed to have access to comparable treatment. To the extent that low-income people are more likely to be in poor health, they could receive a larger share of medical care than their work history would suggest. Medicare's financing is also less regressive than Social Security's, which takes some of the burden off low-income workers. All wage and salary income is subject to the Medicare payroll tax; there is no ceiling to protect the well-to-do. Thanks to the Affordable Care Act, the most affluent Americans pay a higher payroll tax rate for Medicare than do ordinary workers. Other differences work to the detriment of low-income recipients. The egalitarian streak in Medicare means that everyone faces the same deductibles and co-payments. These out-of-pocket expenses can easily add up to thousands of dollars, which is a serious problem for people struggling to make ends meet (Kaiser Family Foundation 2019; US Department of Health and Human Services 2020).

Parts B and D of Medicare are not, strictly speaking, social insurance. Participation is voluntary, not compulsory. Part B helps pay for doctor visits and diagnostic tests; Part D does the same for prescription drugs.[15] These types of medical care are supposed to be more predictable and less expensive than those covered by Part A. Individuals do not face the same risk of financial ruin, and can therefore choose whether to participate or not. Parts B and D are not financed by payroll taxes. Instead, most individuals pay a monthly premium that covers about one-quarter of the cost, with government paying the rest through general revenues.[16] Those revenues come largely from federal income taxes, which means that affluent individuals and to a lesser extent businesses are responsible for taking care of people in these parts of Medicare (Davis et al. 2020; Kaiser Family Foundation 2019).

Even though Parts B and D are funded primarily by other people's taxes, the monthly premiums are not trivial. Part B cost most individuals $135 a month in 2019. The price of Part D depends on which specific drug plan is chosen. A basic plan charged about $33 per month in 2019. (Individuals making over $85,000 a year and couples making over $170,000 paid higher premiums for both parts.) Senior citizens and people with disabilities don't always have an extra $2,000 lying around to pay for medical care each year. Policymakers have tried to make it easier for low-income Americans to afford these benefits. Many of the poorest individuals are dually eligible for Medicare and Medicaid. Recipients with incomes up to 120 percent of the federal poverty line can have their Medicare Part B premiums paid fully by Medicaid. Those with incomes between 120 and 135 percent of the poverty line can get similar support from other government sources. Overall, one out of every five people on Medicare Part B receives assistance with their monthly premiums, which adds up to 10 million people. Beneficiaries with incomes up to 150 percent of the poverty line are eligible for subsidies in Part D. Currently, 13 million Americans qualify, and almost all are fully subsidized. Medicaid pays the monthly premiums for many of them (Davis 2020; Kirchhoff 2020).

Total spending on Medicare was close to $800 billion in 2019, making it one of the largest items in the national budget.[17] Even so, the program does not cover every medical service that recipients might need. Most types of vision care and dental care are excluded. Only 100 days in a skilled nursing facility are covered. And patients are still responsible for co-payments and deductibles. To cover these and related expenses, many people have supplemental medical insurance, either from their employer[18] or from a policy they purchased on their own. The latter are called Medigap policies, and they vary widely in cost and coverage. Low-income people seldom work for companies with generous health benefits, and they cannot afford most Medigap plans. Fortunately, Medicaid will take care of co-payments and deductibles for Medicare recipients living below the poverty line. Medicaid will also pay for some services that Medicare does not (Davis et al. 2020; Kaiser Family Foundation 2019; Kirchhoff 2020).

Medicaid is the primary way government takes care of the medical needs of people with limited incomes. Originally this program covered specific categories of poor people—mostly the elderly, the disabled, and single-mother families with children.[19] Depending on the state, the income threshold was usually well below the official poverty line. For years, many people in poverty could not qualify for Medicaid. Eligibility expanded gradually in the 1980s, especially for pregnant women and young children. The Children's Health Insurance Program (CHIP), established in the late 1990s, extended coverage to more low-income children (Grogan and Andrews 2015; Howard 2007). The biggest change, of course, was the Affordable Care Act. The ACA opened up Medicaid to (almost) everyone making less than 138 percent of the federal poverty line. It no longer mattered whether individuals were young or old, able-bodied or disabled. Lack of income was the chief consideration (Garfield, Orgera, and Damico 2019; Kaiser Family Foundation 2013).[20]

Shortly before the pandemic, 75 million low-income Americans relied on Medicaid to pay their medical bills in any given month (Mitchell et al. 2021).[21] This figure actually understates its importance, since individuals move on and off Medicaid as their income changes, or when they gain or lose job-based health insurance. The Center on Budget and Policy Priorities (2020d) estimates that 97 million Americans used Medicaid at some point during 2018. Total Medicaid spending was close to $600 billion that year. Long-term care, which will be discussed in the next chapter, accounted for one-third of that spending, bringing the bill for medical care closer to $400 billion.[22] Clearly, Medicaid is a critical piece of the social safety net. It is, by far, the largest public assistance program in the United States. For people in poverty, Medicaid is *the* most important source of health insurance.

Medicaid is run jointly by the national and state governments. Key features vary from state to state, making it hard to paint a simple portrait. In terms of financing, state governments pay for 35 to 40 percent of Medicaid, and the national government takes care of the rest. Richer states like Connecticut are responsible for 50 percent of their Medicaid spending, while poorer states like Alabama and New Mexico cover 25 to 30 percent (Mitchell et al. 2021; Rudowitz, Orgera, and Hinton 2019). When we say that governments pay for Medicaid, we really mean taxpayers. State and local tax systems are seldom progressive.[23] The burden of financing Medicaid at the state level is therefore shared by many individuals and businesses. Federal income taxes are much more progressive, and the affluent take care of paying most of the national government's share of Medicaid.

The architects of the Affordable Care Act expected every state to expand their Medicaid program. The national government would pay for almost all the additional cost, and failure to expand could jeopardize funding for a state's existing Medicaid program. A Supreme Court ruling in 2012 made it easier for states to refuse. By the end of 2019, 14 states had chosen not to expand Medicaid. Many of these states are in the South, and all of them are politically conservative (Center on Budget and Policy Priorities 2020d; Kaiser Family Foundation 2013). In these non-expansion states, Medicaid serves fewer of the near poor and fewer able-bodied, working-age adults. The adults who are eligible tend to live in deep poverty.

No matter where they live, most Medicaid recipients would not be expected to have job-based health insurance. They include children (43%), individuals who are blind or disabled (12%), and the elderly (8%).[24] Many recipients, however, are able-bodied, working-age adults (37%). Typically, these individuals are employed full-time or part-time. They might work as cashiers, home health aides, cooks, janitors, or retail salespeople. Either their jobs do not offer health insurance or the workers cannot afford the monthly premiums. Medicaid expansion was designed explicitly to help these individuals. A significant number of adults on Medicaid could be employed but are not because they are in school or caring for a relative. Others are suffering from a partial or short-term disability. Put bluntly, few able-bodied adults on Medicaid spend all day on the couch watching TV or playing Fortnite. This fact did not stop several Republican governors, with support from the Trump administration, from trying to add work requirements to Medicaid. Federal courts rejected some of these efforts, and the Biden administration has not followed Trump's lead (Center on Budget and Policy Priorities 2020d; Garfield et al. 2019; Hurley 2020; Rudowitz et al. 2020).[25]

Eligibility for Medicaid is not based on employment, but it is means-tested. That combination should mean more care for women and racial minorities, and it does. As of 2019, 58 percent of non-elderly Medicaid beneficiaries were female. Twenty percent were Black, and 29 percent were Hispanic; those numbers were higher than their shares of the general population. Medicaid is a crucial source of support for racial minorities. Twice as many Blacks and three times as many Hispanics rely on Medicaid compared to Medicare.[26] Among the non-elderly population, 33 percent of Blacks depend on Medicaid coverage compared to just 15 percent of Whites. Thirty percent of non-elderly Hispanics were on Medicaid as well (Mitchell et al. 2021). Had all states expanded their Medicaid programs after the ACA, insurance coverage for people of color would have been noticeably better. Several states that refused to expand, such as Georgia, Florida, and Texas, have large populations of low-income Blacks and Hispanics (Cross-Call 2020).

All states must offer a broad range of services to Medicaid patients and then can decide which optional services to cover. Mandatory services include hospital care, doctor visits, and diagnostic tests, similar to Parts A and B of Medicare. Behavioral health services for those with mental illnesses or addictions are available.[27] (Medicaid has more extensive coverage for long-term care than Medicare does, which will be discussed in the next chapter.) While prescription drugs are optional under Medicaid, all states cover them. Most states have opted to cover dental and vision care (Center on Budget and Policy Priorities 2020d). Physical therapy is optional, as are hospice care and chiropractic services. States are also allowed to require cost-sharing in some circumstances; Medicaid is not always free to those who receive care. Any co-payments or deductibles are usually modest compared to what Medicare charges, though Medicaid patients typically have much less income available.[28]

To get an idea of how Medicaid differs from state to state, consider a few examples. Children between the ages of one and five are eligible for Medicaid (or CHIP) in Virginia as long as their family income is less than 200 percent of the poverty line. The income cutoff in West Virginia is 300 percent. While dental services are covered in Colorado, chiropractor services are not. Delaware is the opposite. Day treatment for individuals with serious mental health or substance abuse problems is available in Montana but not in Idaho. The Medicaid programs in California and Connecticut both include a drug benefit. California limits the number of prescriptions per month and charges a small co-payment for each. Connecticut has no monthly limits and no co-pays. In no two states is Medicaid exactly alike.[29]

Nationally, Medicaid spending varies markedly among eligible groups. Senior citizens and people with disabilities represent 20 to 25 percent of recipients, but they account for almost half of all Medicaid spending. Many of these recipients cost the government $15,000–$20,000 per year, and potentially more if they reside in a long-term care facility. No matter where they live, the elderly and the disabled often have chronic medical problems that are expensive to treat. A typical child, on the other hand, costs Medicaid $3,000–$4,000 annually.[30] Ear infections and strep throats are easier to deal with.

Apart from Medicare and Medicaid, Workers' Compensation pays the medical bills of people who suffer job-related injuries or illnesses. Though classified as a social insurance program, workers' comp in the US is a strange hybrid of public and private, and has been for over a century (Howard 2002). Most workers' comp programs operate at the state level, without federal regulations or financing. Less than half the states operate compensation funds, and collectively they account for just 15 percent of benefits paid. More often, states require employers to purchase a workers' comp policy from a commercial insurer, or to self-insure. Approximately half the money spent goes to medical care and the other half to income support. In recent years the medical portion has cost close to $30 billion (Boden and Spieler 2015; Murphy et al. 2020).

The fragmented and privatized nature of workers' compensation makes it difficult to find comprehensive data. As of 2014, roughly one-fifth of cash benefits went to households with annual incomes under $24,000. Many and probably most of them were poor. If we assume that medical benefits followed a similar pattern, then those individuals received about $6 billion in medical care in 2018. Almost 40 percent of cash benefits in 2014 went to households with incomes under $42,000, which could translate to $12 billion in medical care. In general, men are more likely than women to receive workers' comp benefits. The racial and ethnic disparities in workers' comp appear to be smaller than in private health insurance. More evident are state-by-state variations. Medical benefits as a share of covered wages are three times higher in Louisiana and Montana than in Massachusetts or Michigan. Those differences partly reflect a state's mix of occupations and industries, some more dangerous than others. They can also reflect which workers are excluded from coverage, or how difficult it is to prove that one's illness or injury is job-related (Boden and Spieler 2015; Moore, Thompson, and Hisnanick 2018; Murphy et al. 2020). Nonetheless, workers' compensation is so small that it cannot have much impact on the overall patterns of medical care for low-income Americans.

In this part of the social safety net, national and state governments take care of millions of Americans by paying most or all of their medical bills. Many of the beneficiaries are poor or near poor. A secondary role for government is regulating the behavior of private employers and insurers. The Affordable Care Act does this in multiple ways.[31] For select groups, the government also acts as medical caregiver. The best-known recipients are current and former members of the military. They come closer than any other Americans to experiencing a European-style national health service.[32]

Active duty military, members of the National Guard and reserves, and their families participate in the TRICARE program. It is not unusual for employers to offer health insurance, especially when that employer is a government agency. With TRICARE, the Defense Department does that and operates hundreds of medical facilities, in this country and abroad. These facilities are typically located on or near a military base and staffed by military doctors and nurses. TRICARE also pays for individuals to be treated by civilian medical providers, so the government is not always their caregiver. Compared to a typical health plan in the private sector, TRICARE covers a broader range of employees and pays for a wider range of services. Nevertheless, TRICARE's co-payments and deductibles are less costly than most private plans. As a result, low-income members of the military have much better access to medical care than do low-income workers elsewhere (Kleykamp and Hipes 2015; Mendez 2020).[33]

Similarly, the Department of Veterans Affairs (VA) operates a series of hospitals and medical facilities around the country. It finances medical care and employs the doctors, nurses, and support staff who provide that care.[34] Funding is limited, and not all veterans can be treated. Priority is given to veterans based on their extraordinary service history—for example, disabled in the line of duty, Purple Heart recipients, former prisoners of war—or their lack of income (Panangala and Sussman 2019). Although these benefits are partly means-tested, they are not limited to veterans living in poverty. The income threshold in 2019 for a single veteran was almost three times the federal poverty line. The threshold for a veteran with three dependents was almost twice the poverty line for a family of four.[35] The VA understands that people living above the poverty line can face serious barriers when it comes to medical care.

Despite the broad definition of "low income," relatively few veterans access the VA this way. In 2017, 1.2 million veterans received medical care based on their income (a smaller number were eligible but did not need treatment that year). The total number of veterans who received care was six million. Most veterans use the VA system because of their service-related disabilities, which range from mild to severe. Individuals with severe disabilities often receive care worth more than $10,000 each year.[36] By serving low-income veterans, the VA system is part of the medical safety net, likely bigger than workers' compensation but far smaller than Medicaid.

The US government also provides medical care to American Indians and Alaska Natives. The Indian Health Service (IHS) employs a few hundred dentists, several hundred doctors and pharmacists, and more than two thousand nurses. As of July 2020, it was operating 24 hospitals, 51 health centers, and a few dozen smaller facilities. Most of these are located on or near reservations. The poverty rate among American Indians and Alaska Natives is unusually high, and many IHS patients have low incomes. However, they are not required to use the IHS; they can seek care from hospitals and health centers that are funded by IHS but run by the tribes themselves, or from private providers. The IHS is simply too small to serve the entire population of three million individuals, scattered across the country. Annual appropriations are $6 billion, which is roughly what the VA health system spends in a month. By any measure, the IHS is a small part of the social safety net.[37]

A much different picture of caregiving emerges once we move down from the national level. State and local governments operate more than 900 hospitals, far more than the Defense Department, the VA, and the IHS combined. The medical staff are public employees, and state and local governments usually pay for hospital construction and renovation. Patient care is financed mostly by Medicaid, Medicare, and private insurers. Many of these public hospitals are located in urban areas. A significant number are connected to medical schools: the Jackson Memorial Hospital, for instance, is operated by Miami-Dade County and serves as the main teaching hospital for the University of Miami medical school. Some state-run hospitals specialize in treating severe mental illnesses and are often located in smaller communities. Public hospitals handle approximately 12 percent of all hospital admissions in the United States. That translated to over four million admissions in 2018.[38]

Historically, state and local hospitals were built to serve disadvantaged populations. That mission continues, and their mix of patients is distinctive. A recent survey of 300+ public hospitals found that privately insured patients were in the minority. Medicaid paid for one-third of all admitted patients and for one-quarter of those treated on an outpatient basis. The figures for Medicare were similar. Like current and former members of the military, these individuals have their medical care paid for and delivered by government. Many public hospitals are located in areas with high levels of poverty and food insecurity. Their patients are often uninsured or underinsured and may have trouble paying their medical bills. The typical public hospital in this survey provided $80 million of uncompensated care in 2018, which was ten times the national average. Any hospital that cares for so many people with low incomes will likely benefit many racial minorities as well. In this survey, 25 percent of public hospital patients were Black and 23 percent were Hispanic (America's Essential Hospitals 2020). For many low-income Americans, particularly in urban areas, public hospitals are crucial caregivers.[39]

Help from Charity

Charitable giving to the health care sector involves tremendous sums of money. Phil Knight, the founder of Nike, and his wife gave $500 million to the Oregon Health & Science University in 2013 for cancer research. Two years later, billionaires Mark Zuckerberg and Priscilla Chan donated $75 million to the San Francisco General Hospital Foundation for the purchase of new equipment and technology. Joseph "Rusty" Walter III and his wife Paula gave $101 million to

Houston Methodist Hospital for neuroscience research in 2017. (Walter, who made his fortune in oil, had been treated for a stroke at that hospital a few years earlier.) In 2018, the Mayo Clinic School of Medicine received $200 million from one wealthy donor, and a family foundation gave the same amount to the Harvard Medical School. Both gifts aimed to promote medical education and research. The following year, three separate donors gave at least $200 million to the Cleveland Clinic, Massachusetts General Hospital, and the Rady Children's Hospital in San Diego, respectively. The main objectives were to promote medical education, fund research, improve technology, and expand existing buildings.[40]

Altogether, charitable donations to health care amounted to $41 billion in 2018. (While major gifts from the ultra-rich grabbed the headlines, most donors gave less than $1,000.) The total amount certainly looks large, until you start making comparisons. Forty-one billion dollars would have funded Medicaid for less than a month. It would have paid for less than three weeks of Medicare. Moreover, much of the donated money went to medical research. Those gifts were directed to specific institutions, like those mentioned above, or to charities such as the American Cancer Society. These donations supplement government funding for research, which is often modest, and they represent an investment in the future. Perhaps in a decade or two, that money will benefit low-income individuals, along with others who have certain medical problems. Besides research, some of the $41 billion went to medical education, and eventually some of those doctors and nurses might treat patients who are poor or near poor.[41] Most charitable donations did not target the immediate financial or medical needs of low-income Americans. In all these respects, 2018 was a typical year (Giving USA Foundation 2019).

Of course, there are exceptions. When the Catholic dioceses of New York sold off a nonprofit health insurance business in 2018, they used the proceeds to create the Mother Cabrini Health Foundation. The Foundation pledged to spend "up to $150 million per year to increase access to healthcare in low-resource and vulnerable communities" (Giving USA Foundation 2019: 241; see also LaMantia 2018). Some individuals donate money to organizations that help pay off medical debt. One of the better-known outfits, RIP Medical Debt, received donations worth $10 million in 2019. On average, one of their dollars can pay off $100 worth of medical debt facing low-income Americans. In December of 2020, billionaire philanthropist Mackenzie Scott surprised the organization by donating $50 million.[42] Wealthy individuals and companies connected to the pharmaceutical industry have been giving millions of dollars to organizations that combat opioid addiction (Giving USA Foundation 2019).[43] While such charitable efforts may be laudable, they represent a tiny share of the financial burden in this part of the social safety net.

Faced with huge medical bills, some Americans go online to beg for money. The polite name for this practice is crowdfunding. While it is certainly used in less desperate circumstances (e.g., to start a new business), crowdfunding has been attempted by cancer patients, parents of premature babies, victims of car crashes, and many others. One recent study found that "medical campaigns make up more than a third of all fundraising efforts on sites like GoFundMe, raising more than $650 million a year" (Kenworthy et al. 2020).[44] Not surprisingly, these campaigns have been more common in states that did not expand Medicaid. Yet crowdfunding is no panacea. The vast majority of campaigns never hit their funding target, and many fail to get halfway. The aggregate sums of money raised are relatively tiny. The kinds of people who are successful at crowdfunding tend to be more affluent, better educated, and more comfortable with computers. They know how to craft a winning appeal. They also tend to be connected, personally or professionally, to more people who can give money. Gender and racial disparities in crowdfunding work against women and racial minorities. For many reasons, crowdfunding is simply not going to help most low-income Americans with medical problems (Berliner and Kenworthy 2017; Kenworthy et al. 2020; Redden 2018; Renwick and Mossialos 2017).

Charitable donations and crowdfunding are used to take care of people who are sick or injured. Free and charitable clinics are responsible for taking care of and caregiving, and they could not survive without all kinds of donations. The United States currently has approximately 1,400 of these clinics.[45] Forty percent are faith-based organizations. Although some clinics have sizable budgets and operate Monday through Friday, most spend less than $500,000 and are open a few days each week. The medical services offered vary from clinic to clinic. Still, these are clinics, not full-fledged hospitals. Free clinics do not require any payment. Charitable clinics charge a flat or sliding-scale fee, based on the patient's income.[46] Roughly ten percent of free and charitable clinics bill third-party insurers such as Medicaid. Nevertheless, most clinics' revenue does not come from patients and insurers. Instead, they rely on cash donations to pay for staff and supplies. That money comes from local individuals, churches, civic groups, companies, and nonprofit foundations. Government grants tend to be small or nonexistent. In addition, clinics try to get their physical space donated, or at least offered at a reduced rent. They often ask drug companies to donate medications (Darnell and O'Brien 2015; National Association of Free & Charitable Clinics 2020; Pugh 2017).[47]

Free and charitable clinics also depend on highly skilled volunteers. In 2019, that group included more than 37,000 doctors, 18,000 nurses, and 13,000 dentists. Almost 6,000 pharmacists volunteered, as did 2,400 mental health providers. They are essential caregivers. An average clinic pays for two full-time and two part-time medical staff, which limits how many patients they can serve. That clinic will also rely on 20–30 nurses and doctors, drawn from the local community, who might agree to work a day or two each month. Many clinics are so small they cannot afford to pay for a full-time dentist or therapist; those services are provided only if qualified professionals volunteer. In addition, tens of thousands of ordinary citizens donate their time, helping with administrative tasks or serving as interpreters (Darnell and O'Brien 2015; National Association of Free & Charitable Clinics 2020; Smietana 2020).

Before the pandemic, these clinics were treating two million Americans each year (the numbers were higher before the Affordable Care Act). The vast majority were low-income and uninsured or underinsured. Many of the uninsured live in states that have refused to expand Medicaid. Some people who visit these clinics are poor immigrants who are ineligible for Medicaid. Some patients are eligible but cannot find a doctor who accepts Medicaid (see below). Many patients are employed but lack job-based health insurance, or they have health insurance but cannot afford the high deductibles and co-payments. According to the National Association of Free & Charitable Clinics, five out of every six patients come from a working household. Similar to Medicaid, clinic patients are mostly female (58%).[48] A national survey from 2015 found that 40 percent of all clinic patients were Black or Hispanic (Darnell and O'Brien 2015; Kamimura et al. 2016; National Association of Free & Charitable Clinics 2020; Pugh 2017; Smietana 2020).

It is unclear how much this care costs. If we assume that visits to free and charitable clinics replace visits to hospital emergency rooms, then clinics provided the equivalent of $10 billion worth of care in 2019. However, without these clinics, some individuals might not get medical attention. Their condition would go untreated, and they would hope for the best. The cost of their care today would be less, but down the road could be much higher (National Association of Free & Charitable Clinics 2020; Smietana 2020). Under any scenario, the cost of free and charitable clinics is far less than Medicaid, which serves many more patients. Though means-tested, these clinics help fewer low-income Americans than Medicare.

One point worth emphasizing is that free and charitable clinics are not available everywhere. Even though the United States has 60,000 food pantries and soup kitchens, people in some parts of the country cannot access them (Chapter 6). This problem is worse with 1,400 clinics. Free and charitable clinics might not be located where patients live, or they might have more demand than they can handle. In Texas, for example, there is one clinic in Abilene. If you head west, toward Midland and Odessa, you will have to drive 450 miles before reaching the next clinic in El Paso. Before the pandemic, the Albany, New York metropolitan area had almost 900,000 people and one free clinic. Not a big one, either: it had one full-time nurse practitioner and was open for parts of Tuesdays, Thursdays, and Fridays.[49]

Spotty coverage is one reason why the Remote Area Medical (RAM) organization exists. It sponsors temporary "pop-up" clinics all over the United States, especially in rural areas. For two or three days, medical professionals volunteer their time and provide free care to hundreds and sometimes thousands of people. Their patients are uninsured or underinsured. Many have chronic conditions like arthritis, diabetes, and high blood pressure. Others might have abscessed teeth. Some have simpler problems, like needing a vision exam in order to obtain a commercial driver's license. These individuals will drive for hours and wait for hours to be examined and treated (Calello 2018; Saslow 2019). In 2018, RAM-sponsored clinics provided medical care to over 45,000 people.[50]

Earlier in this chapter, I noted how public policies shape private health insurance. The same is true with respect to medical charity. For instance, public charities must comply with detailed rules established by Congress and enforced by the Internal Revenue Service. Doing so exempts them from paying federal income taxes, as well as state and local property and sales taxes (Reich 2018). Because free and charitable clinics are often strapped for cash, minimizing their tax obligations is a real benefit.[51] By the same token, individuals who donate goods or cash to charities may be eligible for tax breaks. The tax expenditure for charitable contributions to health organizations was worth almost $4 billion in 2019. Most of the beneficiaries had incomes of at least $100,000 (Joint Committee on Taxation 2019). Donations of time and labor, however, do not receive favorable tax treatment. The US government subsidizes the millionaires and billionaires who support medical research, but not the nurses, doctors, and regular citizens who volunteer at local clinics (Reich 2018). In short, charity does not happen in a vacuum; government can choose whether and how to promote it.

The Business of Caregiving

During his career, Uwe Reinhardt was one of the top health economists in the United States. He liked to remind people about the Cosmic Law of Health Care: "every dollar of health spending is someone else's health-care income, including fraud, waste and abuse" (Reinhardt 2009; see also Reinhardt 2019). Health care is not simply a story about healing the sick and injured; it is also about jobs and paychecks, sales and profits. We know part of this story already. The insurance industry helps take care of most Americans by paying for their medical care. Private health insurance is a trillion-dollar business, and anyone who tries to lower the cost of insurance or increase the role of government will face heavy resistance. One of the first questions asked about any single-payer proposal is what will happen to all the people who work for the insurance industry.

Medical caregiving is big business (Rosenthal 2017). Americans spent $1.2 trillion on hospital care in 2019. If we subtract the monies going to government-run hospitals, the amount is still huge. Physician care and clinical services (e.g., blood tests, x-rays) cost an additional $772 billion. Prescription drugs, $370 billion. Americans spend almost $150 billion each year on dental care. The total cost of medical care in the United States—excluding long-term care, medical research, and public health—is approximately $3 trillion (Martin et al. 2021). That is equivalent to the entire French or British economy.[52]

All that money means jobs. In any given month, five million Americans are employed by hospitals. Close to eight million people work in various doctors' and dentists' offices, outpatient clinics, or diagnostic labs. Health and personal care stores—pharmacies, opticians, and the like—have a million employees. Even smaller segments such as the pharmaceutical industry have plenty of workers.[53] Unlike sectors of the economy that are concentrated in one region or a few states, medical care is important all over the country. Hospital systems are the single largest employer in 18 different states, from Maine to Oregon.[54] Many medical professionals are well paid, and they stimulate demand for other goods and services in the area. Economically, medical care has big ripple effects.

These numbers reflect the entire US health care system and not just the safety net portion. Let's focus for a minute on the caregivers who do business with Medicaid. Hospitals were paid a little more than $200 billion by Medicaid in 2019. Even if you are a trillion-dollar industry, that much money will grab your attention. Medicaid paid doctors, dentists, and labs almost $100 billion. The total bill for prescription drugs was more than $30 billion.[55] Medicaid generates a ton of revenue, which creates a large, motivated constituency (Kronebusch 1997; Olson 2010). Politically, the program seems vulnerable because recipients have so little income and children cannot vote. Caregivers, however, could mobilize to protect Medicaid based on high-minded principle and economic self-interest. Spending cuts hurt their bottom line. Public officials might listen more closely to the CEO of a major hospital than a poor single mother.

Medicaid is not equally important to all caregivers. Doctors and hospitals located in more affluent parts of the country typically see few Medicaid patients. Numerous hospitals have moved from downtown areas to the suburbs, in part to attract more affluent patients (Galewitz 2015). At the other end of the spectrum are public hospitals, discussed earlier, that count heavily on Medicaid. The same is true of community health centers that offer primary and preventive care. Almost 1,400 of these centers operate nationwide. Most have multiple sites, generating over 10,000 facilities that offer medical care. They are usually located in areas that are low-income or medically underserved. They can be found in big cities and rural communities. Many of their patients live in poverty, some are homeless, and many are uninsured. These centers treat 28 to 30 million Americans each year, and the professionals who work there play a vital role in the medical safety net. Medicaid pays for almost half the care provided by community health centers (Health Resources & Services Administration 2020; Johnson 2020; Stone 2020).

Public hospitals, nonprofit hospitals, and community health centers must take Medicaid and Medicare patients in order to justify their tax-exempt status. These organizations contribute to the greater good by caring for the poor, the elderly, and the disabled. Yet a quarter of US hospitals are run for profit, and they do not have to play by the same rules.[56] Most doctors, clinics, and medical labs are in the same position. With the exception of emergency treatment (discussed below), these caregivers have some ability to choose their patients, and many do not want to deal with Medicaid or Medicare.

A major reason is money.[57] Insurance companies reimburse doctors and hospitals at a higher rate than Medicaid or Medicare. Medicare might pay $17,000 for a knee replacement, for instance, whereas private insurers might pay $37,000 (Abelson 2019). According to a recent review of the literature, private insurers pay roughly twice as much as Medicare for hospital services, and 40 percent more for physician services (Lopez et al. 2020). Medicaid payment rates differ from state to state, making it difficult to generalize. Medicaid usually reimburses doctors and hospitals at a somewhat lower rate than Medicare. Everyone in the medical community knows that privately insured patients are more profitable. Doctors and hospitals often make a bolder claim: they lose money by treating Medicare and Medicaid patients (American Hospital Association 2020b; American Medical Association 2020; Gee 2019). According to the American Hospital Association, hospitals suffered a Medicaid shortfall of $23 billion in fiscal year 2017 (MACPAC 2020). While the accuracy of such claims has been challenged (e.g., Lee 2017; Rickert 2012), they remain potent. Anybody who supports "Medicare for All" will probably be accused of putting doctors and hospitals out of business (Abelson 2019).

For taxpayers, the good news is that government can keep medical costs down better than private insurers can. The sheer size of government makes it a powerful negotiator in the Medicare and Medicaid programs. The bad news for employers and employees is they pay higher prices for private health insurance to compensate for people with government insurance. More bad news is that low reimbursement rates could create access problems for people on Medicaid and Medicare. A recent survey found that 71 percent of physicians said they would take new Medicaid patients. In other words, almost 30 percent said they would not. The problem was worse in certain specialties: only 36 percent of psychiatrists said they would see new Medicaid patients. Doctors were more willing to accept new Medicare patients, but were most willing to accept new privately insured patients (Holgash and Heberlein 2019; see also Currie 2006). In short, being covered by Medicaid is no guarantee that individuals can access medical care easily.

Whether or not doctors and hospitals accept Medicaid, many will provide some uncompensated care to their patients. That care has two parts, charity care and bad debt, and both are relevant to the social safety net. Charity care is offered to patients who are uninsured and low-income. Their treatment is free or steeply discounted.[58] Bad debt arises when insured patients fail to cover their deductibles and co-payments. The recent growth of high-deductible plans has made this problem worse. Uninsured patients who do not qualify for charity care can also incur bad medical debt. These patients are typically charged higher prices than those with private insurance, making repayment difficult. Some hospitals have been extremely aggressive in trying to collect on bad medical debt. At times this has meant putting liens on patients' homes or driving them into personal bankruptcy (American Hospital Association 2020a; Hancock and Lucas 2019; Meyer 2019; O'Brien 2018; Rau 2019).

With so many different organizations involved with medical care, it is hard to know exactly how much uncompensated care is given. Hospitals provide the bulk of this care. People who are admitted to hospitals often incur enormous bills, and those who show up at emergency rooms often lack health insurance. The American Hospital Association (2020a) estimates that hospitals provided $41 billion worth of uncompensated care in 2018. Slightly more than half of that was charity care. Community health centers are the second most likely source of uncompensated care, which makes sense given their mission and clientele. Doctors' offices are a somewhat distant third (Bruch and Bellamy 2020; Coughlin et al. 2014).

Government is one reason why hospitals provide charity care, and government has tried to compensate them for some of these expenses.[59] The Emergency Medical Treatment and Labor Act of 1986 requires hospitals with emergency departments to stabilize and treat anyone who comes to them with an urgent medical condition (e.g., a woman in labor, someone having a heart attack). These patients cannot be "dumped" on another hospital because they are unable to pay (Meyer 2016). Historically, the US government has paid for some charity care by reimbursing hospitals that served a disproportionate share of the uninsured. Those payments were supposed to be cut back by the Affordable Care Act. The ACA would reduce the number of uninsured Americans, and thus lessen the need for charity care. In Medicaid-expansion states, that is exactly what happened. But several states did not expand Medicaid, and the cuts were postponed (Garfield, Orgera, and Damico 2019; MACPAC 2020; Schubel and Broaddus 2018).

At the end of the day, medical care in this country is a business, not a charity. Hospitals may provide $41 billion in uncompensated care, but that represents just three percent of their total revenues. Charity care is an even smaller percentage. Some uncompensated care is bad medical debt, which hospitals are trying hard to collect. And hospitals are partly reimbursed by the federal government for their charity care. Doctors provide less charity care than hospitals do. Granted, some hospitals and some doctors are unusually generous when dealing with people who cannot afford medical care. Nevertheless, the Cosmic Law of Health Care has not been repealed. Most Americans living in or near poverty will receive far more help from Medicaid than they will from corporate charity.[60]

Discussion

In the middle of the 20th century, health insurance changed dramatically. Job-based insurance spread quickly in the United States and became the foundation. Medicaid and Medicare were added to fill in some of the gaps. The public–private mix for financing medical care favored the private sector (Hacker 2002; Quadagno 2005). This pattern holds true today. Most Americans have private health insurance, typically from their employer (Table 8.1). To the extent that taking care of something means paying for it, then employees, employers, and private insurance companies have primary responsibility for medical care. While Medicaid and Medicare have grown, they still serve a minority of the population.

Public and private are not mutually exclusive. Private health insurance is shaped by a variety of government tax breaks and regulations. Moreover, some individuals carry public and private insurance, which is why the rows in Table 8.1 add up to more than 100 percent. Older Americans, for example, might still be employed and thus have Medicare and job-based health insurance. Or they might combine Medicare with a private Medigap policy.

The public–private mix varies considerably from group to group. For people living in poverty, government is much more likely to pay for their medical care. Similarly, more of the near poor are publicly insured than privately insured (Table 8.1). Medicaid is a crucial source of health insurance for low-income Americans, which means that taxpayers, many of them affluent, are the ones paying. As we go up the income ladder, private insurance becomes increasingly important. Those with full-time employment are also more likely to have private insurance.[61] Blacks and Hispanics are less likely. The differences between men and women (not shown) are very small.[62]

Despite the enormous sums spent on private and public health insurance, millions of Americans are uninsured. According to the Census Bureau's Current Population Survey, 26 million Americans (8.0%) did not have health insurance in

Table 8.1 **THE INSURED AND THE UNINSURED (2019)**

Group	Insured		Uninsured	
	Privately	*Publicly*	*Percent*	*Number*
Total	67.4 %	35.4 %	9.2 %	29.7 million
Income				
below poverty line	26.6	65.2	16.0	6.7
1x–2x poverty line	42.6	53.4	15.2	8.4
2x–4x poverty line	70.0	32.2	10.5	10.0
over 4x poverty line	87.6	21.9	3.9	4.9
Employment (ages 15–64)				
full-time	84.6	7.4	10.2	10.9
part-time	66.4	21.0	15.8	8.4
unemployed	49.6	42.6	14.7	6.8
Race/ethnicity				
White, non-Hispanic	74.7	34.3	6.3	12.2
Asian	74.7	25.6	6.6	1.2
Black	55.7	43.5	10.1	4.1
Hispanic	50.1	36.3	18.7	11.0

Notes: Some people have private and public health insurance; adding up the income, employment, or race/ethnicity numbers of the uninsured may not result in the total number due to rounding.

Sources: Katherine Keisler-Starkey and Lisa N. Bunch, *Health Insurance Coverage in the United States: 2019*, U.S. Census Bureau Current Population Reports, pp. 60–271 (Washington, DC: Government Printing Office, 2020), Table A-2; U.S. Census Bureau, *Health Insurance Historical Tables*, https://www.census.gov/data/tables/time-series/demo/health-insurance/historical-series/hic.html, Table HIC-5.

2019. The American Community Survey, also conducted by the Census Bureau, estimated that almost 30 million Americans were uninsured that year (9.2%). The first survey was administered between February and April of 2020, just as the pandemic was hitting. The response rates were lower than usual, particularly among people with lower incomes. The American Community Survey is the more accurate source for 2019 (Broaddus and Aron-Dine 2020; Keisler-Starkey and Bunch 2020).

The last column of Table 8.1 shows that the medically uninsured are a diverse bunch. About half are poor or near poor, but half are not. Millions of Americans are too "rich" for Medicaid, too young for Medicare, and working at a job where health insurance is unavailable or unaffordable. Over ten million full-time workers lack health insurance. More than 40 percent of the uninsured are non-Hispanic Whites. The lack of health insurance affects a wider range of people than food insecurity (Chapter 6).

That said, some groups definitely have a higher chance of being uninsured, and low-income Americans are one of them (Table 8.1). Even with Medicaid, Medicare, and private insurance, 16 percent of people living in poverty are uninsured. People living somewhat above the poverty line have a similar experience. We know some of the reasons why. Many jobs held by low-income workers do not include health benefits. The uninsured rate is substantially higher in states that have not expanded Medicaid; the rate in Texas, for example, is more than double that in California (Broaddus and Aron-Dine 2020; Keisler-Starkey and Bunch 2020). There are other reasons, including the administrative burdens of qualifying for Medicaid and remaining eligible (Herd and Moynihan 2018; Michener 2018). But the main point is that the medical safety net has a sizable hole.

Blacks and especially Hispanics are more likely to fall into this hole (Table 8.1). Compared to native-born citizens, immigrants have higher rates of being uninsured; this helps account for the elevated rate among Hispanics (18.7%). Working-age adults are more likely to be uninsured than are children or senior citizens (Keisler-Starkey and Bunch 2020). Medicaid and Medicare have made huge strides toward covering the latter groups. The failure to expand Medicaid since the ACA has impacted low-income, working-age adults the most. Finally, men are somewhat less likely to be insured.[63] Women have a greater chance of being poor, but they are also more likely to have health insurance.

Being officially "insured" covers a wide range of people—probably too wide. Since 2005, the Commonwealth Fund has been conducting detailed surveys of health insurance among US adults between the ages of 19 and 64. They have found that approximately ten percent of adults who were insured at the time of the survey lacked coverage at some point in the previous year. The Census Bureau would have counted such individuals as insured. The average length of coverage gaps has shortened since the Affordable Care Act, but they usually last for months and not weeks. Coverage gaps are more common among people with low incomes, part-time workers, Blacks, and Hispanics (Collins, Bhupal, and Doty 2019).

The Commonwealth Fund counts as "underinsured" anyone with health insurance all year who had large out-of-pocket medical costs. This group includes people whose deductible was at least five percent of their household income; people with incomes below 200 percent of the poverty line whose total out-of-pocket costs exceeded five percent of their income; and anyone else with out-of-pocket costs that exceeded ten percent of their income.[64] By this definition, 23 percent of American adults were underinsured in 2018. That number has been growing, largely because of changes in private insurance such as the rise of high-deductible plans. Once again, people with low incomes are more likely to be underinsured. However, being underinsured is one of the few measures of well-being where non-Hispanic Whites fare worse (Collins, Bhupal, and Doty 2019). This is probably because more Blacks and Hispanics are uninsured or have coverage gaps, which by definition means they cannot be underinsured.[65]

When we account for coverage gaps and underinsurance, health insurance in the United States looks much more tenuous. In 2018, only 55 percent of working-age adults had health insurance consistently for the past year and were not underinsured. In other words, a little over half of them had reliable and somewhat affordable health insurance. The figures for non-Hispanic Whites (58%) and full-time workers (59%) were a bit higher; health insurance is a problem even for the more advantaged groups in society. Less than half of part-time workers and Hispanics and less than 40 percent of the poor and near poor had reliable, affordable health insurance. Most of them were uninsured, underinsured, or dealing with coverage gaps (Collins, Bhupal, and Doty 2019). Calls for comprehensive health reform are appealing when so many Americans struggle with the status quo.

In theory, people can receive medical care in this country without good insurance coverage. We have many free and charitable clinics and even more community health centers. Hospitals and doctors provide charity care. All these parts of the medical safety net must make some difference. Whether the poor and near poor have adequate, reliable health insurance might not be the central issue. What matters is whether they receive the medical care they need.

In fact, they do not. Table 8.2 offers a snapshot of access problems (circa 2018). The two general categories are treatment and prevention, and the individuals surveyed were working-age adults. Many Americans say they cannot afford the medical care they need. One in five adults did not visit a doctor or clinic when they had a medical problem, because of the cost. One in five who needed a prescription filled did not, because of the cost. One-third of adults delayed or did not get the dental care they needed for the same reason. These are signs of general distress; medical care in America is too expensive (Reinhardt 2019; Rosenthal 2017).

Yet these problems are far more common among the uninsured. Half of uninsured adults are not visiting a doctor or clinic whenever they have a medical problem. Less than half are going to the dentist whenever their teeth need work. People with low incomes fare better than the uninsured, but they still have more trouble than the average person when trying to get medical treatment (Collins, Bhupal, and Doty 2019). I call attention to these examples because they do not require a specialist or hospitalization. These types of care are supposed to be available for little or no cost at free and charitable clinics all over the country. Community health centers are also viable options. While many people are benefitting from these services, so many are going untreated. Numerous studies have found results similar to those in Table 8.2, affecting people of all ages

Table 8.2 ACCESS TO MEDICAL CARE (2018)

	Total US (ages 19–64)	Uninsured	Income level	
			below 133% of poverty	133–249% of poverty
Went without needed care inpast year because of cost:				
delayed/did not get dental care	33%	56%	39%	43%
had medical problem, butdid not visit doctor/clinic	21	49	24	28
did not fill prescription	19	32	24	22
Preventive care:				
regular source of care	89	68	88	88
blood pressure checked inpast two years*	91	72	88	89
cholesterol checked in past five years	72	44	63	63
mammogram in past twoyears (women age 40+)	65	32	56	48
dental exam in past year	60	32	43	49

* checked in past year if person has high blood pressure.

Source: Sara R. Collins, Herman K. Bhupal, and Michelle M. Doty. *Health Insurance Coverage Eight Years After the ACA: Fewer Uninsured Americans and Shorter Coverage Gaps, But More Uninsured* (New York: Commonwealth Fund, 2019). https://www.commonwealthfund.org/publications/issue-briefs/2019/feb/health-insurance-coverage-eight-years-after-aca.

(e.g., Garfield, Orgera, and Damico 2019; Hodgkinson et al. 2017; Institute of Medicine 2009; Woolhandler and Himmerstein 2017).

By the same token, many Americans are not getting as much preventive care as they should (Table 8.2). The problems are generally worse for the uninsured, the poor, and the near poor. Low-income Americans can access simple types of care, like having their blood pressure checked every two years.[66] As soon as diagnostic or lab tests need to be run, the story changes. Poor women are less likely to get mammograms. Poor men and women are less likely to have their cholesterol checked or be screened for colon cancer. Most are not receiving regular dental check-ups. Among the uninsured, only about one-third are being tested or examined at the recommended intervals (Collins, Bhupal, and Doty 2019). If your goal is to keep people healthy and reduce long-term medical costs, then the lack of preventive care is a serious concern.

For people struggling to make ends meet, the high cost of medical care forces them to make difficult trade-offs. The uninsured or underinsured might have to choose between having a tooth pulled or buying groceries for their family. Standard blood tests would help identify medical problems, but the phone bill might be more pressing. Do you get weeks of physical therapy, like your doctor recommended, or do you pay next month's rent? Medicaid coverage can make these trade-offs easier, but even some of those patients do not get the care they need (Collins, Bhupal, and Doty 2019). They might have trouble finding a doctor who accepts Medicaid. Additional trade-offs confront the working poor. Can I afford to miss a shift in order to keep a medical appointment? Just the travel time and the wait time could take hours (Lewis, Abrams, and Seervai 2017). Can I afford to have this procedure if it means missing a few days of work while I recover? People with good-paying jobs and adequate health insurance rarely have to think about such questions. Millions of Americans do not have that luxury.

Daily Care

In the late 1950s, medical staff at the Benjamin Rose Hospital in Cleveland investigated how well their patients were recovering from hip fractures. In particular, they wanted to know how many of their older patients could live independently after being discharged from the hospital. The team, led by Dr. Sidney Katz, created an index based on specific activities of daily living (ADLs) such as getting in and out of bed, bathing, and feeding one-self. Individuals received one point if they could perform each activity or zero points if they could not. The maximum was six points. It turned out that patients who scored higher on this index were less likely to end up in a nursing home, and their mortality rates were lower as well (Staff of the Benjamin Rose Hospital 1959, 1960).

The ADL index has become a powerful diagnostic tool for doctors, nurses, social workers, and gerontologists. Some versions of the index include a greater or lesser number of activities. Some versions score each activity on a continuum from dependent to independent. A related index of instrumental activities of daily living (IADLs) is now widely used. IADLs range from shopping for groceries and clothes to preparing meals, paying bills, and managing medications (Colello 2019; Gaunt 2020; Mlinac and Feng 2016). Despite their differences, all these measures are trying to answer the same questions. How well can people take care of themselves on a daily basis? What kinds of assistance might they need? The key issue is functioning, not flourishing.

We normally ask these questions about adults with disabilities. Their impairment might be temporary or permanent, partial or extensive. Disabilities often result from aging. They can also be due to illness or accident. Individuals might have adequate income and reliable shelter; however, if they cannot get out of bed or feed themselves, they face serious hardships. Some people could have good health insurance coverage, but if they cannot remember when to take their medications, the consequences could be disastrous. Daily care is therefore distinct from other basic needs discussed in the previous chapters.

Who Cares. Christopher Howard, Oxford University Press. © Oxford University Press 2023.
DOI: 10.1093/oso/9780190074456.003.0010

Long-term care is one type of daily care, and the most expensive. Policy experts and practitioners often use a different phrase, long-term services and supports (LTSS), but the meaning is the same: "the broad range of paid and unpaid medical and personal care assistance that people may need . . . when they experience difficulty completing self-care tasks" (Reaves and Musumeci 2015: 1).[1] Much like medical care, the cost of long-term care varies enormously. It might be as small as paying someone to deliver your groceries, or it could take your entire life's savings. In 2019, the average annual cost of a private room in a nursing home was $102,000. Even a semi-private room cost $90,000. Someone who hired a home health aide for 40 hours a week could easily spend $50,000 a year.[2] No one who is poor or near poor can afford to pay for such care. At these prices, almost everybody will need help.

Some adults will be lucky enough to function independently until the day they die. All infants and children, however, must receive daily care from others. They cannot take care of themselves. Infants have, in effect, very low ADL scores. Children are unable to perform most of the IADLs.[3] Infants and children may not be disabled, but they are highly dependent. Parents have the lead responsibility as caregivers, and many of them must also earn a paycheck. To balance work and family, they will need help with child care. On average, parents who paid for child care spent $9,000–$10,000 per child in 2019.[4] That is a huge expense for low-income parents, comparable to their rent. Having two young kids in a child-care center could consume their entire paycheck. Low-income parents will need help from somewhere in order to afford decent child care.

When individuals need daily care, government focuses more on taking care of than caregiving. National and state governments are a major source of funding for long-term care, primarily through Medicaid. Because Medicaid is means-tested, it offers important benefits for people with low incomes, regardless of their work history (Chapter 8). Government plays a much smaller role in child care, with some monies targeted at the poor and near poor. Government pays for-profit and nonprofit organizations to be the caregivers. Long-term care is a large and growing industry; nursing homes, assisted living facilities, and home health agencies can be quite profitable. For their part, child-care providers range from national chains with hundreds of franchises to local churches and families that operate a single facility.

The need for daily care is most evident in the first and last years of our lives. Occasionally we need help caring for ourselves or loved ones during our working years. We might have to leave our job temporarily in order to devote more time to caregiving or care-receiving. Such absences might be justified as maternity leave, parental leave, family leave, medical leave, or bereavement leave. Governments and employers determine how long these leaves can last and whether they are paid or unpaid. For obvious reasons, unpaid leave is not going to provide much help to people who are struggling to make ends meet.

Governments, businesses, and nonprofits are not the whole story, or even the main story. Daily care is commonly provided by relatives, without charge. Family members perform double duty, taking care of and giving care to some of the most vulnerable members of society. As we shall see, the extended family is unusually important in this part of the social safety net.

Daily care is seldom discussed in the welfare state literature. That research focuses on economic risks associated with capitalism and industrialization, and the need for daily care goes back to the dawn of humankind. Political theorists and feminist scholars have paid considerable attention to daily care (Boris and Klein 2012; Duffy 2011; Glenn 2010; Levitsky 2014; Tronto 1993, 2015). They have highlighted the crucial role that women play as unpaid caregivers. Mothers have traditionally devoted more time than fathers to child care. Women have been more likely to care for elderly relatives who cannot live independently. Giving daily care can be physically and emotionally draining. The time demands can be unpredictable. And yet all the work involved is often taken for granted. Women, especially women of color, are also more likely to be employed as caregivers. They are working for nursing homes, home health care agencies, and child-care centers. Few of these jobs pay well. In this part of the social safety net, we expect gender to be highly salient.

Long-term Care

Long-term care is closely tied to the concept of disability, which is ambiguous (Meyer and Stevens 2020; Stone 1984). In the United States, disability must be either job-related or severe and long-lasting before government will provide income support. Only a small fraction of Americans are impaired enough to qualify for Disability Insurance or Supplemental Security Income (Chapter 5). Many of these individuals need daily care as well. A government check, by itself, cannot help them get dressed in the morning, and it won't cook their dinner. In some cases, around-the-clock care will be essential. Imagine someone with a degenerative disease like Alzheimer's or Huntington's, or someone who barely survived a terrible car accident.

We often equate disability with extreme forms of impairment and dependence. Disabilities can be less severe and still make caring for oneself difficult. According to the US Centers for Disease Control and Prevention (CDC), one-quarter of non-institutionalized adults—over 60 million people—had at least one physical or cognitive disability in 2016.[5] Fourteen percent of adults reported having trouble when walking or climbing stairs. Eleven percent said they had "serious difficulty concentrating, remembering, or making decisions"; ten percent had significant problems hearing or seeing; seven percent had trouble running errands alone; and four percent had difficulty dressing or bathing themselves. Millions of Americans were living with two or more of these disabilities (Okoro et al. 2018). Some disabilities can be handled fairly simply, such as taking the elevator instead of the stairs whenever possible. Others are more difficult to deal with. The AARP organization estimated that 14 million adults were impaired enough in 2018 to need help with their daily care (Hado and Komisar 2019).

Disabilities are not distributed equally. They are much more common among people with lower incomes. For instance, 29 percent of all adults aged 45–64 had at least one disability in 2016. If those adults were also living in poverty, the rate doubled. Similar gaps between the poor and non-poor were evident for each type of disability tracked by the CDC. Altogether, nearly half of all adults living in poverty are dealing with some type of disability. The racial gaps are smaller but still significant: in every age group, Blacks and Hispanics are more likely to be disabled than are Whites or Asians. The highest rates belong to American Indians and Alaska Natives. Women are somewhat more likely than men to be disabled (Okoro et al. 2018; see also Meyer and Stevens 2020).[6]

Not surprisingly, disabilities occur more frequently among senior citizens. As we age, we naturally lose some of our physical and cognitive abilities. Years spent battling chronic diseases or failing to receive adequate medical care can add to the toll (Gonyea 2014). Over 40 percent of senior citizens had some type of disability in 2016, which was more than twice the rate of younger adults (Okoro et al. 2018). In 2017, 22 percent of individuals age 85 and older needed help with personal care, compared with only three percent of individuals between the ages of 65 and 74 (Tuck and Moore 2019). Any single-year snapshots like these will understate the lifetime risk. A different study, using data from 1995 to 2014, found that 70 percent of adults who reached the age of 65 would need some long-term service or support before they died. One-quarter of them would require care for at least four years (Johnson 2019).

The aging of the population is an important reason why the need for long-term care has been growing and will continue to do so. Since the middle of the 20th century, life expectancy has slowly but steadily increased. Americans born in 1950 could expect to live for 68 years; the average person born in 2000 will live to be 77. Life expectancy has also grown for those who manage to reach 65 or 75. In 2016, 49 million Americans were age 65 or older, and they constituted 15 percent of the population. By 2040, the Census Bureau estimates that this group will total over 80 million and comprise a larger share (22%) of the population. The number of people age 85 and older is projected to increase rapidly, from 6.4 million to 14.4 million.[7] In the process, more and more of the elderly will be racial and ethnic minorities (Houser, Fox-Grage, and Ujvari 2018).

These years will be golden for some and a struggle for others. Poverty rates among the elderly increase as they get older. Despite the powerful impact of Social Security (Chapter 5), poverty among Americans age 80+ is often higher than the national average. The reasons are not hard to figure out: earnings, savings, and job-based retirement pensions diminish over time; out-of-pocket medical expenses tend to increase. Poverty rates among the elderly are also higher for women and significantly higher for Blacks and Hispanics. Approximately one-fifth of all Black and Hispanic women aged 65 + were officially poor in 2019 (Li and Dalaker 2021; Mudrazija and Angel 2014). In other words, the same people who are more likely to have disabilities are the same ones with less money to pay for care.

If we know that disability is likely at some point in our future, then rationally we should plan ahead for whatever care we might need. That is easier said than done. The severity and duration of disabilities are hard for anyone to predict years in advance. We might end up needing nothing for long-term care or having to pay well over $100,000. This seems like an ideal spot for private insurance; after all, homeowners and car owners buy insurance knowing they might never file a claim, or they could experience a total loss. Although some job-based health insurance policies include limited coverage for long-term care, low-income workers rarely have those kinds of policies. Stand-alone long-term care policies exist, but fewer and fewer insurers are selling them, and the annual premiums typically cost $2,000 to $4,000 (Colello 2020; Houser, Fox-Grage, and Ujvari 2018; Stark 2018).[8] The poor and near poor already have difficulty saving a few hundred dollars for emergencies, and they aren't accumulating large pensions from their employers. Setting aside thousands of dollars for long-term care is practically impossible (Reaves and Musumeci 2015; Chapter 5 of this book).[9]

Most adults who need help will rely instead on family (or friends). This pattern reflects both cost considerations and a widespread belief that relatives should be responsible for daily care. From this perspective, it is totally appropriate to purchase food, housing, and medical care. Daily care is different. Paying for that care, or expecting government to pay, could signal a failure of family members to perform their normal duties (Levitsky 2014; Warraich 2017). The sense of responsibility cuts both ways. Many family members feel that caregiving gives them a sense of purpose in life. Many also say they had no choice in the matter (AARP and National Alliance for Caregiving 2020).

The AARP and the National Alliance for Caregiving have conducted surveys of unpaid caregiving over the last two decades. (Routine child-care responsibilities are excluded.) The most recent survey, conducted in 2019, found that 39 million

Americans were providing unpaid care to an adult relative or friend; five million were caring for a child with special needs; and another nine million were
caring for at least one adult and one child. This last group is often known as
the "sandwich generation" because they are being pressured from both sides.
All told, 53 million adults were acting as unpaid caregivers.[10] The weekly time
commitment varied, with some caregivers devoting less than eight hours and
others devoting over 40 hours. The median was 15 to 20 hours per week. Almost
30 percent of those providing unpaid care have done so for five or more years
(AARP and National Alliance for Caregiving 2020).

Most unpaid caregivers help with at least one ADL, such as getting out of bed
or getting dressed. Virtually all of them assist with numerous IADLs. They routinely provide transportation, shop for groceries, perform housework, prepare
meals, and help manage finances. The work does not end there. Most caregivers
spend time communicating with medical professionals or advocating with
agencies on behalf of care recipients. Unpaid caregivers also function, sometimes
uncomfortably, as extensions of the health care system. More than half perform
tasks such as monitoring blood pressure, giving injections, changing wound
dressings, or caring for catheters and colostomy bags.[11] While many caregivers
have paid help, two-thirds of them report being on their own or sharing responsibility with other family members (AARP and National Alliance for Caregiving
2020; Reinhard et al. 2019b).

Unpaid caregivers come from all walks of life. In 2019, 61 percent were
women and 39 percent were men. Women were also more likely to be the primary caregiver and more likely to be caring for two or more adults. The gender
gap is smaller than it was a generation ago, but it still exists. Roughly 60 percent
of caregivers were White and 30 percent Black or Hispanic, which was close to
their shares of the US population. Caregiving hours were greater for Blacks than
Hispanics, and greater for both than for Whites. On average, Black caregivers
perform a wider range of duties than their White counterparts. Whites tend to
care for older recipients. The average age of caregivers was almost 50, with one-
quarter being younger than 35 and one-fifth older than 65. (The older ones are
usually looking after their spouse or partner.) Most unpaid caregivers also have
a paying job (AARP and National Alliance for Caregiving 2020; Reinhard et al.
2019b).

These surveys tell us less about care recipients. The exact number is unknown, because each recipient could have more than one caregiver. Almost half
of caregivers reported being the sole caregiver, which makes 30 million care
recipients seem like a conservative estimate. The vast majority of recipients are
relatives, typically elderly parents. Two-thirds are over the age of 65. Women
outnumber men (61–39), in part because women outlive men. While many
recipients live with their caregiver, most do not (AARP and National Alliance

for Caregiving 2020). A similar survey, conducted in 2018, found that Whites tend to be overrepresented and Hispanics underrepresented among recipients of unpaid care (Reinhard et al. 2019b).[12]

We know a few things about recipients' health. Over 60 percent have a long-term physical condition that requires care. Old age/frailty is the main example. Thirty percent have short-term physical conditions, such as recovering from surgery. Almost one-third of recipients have memory problems. Over 25 percent are dealing with emotional or mental health issues. Smaller numbers have behavioral issues or developmental/intellectual disorders. Note: these figures add up to more than 100 percent because many recipients have multiple problems (AARP and National Alliance for Caregiving 2020; see also Reinhard et al. 2019b).

The world of unpaid caregiving has been changing. The number of caregivers has grown in recent years, and a larger number are caring for multiple people. Memory problems and mental health issues have become more common reasons why daily care is needed. The duration of unpaid care for a typical recipient has increased. More recipients live with their caregivers, and this is particularly true for African Americans. Overall, the trend line is pointing in the direction of more need, not less (AARP and National Alliance for Caregiving 2020).

Unpaid caregiving is so widespread, we cannot include all of it in the social safety net. Most caregivers are not poor. Their median household income in 2019 was $67,500, which was similar to the general population. One-fifth of caregivers had incomes below $30,000. Roughly ten million caregivers (one-fifth of 53 million) might qualify as low income, and that is a sizable number. In this group, African Americans and Hispanics are overrepresented. The family members of low-income caregivers tend to have more health problems than average, which makes the burden of caring for them greater. The financial strain is greater, too: they are more likely to deplete their savings or take on more debt in order to make up for lost wages. Not surprisingly, low-income families are less likely to hire paid caregivers. These families feel particularly stressed when performing medical tasks. A visiting nurse is not cheap, so they try to make do on their own (AARP and National Alliance for Caregiving 2020; Levitsky 2014; Reinhard et al. 2019b).

In-depth studies of poverty can put a human face on these patterns. One recurring theme emphasizes the tensions between caregiving and employment. While investigating the lives of poor women after the 1996 welfare reforms, Sharon Hays

> encountered a number of welfare mothers who were taking care of disabled others. You will perhaps recall, for instance, the mother in the Arbordale waiting room who cared for both her grandchild on a lung

machine and her terminally ill father. There was Sheila who was afraid to
leave her wheelchair-bound mother at home alone. (Hays 2003: 166)

Katherine Newman's portrait of the working poor in New York City spelled out
the consequences in more detail.

> When chronic, long-term health problems threaten the independence
> of a fifty-year-old grandmother, her daughter and grandchildren may be
> staring a twenty-year problem in the face, one that inevitably threatens
> their own careers. Workdays are missed, school days are interrupted,
> savings accounts are drained to pay for doctors and medicine, families
> double up to provide personal care. No element of life is left unscathed.
> (Newman 1999: 208)

Providing daily care is especially difficult for those living paycheck to paycheck,
or whose jobs come with unpredictable hours and few sick days, which is the
reality for many of the working poor (Desmond 2018; Levitsky 2014; Chapter 5
of this book).

Alternatively, people who need long-term care can turn to government for
assistance. Americans spent a little over $400 billion on long-term care in 2018.
Medicaid (44%) and Medicare (20%) were responsible for almost two-thirds of
that total. Medicaid alone paid for more long-term care than all private insurance
and individual out-of-pocket spending combined (Colello 2020).[13] Medicaid is
a public assistance program, with funding shared between the national and state
governments. Given that most of the money comes from the national government, and most of that from income taxes, affluent Americans are heavily involved in paying for the long-term care of people with low incomes.

As noted in Chapter 8, Medicaid is a complicated program with lots of variation from state to state. The long-term care segment of Medicaid is no exception. All states cover everyone who qualifies for Supplemental Security
Income, which has strict standards for disability, income, and assets. States have
the option of extending coverage to people with lesser degrees of impairment
and somewhat greater financial resources. Most states do this to some degree.
Disability is typically based on how many ADLs an individual can perform independently, and states can choose the threshold number. If individuals have high
medical expenses, states can deduct some portion of them when determining
income eligibility. People who were middle class for much of their lives might
eventually receive long-term care from Medicaid. They could start by paying for
LTSS out-of-pocket or with insurance, "spend down" their assets, and then tran-
sition to Medicaid. The exact path will not be the same in every state. To varying
degrees, this part of the social safety net extends well beyond the chronically

poor (Grogan and Andrews 2015; Meyer and Stevens 2020; Mitchell et al. 2021; Reaves and Musumeci 2015; Thach and Wiener 2018).

Medicaid has historically favored nursing homes, which provide comprehensive care for the seriously disabled. In recent decades, many states have been granted federal Medicaid waivers to shift some LTSS spending to home and community-based services (HCBS).[14] Familiar examples include home health aides and adult daycare centers. Medicaid will allow individuals to be cared for without being institutionalized, which is what many prefer. This is an important trend because Medicaid now spends more money on HCBS than on institutional care. Most people who benefit from Medicaid LTSS receive care in their own home or the community, not in a nursing home. The use of these waivers varies by state, as does the length of the waiting list for these services (Eiken et al. 2018; Meyer and Hausauer 2015; Mitchell et al. 2021; Reaves and Musumeci 2015; Thach and Wiener 2018).[15]

Geographic differences in Medicaid LTSS are not closely related to whether states chose to expand Medicaid as part of the Affordable Care Act. That decision has had a bigger impact on working-age adults than people with disabilities. Nevertheless, state-level differences in LTSS are significant. For instance, as of 2018, the asset limit for an individual with disabilities was $2,000 in Illinois but $10,000 in Iowa.[16] The state of New York had a Medicaid waiver to provide home and community-based care to individuals with physical disabilities, provided their incomes were below 84 percent of the federal poverty line. The threshold for this same group was 300 percent of the poverty line in Connecticut and New Jersey. Two-thirds of the states allowed Medicaid to pay for personal care in the home, such as help with bathing and meal preparation. One-third did not (Musumeci, Watts, and Chidambaram 2020; Thach and Wiener 2018; Watts, Musumeci, and Chidambaram 2021).

Details about long-term care recipients are hard to pin down because of how Medicaid data are collected and reported.[17] At last count, about two million Medicaid recipients were receiving LTSS in institutions. Most were living in nursing homes or specialized facilities for individuals with intellectual and developmental disabilities. While they represent a tiny fraction of all Medicaid recipients, the cost to care for them is very high. An additional five million people (or so) were receiving some form of home or community-based care that was paid by Medicaid. Depending on the type of care and the extent of impairment, the annual cost could range from $8,000 to over $40,000 per person. That is still less than the cost of institutionalization, which helps explain why so many Medicaid waivers have been sought and granted. Women are more likely than men to receive almost any type of long-term care from Medicaid. Women tend to live longer, and they don't have as much income. While Blacks and Hispanics are more likely to benefit from Medicaid overall (Chapter 8), it is unclear how much they benefit from the long-term care portion given their shorter lifespans. In the general population, Hispanics appear to be underrepresented in nursing homes and hospice care and overrepresented in adult daycare centers. Relatively few Blacks or Hispanics are being cared for in assisted living facilities, which are less comprehensive than nursing homes but still expensive (Centers for Medicare & Medicaid Services 2020; Eiken et al. 2018; Harris-Kojetin et al. 2019; Watts, Musumeci, and Chidambaram 2020).

Medicare subsidizes long-term care—not as much as Medicaid, but more than private insurance. Eligibility for Medicare is based on prior employment, not need. As a social insurance program, Medicare benefits a wide range of people, some of whom are low income (Chapter 8). Nevertheless, there are important limits as to what this program can do. One constraint is that Medicare excludes non-elderly people who have impairments but do not qualify for Disability Insurance. Moreover, Medicare will not pay for the types of personal care associated with ADLs and IADLs if that is all the care needed. Senior citizens who are generally healthy but frail or forgetful will have to find assistance elsewhere.[18]

Medicare will pay for services provided by medical professionals such as nurses and physical therapists. But not for very long. If individuals require a skilled nursing facility, then Medicare will cover all costs for the first 20 days.[19] Beneficiaries will owe a large co-payment ($185.50 per day, as of 2021) for the next 80 days. Medicare pays nothing for institutional long-term care after 100 days. Such a benefit will be useful to individuals with temporary disabilities, perhaps after they have been discharged from a hospital and before they are ready to go home. This might be classified as rehabilitation or post-acute care. Medicare can buy people a little time to figure out whether family members, Medicaid, private insurance, or savings will be called upon in the near future. The short-term emphasis is reinforced by Medicare's coverage of palliative hospice care, provided that recipients have no more than six months to live.[20]

Consequently, Medicare is far less important than Medicaid in this part of the social safety net. Twelve million low-income Americans may be eligible for both programs, but the division of labor is pretty clear-cut. Medicare pays for acute and post-acute care, while Medicaid pays for long-term care. This is not a strict separation: Medicaid can take care of co-payments owed to Medicare (Chapter 8), and Medicare can cover the first few months of LTSS. Even so, much of Medicare's long-term care spending helps people who are not and will not be poor.[21]

National and state governments have the lead responsibility for funding long-term care. Tens of thousands of for-profit and nonprofit organizations are in charge of caregiving. Except for adult day centers, which comprise a small share of the total, most of these organizations operate for profit. As of 2016, more than

15,000 nursing homes were providing care; over two-thirds were for profit and over half were owned by regional or national chains. There were almost 29,000 residential care communities, and 80 percent of them were run for profit, mostly by chains. Eighty percent of the 12,000 home health agencies operated for profit (Harris-Kojetin et al. 2019). According to the Bureau of Labor Statistics, employment of home health or personal care aides is growing faster than almost any other occupation. Over three million Americans are employed in these jobs.[22] Daily care is big business in this country—not on the scale of medical care, but still big.

These organizations have something of a Jekyll-and-Hyde reputation for caring. The nurses, aides, therapists, and social workers are generally viewed as essential caregivers. They help feed and bathe the most vulnerable. They literally pick us up after we have fallen, and they could be the last people we see before dying. These caregivers are frequently overworked, underpaid, or both. Many of them earn $10–$15 per hour. Reports of wage theft by employers are common. Staff turnover is high. To many observers, the poor working conditions are no coincidence given that paid caregivers are overwhelmingly female and disproportionately Black or Hispanic. Many are immigrants as well (Buch 2018; Duffy 2011; Gandhi, Yu, and Grabowski 2021; Gollan 2019; Schweid 2021; True et al. 2020).

The owners are portrayed less sympathetically. The profit motive leads many of them to keep a tight lid on labor costs. Low wages, turnover, and staff shortages make life hard for workers and can jeopardize the quality of patient care. A growing number of nursing homes are owned by private equity groups intent on maximizing returns for their well-heeled investors. Alternatively, some owners control a web of companies that supply goods and services to their long-term care facilities; those companies are paid more than if they truly operated in a competitive market. Either way, owners and investors can make millions of dollars from nursing homes (Cenziper et al. 2020; Meyer 2020; Olson 2010; Rau 2018; Warraich 2021).[23] For their part, home health care agencies often turn a profit, and they have been touted as a great business opportunity for franchisees. A caring disposition might help when entering the long-term care business, but it is not a requirement.[24]

Despite the potential for profit, many companies claim they are struggling to stay afloat. Over 500 nursing homes closed their doors between 2015 and 2019 (Flinn 2020). Perhaps the most cited problem is Medicaid. Similar to hospital care, Medicaid pays less for long-term care than either Medicare or private insurance. While estimates vary and states differ, nursing homes typically receive 70%–80% as much from Medicaid as they do from private payers.[25] A leading trade association makes a stronger claim: nursing homes consistently lose money when caring for Medicaid clients. This is a huge problem when most of your clients are covered by Medicaid.[26] Nursing homes can stay in business only because higher reimbursements from private payers and Medicare offset these losses. If two people are waiting for a spot to open and one of them is covered by Medicaid, nursing homes have a strong incentive to admit the other person (Gleckman 2020a; Meyer 2020; Quadagno 2020).[27] Not everyone is convinced by these numbers. They question whether the losses reported by nursing homes have been exaggerated (Harrington et al. 2013, 2021). This is not the place to resolve these arguments. I mention them to show how closely connected are the public and private strands of the social safety net, and to highlight frictions between those who pay for care and the caregivers.

Child Care

Child care creates some boundary issues with respect to the social safety net. Policy experts and providers often refer to early care and education (ECE) rather than child care. ECE is supposed to remind us that infants and young children are getting more than fresh diapers and food each day. They are also being prepared for school by learning how to recognize shapes and colors, play well with others, and follow directions. In the Introduction to this book, I distinguished between safety net programs that help care for our basic needs and educational programs that help us climb ladders of success. That line will be fuzzy for the next few pages. Organizations that offer child care/ECE often provide the types of daily care found in a nursing home. They also might follow a standard curriculum of instruction.[28]

Compared to long-term care, the need for child care is more predictable. Parents do not wonder if their newborn will require help someday. They understand that all infants and young children must receive daily care. The problem is figuring out a good mix of care from parents and other adults, whether paid or unpaid.

In recent years, about 40 percent of all children under the age of five were being cared for exclusively by their parents (Swenson and Simms 2020). One parent might work full time while the other stays home with the kids, or both parents work part-time and share the caregiving duties. Low-income families have a hard time taking this approach. Obviously, living on one paycheck will be easier for families with average or above-average incomes.[29] Finding part-time employment with predictable hours is difficult for anyone, especially workers with low-wage jobs. In addition, most poor children are growing up in single-parent families. In 2018, 11.7 million children were officially poor and 7.7 million of them were living in single-parent (usually single-mother) families. A majority of young children in poverty were also living in single-parent families (Semega et al. 2019).[30]

The growing number of single-parent families and two-earner couples has increased demand for paid child care. An extreme example is the uber-rich family spending $50,000–$100,000 per year on a live-in nanny. Less expensive options include a spot at a child-care center or family child-care home. Less expensive does not mean cheap, or even affordable. As mentioned earlier in this chapter, these options impose a huge financial burden on low-income families. Those parents cannot afford to spend half their paycheck on child care. (The Department of Health and Human Services recommends that families spend no more than seven percent of their income on child care.) They will have to get financial help, most likely from government. Otherwise, they will count on their family safety net.[31]

In the public safety net, it is easy to find programs that spend at least $50 billion per year. The portion of Medicaid dedicated to long-term care is close to $200 billion. In contrast, child-care subsidies for low-income families add up to around $10 billion. Most of the money comes from the national government and some from the states. About two-thirds is distributed through the Child Care and Development Fund (CCDF) and the rest through TANF and the Social Services Block Grant. States' involvement means that eligibility rules and benefits will vary across the country (Chien 2020; Currie 2006).[32]

Eligibility is based on a combination of need and work. According to federal guidelines, the family's income must not exceed 85 percent of their state median (adjusted for family size), and the child must be under the age of 13. State guidelines are often more restrictive. As a result, the average income limit for recipients was a little over half the state's median income in 2017. Child-care subsidies are effectively targeted at low-income families. They also come with behavioral requirements—for the parent, not the child. "Child care subsidies help parents pay for child care so parents can work or participate in education and training activities" (Chien 2020). After the 1996 welfare reforms, for instance, states shifted TANF money away from cash benefits and toward work supports like child care. These eligibility requirements favor the working poor; government will not pay for child care to help mothers and fathers enjoy some free time.[33] Nonetheless, the budget outlays are so small that it is hard to see child care as a major victory for the working poor.

Through these programs, government subsidizes care for two million low-income children. Two-thirds of them are under the age of six. The rest are between the ages of six and 12, enrolled in before-school or after-school programs.[34] These children represent a small fraction of those who are eligible. Based on federal guidelines, over 13 million children qualify for assistance; under more restrictive state guidelines, the number is closer to nine million.[35] Much like housing assistance, states ration child-care subsidies. The lower the family's income, the more likely they are to receive help. Families currently on TANF or at risk of needing TANF are normally given priority, as are families with special-needs children. States usually expect parents to pay part of the costs, but the exact amounts vary and some of the poorest families pay nothing. Among those who are eligible, Black children are more than twice as likely as White or Hispanic children to receive a child-care subsidy. Most of the beneficiaries are Black or Hispanic. Eighty percent live in single-parent families (Chien 2020; Children's Defense Fund 2021; Lynch 2019a).[36] In a program aimed at the poorest children, these patterns should not be surprising.

Paid caregivers work in a variety of settings. Most of the $45–$50 billion that Americans spend on child care each year goes to approximately 75,000 child-care centers. Three-quarters of these centers are run for profit. They might be national chains like KinderCare or Bright Horizons, or they could be local businesses. Generally speaking, the potential for profit-making is lower here than in long-term care. The remaining child-care centers are run by nonprofits such as the YMCA, The Salvation Army, and individual churches.[37] A typical center, whether for-profit or nonprofit, has a dozen employees. Most child-care establishments, however, are family child-care homes with a single employee. They are truly small businesses. Though the numbers fluctuate, there were almost 600,000 family child-care homes as of 2016. As a group, these homes care for considerably fewer children than centers do, and their share of the market has been declining (Committee on Economic Development 2019; Swenson and Simms 2020; Workman and Jessen-Howard 2018).[38]

Regardless of the setting, the profile of caregivers is similar to long-term care (Child Care Aware of America 2019; Ewing-Nelson 2020; Gould 2015). Paid child-care workers are almost always women, and they are disproportionately racial minorities and immigrants.[39] The average pay is $10–$15 an hour. One difference is that job-based health insurance is less common among child-care workers. In addition, fewer people are employed in child care, and little job growth is expected in the next decade.[40]

Government subsidies for child care usually function like vouchers, allowing low-income parents to choose a provider. The number of options depends on local conditions, and many parts of the country have been labeled "child-care deserts" for their lack of providers. These deserts are common in rural areas and places with large Hispanic populations (Malik et al. 2018). In the largest program, the CCDF, three-quarters of the vouchers are used in child-care centers and most of the rest in family child-care homes. A small fraction of these subsidies pay relatives to care for a child.[41]

The Head Start program straddles the line between safety net and education. According to the Department of Health and Human Services, "Head Start promotes school readiness for children in low-income families by offering educational, nutritional, health, social, and other services."[42] Head Start, like any preschool, is trying to promote cognitive development, social skills, and emotional well-being. A sizable fraction of participants are infants and toddlers.[43] Equally important, Head Start is free for low-income parents. As we have seen, the supply of child-care subsidies is seriously lacking, and low-income parents cannot afford to pay for full-time or even half-time child care. Head Start gives them another option. With their children enrolled, parents will have more time to further their education, acquire job training, or hold down a job. In short, the program benefits children and their parents.

Head Start serves approximately one million children. Almost all have family incomes below 130 percent of the federal poverty line, and most live in poverty. A majority of Head Start families identify as Black/African American or Hispanic/Latino. More than 20 percent of the parents speak primarily Spanish at home. Depending on where they live, the children might attend Head Start full time or part-time, year-round or part of the year. The price tag of Head Start is about $10 billion, funded by annual appropriations from the national government. Once again, taxes paid by the affluent help take care of the poor and near poor. Still, with its modest budget, Head Start serves less than half of all poor children under the age of five.[44]

Most Head Start programs are operated by community action agencies, local nonprofits, or school districts. Profit-making firms are much less prevalent than in child care.[45] Many organizations incorporate Head Start children into some larger ECE program, and therefore receive tuition payments from other parents or funding from state and local governments as well. Virtually all (98%) Head Start teachers are women, and half are Black or Hispanic. Most teachers graduated from a four-year college. The teachers employed by school systems are, on average, paid much better ($40,000–$45,000/year) than those who work for community action agencies or local nonprofits ($25,000–$30,000). Nevertheless, no one is getting rich working for Head Start, and staff turnover among lead teachers can be 20 to 25 percent each year (Bernstein et al. 2019). Head Start also relies on unpaid caregivers from the local community. Almost one million Americans are helping out in Head Start classrooms. Most of them are parents of children currently enrolled, but other relatives and parents of former students also contribute.[46] With so much outside involvement, Head Start is not exclusively part of the public safety net.

For low-income families who cannot benefit from government subsidies or Head Start, child care is prohibitively expensive. These families could easily spend one-third of their income on child care, far above what the government recommends (Malik 2019).[47] Paying that much is simply not feasible for most parents, and therefore they turn to the family safety net. In single-parent families, the non-custodial parent (most likely the father) might help take care of the children financially, and that money could help pay for child care. Child support can be ordered by the courts and paid on a regular basis, or it might be more informal and irregular. In low-income families, child support is far from guaranteed. Sixty percent of custodial parents who were living in poverty did not receive the full amount of child support they were legally owed in 2017. Almost one-third received no payments at all.[48] Where a history of abuse or bitterness exists, the custodial parent will probably feel strongly about keeping the non-custodial parent out of the picture. In practice, many single parents do not file for child support (Collins and Mayer 2010; Edin and Lein 1997; Edin and Shaefer 2015; Grall 2020).

Family members are more likely to be enlisted as caregivers. Grandparents, aunts, uncles, and other relatives are the primary caregivers during the work week for about one-fifth of children under the age of five. For low-income families, relatives are even more important. In 2015, relatives were the primary caregivers for young, low-income children more often than were child-care centers, and much more often than family child-care homes. Some of these relatives were paid, either by the parents or government; three-quarters of them were unpaid. These numbers actually understate the importance of extended family because many parents piece together combinations of child care. Their kids might be enrolled at a child-care center during the morning and then go to a relative's home in the afternoon (Malik 2019; Swenson and Simms 2020).

Along with significant cost savings, the family safety net offers other benefits. Children get a chance to develop closer bonds with their relatives. Grandparents or other kin might be more secure financially or more experienced as parents, which could make them good caregivers. For families living in a child-care de-sert, extended family could be one of the few options available.

A major advantage of the family safety net is its flexibility. Many low-income parents have jobs with unpredictable schedules (Chapter 5), making it hard to arrange in advance for paid child care. Finding a relative or friend may be their best option on short notice. Some low-income parents work nights or weekends, when very few child-care establishments are open. Luckily, a sister or cousin is willing to pitch in. Children sometimes get sick at day care or school, and they need to go home. Low-income parents might not be able to get time off from work on such short notice; Nana or Grandpa will have to pick them up and care for them the rest of the day. Working parents frequently need someone to watch their school-age children during the summer months. In-depth studies of pov-erty are filled with examples of family members helping out with child care on a regular or as-needed basis. Without their help, low-income parents could lose their jobs, or their children could be left at home alone (Collins and Mayer 2010; Edin and Lein 1997; Edin and Shaefer 2015; Henly 2018; Hicks-Bartlett 2000).

That said, the family safety net has its limitations. For one thing, not everyone lives near their relatives. If family members are in the area, informal norms of reciprocity dictate that those who receive help should also give it. Parents who benefit from unpaid child care may be called upon to care for a relative's kids in the future. They might be expected to share food with family members in exchange for child care. They might be asked to run errands or provide transportation (Edin and Lein 1997). While these exchanges can be mutually beneficial, parents can't always predict when a relative will call in a favor.

Another complication is that family members can clash over parenting styles (Kalil et al. 2000). Someone might not ask their sister for help, for example, if she seems too strict or too permissive with kids. Others might resent how they were treated as a child, making it harder to ask their own parents (now the grandparents) for help. Finally, friends and relatives do not have to be specially trained or licensed, which makes the quality of care more variable. In the worst-case scenario, some children are neglected or abused. Low-income parents are frequently connected to people whose lives are turbulent and who are ill-suited to be caregivers. But desperate parents don't always have good options or make good choices (Edin and Shaefer 2015).

The Working Years

Everybody starts out life being highly dependent on others for daily care. We could be somewhat or highly dependent in our later years as well. In between, we are supposed to be independent. Employment is a major source of independence, and we have seen what types of income support are available to those who are unemployed or severely disabled (Chapter 5). Those who are employed, however, may find that their ability to work is periodically compromised by their need to give or receive daily care. Familiar examples include illness (either the worker's or a family member's) and the birth/adoption of a child. Employees would like to be able to step away from their normal job duties for a relatively short period of time, focus on care, then return to work. Employers and governments can make it easier or harder for workers to deal with these situations.

Probably the best-known policy is the Family and Medical Leave Act (FMLA). This Act was hailed as a milestone when it was enacted in February 1993. President Clinton made it the first piece of legislation he signed into law. Millions of American workers were now guaranteed time off from work to care for themselves or their relatives (i.e., child, spouse, or parent). Any health insurance they had before taking leave would continue during their leave. Covered workers were also guaranteed a comparable job with their employer when they returned.[49] The US government did not have to raise taxes or increase spending to make any of this possible. The FMLA is a social regulation, one where government tells employers how to treat their employees.

Clinton portrayed the new law as a combination of social policy and economic policy. He praised the FMLA for helping workers to care for a newborn
or adopted child, or to care for a relative with a serious medical problem. "It is
neither fair nor necessary to ask working Americans to choose between their
jobs and their families—between continuing their employment and tending to
their own health or to vital needs at home."[50] Many types of workers faced this
dilemma, and their numbers were growing; a government response was long
overdue, he said. Clinton argued that companies would benefit, too, from lower
turnover, better employee morale, and higher productivity. Finally, he pitched
the FMLA as a smart move for taxpayers. Without these new rules, spending
on medical care and public assistance would go up.[51] Once again, a prominent
Democrat was trying to help workers and their families.

Whether the Act truly qualifies as a milestone is debatable. The original law
was limited in scope. Although it covered all government workers, the FMLA
did not apply to private-sector businesses with fewer than 50 employees. Most
part-time workers and recent hires were excluded. Leave time was limited to 12
weeks per year, and that leave would be unpaid.[52] As a result, many low-income
workers were not covered by the FMLA, and those who were covered found
it hard to make ends meet without a paycheck. Virtually every country in the
world was offering paid parental leave in the 1990s, but not the United States.

Despite numerous calls to expand coverage and require paid leave, the FMLA
remains essentially unchanged. The inequities are quite predictable. A recent
study, commissioned by the Labor Department, focused on the experiences
of low-wage workers making less than $15/hour. Only 38 percent of all low-
wage workers were covered by the FMLA, compared to 63 percent of workers
who were better paid. Two barriers loomed large. Low-wage workers were
more likely to be recent hires and more likely to be employed part-time. They
were also more likely to be "gig" workers who were classified as independent
contractors, not employees, and therefore exempt from the FMLA.[53] Among
the low-wage workers who were covered by the FMLA and needed a leave but
did not take it, almost two-thirds worried they might lose their job. An even
higher percentage said they could not afford to take unpaid leave (Brown, Roy,
and Klerman 2020).[54] A separate study found that the average woman in a low-
income household (<$30,000) took six weeks of leave following the birth or
adoption of a child. A woman living in a high-income household ($75,000+)
took 12 weeks (Horowitz et al. 2017).

Just as many employers offer starting wages above the legal minimum, many
employers go beyond the FMLA and offer paid leave. Low-income workers remain disadvantaged. Eighty percent of higher-paid workers had access to paid
leave for their own illness in 2018, compared to 52 percent of low-wage workers.
The proportion was even lower for the poorest workers.[55] As a job benefit, paid

sick leave is far more common than paid family leave. Less than 20 percent of workers in the private sector have access to paid family leave. Coverage is much greater among workers in the top quartile than the bottom quartile of wages (30% versus 8%). Likewise, full-time workers are much more likely to benefit than part-time workers (Donovan 2020). Keep in mind that paid leave does not necessarily mean full pay. Only 22 percent of low-wage workers received full pay during their leave; the figure was 53 percent for higher-wage workers. To cover their lost wages, low-wage workers were almost twice as likely to borrow money and were three times more likely to receive some form of public assistance (Brown, Roy, and Klerman 2020). Another study found that low-income parents who took unpaid leave were more likely to delay paying their bills and to borrow money from family or friends (Horowitz et al. 2017).

In the public safety net, we typically find the US government playing a bigger role than state governments in taking care of the poor and near poor. Leave policies are an exception. Some state governments have extended eligibility for unpaid leave to a larger group of workers than the FMLA requires. Other states have expanded the types of relatives who count as the worker's family (Reddy 2018). Notably, a number of state governments have enacted paid leave policies. These policies are based on social insurance principles, not public assistance, which means that low-income workers benefit as part of a larger population. The events triggering family or medical leave are considered short-term disabilities and thus appropriate for social insurance. Five states—California, New Jersey, New York, Rhode Island, and Washington—were running programs for paid medical leave and family leave before the pandemic. Eligibility is based on work history, but the threshold is usually lower than for the FMLA. Depending on the state, the leave period lasts for six to 52 weeks; medical leaves are typically covered for a longer period than family leaves. The benefits average around two-thirds of the employee's prior weekly wage and are financed by payroll taxes. Three other states (Connecticut, Massachusetts, Oregon) and the District of Columbia were in the process of implementing paid leave policies as of February 2020 (Donovan 2020).[56] Many of these same states have passed laws requiring employers to offer paid sick days to their employees (Reddy 2018). It is no coincidence that these places are Democratic strongholds.

Family and medical leave benefits are inclusive, not targeted. There is no equivalent to Medicaid and long-term care, nothing that resembles Head Start. Inclusive policies can have a profound effect on poverty, with Social Security as the best example (Chapter 5). But simply being inclusive is not enough. When family and medical leave is unpaid, the big winners are couples who can afford to live on one paycheck, or individuals who can afford to live off their savings. The big winners have above-average incomes.

For low-income workers, the Family and Medical Leave Act is clearly better than nothing. Being able to take leave without losing your job is important. Paid leave would make it much easier to care for themselves and their loved ones. Studies have found that paid parental leave is associated with lower rates of infant mortality and postpartum depression. Poor children are more likely to be immunized on schedule when their parents have paid leave. In California and Rhode Island, families were less likely to need SNAP or other forms of public assistance when covered by paid leave (Donovan 2020; National Partnership for Women & Families 2019; Veghte et al. 2019). Paid family leave allowed Black mothers to extend their leaves by four to six weeks in California. The added time for Hispanic mothers was a bit smaller but still noticeable (Rossin-Slater, Ruhm, and Waldfogel 2013; see also Bartel at al. 2019).

Discussion

Mapping this part of the social safety net is complicated because so much daily care is provided by family members. We cannot track their actions as readily as government spending, job-based benefits, or charitable giving. The family safety net appears to be more important for daily care than it is for income, food, housing, or medical care. By the same token, the family safety net is more important than the public safety net for long-term care and child care. One study by the AARP estimated that family members contributed the equivalent of $470 billion in unpaid care while tending to their adult relatives in 2017.[57] That sum was far greater than what Medicaid spent on long-term care. In fact, it exceeded all public and private spending on long-term care that year (Reinhard et al. 2019a). Finally, it is quite clear that government takes care of poor disabled adults, most of whom are elderly, more than poor children. Spending on long-term care by Medicaid far exceeds spending on various child-care programs targeted at low-income families.

A better understanding of daily care complicates our understanding of work and the safety net. Family leave policies and child-care subsidies help paid workers balance their job and family responsibilities. They favor the working poor over the nonworking poor. In contrast, the main long-term care program, Medicaid, does not link eligibility or benefits to paid employment. Need is what matters most. Need is also what leads more than 50 million Americans to provide daily care for their relatives (and friends). That includes millions of unpaid caregivers living in or near poverty. Unpaid caregiving is a part-time job for most and a full-time job for many. The paychecks may be small, but the responsibilities are not.

One obvious part of this story is the central role of women as caregivers. Women still do most of the work of unpaid caregiving within their families.

Women are, by a wide margin, the people who are employed in long-term care and child care. Most of those jobs pay enough to lift one adult above the poverty line. But if a single mother is a paid caregiver and trying to support one or two children, her family will struggle to stay out of poverty.

Each chapter in this section of the book has concluded by shifting attention to the care recipients. Frankly, it is difficult to measure the adequacy of daily care. The US government routinely surveys adults about their income, food security, housing, and health insurance. However, children and disabled individuals may be unable to answer questions about their daily care. We might not fully trust their caregivers, either. How many people will admit to leaving their elderly parent in bed for a week, or to failing to feed their infant child?

Instead, professional caregivers are supposed to speak up when they see signs of trouble. The Child Abuse Prevention and Treatment Act of 1974 "requires each State to have provisions or procedures for requiring certain individuals to report known or suspected instances of child abuse and neglect."[58] While mandatory reporters vary from state to state, they usually include child-care workers, teachers, doctors, nurses, and mental health professionals. Similar laws exist to protect the elderly and adults with disabilities. Medical professionals and paid caregivers working for nursing homes, assisted living facilities, and home health care agencies are typically classified as mandatory reporters.[59] States also make it possible for ordinary citizens to report their concerns, perhaps through a telephone hotline. The job of investigating these claims belongs to the relevant child welfare or adult protective services agency, or to local law enforcement.

Table 9.1 presents a few statistics about the mistreatment of children, and all these numbers come with caveats. Federal law does not define child abuse or child neglect in much detail. State laws are more specific, but they vary. Many states distinguish between neglect and medical neglect of children, for example, while some states simply have a single category called neglect. All states report cases where children were sexually abused, but not all states report when children were victims of sex trafficking. States do not always record the same demographic data concerning victims or perpetrators. And some states are more willing than others to seek an "alternative response" to reports of mistreatment, which usually involves offering needed services to a family. Parents who did "X" could be labeled as neglectful in one state but not in another (US Department of Health & Human Services 2021).

Apart from inconsistencies at the state level, the numbers could be biased nationwide because of the reliance on mandatory reporters. In 2019, over two-thirds of the reports came from professional caregivers. Overwhelmingly, the alleged perpetrators were the child's parents or relatives. Documented cases of abuse or neglect in child-care centers or other institutions were very rare (US Department of Health & Human Services 2021). One might wonder if paid

Table 9.1 **NEGLECTED AND ABUSED CHILDREN (2019)**

	Number	Percent	States reporting
Total victims	656,243		52*
Girls	337,163	51.4	52
Boys	316,972	48.3	52
Unknown	2,108	0.3	52
White	279,332	43.5	50
Black	133,838	20.9	50
Hispanic	150,762	23.5	50
Total victims with caregiver risk factors	626,159		47
Public assistance	99,383	26.9	29
Financial problems	54,545	13.7	31
Inadequate housing	40,120	9.6	38

* includes District of Columbia and Puerto Rico.

Note: the percentages are based on the total number of victims in the states that reported the relevant data.

Source: U.S. Department of Health & Human Services, Administration for Children and Families, Administration on Children, Youth, and Families, Children's Bureau. 2021. *Child Maltreatment 2019.* https://www.acf.hhs.gov/cb/report/child-maltreatment-2019.

caregivers are consistently willing to report a co-worker's bad behavior. On the other hand, young children who are cared for exclusively by family members, and largely invisible to mandatory reporters, could be harmed without anyone filing a report. Last but not least, the child welfare system has often been accused of racial bias. Many minority parents—especially those with low incomes—feel they are subject to extra scrutiny and harsher judgments. As a result, they are more likely to be labeled as neglectful or abusive parents (Fong 2020; Joyce 2019; Meyerson 2018).[60]

Over 650,000 children were officially mistreated in 2019 (Table 9.1). Three-quarters of them were neglected, meaning the responsible caregiver had failed to provide a minimal level of food, medical care, daily care, or other basic need. Abuse cases were less common but more severe; they typically involved intentional acts of physical or psychological harm. Girls were slightly more likely than boys to be the victims of neglect or abuse. Almost 25 percent of all children were Hispanic, and almost 25 percent of the victims were Hispanic. Black children, however, were disproportionately likely to be victims. While 14 percent of all children in the United States were Black or African American, they represented

21 percent of abuse and neglect victims. White children, in contrast, were less likely to be victimized than their share of the total population would indicate (US Department of Health & Human Services 2021).[61]

The bottom rows of Table 9.1 suggest that the Black–White gap is related to income. Based on data from most states, a large fraction of caregivers were receiving some form of public assistance (e.g., Medicaid, SSI, TANF) when they were accused of neglecting or abusing children. Tens of thousands reported having financial problems or were dealing with "substandard, overcrowded, or unsafe housing conditions, including homelessness" (US Department of Health & Human Services 2021: 23). Parents struggling to make ends meet might not have enough money for food or child care, and their kids might be hungry or left alone from time to time. Parents could be accused of neglect simply because they were poor. The daily grind of survival could lead some parents to be abusive. To be clear, most low-income parents and most Black parents do not mistreat their children. Some White parents and some affluent parents do. My point is that a lack of income will make it harder for anyone to take proper care of children. In this country, Black families are much more likely to be poor or near poor (Chapter 5).[62]

The adequacy of care for adults is even harder to figure out. While national and state governments pay attention to elder abuse, we know that many older Americans do not need help with daily care, and that many disabled adults who need help are not elderly. The various definitions of elder abuse cover a wide range of problems, some of which do not involve caregivers (e.g., when strangers try to swindle older Americans out of their savings). In addition, the gender, race, and ethnicity of victims are reported more often than their income, making it difficult to know how the poor and near poor are faring. For the purposes of this chapter, the most relevant type of abuse is elder neglect, which is defined much like child neglect. Unfortunately, studies have found that only a tiny fraction of neglect cases involving older Americans are ever reported.[63]

We might expect useful data from nursing homes. Their employees are usually considered mandatory reporters under state laws and thus obligated to report suspected cases of abuse or neglect. Residents of nursing homes may have family members who visit from time to time and who can monitor their care. Nursing homes are reimbursed by government for most of their residents, which means they must abide by certain standards and document how the money was spent. In case these safeguards are not enough, the national government created a standard rating system for nursing homes in 2008. Homes that received five stars had the best staffing ratios, allowing for more individual attention. They also had fewer residents experiencing medical problems. Nursing homes that received just one star were supposed to be much lower quality. The timing of the star system was no coincidence: lawmakers were concerned that the wave of private equity firms buying nursing homes would lessen the quality of care. Advocates for the elderly applauded the new system (Silver-Greenberg and Gebeloff 2021). Given that nursing homes rely heavily on Medicaid patients, these ratings should help us understand the quality of long-term care for low-income individuals.

Nevertheless, ratings are only as accurate as the underlying data. According to a detailed investigation by the *New York Times*, many nursing homes have tried to game the system. Their owners found that higher ratings increased demand for their services and profits. Thus they had a financial incentive to underreport problems. Based on records from over 10,000 nursing homes, reporters from the *Times* found a huge number of factual errors—almost all of which made the quality seem better than it actually was. Other studies have uncovered similar problems. "In 2019, the inspector general of the US Department of Health and Human Services found that nursing homes reported only 16 percent of incidents where residents were hospitalized for 'potential abuse and neglect'" (Silver-Greenberg and Gebeloff 2021). Another study concluded that 40 percent of all serious falls in nursing homes were not reported to Medicare between 2011 and 2015. A separate evaluation found that "half of nursing homes underreported potentially deadly pressure ulcers, or bed sores, by at least 50 percent" (Silver-Greenberg and Gebeloff 2021). For the most vulnerable members of society, caregiving and profit-making are a risky combination. The care received may be far less than advertised.[64]

Conclusion

Maps appeal more to the head than the heart. Good maps are useful: they simplify complex phenomena, highlighting certain features while ignoring others; and they help readers navigate unfamiliar terrain. With so many in-depth studies of poverty available, now seems like the right time to create a comprehensive map of the social safety net. In this book, the main sections of the map cover what we say and what we do about material hardship. This map does more than highlight the views of public officials and the workings of government programs. It also calls attention to low-income workers, extended families, charities, taxpayers, and profit-making businesses. In other words, this book combines "top-down" and "bottom-up" perspectives on the social safety net (Michener, SoRelle, and Thurston 2020). The core needs include income and medical care, both mainstays of the welfare state literature. Food, housing, and daily care, which are often overlooked in that literature, receive equal consideration. With so many pieces, this project could easily become a jumbled assortment of random facts. By organizing the pieces around the theme of care, I hope to produce a comprehensive and coherent map.

This final chapter will summarize the main patterns of care in the US social safety net. To recap, the four stages identified by Tronto (1993, 2013) are caring about, taking care of, caregiving, and care-receiving. *Caring about* refers to how much attention we pay to a general group or problem. When we care deeply about something, we are more inclined to take action. *Taking care of* denotes responsibility. Which parts of society should address problems related to poverty? Who pays for whatever care is given? The third stage, *caregiving*, features the individuals and organizations that provide essential goods and services. They could be preparing subsidized lunches at a public school or volunteering at a food pantry. They could be family members watching over disabled relatives for free, or for-profit nursing homes performing similar tasks. Finally, *care-receiving* helps us recognize how well different needs are being met. After all the care is given, how many people are still poor? Who is still homeless or medically uninsured?

Who Cares. Christopher Howard, Oxford University Press. © Oxford University Press 2023.
DOI: 10.1093/oso/9780190074456.003.0011

One advantage of the care approach is that it sheds light on those who support the social safety net as well as those who benefit from it. In the process, we come to realize that the world is not divided neatly into caregivers and care-receivers (or into "makers" versus "takers"). Many of the working poor are paying taxes at the same time they are relying on SNAP. Someone can be living in subsidized housing and providing unpaid care to relatives. People who spend a lifetime in the middle class might eventually need Medicaid to pay for a home health aide or a bed in a nursing home.

This map is based on evidence from the last two decades. Most of the facts and figures in Part II came from 2014–2019, when the economy was healthier than usual. Rates of poverty, food insecurity, homelessness, and other social ills should have been relatively low. The world changed dramatically in 2020, and it would be strange to ignore Covid-19 completely. The pandemic disrupted everyday life more than anything since World War II. The postscript to this book will explore the initial impact of the pandemic on the social safety net.

What We Say

Based on Part I of the book, it would be easy to conclude that Americans do not care much about poverty-related issues. In any given year, only five percent of adults have named poverty, hunger, homelessness, or welfare as the country's most important problem (Chapter 1). The failure of the AFL-CIO (Chapter 2) and the Democratic Party (Chapter 4) to mention these issues at their national conventions is striking. Those organizations have long claimed to advocate for the downtrodden and the marginalized. If labor leaders and Democratic officials are largely silent, then we can hardly expect business leaders and Republicans to care much, either.

My reading of the evidence is a bit different. It appears that Americans have two vocabularies, one based on work and the other on need. The world of business and labor organizations is dominated by employers and workers, paychecks and profits. Leaders of these organizations often disagree about how to generate good-paying jobs, but they agree that steady employment will remedy many of life's problems. They are so sure of this path they have trouble uttering the phrase, "working poor." Elected officials from both parties speak the same language. They care about workers and working families. They look for ways to take care of workers and working families. People with low incomes are seen primarily when they are part of some larger group of workers. They are not recognized as the working poor. The two parties are certainly not identical. Democrats have declared that anyone who works full time should not be poor, and Republicans have not. Republicans have been more interested in attaching work requirements to public assistance programs.

Charities talk about needs all the time (Chapter 3). Granted, some of these needs are unrelated to the social safety net: churches care deeply about spiritual needs, and many secular charities are devoted to environmental, educational, or artistic needs. Nevertheless, all the major faiths in the United States are attentive to people who are poor, hungry, sick, or otherwise afflicted. The dominant religion is Christianity, and the Bible contains many passages urging the faithful to care about and take care of the neediest members of society. Contemporary churches continue to espouse these principles. They do not consider people to be worthy or unworthy of care based on employment. Major charities such as the United Way and The Salvation Army believe that needy individuals can be found everywhere, not just among the poor. Their mission is to meet those needs as best they can. No one has to show a paycheck in order to receive groceries from Feeding America or medical care from St. Jude's Hospital.

These are broad generalizations, and some organizations speak the languages of work and need. Many employers disagree with Milton Friedman about the value of corporate charity, and they try to be attentive to unmet needs in their communities. The Service Employees International Union (SEIU) frequently mentions poverty and need among low-income workers. Habitat for Humanity requires beneficiaries to have below-average incomes and to donate their labor during the construction or renovation of their homes. Beneficiaries will also need a steady job to handle the mortgage payments.

Nowhere are the precepts of work and need combined more thoroughly than in public opinion (Chapter 1). On the one hand, Americans consistently mention jobs or the economy as higher priorities than anything related to poverty. The public favors work requirements for adult welfare recipients. On the other hand, most Americans believe that government should take care of people who cannot take care of themselves. Most believe that government should guarantee everyone enough food to eat and a roof over their heads. In short, government should respond to certain needs. The dual emphasis on work and need can make public opinion hard to interpret. The combination is understandable, given that Americans spend their daily lives connected to some realms that emphasize work and others that emphasize need.

One point easily overlooked is how Americans quantify need. The general public believes that the US poverty rate is three times larger than the numbers reported by the US Census Bureau. When people say that poverty should be a top priority for public officials, they want government to help over 100 million of their fellow Americans. The public's estimates are not outrageously high. The United Way has developed a series of "bare bones" household budgets that it claims are more realistic than the government's poverty thresholds. According to their calculations, 40 percent of Americans cannot afford basic expenses. That figure is right in line with the public's views.

So far it appears that churches, secular charities, and some members of the general public care deeply about poverty-related issues. I do not want to exaggerate the level of concern. Churches are dealing with all kinds of issues such as racial justice, same-sex marriage, and climate change. Many denominations are worried about declining membership—they have only so much time for poverty, hunger, and homelessness. Some major charities (e.g., United Way, St. Jude's Hospital) try to meet needs regardless of recipients' income. The poor and near poor are not their only clients. For their part, ordinary Americans say that many issues should be a top priority for the president and Congress. It is hard for poverty to stand out in such a crowded field. Moreover, poll data indicate that some people care about the needy as long as the costs of doing so are minimal. In short, *caring about* is relative, and we should make comparisons across issues or groups before reaching a final judgment.

Taking care of the poor and needy means, at a minimum, assigning responsibility for whatever care is given. Americans believe that responsibility ought to be shared. Few people think that responsibility should be borne only by individuals or only by government. Exactly how to share that responsibility is contested. Labor leaders and Democratic officials favor a combination of workers, strong unions, and activist government. Groups representing small business (e.g., the NFIB) are usually more reluctant to involve government than groups representing big business (e.g., the Business Roundtable). Republican officials are not keen on unions and want to scale back government's role without eliminating it. They generally expect more from individuals and charities. Leaders from the voluntary sector have made it very clear that churches and charities lack the resources to eradicate poverty and need. They see themselves working alongside government, and sometimes directly with government. They understand the importance of the public safety net and regularly oppose cuts to public assistance programs.

Figuring out how ordinary Americans allocate responsibility is tricky. Opinion polls usually frame the choice as individual versus government responsibility. Most Americans put themselves somewhere between these two poles, with the exact position depending on the question. Americans consider government's responsibility for the elderly to be greater than for working-age adults, and greater for food or housing than for jobs or income. However, when given a wider range of options, a sizable number of Americans expect family members, churches, or charities to take the lead in fighting poverty. Government is the public's top choice, but a majority are counting on other parts of society to step up.

Whether the general public wants government to have more responsibility also varies. Americans are more likely to favor greater government spending on poor people than on welfare recipients. These views are part of a larger pattern in which attitudes toward poverty are more favorable than attitudes toward welfare. In the past, scholars have argued that racial stereotypes help explain this pattern, with many Whites viewing Blacks as lazy and therefore too willing to accept welfare over work (Gilens 1999). Some evidence from Chapter 1 indicates that stereotypes about Blacks and welfare have weakened a bit without disappearing.

Americans are seldom of one mind concerning the proper role of government. Compared to Whites, a larger share of Blacks and Hispanics feel that helping the poor and needy should be a top priority for the US government. Women express more support for government involvement than men do. The partisan gaps are even wider. Self-identified Republicans are much less likely than self-identified Democrats to say that fighting poverty should be a top priority for government. Republicans are also much less likely to say that government should take the lead in fighting poverty. Many Republicans believe that "we" are spending too little to assist the poor, but they do not support greater government spending. Logically, Republicans must feel that families, churches, and charities ought to spend more.

What We Do

Taking care of someone can also mean helping to pay for their care. When parents take care of college tuition for their children, that is a significant act. When donors give money to the American Red Cross, they are helping take care of strangers who need medical attention or disaster relief. One of the distinctive features of this book is showing who finances the social safety net as well as who benefits from it.

If I have done justice to this topic, then readers should understand how hard low-income people try to take care of themselves and their families. They accept part-time jobs when full-time work is unavailable. They cope with unpredictable work schedules. Most of their jobs do not come with health and retirement benefits, or their employers contribute so little that low-income workers cannot afford those benefits. Few of their employers offer paid family and medical leave. Housing, long-term care, and child care are expensive for members of the middle classes; the poor and near poor have great difficulty paying market prices for these goods and services. They might ask family members to help take care of these needs for little or no pay. The family safety net has its limits, and millions of Americans must look elsewhere for assistance.

Government has the resources to take care of many of them. The public safety net relies on a variety of social insurance and public assistance programs, as well as some tax expenditures and social regulations. For now, we can set aside social regulations (e.g., minimum wage laws, Family and Medical Leave Act), which do not require financial support from government. Social insurance programs like Social Security and Unemployment Insurance are financed with payroll taxes. Almost all employers and employees pay these taxes. However, the effective tax rate tends to be higher for low-income workers. If they want to benefit from social insurance, they will have to work for it and pay for it.

Public assistance programs and tax expenditures are financed much differently. They rely heavily on federal income taxes, which are paid primarily by affluent Americans (Joint Committee on Taxation 2019). Because of the Earned Income Tax Credit, many of the working poor will not owe any income taxes, and millions of them will receive a tax refund. Some public assistance programs, notably Medicaid, are financed partly by state governments, and their tax systems are not as progressive. On balance, though, public assistance programs and the EITC are highly redistributive. Individuals earning more than $200,000 a year are taking care of those earning less than $30,000. Unlike social insurance programs, which in this country largely provide income support and medical care, public assistance programs can be found throughout the social safety net. Part II of this book features at least one public assistance program in every chapter. Basically, we are counting on rich people to help reduce many types of hardship.

The social safety net extends beyond the public safety net. Charities are important in some parts of the social safety net, especially food and medical care. Charities rely on private donors for most of their funding.[1] Out of the $428 billion given to charity in 2018, roughly two-thirds came from individuals. The rest was donated by foundations, death bequests, and corporations. Before the pandemic, a little more than half of US households were donating to charity, and that share has been declining since 2000. Typically, charitable gifts follow a U-shaped pattern in which poor and rich Americans donate larger shares of their incomes than do members of the middle class (Giving USA 2019; Indiana University Lilly Family School of Philanthropy 2019; Reich 2018). In terms of dollars, the rich play an outsized role. Ninety percent of households with incomes over $200,000 (or a net worth over $1 million) made charitable donations in 2017, well above the national average. Among donors, the typical affluent household gave approximately $30,000, compared to $2,500 from the general population. One recent study estimated that households in the top one percent of income were responsible for one-third of all charitable giving.[2] The US government offers a tax deduction for charitable giving, one that was worth $44 billion in 2019. Taxpayers with at least $200,000 in income receive the lion's share, partly because they make large donations and partly because they pay most of the taxes (Joint Committee on Taxation 2019). Rich people in America are a crucial source of charitable donations for the same reason as tax revenues—they have an enormous amount of income and wealth.

Most charitable donations do not benefit people with low incomes. Those monies flow in many directions such as helping universities build athletic facilities and academic buildings, supporting art museums and symphonies, and trying to protect endangered species. Some charities focus on poverty-related needs in developing countries. Religious organizations are the largest recipients of charity in the United States, yet most of that money pays for clergy salaries and other operating costs (e.g., utilities, building maintenance). Roughly five percent of their donations go to the social safety net, supporting food pantries and the like. Churches might have a bigger impact on the supply of volunteer caregivers than on the amount of money used to take care of the needy (Giving USA 2019; Reich 2018; Wuthnow 2004).

Although precise numbers are lacking, a reasonable estimate is that less than half and probably closer to one-third of all charitable donations help finance the US social safety net (Matthews 2013; Reich 2018).[3] Lately, that works out to $150–$200 billion each year. Medicaid alone exceeds that amount. When we add in the other public assistance programs discussed in Part II, as well as the relevant parts of social insurance programs, annual spending by government easily surpasses $1 trillion. Without question, government funds the social safety net much more than organized charities do.

Besides donating money to charities, individuals volunteer in their communities. They donate their time and skills, and thus help take care of other people. It is very hard to know how many of these volunteers are active in the social safety net, and who they are. An estimated 77 million Americans volunteered through a formal organization in 2018, contributing almost seven billion hours of their time. Much of their effort, however, was devoted to matters like education, youth sports, and the arts. Many people volunteered at church, serving as ushers or lay readers. None of those actions are relevant here. Approximately one-third of volunteers were involved in the collection, preparation, and distribution of food, and many of them probably worked in food pantries or soup kitchens. But not all. Some may have prepared food for church functions or their kids' classrooms. Similarly, we do not know how many Americans volunteered at free and charitable clinics. As a (very) rough estimate, perhaps 30 million volunteers were involved with the social safety net, donating a bit less than three billion hours. Depending on how we value that time, those volunteers could have given the equivalent of $50 billion to the social safety net. That is a small fraction of what government spends.[4]

Those who take care of others in the social safety net may or may not be the caregivers. With income support, government usually performs both functions, raising tax revenues and issuing benefit checks. That is how Social Security,

Disability Insurance, Unemployment Insurance, SSI, and the EITC operate.[5] Medical professionals who donate their services to free and charitable clinics are, in effect, taking care of medical needs and giving care. In the realm of daily care, many family members agree to work for free, tending to the needs of their young or disabled relatives. Otherwise, someone would have to pay for that care.

Apart from income support, government usually pays other organizations to be the caregivers.[6] SNAP cards are used to buy food in regular grocery stores. Vouchers help pay the rent in privately owned apartments. Medicaid and Medicare reimburse a huge number of hospitals, doctors' offices, diagnostic labs, nursing homes, and home health care agencies. Thousands of child-care centers receive federal funding but are not run by government. The public-private partnerships are everywhere. You'd have to be living in a really small town if no stores accepted SNAP, and no medical professionals dealt with Medicaid or Medicare.

Most of these organizations are run for profit. We may not think of care-giving as a business, but in many parts of the social safety net, it is. The obvious examples are medical care and long-term care. Medicaid and Medicare pay private companies hundreds of billions of dollars every year to care for low-income patients. These companies employ millions of workers, from personal care aides to surgeons. Their economic impact in many parts of the country is huge. Some of these companies are quite profitable. Many hospitals and nursing homes rely heavily on government for their revenue; some would go out of business without government support. This is an important difference between income support and medical care, which are the two largest sections of the social safety net: income support is largely handled by government, whereas medical care relies on a complex mix of public, for-profit, and nonprofit organizations.

Corporate caregiving raises all kinds of questions that are beyond the scope of this book. Is the profit motive more likely to promote better care, or just cost-cutting? The experience of nursing homes is not encouraging. (Then again, maybe Medicaid's low reimbursement rates would keep anyone from providing decent care.) Could companies offer political support for safety net programs, helping to block cuts and perhaps even promote expansion? Given the weakness of interest groups advocating for the poor, and the reluctance of both parties to fight poverty, a few corporate allies could be important. From a more historical perspective, we might wonder if government jobs programs truly ended in the New Deal or were replaced by a vast network of government contracts with businesses and nonprofits.

Caregiving by charities also varies from one part of the social safety net to the next. Few religious or secular charities hand out cash, and when they do, the amounts are usually small. Some churches operate temporary homeless shelters during the winter months. Otherwise, they do not provide much in the way of low-income housing. Some churches operate child-care centers on site. Charities are much more prominent in food and medical care. Food banks, food pantries, and soup kitchens play important roles in the social safety net. Nevertheless, they do not come close to providing as many meals as SNAP pays for. Companies donate food, and individuals volunteer their time in order to keep these organizations up and running. Every month, millions of Americans are able to eat a few more meals thanks to charity. On a smaller scale, free and charitable clinics provide medical care to Americans who do not have private insurance, are unable to get Medicaid, or who live too far away from providers that accept Medicaid patients. In essence, food and medical charities help care for people who have fallen through holes in the public safety net.

The number of caregivers involved with the social safety net is remarkable. Millions of Americans are paid caregivers, and millions more are unpaid. Caregivers are a diverse group. They range from highly trained professionals to untrained family members. Many volunteer caregivers are mobilized by religious organizations; many are not. Some people are caregivers full time, some part-time. They might have face-to-face contact with care recipients, or they might not.[7]

Many people see themselves as caregivers, such as nurses and child-care workers. Other people have more ambiguous roles. Consider the manager of a grocery store that participates in the SNAP program. He will get regular reports about SNAP purchases at the store, but that does not necessarily mean he has a caring disposition or identifies as a food caregiver. Though the store's cashiers have more face-to-face contact with SNAP recipients, they probably do not know who those recipients are, now that debit cards have replaced paper stamps. Or think about the computer experts who make sure that Social Security checks are electronically deposited in recipients' bank accounts every month. Those government workers will never meet the recipients, and recipients will probably never know the names of the people who transferred income to their accounts.

Previous studies of caregiving have focused heavily on daily care. The caregivers are easy to identify because they have regular, direct contact with care recipients. The caregivers are usually women. Mothers provide unpaid care for their young children, and adult daughters do the same for their aged parents. A large majority of nurses, home health aides, and child-care workers are women. They are disproportionately women of color, and their jobs do not pay well. These patterns are still evident (Chapter 9).

In other parts of the social safety net, identifying the relevant caregivers becomes more complicated. Now we are dealing with large bureaucracies. We run into all sorts of public–private partnerships where caregivers and care recipients may not encounter or recognize each other. Sometimes care is given electronically and sometimes in person. It is not obvious who qualifies as a caregiver and who does not. Many of them could be men. Future studies may need to distinguish between direct and indirect caregivers, or argue that only those who have regular, direct contact with recipients should count as caregivers. In the meantime, I will refrain from making any additional statements about gender and caregiving in the social safety net. When concepts are fuzzy and crucial data are missing, such caution is appropriate.[8]

As we finish our tour of the social safety net, we encounter something of a paradox. Thanks to taxpayers and charitable donors, the United States generates hundreds of billions of dollars every year to take care of people living in or near poverty. Millions of Americans are employed as caregivers, working for government agencies, nonprofits, or the private sector. Millions more function as unpaid caregivers for family members or close friends. These sound exactly like the components required for an effective social safety net. And yet, when we look closely at care-receiving, we realize how many people are still struggling to meet their basic needs.

Each chapter in Part II ends with numerical measures of the adequacy of care, along with some discussion of the limitations of those measures. Without question, the social safety net is riddled with holes. More than 40 million Americans were living below the poverty line in 2018—one out of every eight people. Almost 50 million Americans were living in near poverty that year, meaning their incomes were between 100 and 150 percent of the poverty threshold.[9] Over one-quarter of the US population was poor or near poor that year, even though unemployment and inflation were quite low. Without government programs, particularly Social Security and the EITC, income poverty would have been much higher (Fox 2019). Even so, 90 million Americans were living in or near poverty when the economy was supposed to be in good shape (Chapter 5).

Poverty rates are not the only indicator of distress. In 2018, 14 million households were food insecure. Despite the means-tested SNAP program and thousands of charitable food pantries, many of the food insecure had low incomes. A separate group earned too much to qualify for SNAP and was also food insecure (Chapter 6). In other words, income poverty is not perfectly correlated with other types of need. Although a tiny fraction of Americans are homeless at any given time, millions are coping with high housing costs. In 2017, almost eight million low-income households were severely cost burdened, meaning they spent at least half their income on housing. These individuals have major problems paying their other bills. People who spend 30 to 50 percent of their income on housing often have similar problems. Low-income people across the country worry about falling behind on their rent and being evicted. Government assistance is limited, with long waiting lists for public housing units and rental vouchers. Without the family safety net, the number of Americans who are severely cost burdened would be larger (Chapter 7).

We are particularly vulnerable when sick, disabled, or very young. The Affordable Care Act (ACA) was a policy milestone, extending health insurance coverage to millions of Americans. Nevertheless, 30 million people were uninsured as of 2019. Roughly half of them were poor or near poor, and the failure of many states to expand Medicaid was a big reason why. Without health insurance, many Americans do not get the medical care they need. Even with insurance, some people with low incomes will not get medical tests or treatments because they cannot afford the co-payments and deductibles (Chapter 8).

Unfortunately, we lack good measures of the adequacy of daily care, partly because states differ in how they handle cases of neglect and abuse, and partly because so much care is provided by family members, out of public view. Officially, one percent of all children were neglected or abused in 2019, and about one-quarter of those children were in families receiving public assistance. We have good reason to believe that most cases of neglect are unreported, both in domestic and institutional settings. Although government does little to pay for child care, Medicaid is the single most important payer for long-term care, public or private. Those who are disabled and need long-term care are more likely to be helped by government if they are also poor. If appropriate care is not available in their area, or providers hesitate to accept Medicaid clients, then people with disabilities will have to rely on relatives for their daily care (Chapter 9).

Patterns of Care

According to many observers, work separates the deserving poor from the undeserving poor. This distinction definitely holds true with respect to income support. All social insurance programs link eligibility to employment, and most of them link benefits to wages.[10] Social Security, a broadly inclusive program, is vital to millions of low-income retirees and is a crucial part of the social safety net. By the same token, only wage earners and their families can benefit from the Earned Income Tax Credit. The main justification for minimum wage laws is to boost the incomes of the working poor. Since the 1990s, individuals who want cash welfare (i.e., TANF) have faced greater work requirements. About the only exception to this pattern is SSI, which transfers income to low-income people who are severely disabled, blind, or elderly, and therefore are not expected to work. As mentioned above, charities care for people based on need, not work, but few charities hand out cash.

Once we explore other parts of the social safety net, we find that millions of Americans are receiving care without having to work for it. The United States has no social insurance programs for food or housing. Most people who benefit from SNAP, WIC, and subsidized housing are not subject to work requirements.[11]

Medicaid is the most important source of health insurance and long-term care, and it does not have work requirements, either. Individuals who receive food or medical care from charities do not have to be employed. It would be incorrect to say that income support is always based on work, and every other form of care is always based on need. Some of the working poor have health insurance from their employers, and most will benefit from Medicare when they turn 65. But paid work is far more important in the realm of income support than it is for food, housing, medical care, or daily care.

These differences suggest a certain level of distrust. When we know exactly which needs are being met, we do not expect people who are poor or near poor to work for their benefits. When we offer income support, which recipients could spend as they choose, then we do expect work.

Another possibility is that demographic characteristics—notably race, ethnicity, and gender—determine who receives more care. In the social safety net, Blacks and Hispanics consistently fare worse than Whites. Poverty rates are twice as high among Blacks and Hispanics. In 2018, almost half (45%) of all Hispanics in this country were poor or near poor. The numbers were similar for Blacks (42%), but much lower for Whites (19%). Blacks and Hispanics are also more likely to live in deep poverty. Racial minorities are disproportionately likely to be food insecure, homeless, and severely burdened by housing costs. Hispanics were three times more likely than Whites to be medically uninsured in 2019.[12] Because non-Hispanic Whites are 60 percent of the population, it will not be surprising to learn that most people in poverty are White. Millions and millions of Whites are struggling in the United States. The chances of experiencing hardship, however, are significantly greater for Blacks and Hispanics.[13]

This is an old story. Poverty rates for Blacks and Hispanics have been two to three times higher than Whites since at least the 1970s. Large gaps have persisted whether the economy was strong or weak, and regardless of which party was in the White House (Creamer 2020). Before the Affordable Care Act, Hispanics were almost three times more likely than Whites to be uninsured (DeNavas-Walt, Proctor, and Smith 2010). While more Whites, Hispanics, and Blacks have gained health insurance coverage since then, sizable inequalities remain.

Gender gaps in the social safety net cut both ways. Women are slightly more likely than men to live in poverty and deep poverty. The same pattern holds for food insecurity.[14] Girls are slightly more likely than boys to be neglected or abused. On the other hand, men are much more likely than women to be homeless. Men are less likely to have health insurance, partly because Medicaid expansion has been blocked in some states (many low-income women were already on Medicaid before the ACA).[15] Men are also less likely to receive long-term care, most of which is funded by Medicaid. Women represent two-thirds of nursing home residents and over 60 percent of home health care recipients. These gaps are due in part to shorter life expectancies for men and to greater rates of disability among women.[16] Overall, being Black or Hispanic is a bigger disadvantage than being female among low-income Americans. I am not saying that gender inequalities are trivial or should be ignored. But racial and ethnic inequalities are consistently larger.

At several points in Part II, it became evident that geography affects caregiving and care-receiving. In 2018, a poor family with one parent and two children could get no more than $300 a month from TANF in a dozen states. A similar number of states set the maximum cash benefit somewhere above $600 (Falk and Landers 2019). As we saw in Chapter 8, affordable housing is not equally available around the country. The poor and near poor are more likely to double up with relatives in some states compared to others. Rates of child abuse and neglect range from 0.2% in Pennsylvania to 2.0% in Kentucky (US Department of Health & Human Services 2021). Weir and Schirmer (2018) found regional variations in how nonprofits work with local governments and businesses when assisting the poor. Outcomes can vary within states, too. Depending on where you live in South Dakota, the rate of food insecurity could be less than 10 percent or more than 25 percent.[17]

Sometimes the patterns seem obvious. Conservative/Republican states have been less likely to expand Medicaid, and those states usually have higher rates of uninsured residents. Liberal/Democratic states have been more likely to introduce paid family or medical leave programs. States with lower per capita incomes (e.g., Mississippi, New Mexico) often have more food insecurity, while wealthier states (e.g., Massachusetts, New Jersey) have less.[18] But affluence is no guarantee of adequate care. New York is one of the richer states in the country; it also has one of the highest rates of homelessness.[19] Nor is political ideology always a reliable indicator. Unemployment benefits in 2019 replaced a smaller share of wages in liberal California than in conservative Idaho.[20] Apart from ideology and affluence, racial and ethnic variables may be closely associated with state-level variations in social policy (Hero 1998; Johnson 2003; Soss, Fording, and Schram 2011). While all these differences might be a boon to academic researchers, they raise fundamental questions about equity and fairness.

With so many variations from place to place, and from one need to another (income, food, etc.), "the" social safety net might not exist. It would be reassuring to imagine that certain principles or organizations are uniting these discrete strands into a single net. Given the evidence, one could just as reasonably view the status quo as a series of improvised remedies, or as a building with multiple architects employed by different firms. With so many needs unmet, it seems highly misleading to refer to any part as a "safety net." That phrase implies a level of care that is not being delivered. Millions of Americans still lead precarious

lives. Our collective efforts have lessened human misery, but so much work remains to be done.

Words versus Deeds

Chapter 1 raised the possibility of cheap talk. Individuals (and organizations)
could say they care about the poor and the needy without really meaning it. One
way to detect cheap talk is by comparing rhetoric with behavior. It turns out that
actions go way beyond words in parts of the social safety net, which is the opposite of what we might expect.

First, public officials take care of low-income Americans much more than
their rhetoric would suggest. Over the last two decades, statements about poverty, hunger, and homelessness have largely been absent from party platforms.
Presidents have seldom mentioned poverty-related topics in their State of the
Union addresses (Chapter 4). Nevertheless, every year, the budget for public
assistance programs has been substantial. The national government spent over
$900 billion on programs targeted at low-income people in fiscal year 2018.
If we subtract monies spent on education, employment and training, and energy assistance, the total was closer to $850 billion (Lynch et al. 2020). That
sum represented 20 percent of all federal outlays.[21] If we include the relevant
portions of Social Security, Medicare, Disability Insurance, and Unemployment
Insurance, then federal spending on the poor and near poor easily exceeded $1
trillion, which was approximately 25 percent of the budget. Public officials never
come close to spending 25 percent of their time talking about poverty-related
issues.

By way of analogy, let me suggest one reason for the huge gap between words
and deeds. My wife and I pay our mortgage bill every month. It is one of our biggest
expenses, yet rarely do we talk about the importance of being homeowners. That
question was settled years ago when we agreed to buy a house. Public officials
might be in a similar position. At different points in the past, they decided to
fund social programs that benefit low-income Americans. (In most cases, the initial impetus came from Democrats.) Many of those programs were designated
as budgetary entitlements, also known as mandatory spending. They do not require annual appropriations and can grow more or less automatically. Currently,
80 percent of federal spending that is targeted at low-income people is classified
as mandatory spending (Lynch et al. 2020). Some of the largest public assistance programs—Medicaid, SNAP, SSI—are budgetary entitlements.[22] All tax
expenditures, including the EITC and Child Tax Credit, are entitlements. Social
insurance programs like Social Security and Medicare, which help the poor and
non-poor, are also entitlements. Seldom do public officials debate fundamental

changes to entitlement programs. If government's role feels settled, then we might not hear many references to poverty-related issues in official statements.

A related point is that rich people take care of low-income Americans more than we might expect. We saw in Chapter 1 that income is associated with policy priorities: affluent people are less likely to call poverty a top priority for the president and Congress. The affluent are also less likely to favor increased federal spending on the poor.[23] And yet these same people provide most of the money used to finance public assistance programs. Charities usually try to make donors care about certain issues in order to inspire donations. Government does not have to appeal to anyone's emotions. With taxation, government can compel the rich to take care of people with low incomes. It would be nice if the rich cared about poverty-related issues, but it is not essential.

My attention to taxes is not intended to generate sympathy for the rich. Their incomes have been growing faster than everyone else's. In 1980, the top 20 percent of US households had 46 percent of the country's pre-tax income. By 2017, that group had 55 percent. The richest one percent of households almost doubled their share of pre-tax income during this period (from 9.0 to 16.7%). The federal tax code gives the affluent sizable deductions for their charitable contributions and many other ways to lower their taxes. Their share of after-tax income has been growing just as fast as their share of pre-tax income.[24] Republican tax cuts enacted in 2017 are reinforcing these trends.[25] In essence, the government is allowing the rich to get richer as long as they help finance the public safety net (and the military). Whether this qualifies as a good trade-off is an open question.

Comparing words and deeds for business is complicated. As noted in Chapter 2, peak associations do not pay much attention to poverty-related issues. They usually want government to boost the economy by lowering taxes, cutting regulations, slowing down the growth of entitlements, and promoting international trade. Among specific industries or companies, we found greater attention to Medicaid expansion and the minimum wage.

Businesses do relatively little to take care of people in the social safety net. Wages and salaries do not count; those are payments for services rendered. Corporations donated a total of $20 billion to charities in 2018. Many of those donations were directed to education, the arts, and the environment. Only one-quarter of corporate gifts went to health and social services, and we don't know what portion of that ended up in the social safety net (Giving USA 2019).[26] Corporate income taxes are not a major source of revenue for public programs, either. In 2019, companies paid $230 billion in federal income taxes, whereas individual income taxes amounted to $1.7 trillion.[27] Payroll taxes for social insurance programs raise much more revenue than corporate income taxes. Although employers appear to pay half or more of these taxes, economists believe that workers ultimately bear most of the burden. Employers have certain monies available for compensation, and more money spent on payroll taxes means less money for wages, salaries, and benefits.

There is a rough equivalence between how much businesses care about poverty-related issues and how much they take care of people in the social safety net (i.e., not much). The picture changes dramatically when we shift to caregiving. The US social safety net relies heavily on for-profit companies as caregivers. In medical care, daily care, food, and housing, corporate caregivers deal with a larger number of needy individuals than government agencies or nonprofits do. These companies depend—sometimes a little, sometimes a lot— on government funding. It is in their economic self-interest to be part of the social safety net.

Collective endeavors rely on a variety of incentives and commands, aka "carrots and sticks." The social safety net is no exception. Government requires the rich to take care of the poor, via income taxes, and it requires almost all employers and employees to finance social insurance programs. Most companies must abide by minimum wage laws. Those are some of the sticks. The government offers tax deductions for individuals and corporations that donate to charity; even bigger tax breaks to companies that provide retirement pensions and health insurance to their workers; and government pays many companies to provide care to the poor and needy. Those are the carrots. Charities may rely on the kindness of strangers, but national and state governments definitely do not. A social safety net based heavily on altruism and compassion would be much smaller than what we have today.

Noting that our actions surpass our rhetoric isn't necessarily a compliment. Imagine someone who never talks about charity but puts one dollar in a Salvation Army kettle every December. Would we be impressed? Unless that person was dirt poor, probably not. The US social safety net, in its present form, does not require elected officials, labor unions, businesses, or the general public to care much about material hardships. While the social safety net helps millions of Americans, the care received is often inadequate. If we want the social safety net to perform better, then we have to declare, publicly and repeatedly, how important it is to reduce human misery. We have to talk about problems like poverty and food insecurity more often. Of course, rhetoric alone will not make housing more affordable or health insurance more available; it will not be enough to move people out of deep poverty. But it is hard to imagine how benign neglect can lead to meaningful improvements.

Postscript: The Social Safety Net and the Pandemic

The Covid-19 pandemic disrupted lives all over the world. In the United States, hospitals and nursing homes were quickly overwhelmed. State governments issued stay-at-home orders, and social distancing became the norm. Students and teachers were forced to adapt to virtual learning. Religious services moved online. Sporting events and concerts were canceled. Many businesses closed temporarily, then permanently. Millions of workers were laid off; many others had their hours reduced. The unemployment rate in 2019 hovered below four percent; by April 2020, it was close to 15 percent.[1] Approximately 385,000 Americans died from Covid in 2020.[2] Average life expectancy declined by 1.5 years, the largest single-year drop since World War II (Arias et al. 2021).

After a historic effort, vaccines became available to the public during the first months of 2021. Nevertheless, millions of Americans refused to be vaccinated. The pandemic had become highly politicized, a battleground for those who distrusted medical experts, government, or Democrats (Ivory, Leatherby, and Gebeloff 2021; Sparks, Kirzinger, and Brodie 2021). Almost 450,000 Americans had Covid listed as their cause of death in 2021.[3] Overwhelmingly, those who were hospitalized with Covid or died from it had not been vaccinated. Daily life was increasingly different in vaccinated versus unvaccinated parts of the country (Mandavilli and Mueller 2021; Yan and Holcombe 2021).

It is too soon to identify all the ways Covid-19 affected the social safety net. What follows are some initial observations, based on the care framework employed in this book. There are elements of continuity and change, and I cannot predict which of these will endure after the pandemic has ended. In many ways, Covid-19 exposed middle-class Americans to problems that the poor and near poor have been dealing with for years. The pandemic might prompt a serious overhaul of the social safety net. It could just as easily be dismissed as a freak occurrence, akin to a natural disaster.

Who Cares. Christopher Howard, Oxford University Press. © Oxford University Press 2023.
DOI: 10.1093/oso/9780190074456.003.0012

Thus far, the general public does not appear to care about poverty-related needs any more or less than they did before the pandemic. In the election month of November 2020, one percent of Americans named poverty, hunger, or homelessness as the most important problem facing the country, and one percent cited "lack of money." A year later three percent of Americans named poverty, hunger, or homelessness as the most important problem facing the country, two percent cited lack of money, and less than one percent said welfare. Those numbers are right in line with what we saw in Chapter 1. (The top priorities in 2020 and 2021 were usually the coronavirus and the government/poor leadership.) Asked in January 2021 about policy priorities for President Biden and Congress, 53 percent of Americans agreed that the problems of poor people should be a top priority, and 39 percent said those problems were important but not a top priority. That may seem like a small drop from 2019, but Pew changed the question wording. Instead of asking about the poor and needy, the 2021 poll only mentioned poor people.[4]

Americans are still divided about the proper role of government. When asked whether the federal government has a responsibility to provide an adequate standard of living for everyone, three-quarters of Democrats, Blacks, and low-income respondents agreed in April 2021. By contrast, less than half of Whites and upper-income respondents—and just one-third of Republicans—shared this view. Similar questions about government's responsibility for retirement income and health insurance produced similar gaps (Pew Research Center 2021).

Business interests developed a new appreciation for the public sector. Before the pandemic, the National Federation of Independent Business (NFIB) declared that government should stay out of the way so entrepreneurs could grow the economy (Chapter 2). The NFIB then spent much of 2020 lobbying government officials for hundreds of billions of dollars in small business loans. It also supported generous loan forgiveness policies. In December of that year, the organization proudly announced that "at every stage of this crisis, NFIB has fought tirelessly to secure the relief and resources that America's small businesses deserve. . . . NFIB's around-the-clock legislative outreach, lobbying, and public relations campaigns helped secure financial lifelines for millions of small businesses."[5] A staunch defender of free markets was now describing government assistance as essential and justified.

The NFIB did not change its tune completely. The organization rarely referred to poverty, poor people, hunger, or homelessness during the pandemic. Instead, it talked about helping employers and workers be part of the country's economic recovery. The unemployed were someone else's problem: the NFIB opposed higher unemployment insurance taxes on employers as a means of paying for the spike in benefits. About the only time the organization mentioned poverty was in connection with minimum wage laws, claiming that a substantial increase would not help the poor. Basically, the NFIB leadership was happy to receive government's carrots but resisted the sticks.[6]

The Business Roundtable issued a statement in 2019 urging corporations to care more about their workers and local communities. Shareholders shouldn't be the only stakeholders who matter. Critics at the time wondered whether this was merely a symbolic gesture (Chapter 2). The pandemic made these critics look prescient. Many of the CEOs who signed on to that document furloughed workers in 2020 while continuing to pay dividends to shareholders and large salaries to senior executives. Unemployment jumped, and yet many of the country's largest companies managed to turn a profit. Indeed, lower labor costs helped them make money. The stock market had a terrific year in 2020, with the S&P 500 up 16 percent and the Nasdaq Composite index up by more than 40 percent (Goodman 2020; MacMillan, Whoriskey, and O'Connell 2020; Shaban and Long 2020). The stock market experienced another bullish year in 2021, fueled by huge corporate profits (Jackson and Schmidt 2022; Telford and Siegel 2021).

During the pandemic, the AFL-CIO continued to focus on workers. It portrayed Covid-19 as a threat to the health of essential, frontline workers, and to the finances of those who were now unemployed. Labor leaders called on the national government to take better care of workers and criticized the Trump administration for paying too much attention to corporate executives and shareholders.[7] For their part, religious organizations continued to talk about low-income people, regardless of employment. They supported a higher minimum wage as well as more money for food and housing assistance programs.[8] They reminded officials that charity alone could not take care of the poor and needy. According to the ecumenical Circle of Protection (May 2021), "our churches are on the frontlines of hardship, providing food, shelter, and health services, but we cannot meet the need without robust partnership from the federal government."[9]

Both political parties held socially distant conventions in the summer of 2020. Republicans made history by failing to adopt a new platform. Instead, GOP officials reiterated their support for the 2016 platform and cut short any attempts to question Trump's record as president. Trump lost his re-election bid, which means that Republicans have not offered a new party platform or State of the Union address since the pandemic started. Democrats have, and their rhetoric has changed in certain ways.

The 2020 Democratic platform included more references to poverty, poor people, and low-income people than any platform from 2000 to 2016 (by either major party). It also mentioned the homeless more often than any recent platform. In 2012 and 2016, Democrats had stated that ending poverty should be a national priority, and they repeated that pledge in 2020. They also

declared that no American should go hungry, which was part of the 2016 platform, and added similar language regarding homelessness. Democrats continued to embrace Medicaid expansion as a crucial way to reduce the number
of uninsured Americans. They promised to increase spending on food assistance programs. Technically, incoming presidents don't give a State of the
Union address as soon as they are elected, but they usually give an equivalent
speech. President Biden delivered his in late April 2021. While the pandemic
was foremost on his mind, he did mention two poverty-related goals: cutting
the child poverty rate by half; and ensuring that no one who worked full-time
lived in poverty. Those were specific and ambitious goals.[10] In the first half of
2021, Democrats in Congress were talking openly about promoting economic
recovery and fighting poverty at the same time (Snell 2021; Werner 2021). All
in all, Democratic officials seemed to care more about material hardship than
they had in at least two decades.

Of course, political parties do not transform overnight. The 2020 Democratic
platform mentioned workers (in some form) three times more often than
poor people and low-income people. Biden's April speech also referred to
workers more often. According to the 2020 platform, "Democrats believe that
it is a moral and an economic imperative that we support working families."
Democrats still emphasized the importance of strong unions and equal pay for
women. Democrats still supported a big increase in the minimum wage. Neither
the 2020 platform nor Biden's speech made any reference to the "working poor."
In short, Democrats continued paying more attention to people with jobs than
to people with low incomes.

When the pandemic shut down much of the US economy, millions of workers
were laid off, furloughed, or assigned fewer hours. With their incomes reduced,
many Americans soon had trouble paying their bills. Some tried to take care of
themselves by tapping into their own savings or retirement accounts. A national
survey from August 2020 found that almost half of lower-income households
used this strategy (Parker, Minkin, and Bennett 2020). The amounts available were likely small, and many of these people would not have had savings
to fall back on (Chapter 5). Some of those affected by the pandemic relied on
the family safety net and moved back in with relatives, while others resorted to
shared housing with strangers (Dougherty 2021).

Charitable organizations continued to take care of the needy. Total charitable
giving in 2020 was five percent higher than in 2019. Individuals remained the
largest source, and their giving increased by two percent. A surge in foundation gifts helped offset a decline in corporate giving. Civil rights and environmental charities benefitted from a big jump in donations, whereas health-related
charities received less than the year before (Marcos 2021). It is impressive that
donations increased at all in 2020. Nevertheless, charities were still financing

a small piece of the social safety net. The increase in total giving did not come close to matching the escalation of material hardship across the country.

The big story was how much more the national government did to take care of those affected by the pandemic. Washington was already financing a variety of social insurance, public assistance, and tax expenditure programs, and that money continued to flow. Some entitlement programs quickly expanded in response to new needs. When Americans lost their jobs, they often lost their health insurance (Stolberg 2020). Medicaid was there to catch many of them.[11] Enrollment in Medicaid grew by 12 million people between February 2020 and June 2021. Realizing that state governments were facing revenue shortfalls, the national government also increased its share of Medicaid financing. Federal spending on Medicaid increased by 20 percent during the first year of the pandemic (Corallo 2022; Guth, Rudowitz, and Garfield 2021). Likewise, enrollment in SNAP rose from 37 million individuals in February 2020 to 43 million by February 2021. The national government temporarily increased benefit levels at the end of 2020 and again in March 2021. As a result, a low-income family of four could receive an extra $100 per month in food assistance.[12]

More importantly, the national government enacted massive relief packages in March 2020 ($2.0 trillion), December 2020 ($900 billion), and March 2021 ($1.9 trillion), along with a few smaller relief bills. Support in Congress was bipartisan when Trump was president, but much more partisan during Biden's first year in office.[13] Virtually all these efforts were financed through deficit spending, pushing the cost into the future. Historically, such deficits have been paid off with spending cuts, tax increases, or both. The spending cuts could affect everyone from defense contractors to welfare recipients. If more income tax revenue is needed, then corporations and affluent individuals will help fund Covid relief. Some experts believe the burden will be so heavy that additional taxes (e.g., wealth, value-added, pollution) will be needed (Gleckman 2020b; Sachs 2021). For now, it is unclear who will end up paying for these relief packages. What we do know is that charities and state governments could never have taken care of needs on this scale.

The national government played to its historic strength—cutting checks. A large chunk of relief money went to businesses in the form of loans. An unknown portion of those loans helped employers keep low-wage workers on their payrolls during the pandemic.[14] The Biden administration's American Rescue Plan included big increases to the Child Tax Credit and Earned Income Tax Credit, but only for 2021. Many low-income families were able to claim the Child Tax Credit for the first time. Benefits were paid out monthly instead of annually, giving low-income families a steady stream of income support.[15]

Even though the Great Recession (2007–09) had exposed shortcomings in Unemployment Insurance (UI), states did virtually nothing to correct them

(Porter 2021). States' UI programs were quickly overwhelmed by the pandemic, and the national government had to step in. UI was expanded several times between March 2020 and March 2021. The total cost of these changes exceeded $750 billion, which was far greater than in any previous recession. Elected officials made it temporarily easier to qualify for benefits, which helped many low-wage workers; to collect benefits for a longer period of time; and to receive larger benefits. Because many low-wage workers were laid off during the pandemic (Iacurci 2020; Parker, Minkin, and Bennett 2020), Unemployment Insurance became a much larger part of the social safety net.

Traditionally, UI benefits have been linked to past wages (i.e., higher wages, bigger benefits). While benefit levels vary by state, they usually replace less than half of workers' wages. One of the most remarkable parts of the first relief bill, known as the CARES Act, was an additional $600 per week for unemployed workers in every state. That provision expired during the summer of 2020. An extra $300 per week in benefits was included in the December 2020 and March 2021 relief packages. Even the $300 increase managed to double the value of unemployment checks for many low-wage workers.[16] Several Republican-led states decided that these amounts were too generous and were discouraging people from finding a job. These states started to cut their UI benefits during the summer of 2021 (Cohen and Ember 2021). Partisanship and federalism continued to shape the public safety net.

Finally, the US government issued stimulus checks (aka Economic Impact Payments) to millions of lower, middle, and upper middle-income Americans. In the first round (March 2020), the maximum amount was $1,200 per adult and $500 per child. The second round, in December, topped out at $600 for each eligible adult and child. The third round (March 2021) paid out up to $1,400 per adult and per child. Recipients could be employed or unemployed; their incomes could be below the poverty threshold or well above it. The maximum was generally available to individuals with incomes below $75,000 and to married couples with incomes below $150,000. The check amounts phased out so that individuals with at least $100,000 and couples with at least $200,000 could not benefit. Between March 2020 and March 2021, the US government agreed to spend more than $850 billion on these stimulus checks. That money was supposed to boost the economy by stimulating consumer demand, and to help individuals and families who were struggling to pay their bills.[17] A family of four living in or near poverty could have received over $10,000. The stimulus checks by themselves could not move anyone above the poverty line. Nonetheless, they came as close to a guaranteed income as the United States ever had.

Before the pandemic, the public safety net for housing was small. Public housing and vouchers already had long waiting lists (Chapter 7). These programs are not budgetary entitlements, so they do not grow automatically when housing needs increase. In short, government had much less to build on than it did with medical care or food assistance. The need, however, grew rapidly in 2020 as millions of Americans lost income from work and had trouble paying their rent or mortgage. The potential for mass evictions was real.

Government officials adopted a multi-pronged approach. At the national level, the stimulus checks and additional unemployment benefits would be large enough to help many Americans pay for housing. General income support would substitute for housing-specific assistance. Second, the major relief packages distributed hundreds of billions of dollars to state and local governments, and they were encouraged but not required to use some of that money to prevent evictions. Two relief packages allocated money to pay for overdue rent, totaling over $45 billion (though that money was slow to be distributed).[18]

Another, more contentious approach relied on regulation instead of spending. National and state governments approved eviction moratoriums, effectively telling landlords and lenders how to behave during the pandemic. The national government protected homeowners against foreclosure if their loans were guaranteed by the FHA, VA, or other government agency. The CARES Act included a temporary eviction moratorium that applied to low-income rental housing subsidized by the national government. When that lapsed, the CDC issued a more comprehensive moratorium in September 2020. Public health officials argued that evictions would force more Americans to live in homeless shelters or double up with other households. Social distancing would be compromised, making it easier for Covid-19 to spread. The CDC moratorium protected most of the same people who were eligible for the stimulus checks. It was extended a couple of times, then allowed to expire at the end of July 2021 (McCarty and Perl 2021; National Housing Law Project 2021a, 2021b; Totenberg and Arnold 2021). Many states enacted their own eviction moratoriums in the first months of the pandemic, and some states promised to preserve their moratoriums for at least a few months after the CDC order ended (Hernández 2021). None of these laws allowed individuals to default on whatever rent they still owed.

During the pandemic, the national government engaged in socially distant caregiving by distributing hundreds of billions of dollars directly to individuals. Little face-to-face contact was required. The impersonal side of government proved to be something of an asset. However, certain parts of the social safety net—medical care and daily care—have always relied on direct, personal forms of caregiving. These parts depend on myriad businesses, nonprofits (including charities), volunteers, and families to be caregivers. While their tasks became far more complicated, we do not know much yet about how they coped with Covid-19.

A few developments seem clear. First, needy individuals relied more on the family safety net. As Covid-19 ravaged long-term care facilities, people with serious disabilities looked increasingly to family members for daily care. With schools and child-care centers closed, parents and other relatives had to provide full-time child care.[19] Many of them were trying to work from home as well. When child-care centers re-opened, they were not allowed to take in as many children, for public health reasons, and many parents hesitated to send their kids back for the same reasons. Women often quit work or reduced their hours in order to provide more unpaid care to family members (Gogoi 2020; Lee 2021; Mathews and McGinty 2020; North 2020).

The pandemic hurt a significant number of child-care providers. They could not stay in business while operating at reduced capacity; family homes or stand-alone centers have to be full or almost full in order to survive. Between December 2019 and March 2021, almost 16,000 child-care centers and family homes shut down. If those jobs do not come back, then many women and racial minorities who worked in child care will have to look elsewhere for employment. Moreover, many low-income parents will find it harder to stay employed if they cannot find child care in their area. The relief bill passed in March 2021 included $25 billion to help child-care providers cover higher expenses associated with the pandemic. The Biden administration proposed spending an additional $225 billion on child care over the next ten years as part of its American Families Plan. Some of this money would boost the pay of child-care providers, and some would subsidize low-income parents. The reaction from congressional Republicans was somewhere between chilly and dismissive (Leonhardt 2022; Malik et al. 2020; Mongeau 2021; Rockeman and Saraiva 2021).

Finally, the stress on caregivers was extraordinary. Doctors, nurses, home health aides, and other medical professionals put their lives at risk every day. For months, they did not know exactly how contagious the virus was or what measures were most effective in preventing its spread. Protective personal equipment was sometimes scarce. To be safe, many on the front lines stayed away from their own family members. Despite taking precautions, over three thousand medical caregivers died from Covid-19 by the summer of 2021. Those working in hospitals and nursing homes watched their patients suffer and die at alarming rates. In such a hostile environment, burnout and PTSD became all too common (Clement, Pascual, and Ulmanu 2021; Jacobs 2021; Kim 2020; Pflum 2021).

Unpaid caregivers experienced more stress as well. In one national survey, two-thirds of adults who were unpaid caregivers said they were dealing with mental health challenges such as anxiety and depression. Among adults who were not caregivers, one-third reported having similar problems. Another study found that low-income caregivers were more likely to experience loneliness and to worry about paying for food. Because women provided most of the unpaid care, they experienced most of the stress (Beach et al. 2021; Chatterjee 2021; Gogoi 2020; Ranji et al. 2021).

During the pandemic, numerous analysts and organizations tried to track income poverty, food insecurity, and other indicators of well-being. Doing so was complicated for a variety of reasons (e.g., time lags in reported data, sudden changes in public policy). In August 2020, for example, the temporary federal moratorium on evictions had just expired. Housing expert Matthew Desmond was warning anyone who would listen about an impending crisis in evictions. By October he sounded hopeful, mostly because the CDC had issued a broader eviction moratorium in September (Desmond 2020; Holpuch 2020). By the end of 2021 those protections had expired, and evictions across the country were on the rise (Kasakove 2021). The Urban Institute initially projected that the supplemental poverty rate would be 13.7 percent in 2021. Five months later it issued a much lower estimate of 7.7 percent. In between, the American Rescue Plan passed, many more Americans were vaccinated, and the economy improved (Giannarelli, Wheaton, and Shantz 2021; Wheaton, Giannarelli, and Dehry 2021). Readers should understand that the patterns of care-receiving described below could have changed by the time this book is published.

One of the biggest headlines is that material hardships may not have increased overall. Even with major disruptions to every part of society, the country didn't go to hell. The official poverty rate rose from 10.5 percent in 2019 to 11.4 percent in 2020. Even so, poverty was less common than during the Great Recession (Shrider et al. 2021). The Supplemental Poverty Measure, which is a more accurate indicator (Chapter 5), actually dropped from 11.8 percent in 2019 to 9.1 percent in 2020. Stimulus checks and expanded unemployment benefits kept millions and millions of Americans out of poverty (Fox and Burns 2021). Another study, using a new method to track monthly changes in poverty, found that the national rate was just slightly higher in June 2021 than it had been in January 2020 (Han, Meyer, and Sullivan 2021).

Other indicators tell a similar story. The government's annual Report on the Economic Well-Being of US Households found that three-quarters of American adults said they were doing okay financially or living comfortably in November 2020. That number was unchanged from a year earlier. More households saw their incomes increase than decrease in 2020. The share of Americans who said they had $400 on hand to cover an emergency expense did not drop in 2020 (Board of Governors of the Federal Reserve System 2021). According to researchers at the Urban Institute, "despite a steep drop in employment, we find the share of nonelderly adults reporting food insecurity and problems paying utility and medical bills *declined* between 2019 and 2020" (Karpman and Zuckerman 2021: 1; italics in original). Outpatient visits for medical care experienced a huge and predictable decline at the start of the pandemic. By October 2020, the number of visits were close to normal (Mehrotra et al. 2021).

Taken together, these findings represent a remarkable achievement, and much of the credit belongs to the national government. Multiple studies found that policy changes such as the stimulus checks and expansions to Unemployment Insurance and SNAP helped counteract the negative effects of the pandemic. Government aid replaced lost income from work. After those checks had been spent or the unemployment benefits expired, hardship increased (Board of Governors of the Federal Reserve System 2021; Cooney and Shaefer 2021; DeParle 2021; Han, Meyer, and Sullivan 2021; Wheaton, Giannarelli, and Dehry 2021). Some credit also belongs to nonprofit food banks and food pantries. Despite all the difficulties of acquiring and distributing food safely, the Feeding America network provided more meals to more people in 2020 than it had in 2019. It expected to serve even more in 2021.[20]

Nevertheless, some people fared badly during the pandemic. The most obvious group to suffer were residents of long-term care facilities. All were disabled, many were elderly, and many were low-income. While the exact number of deaths is unknown (and may never be known), the Covid Tracking Project reported that eight percent of these residents had died from Covid-19 by March 2021. The figure was higher for nursing homes. Less than one percent of the US population resided in long-term care facilities, yet they accounted for one-third of Covid deaths during the first year of the pandemic.[21] By December 2021, more than 140,000 nursing home residents had been killed by Covid-19. More than 2,000 nursing home staff had died from it as well.[22] Several studies found that for-profit facilities were more likely than nonprofit facilities to have Covid cases and deaths. Low staffing levels and high staff turnover likely contributed to this tragedy (Abelson 2021; Jaffe 2020; Ochieng et al. 2021; Silver-Greenberg and Gebeloff 2021). The American Jobs Plan, proposed in the spring of 2021, originally included $400 billion of additional spending on long-term care, spread out over eight years. Most of that money would support home and community-based care, not nursing homes. Again, Republicans balked (Graham 2021).

The pandemic did not affect all workers equally. Most white-collar professionals found ways to work from home. They kept their jobs and their paychecks. Many of these workers also received government stimulus checks. In contrast, low-wage workers were much more likely to be unemployed or have their hours reduced. Their jobs usually required close personal contact; no one needed virtual cooks, hotel maids, or cashiers. Some of their employers went out of business, prolonging their unemployment. These workers faced much greater hardship. If we compare workers who lost their jobs in 2020 to those who had no negative impact on their employment, the former were twice as likely to be food insecure, three times more likely to have trouble paying utility bills, and four times more likely to have trouble paying the rent or mortgage (Karpman and Zuckerman 2021; see also Board of Governors of the Federal Reserve System 2021).

Likewise, material hardships varied by income. If we compare low-income households (<$35,000 in income) to households with above-average incomes ($75,000–$150,000), the former were eight times more likely to have trouble getting enough food to eat at the start of 2021. Almost half of low-income households were behind on their housing payments (Root and Simet 2021). By the summer of 2021, 23 percent of low-income households said they often or sometimes lacked enough food to eat. The figure was less than three percent among those with above-average incomes. Low-income renter households were three times more likely to be behind on their monthly payments. Almost one out of four low-income households borrowed money from friends or family to pay their bills in the previous week. Among above-average households, the rate was closer to one in twenty. Low-income households were three times more likely to report being medically uninsured.[23]

Racial and ethnic inequalities are still very apparent. The decline in life expectancy from 2019 to 2020 was much greater for Hispanics (3.0 years) and Blacks (2.9) than for Whites (1.2). Hispanic men (3.7 years) and Black men (3.3) fared especially badly (Arias et al. 2021).[24] Blacks and Hispanics were more likely than Whites to be infected with Covid-19, and they were more likely to be hospitalized. Among individuals with Covid-19, Blacks and Hispanics were twice as likely as Whites to die.[25] Social and economic factors made racial minorities more vulnerable. They often lived in smaller apartments or shared housing with more people, making it easier for the virus to spread. They were more likely to use public transportation. Without health insurance, many were accustomed to postponing medical treatment as long as possible. Many Blacks and Hispanics kept working at hospitals, nursing homes, home health agencies, or factories where social distancing was hard to sustain. They were almost literally in the line of fire (Centers for Disease Control and Prevention 2021; Oppel at el. 2020; Romano et al. 2021).

The disparities did not end there. In 2021, people of color were more than twice as likely as Whites to have trouble getting enough to eat. Blacks were twice as likely as Whites to fall behind on their rent. Compared to Whites, Blacks were twice as likely to be medically uninsured; Hispanics/Latinos were three times as likely.[26] These gaps are very similar to those described in Chapters 6–8, before the pandemic hit. Based on the supplemental measure, poverty rates dropped for Whites, Blacks, and Hispanics in 2020, yet sizable racial gaps remained (Fox and Burns 2021). One silver lining can be found in the Urban Institute's poverty projections. If they are correct, then Black and Hispanic poverty rates will drop to all-time lows in 2021. White poverty rates will continue to be lower, but the racial gaps could be smaller than in the past (Wheaton, Giannarelli, and Dehry 2021).

In many ways Covid-19 exposed preexisting holes in the US social safety net. Those familiar with long-term care were saddened but not surprised when deaths spiraled out of control in nursing homes. The adequacy of that care has long been suspect. Policy experts have been pointing out structural flaws in Unemployment Insurance for years. The lack of affordable housing in many parts of the country is no secret. Charities have had trouble before when dealing with a big jump in hardship. It would be misleading to compare Covid-19 to a natural disaster that demolished even the strongest buildings. The social safety net was compromised before the pandemic hit.

Prospects for Change

We do not know yet whether Covid-19 will produce long-term changes in the social safety net, or what they will be. There is no typical or natural response to crises like this one. The horrible flu pandemic of 1918 eventually led to changes in medical care and public health in this country, but not to national health insurance. Several years passed between the stock market crash of 1929 and the Social Security Act of 1935. World War II had a much bigger influence on social policy in Europe than in the United States. More recently, the Great Recession of 2007–09 had little impact on Unemployment Insurance or charitable giving. The main innovation was the Affordable Care Act, even though health insurance coverage and medical costs did not get much worse during the recession.

Democrats have been trying to mend the public safety net ever since the pandemic started. Those efforts escalated after President Biden was elected, with the biggest known as Build Back Better. The original proposal included $400 billion of new money for long-term care, especially home- and community-based services, along with substantial increases in child-care subsidies. (It also embraced free and universal preschool for 3- and 4-year-olds.) The national government would, for the first time, guarantee 12 weeks of paid parental leave. Other parts would expand health insurance coverage for low-income people living in states that refused to expand Medicaid; reduce out-of-pocket costs for prescription drugs covered by Medicare; provide much-needed repairs to public housing units; make permanent some temporary expansions of the Earned Income Tax Credit and Child Tax Credit; and allot more money to feed low-income children during the summer months. All those changes would reduce hardships for millions of Americans. Most of the money for Build Back Better would come from higher income taxes on corporations and the rich, as well as greater efforts to crack down on tax avoidance by the affluent.[27]

Over the course of 2021, several parts were whittled down or dropped. Republicans in Congress refused to offer any support, and some centrist Democrats balked at the overall price tag. By the time Build Back Better passed the House in November, the long-term care benefits had been significantly reduced. Only four weeks of paid parental leave would be covered, and increases to the Child Tax Credit would expire after one year. And yet, navigating through the House was supposed to be the easy part. Most observers predicted that the path through the Senate would be more difficult (Bolton 2021; Cochrane and Weisman 2021; Prokop 2021). By the middle of 2022, Build Back Better had stalled out in the Senate.

In keeping with the bird's-eye approach, I will not second-guess Biden's decision to combine so many initiatives, including clean energy, into one bill. Nor will I try to analyze Senator Manchin's motives and actions. Let's stay focused on broader patterns of rhetoric and policy. Time and time again, Democrats touted Build Back Better as a major improvement in the lives of working families and the middle class.[28] Explicit references to the poor, near poor, or working poor have been scarce. Individuals with lower incomes were supposed to benefit, but only as part of a larger effort. According to the White House website,

> President Joe Biden believes that there's no greater economic engine in the world than the hard work and ingenuity of the American people. But for too long, the economy has worked great for those at the top, while working families get squeezed. President Biden promised to rebuild the backbone of the country—the middle class—so that this time everyone comes along. The Build Back Better Framework does just that.
>
> This framework will . . . grow our economy from the bottom up and the middle out.[29]

Likewise, advocates have seldom touted Build Back Better as a remedy for poverty, food insecurity, or evictions. Instead, they have highlighted problems that affect low-income and middle-income Americans, such as the high costs of child care and long-term care.

In most facets of life, it is safer to bet on continuity than change. Despite a Great Recession, a turbulent Trump presidency, and a global pandemic, Democratic officials have not changed how they talk (or don't talk) about poverty-related issues. For their part, Republican officials have shown little interest in elevating these issues. They prefer to rile up their base by harping on mask and vaccine mandates, Critical Race Theory, and the like. Calls for "compassionate conservatism" seem like a distant memory. It doesn't take much courage to predict these patterns will continue in the next few years.

Actions, as the old saying goes, speak louder than words. Although their rhetoric may not have changed, Democrats adopted an unusual strategy when designing Build Back Better. The public safety net relies mainly on two types of
programs, public assistance and social insurance. Build Back Better is more of
a hybrid model: it combines the financing of public assistance with the widely
available benefits of social insurance (Howard 2022). Wealthy individuals and
corporations are expected to pay billions more in income taxes. But instead
of targeting that money to assist low-income Americans, Build Back Better
promises to help a wide range of people, from the poor to the upper-middle
class. This design is most evident in benefits for families with children (e.g., paid
parental leave, child-care subsidies, universal preschool).

The fact that Democrats chose not to stick with the standard social insurance
or public assistance models is noteworthy. Other countries use social insurance
to pay for parental leave, and one can readily imagine adding long-term care insurance to Medicare, Social Security, or Disability Insurance.[30] Going this route
would require higher payroll taxes, and most Democrats have been resisting that
option for decades (Campbell and Morgan 2005). One reason is that payroll
taxes weigh more heavily on workers with average and below-average incomes,
many of whom vote Democratic. The Affordable Care Act, which is financed
in many different ways, did not increase payroll taxes for the vast majority of
workers. We know that the largest social insurance program, Social Security, is
the single most important part of the public safety net. If new social insurance
programs are off the table, then a better public safety net could require different
types of programs. Otherwise, we may need to increase payroll tax revenues
from the affluent.[31]

The public assistance model assumes that the poor and near poor are quite
different from everyone else. Increasingly, it has become clear that members
of the middle class also have trouble paying for child care, long-term care, prescription drugs, and housing. Targeting benefits exclusively at people with low
incomes could be bad policy, because legitimate needs would be ignored, and it
could be bad politics, because middle-class voters would feel resentful. Hence
the impetus to design social programs with broader eligibility.

Whether or not parts of Build Back Better are enacted, it offers one future
path for the public safety net. Collect tax revenue from millionaires, billionaires,
and wealthy corporations, then distribute benefits widely across class lines. In
other words, insist that the fortunate few take care of the rest of society.

What general principle(s) could justify such an approach? The Biden administration has not really addressed this question. Historically, the public safety
net has been guided by two principles: individuals must need assistance to
cope with material hardships, or they must earn benefits based on paid employment. For this hybrid model to take root, we might have to expand our notion of

hardship. We would reform or replace the official poverty line because it badly underestimates the extent of need in this country. The government might define the needy as those who pay more than a certain share of their income for expenses such as child care, long-term care, housing, or medical care.[32] Alternatively, the hybrid model could be based on a broader notion of how individuals earn their benefits. Paid work is one way; unpaid caregiving would be another. This would not be a new argument. Progressive Era reformers portrayed child-rearing as a valuable service to society and drew analogies between mothers' pensions, old-age pensions, and veterans' pensions (Orloff 1991; Skocpol 1992).

A more radical principle would be based on rights. Just as every child is guaranteed a public education, every person would be guaranteed adequate food, shelter, medical care, and the like. Public opinion polls show considerable support for some social rights, less for others (Chapter 1). Despite growing interest in a guaranteed income policy, my sense is that a rights-based justification is the least likely outcome. The United States has failed to recognize a right to medical care for so long, it is hard to imagine similar rights to child care or housing taking hold. At least, not in my lifetime.

As a practical matter, any major departure from the status quo should be informed by past experience. We have learned that different types of programs can have powerful effects on poverty-related needs. Three of the most important parts of the social safety net—Social Security, Medicaid, and the Earned Income Tax Credit—represent social insurance, public assistance, and tax expenditures, respectively. These three programs have taken root and grown because their benefits are not limited to people with low incomes. Social Security helps almost every retiree; Medicaid is a crucial source of income for healthcare providers; and many low-wage employers favor the EITC over a higher minimum wage. The future of the social safety net depends on forging these sorts of cross-class alliances, on uniting compassion for others with self-interest.

It should be evident by now that the public safety net is the core of the social safety net. Employers, charities, and extended families play important supporting roles. I do not foresee a major expansion of their efforts anytime soon. There is currently little interest in requiring companies to provide health insurance or retirement pensions to all employees, including those working part-time or for low wages. Only a few employers have promised to do something about affordable housing, and many of them are thinking about their own middle-class workers. Charitable organizations help fill in the gaps for food and medical care, supplementing SNAP and Medicaid. They have a much smaller impact on income support and housing. In many respects, charities do a remarkable job, but they cannot keep pace when times are hard. The decline of religious affiliation in the United States means that churches will have a harder time finding volunteers to serve in the community. The number of millionaires and multimillionaires is growing, which could mean more charitable giving for higher education, medical research, and the arts; however, reducing chronic hardship is typically a lower priority. If churches and secular charities can sustain their current role in the social safety net, that would be something of an accomplishment.

One silver lining of the pandemic is that it revealed just how much we depend on the family safety net. But the message from unpaid caregivers is not, "thanks for the recognition; we plan to do even more." The message is closer to, "hey, we're stretched to the breaking point, how about some help." A national poll conducted in September 2021 asked how important it was for Congress to pass specific pieces of legislation. Seventy percent of Americans felt that it was extremely or very important for the federal government to require employers to provide paid family and medical leave. Almost three-quarters responded that larger child-care subsidies were extremely or very important. And more than 80 percent said the same thing about greater federal spending on long-term care.[33] Americans want government to relieve strains on the family safety net. They seldom want Uncle Sam to be the primary caregiver for their young children or elderly parents. But Americans would like government's help in taking care of their vulnerable relatives.

My hope is that a devastating pandemic somehow leads us to reinforce the social safety net. Too many people have been receiving too little care. Although the net's weak spots have existed for a long time, maybe now they are more visible. Perhaps the need for change has become more compelling. Unfortunately, the one part of society best equipped to make improvements—the national government—is not functioning well these days. Core democratic institutions have been weakened, often deliberately (Levitsky and Ziblatt 2018; Snyder 2021). And the one political party most likely to care about the social safety net is also trying to defend those institutions. Democrats in Washington are spending much of their time ensuring that elections are truly fair and that lawbreakers are held accountable. In the near term, they may have to care for the political system before they can take better care of individuals living in or near poverty.

NOTES

Introduction

1. For important exceptions to this generalization, see Boris and Steuerle 2017 and Smith and Lipsky 1993.
2. For evidence that Democrats have sometimes tried to cut back on social programs, or that Republicans have tried to expand them, see Berkowitz and DeWitt 2013, Bertram 2015, and Howard 2007.
3. Thanks to Sarah Halpern-Meekin for this reminder.
4. Not everyone qualifies, which makes social insurance broadly inclusive rather than truly universal.
5. Although scholars do not agree about how to define the welfare state, most would include two core functions: compensating for sudden drops in income that are common in capitalist economies (e.g., due to unemployment, illness, disability, or retirement); and alleviating the hardships of poverty. In the American context, it is often assumed that the upper tier of social insurance programs performs the first function while the lower tier of public assistance programs performs the second function. That's too simple. As we will see in Part II of the book, social insurance programs do both.
6. See https://www.presidency.ucsb.edu/documents/2020-democratic-party-platform.
7. The social safety net does not have natural or fixed boundaries. I can imagine plausible arguments for why programs like subsidized school meals (Chapter 6) and Head Start (Chapter 9) might belong.
8. See, e.g., https://www.worldbank.org/en/topic/safetynets#1, http://pubdocs.worldbank.org/en/836361575490788719/SPJCC19-SSN-D7S1-Bowen-Adaptive-SP.pdf, and https://www.worldbank.org/en/news/feature/2017/01/10/how-safety-nets-are-becoming-game-changers-in-disaster-response-in-southern-africa.
9. Some disasters could be natural and man-made, such as when zoning laws allow construction in flood-prone areas or a hurricane damages an offshore rig and triggers a major oil spill.
10. With Social Security, employers play a small role by helping the government keep track of wages subject to payroll taxes. Many free and charitable health clinics do not receive a dime of revenue from national or state governments. Nevertheless, their building could receive a property tax exemption, and their doctors and nurses are regulated by state medical boards.
11. "Poor relief" was commonly used in the 19th century, and it sets a lower bar by promising relief instead of safety. That phrase seems more honest than "safety net." However, many people who are struggling to make ends meet in the 21st century are not officially poor.
12. There is also a decent chance that I lack the emotional intelligence to do that kind of research well.
13. In the English language, this sense of burden is the original meaning of care (Tronto 1989).
14. See https://www.rosalynncarter.org/about-us/.

15. While this definition is quite broad, it has limits. "Among the activities of life that do not generally constitute care we would probably include the following: the pursuit of pleasure, creative activity, production, destruction" (Tronto 1993: 104). Tronto concedes that some versions of these activities could qualify as care.

16. In general, context and flexibility are central to care ethics. Theorists who embrace this approach deliberately avoid creating general rules for ethical behavior that apply to all people in all situations. Depending on one's perspective, this is a notable strength of care ethics or a major weakness.

17. For an important exception, see Campbell and Morgan 2005.

18. Quality matters, and I agree with Tronto that not all care is good care. Some parents care for their children badly. In extreme cases, they can be charged with child neglect or abuse. By the same token, some government programs can make recipients feel powerless or disrespected (Hays 2003; Michener 2018; Soss 2000). Care could be highly paternalistic if those who take care of and give care never listen to those who receive care. Caregivers could be exploited through low pay or feelings of guilt. Evaluating the quality of care in the social safety net is important but beyond the scope of this project.

19. For instance, some theorists argue that trust can be understood as relying on someone to take care of what we care about (Sevenhuijsen 2003).

20. Jefferson made this statement shortly after stepping down as President in 1809. See https://founders.archives.gov/documents/Jefferson/03-01-02-0088.

21. I simply note in passing a similarity between this part of Tronto's argument and Robert Putnam's discussion of social capital, generalized reciprocity, and well-functioning societies (Putnam 1993).

Chapter 1

1. Most of the poll results in this chapter were accessed through the Roper iPoll database, maintained by the Roper Center for Public Opinion Research.

2. Despite frequent use of this survey question, not everyone is convinced that it accurately measures the salience of specific issues (Wlezien 2005).

3. For the 2016 exit poll data, see http://www.foxnews.com/politics/elections/2016/exit-polls and https://www.nytimes.com/interactive/2016/11/08/us/politics/election-exit-polls.html.

4. In November 2017, the Associated Press asked Americans how much effort they wanted the federal government to devote to solving a variety of problems. Almost one-half said they wanted "a great deal" of effort when asked about poverty, hunger, and homelessness. One-third wanted "a lot" of effort.

5. Strangely, this question is seldom asked by pollsters.

6. In their 2020 party platform, Democrats recognized that the official poverty measure underestimated the number of Americans living in poverty. See https://www.presidency.ucsb.edu/documents/2020-democratic-party-platform.

7. For a critique of standard ways of measuring political knowledge, see Lupia 2015.

8. This figure is so high partly because the United Way accounted for sizable differences in cost of living across the country. The government's poverty threshold only makes a few adjustments for Alaska and Hawaii, but treats places like New York City and Omaha, Nebraska alike. The original United Way study can be found at https://www.unitedwayalice.org/home.

9. The General Social Survey and American National Election Studies data mentioned in this chapter were accessed and analyzed via the Survey Documentation and Analysis website at the University of California, Berkeley (https://sda.berkeley.edu/).

10. This sentiment is not as strong as it appears: about 25 percent strongly agree with that statement, while roughly 40 percent somewhat agree (Howard et al. 2017).

11. Missing from almost all these polls is some indication of why Americans think that caring for the poor is anyone's responsibility. Some people might think in terms of basic human rights, which would lead to government action. Among certain individuals we might find a sense of noblesse oblige toward the poor, which could lead to public or private action. Religious teachings might compel some of us. Or, perhaps helping the poor is seen as a good investment,

making them and the whole economy more productive. Other people might link responsibility to specific conditions, saying that we should help the poor only if we can afford to and know how to. And we should not dismiss fear: maybe fighting poverty is for our own security, so the poor don't take to the streets and start a rebellion. We will learn more about these sorts of reasons in Chapters 2–4.

12. The introduction to these ANES questions goes like this: "We would like to get your feelings toward some of our political leaders and other people who are in the news these days. We will show the name of a person and we'd like you to rate that person using something we call the feeling thermometer. Ratings between 50 degrees and 100 degrees mean that you feel favorable are warm toward the person. Ratings between 0 degrees and 50 degrees mean that you don't feel favorable toward the person and that you don't care too much for that person. You would rate the person at the 50-degree mark if you don't feel particularly warm or cold toward the person. If we come to a person whose name you don't recognize, you don't need to rate that person."

13. To capture the typical response, I used the median score instead of the mean because responses to feeling thermometer questions are seldom distributed normally.

14. Some readers might not want to rely so heavily on a single feeling thermometer score. Social psychologists have created a 12-item scale, with each item representing a separate statement about one's feelings toward the poor (e.g., "poor people make me feel uncomfortable"). Respondents had to indicate their level of agreement or disagreement with each statement. The composite scale ranged from 1 to 5, with negative feelings at the lower end. This survey was given to a few hundred college students, and their average score on the overall scale was 3.53. A follow-up study, using the same scale on a similar pool of college students, produced an average score of 3.63 (Cozzarelli, Wilkinson, and Tagler 2001; Tagler and Cozzarelli 2013). Those results are consistent with the feeling thermometer scores.

15. Spencer Piston (2018) has analyzed specific feelings toward the rich and poor, using three national surveys. While he was most interested in feelings of sympathy and resentment, he also asked people how angry or compassionate they felt. It seems reasonable to classify sympathy and compassion as warm or favorable emotions, and anger and resentment as cold or unfavorable emotions. Depending on the survey, 60–85 percent of Americans said they felt sympathy for the poor about half the time, most of the time, or always. Feelings of compassion for the poor were even more common. Only ten percent of Americans said they resented the poor. Feelings of sympathy or compassion for the rich were much less common, somewhere between 10 and 20 percent. I thank Prof. Piston for sharing with me detailed data from his book.

16. See Fiske, Cuddy, and Glick 2007 for a concise summary of this stereotype content model. From an evolutionary perspective, being able to make quick judgments about who intends to help or harm us (warmth) and who could do so (competence) would enhance our chances of survival.

17. In-depth interviews with the poor reveal a clear preference for work over welfare (e.g., Edin and Schaefer 2015).

18. The two national surveys were conducted by the Public Religion Research Institute (April 2017 and September 2016), and were accessed via iPoll. The specific wording of this question, "in your own community," leaves open the possibility that people might see poverty differently if asked about the whole country.

19. Kinder and Kam (2010) used several feeling thermometer scores to develop a measure of ethnocentrism for Whites, Blacks, Hispanics, and Asian Americans. In general, ethnocentrism reflects a tendency to see the world as a virtuous "us" pitted against a less worthy "them." The most ethnocentric individuals would have much warmer feelings and positive stereotypes about their own group than about other groups. Kinder and Kam analyzed the impact of ethnocentrism on a wide variety of policy issues, foreign and domestic. They found that ethnocentrism shaped attitudes toward social policy for White Americans only. More ethnocentric Whites tended to have negative attitudes toward policies aimed at the poor but felt much more positively toward Social Security and Medicare. The difference, they argue, was due not just to self-interest. Ethnocentric Whites see poverty through a racial or ethnic lens, and that leads them to feel and think negatively about programs for the poor, who are undeserving because they belong to the "wrong" ethnic or racial group.

20. We will examine poverty rates more fully in Chapter 5.
21. Although these differences were not statistically significant by the usual standard ($p \le .05$), they were significant at the .10 threshold.
22. It appears that support for a national goal of cutting poverty in half within 10 years was stronger among African Americans (87%) and Latinos (79%) than Whites (65%). Nevertheless, strong majorities were present in all three groups (Half in Ten Education Fund and the Center for American Progress 2014).
23. All the partisan differences cited in this section are statistically significant.
24. Hopkins (2009) found that structural explanations of poverty are less likely, and individualistic explanations more likely, in areas of the country that are strongly Republican.
25. In a 2014 poll, 54 percent of Republicans supported the goal of cutting poverty in half within ten years, which would require a major effort. Here the role of government was ambiguous; the question stated that Congress and the president would embrace such a goal, but not what the national government would do to achieve that goal. Republican support was considerable, but it fell far short of the 90 percent of Democrats who embraced this goal (Half in Ten Education Fund and the Center for American Progress 2014).
26. Another possibility is that public opinion has little impact because the relevant information never reaches policymakers. Media coverage often helps issues become more visible, and we can track how often poll data about poverty appeared in major newspapers. Consider the 2016 General Social Survey, which was cited a few times in this chapter. Because the GSS data were not available publicly until March 2017, I used the LexisNexis Academic database to search the *Washington Post* and *New York Times* for reference to any GSS questions between March 2017 and March 2018. During this period, the *Post* ran dozens of stories that mentioned results from this survey, meaning that reporters were aware of the GSS as a resource. These stories discussed abortion, crime, racial attitudes, sexual activity, legalizing marijuana, gender roles, gun control, gay marriage—but not poverty. The *Times* published fewer stories that mentioned the GSS, and the basic pattern was the same. The stories conveyed the public's views toward religion, gender roles, interracial marriage, personal happiness, and several other topics, but not poverty.

An especially revealing example comes from the special poverty survey commissioned by the Half in Ten Education Fund and the Center for American Progress (CAP). The results were made public in January 2014. Because that year was the 50th anniversary of the War on Poverty, the media should have been unusually interested in stories about poverty. This time I used LexisNexis to search for any mention of this survey or the accompanying report in any US newspaper during 2014. The silence was deafening. A handful of stories quoted CAP staff in connection with poverty, but almost always when discussing poverty rates or programs, not public opinion. A few advocacy groups took note of the opinion data, and that was about it. Thus, when organizations release their latest polls related to poverty, the result could be much like the proverbial tree that falls in a forest with no one around to listen.

Chapter 2

1. See https://www.labor-studies.org/by-education-level/elementary/labor-quotes/ and http://www.dclabor.org/union-city-radio/tuesday-august-25-2015?view=full.
2. Stern quoted in 2006 (https://www.cbsnews.com/news/andy-stern-the-new-boss/).
3. Rev. King gave this speech at the annual convention of the Illinois state AFL-CIO on October 7, 1965. http://www.ilafl-cio.org/documents/MLKNewsletter.pdf.
4. President Carter made this statement in 1980: https://www.jimmycarterlibrary.gov/digital_library/sso/148878/175/SSO_148878_175_01.pdf.
5. This quotation dates from January 28, 2016. https://twitter.com/nfib/status/692902302823358464.
6. These figures come from the AFL-CIO website (https://aflcio.org/about-us/our-unions-and-allies).
7. The documents discussed in this section were found on the AFL-CIO website (https://aflcio.org/about-us/leadership/afl-cio-conventions and https://aflcio.org/reports/afl-cio-constitution).

8. I counted "poor" if it referred to individuals, wages, or benefits, but not to performance (e.g., poor economy, poor leadership). The link to one resolution from 2009 was broken, meaning I was able to analyze 196 resolutions from these five national conventions.

9. I searched these resolutions for mention of "working" and "worker." I excluded references to "working" when used as a verb (e.g., "working with local allies") and included references when used as an adjective (e.g., working families, working people).

10. See, e.g., http://www.workingpoorfamilies.org/ and https://politicsofpoverty.oxfamamerica.org/2016/09/5-myths-about-the-working-poor-in-america/.

11. One can imagine a few reasons for this silence. One is that the AFL-CIO genuinely does not care about the working poor. Union members in the United States are mostly middle class, so labor leaders rationally focus on preserving those jobs and boosting those wages and benefits. Statements like, "the mission of organized labor is to improve the lives of our members" (Resolution 9, 2015) are common. Labor leaders might be worried more about inequality, especially the growing gap between the rich and ordinary workers (e.g., Resolution 6, 2001; Resolution 9, 2013), than they are about poverty. A second possibility is that labor leaders are sympathetic to the problems of the working poor but find the whole subject too difficult to discuss. Millions of Americans could be working but poor because labor unions failed to organize them, or because unions could not raise wages enough for those who joined. Labor leaders do not want to highlight their failures and therefore rarely mention the working poor.

Alternatively, labor leaders might have felt that the best way to fight poverty was not to talk about it. Discussions about poverty trigger so many strong emotions—about the character of the poor, the fairness of the economy, race, gender, and the nature of needs versus wants versus rights—that the outcome is seldom productive. Furthermore, most people worry about themselves, not others. Better to talk about specific policies that help a broad swath of the population, including the poor (e.g., Skocpol 1991). In that case, perhaps the failure to mention the poor or the working poor does not actually reflect a lack of care. It could be part of a larger political strategy.

12. The Executive Council Reports can be found at https://aflcio.org/about-us/leadership/afl-cio-conventions.

13. After Barack Obama was elected President in 2008, the AFL-CIO made the Employee Free Choice Act its top legislative priority. That Act, which stalled in the Senate, would have made it easier for workers to unionize and to bargain collectively with employers (Greenhouse 2019; Hacker and Pierson 2010).

14. Labor leaders have known this for decades (Hacker 2002; Roof 2011).

15. Similarly, on the AFL-CIO website, the opening line from the Issues section declares that "all working people deserve good jobs and the power to determine their wages and working conditions." https://aflcio.org/issues.

16. This quotation comes from Resolution 20. https://aflcio.org/resolutions/resolution-20-full-employment-and-15-minimum-wage.

17. See https://www.aft.org/about.

18. See https://www.aft.org/about/sotu.

19. See https://www.aft.org/sites/default/files/sotu_2018.pdf.

20. See https://www.afscme.org/union/about.

21. See https://www.afscme.org/members/conventions/resolutions-and-amendments/2018/resolutions.

22. See https://www.afscme.org/members/conventions/resolutions-and-amendments/2018/resolutions/19-opposing-medicaid-cuts. For similar language, see also https://www.afscme.org/members/conventions/resolutions-and-amendments/2018/resolutions/49-an-economic-agenda-for-all.

23. See https://www.afscme.org/members/conventions/resolutions-and-amendments/2018/resolutions/54-honoring-dr-martin-luther-kings-legacy-and-the-poor-peoples-campaign.

24. See, e.g., http://www.seiu.org/blog/2016/10/saving-for-retirement-isnt-simple-when-earning-poverty-wages; http://www.seiu.org/2019/05/trump-administration-to-home-care-workers-heres-your-poverty-level-wage-now-let-us-tell-you-how-to-spend-it; and http://www.seiu.org/cards/home-care-and-the-fight-for-15.

25. This quotation comes from http://www.seiu.org/blog/2019/1/kings-dream-and-the-movement-to-end-poverty-wage-work. Sara Nelson, president of a much smaller union of flight attendants, shares Henry's views about poverty-level wages (Kullgren 2019). Based on a very small sample, we have some evidence that female labor leaders are more attuned to poverty than their male counterparts.

26. This quotation comes from http://www.seiu.org/blog/2019/4/seiu-members-not-yet-union-workers-ask-presidential-hopefuls-about-their-plans-to-address-economic-injust ice-at-las-vegas-forum. See also http://www.seiu.org/blog/2019/10/things-must-change-including-our-wages.

27. See http://conventiondocs.seiu.org/resolutions-committee/.

28. See https://apcoworldwide.com/news/apco-reveals-2019-trademarks-study/.

29. The NFIB's Small Business Legal Center does publish an annual report, as do some state-level chapters of the NFIB.

30. The 2016 survey was distributed to a random national sample of 20,000 NFIB members, with additional sampling in California, Ohio, and Texas. The results were based on over 2,800 responses. Almost two-thirds of the responses came from companies with fewer than ten employees.

31. See https://www.nfib.com/advocacy/. One of their other Advocacy sections of this website, Economy, overlaps to some degree with the Taxes section.

32. See, e.g., Duggan 2019; https://www.nfib.com/content/press-release/economy/nfib-to-congress-the-proof-is-in-the-numbers/ and https://www.nfib.com/content/press-release/economy/new-nfib-report-confirms-small-business-economic-relief-thanks-to-tax-cuts-and-jobs-act/.

33. See https://www.nfib.com/advocacy/healthcare/.

34. See https://www.nfib.com/content/nfib-in-my-state/michigan/small-business-applauds-passage-of-medicaid-work-requirement/.

35. https://www.nfib.com/advocacy/.

36. See, e.g., https://www.nfib.com/content/issues/pennsylvania/nsylvani-65122/; https://www.nfib.com/content/news/colorado/into-the-great-minimum-wage-mess-we-charge-75755/; and https://www.nfib.com/content/news/labor/big-congressional-vote-on-the-minimum-wage-tomorrow/.

37. See https://www.nfib.com/content/news/illinois/reaction-president-sounded-like-a-candid ate-not-a-leader-63390/ and https://www.nfib.com/content/news/georgia/nfib-to-georgia-senate-raising-the-minimum-wage-would-hurt-workers-67890/.

38. These speeches can be found on the Chamber of Commerce's website, e.g., https://www.uschamber.com/speech/2019-state-of-american-business-address and https://www.uscham ber.com/speech/2018-state-american-business-address.

39. These reports can be found on the Chamber of Commerce's website, e.g., https://www.uschamber.com/sites/default/files/023587_soab_2019_booklet_inside_final_spread.pdf.

40. We will return to the business of health care in Chapter 8.

41. See https://www.uschamber.com/issues.

42. See, e.g., https://www.uschamber.com/speech/speech-the-american-enterprise-institute-s-summer-honors-conference and https://www.uschamber.com/speech/restarting-the-gro wth-engine-reforming-capital-markets-revitalize-our-economy.

43. See https://www.uschamber.com/sites/default/files/documents/files/2017_health_care_policy_recommendations.pdf.

44. See https://www.uschamber.com/sites/default/files/021654_entitlement_reform_101.pdf.

45. See https://opportunity.businessroundtable.org/wp-content/uploads/2019/09/BRT-Statem ent-on-the-Purpose-of-a-Corporation-with-Signatures-1.pdf.

46. See https://www.businessroundtable.org/media/all-statements.

47. The two quotations in this paragraph are taken from https://s3.amazonaws.com/brt.org/BRT_Social_Security_Reform_and_Medicare_Modernization_Proposals_-_January_2013_FINAL.pdf; see also https://www.businessroundtable.org/getting-serious-about-enti tlement-reform. Note: the Business Roundtable and US Chamber of Commerce have similar ideas about entitlement reform, though the rhetoric of the Chamber indicates a greater sense of urgency.

48. See https://www.uschamber.com/letters-congress/us-chamber-letter-hr-582-the-raise-the-wage-act.
49. Both quotations are from https://www.businessforafairminimumwage.org/news/001474/business-owners-applaud-house-passage-15-federal-minimum-wage-bill; see also https://www.businessforafairminimumwage.org/pressreleases.
50. See https://www.businessroundtable.org/policy-perspectives/building-americas-tomorrow-ready-workforce/federal-minimum-wage-policy.
51. This expansion will be discussed further in Chapter 8.
52. See https://www.nfib.com/content/news/virginia/statement-small-business-owners-say-medicaid-expansion-would-hurt-virginia-64650/ (Virginia); https://www.nfib.com/content/news/maine/nfib-maine-survey-shows-strong-opposition-to-medicaid-expansion-65016/ (Maine); https://www.nfib.com/content/news/arizona/small-business-strongly-opposes-expanding-medicaid-62868/ (Arizona); https://www.nfib.com/content/news/louisiana/nfib-to-legislature-dont-pass-the-buck-on-medicaid-expansion-65406/ (Louisiana); https://www.nfib.com/content/news/healthcare/what-gov-bakers-medicaid-funding-plan-would-mean-for-employers/ (Massachusetts).
    Note: state-level chambers of commerce have not been consistently opposed to or supportive of Medicaid expansion (e.g., Galewitz 2014; Hertel-Fernandez, Skocpol, and Lynch 2016).
53. See https://www.aha.org/system/files/content/12/120217-aha-amici-brief.pdf and https://www.aha.org/news/headline/2018-06-14-hospital-groups-urge-court-reject-latest-aca-challenge. Note: the members of these associations include for-profit and nonprofit hospitals.
54. See https://www.chausa.org/docs/default-source/advocacy/medicaid-expansion-oct-2017.pdf?sfvrsn=2; https://www.aha.org/news/headline/2018-10-15-gao-study-poor-forgo-medical-care-more-states-didnt-expand-medicaid; and https://www.aha.org/news/headline/2017-11-30-study-medicaid-expansion-helped-health-chronically-ill-adults.
55. See https://www.vhha.com/research/2015/10/09/how-failure-to-expand-medicaid-has-impacted-virginia-employment/ and https://www.radioiowa.com/2013/03/13/hospital-association-study-says-medicaid-expansion-adds-2400-jobs-in-iowa/. This line of argument is not new; hospitals have often stressed their economic importance when faced with possible cuts to Medicaid (Olson 2010).
56. See http://www.providermagazine.com/news/Pages/2017/0317/AHCA-Urges-Protections-For-Most-Vulnerable-In-New-Medicaid-Funding-Plan.aspx and http://www.providermagazine.com/news/Pages/2017/0917/Latest-ACA-Repeal-Effort,-Medicaid-Cuts-Face-Gauntlet-of-Opposition-.aspx?PF=1.
57. See https://www.sba.gov/sites/default/files/advocacy/Frequently-Asked-Questions-Small-Business-2018.pdf.

Chapter 3

1. For an interesting exception, with historical and cross-country comparisons, see Morgan 2006.
2. See Pew Research Center (2019b), including the detailed tables. The decline of religious affiliation is also evident in the General Social Survey (GSS), which has been conducted over a longer span of time. According to the GSS, 8 percent of Americans said they had no religion in 1990, compared to 23 percent in 2018.
3. In Congress, over 80 percent of legislators call themselves Christians. https://www.pewforum.org/2019/01/03/faith-on-the-hill-116/ (January 3, 2019).
4. Some readers might not belong to an organized religion, but they might not belong to a labor union or business association, either. All these institutions are still important to study.
5. According to Rev. Leith Anderson, head of the National Association of Evangelicals, "there's something like 2,000 verses in the Bible that talk about the poor and the widow and the orphan and the homeless and the hungry" (quoted in Green 2019).
6. These passages are all taken from the English Standard Version of the Bible.
7. In another version of this sermon, Jesus says "Blessed are the poor in spirit" (Matthew 5:3), rather than simply "Blessed are the poor." Being poor in spirit is usually interpreted as being humble, not evil or irreligious.

8. There is an extraordinary passage in the Book of Acts (4:31–35) describing how true believers reacted to the death of Jesus: "And when they had prayed, the place in which they were gathered together was shaken, and they were all filled with the Holy Spirit and continued to speak the word of God with boldness. Now the full number of those who believed were of one heart and soul, and no one said that any of the things that belonged to him was his own, but they had everything in common. And with great power the apostles were giving their testimony to the resurrection of the Lord Jesus, and great grace was upon them all. There was not a needy person among them, for as many as were owners of lands or houses sold them and brought the proceeds of what was sold and laid it at the apostles' feet, and it was distributed to each as any had need."

   This story sounds remarkably like Karl Marx ("from each according to his abilities, to each according to his needs")—if Marx were filled with the Holy Spirit.

9. The other four pillars are sincerely reciting the Muslim profession of faith, praying correctly five times a day, fasting during Ramadan, and making a pilgrimage to Mecca.

10. To further complicate matters, Jesus is quoted by Matthew (26:11) as saying, "For you always have the poor with you, but you will not always have me." He was responding to followers who were upset that a woman had poured expensive oil on Jesus instead of selling that oil and giving the money to the poor. He explained that the woman was preparing him for burial, and thus acting in good faith. Some readers have taken this story to mean that we should pay more attention to Jesus and our own spiritual lives, and less to material aid for the poor. Others disagree.

11. To learn more about evangelicals, see Fitzgerald 2017, Kidd 2019, Pew Research Center 2019b, https://www.pewforum.org/religious-landscape-study/, the Winter 2017/18 issue of *Evangelicals* magazine (https://www.nae.net/evangelicals-winter-2017-18/), and https://www.nae.net/what-is-an-evangelical/.

12. See https://www.nae.net/topics/.

13. See https://www.nae.net/tag/poverty-domestic/, https://www.nae.net/tag/poverty-international/, and https://www.nae.net/tag/hunger/.

14. In recent years, the media have paid much more attention to what the NAE says about immigration and refugees than about poverty.

15. See https://www.nae.net/topics/.

16. See https://www.nae.net/author/naeboard/.

17. See https://www.nae.net/evangelicals-winter-201516/.
   The best-known evangelical magazine, *Christianity Today*, is not published by the NAE.

18. See, e.g., https://www.nae.net/budget-cuts-poverty-focused-programs/ (June 22, 2017) and https://www.nae.net/letter-to-congress-on-earned-income-tax-credit-and-child-tax-credit/ (July 10, 2015).

19. The term "mainline" appears to refer to denominations that were common around the Main Line suburbs of Philadelphia in the early 20th century. Some Methodists and Presbyterians, however, could be considered evangelicals. Episcopalians and Quakers, probably not.

20. See https://nationalcouncilofchurches.us/member-communions/. Technically, the NCC's full name is the National Council of Churches of Christ in the USA.

21. See, e.g., Wilson 1999 and https://www.pewforum.org/religious-landscape-study/.

22. See https://nationalcouncilofchurches.us/the-ncc-announces-bishop-darin-moore-as-chair-of-governing-board/ (October 12, 2017). Black Protestant churches have a long history of working for social justice, going back at least as far as the civil rights movement.

23. See https://nationalcouncilofchurches.us/joint-action-and-advocacy-for-justice-and-peace/.

24. See https://nationalcouncilofchurches.us/priorities/.

25. See https://nationalcouncilofchurches.us/topics/statements/. Given the declining membership in mainline Protestant churches, it is a bit surprising that the NCC says so little about church finances or leadership.

26. See https://nationalcouncilofchurches.us/topics/news/.

27. See https://faithendpoverty.org/about/.

28. See https://faithendpoverty.org/about/.

29. See https://faithendpoverty.org/campaigns/.

30. See https://faithendpoverty.org/2017/epi-christian-groups-release-statement-president-elect-trumps-policy-agenda-nominees/.
31. See https://faithendpoverty.org/campaigns/ and https://faithendpoverty.org/news/.
32. With respect to other types of Christians, those who are Mormons, Jehovah's Witnesses, Greek Orthodox, and Russian Orthodox collectively account for about three percent of the US population. See https://www.pewforum.org/religious-landscape-study/.
33. Pew estimates that Catholics are 20 percent of the population, while the GSS figure is 23 percent (2018 data).
34. See, e.g., http://www.usccb.org/issues-and-action/index.cfm and http://www.usccb.org/issues-and-action/faithful-citizenship/forming-consciences-for-faithful-citizenship-part-two.cfm.
35. See http://www.usccb.org/about/upload/Strategic-Plan-2017-2020-abbreviated.pdf, pp. 6, 7, 8.
36. The previous strategic plan (for 2012–16) had similar priorities, with slightly less attention to the poor. See https://yakimadiocese.org/files/THENEWEVANGELIZATION.pdf.
37. See http://www.usccb.org/about/catholic-campaign-for-human-development/who-we-are.cfm.
38. See http://www.povertyusa.org/facts; http://www.povertyusa.org/stories; and http://www.povertyusa.org/policies.
39. See http://www.usccb.org/about/general-counsel/rulemaking/upload/Final-OMB-Comments-Consumer-Inflation-Measures.pdf (June 20, 2019).
40. Other faith communities certainly care about poverty. For example, the Union for Reform Judaism represents over 800 congregations in the United States and Canada (which are more numerous than Orthodox Jewish congregations). Social justice is a central concern of Reform Judaism, and this organization regularly speaks out on a variety of issues, including poverty, hunger, and homelessness. "We learn that helping fellow human beings in need, *tzedakah*, is not simply a matter of charity, but of responsibility, righteousness, and justice. The Bible does not merely command us to give to the poor, but to advocate on their behalf." https://rac.org/status-economic-justice-us.
41. See https://www.people-press.org/2012/10/31/in-deadlocked-race-neither-side-has-ground-game-advantage/#politics-from-the-pulpit (October 31, 2012). Earlier poll results were obtained from the iPoll database, maintained by the Roper Center for Public Opinion Research.
42. See https://www.nae.net/about-nae/mission-and-work/. Pope Francis has made a similar claim: "Politics, though often denigrated, remains a lofty vocation and one of the highest forms of charity, inasmuch as it seeks the common good. . . . I beg the Lord to grant us more politicians who are genuinely disturbed by the state of society, the people, the lives of the poor!" (quoted in United States Conference of Catholic Bishops 2015: 13).
43. See https://www.nae.net/christian-leaders-release-videos-by-presidential-candidates-on-poverty/ (July 21, 2015) and https://relevantmagazine.com/current/heres-how-2020-candidates-are-responding-to-a-christian-groups-question-about-poverty/ (December 16, 2019).
44. See http://files.bread.org/pdf/Circle-of-Protection-Signatories.pdf.
45. See http://circleofprotection.us/wp-content/uploads/2019/11/circle-of-protection-letter-to-congress-november-4-2019.pdf (November 4, 2019); http://circleofprotection.us/wp-content/uploads/2019/08/government-shutdown-letter-to-congress-january-2019.pdf (January 22, 2019); http://circleofprotection.us/wp-content/uploads/2019/08/farm-bill-letter-to-congress-september-2018.pdf (September 12, 2018); http://circleofprotection.us/wp-content/uploads/2017/06/circle-of-protection-june-21-2017-budget-statement.pdf (June 21, 2017); http://circleofprotection.us/wp-content/uploads/2016/06/circle-of-protection-poverty-task-force-letter1.pdf (May 26, 2016).
46. See https://www.nae.net/letter-to-congress-on-supplemental-nutrition-assistance-program/ (September 12, 2013).
47. See http://www.usccb.org/issues-and-action/human-life-and-dignity/housing-homelessness/usccb-ccusa-letter-to-senate-on-thud-2018-july-12-2017.cfm (July 12, 2017).
48. See http://circleofprotection.us/wp-content/uploads/2019/08/government-shutdown-letter-to-congress-january-2019.pdf (January 22, 2019).

49. See https://www.allianceonpoverty.org/; https://www.interfaithservices.org/; http://www.sfiwj.org/; and https://www.endpovertyri.org/. Note: these interfaith coalitions are more likely in urban areas where temples and mosques are more common.
50. See https://www.irs.gov/charities-non-profits/charitable-organizations/exemption-requirements-501c3-organizations.
51. See https://nccs.urban.org/project/nonprofit-sector-brief#data, Table 1.
52. See Giving USA Foundation 2019 and https://www.forbes.com/lists/top-charities/#14d9fa175f50.
53. See, e.g., https://independentsector.org/; https://www.councilofnonprofits.org/; and https://nanoe.org/ (National Association of Nonprofit Organizations & Executives).
54. "Most" does not mean "all." The Americares organization, for instance, has helped earthquake victims in Puerto Rico and hurricane victims throughout the United States.
55. Although the United Way sponsors a number of education programs, income support and medical care are also high national priorities, and several local branches help with child care and homelessness. Hence, the United Way is considered part of the social safety net.
56. The Salvation Army, American Red Cross, Feeding America, Habitat for Humanity, and United Way also provide various types of relief to victims of natural disasters, which are not being counted as part of the US social safety net.
57. See https://www.bgca.org/about-us/annual-report. That out-of-school time also includes summers.
58. Technically, The Salvation Amy is an evangelical Protestant church. Most of its resources, however, are devoted to serving the needs of people who do not belong to the church, and most of its volunteers do not belong to the church, which makes it quite different from the Southern Baptist Convention.
59. See https://www.feedingamerica.org/hunger-in-america/food-insecurity.
60. See https://www.habitat.org/stories/what-is-poverty and https://www.habitat.org/impact/need-for-affordable-housing.
61. See https://www.unitedforalice.org/; https://www.unitedforalice.org/national-overview; and https://www.unitedforalice.org/methodology.
62. See Semega et al. 2019; https://humanneedsindex.org/; https://www.salvationarmyusa.org/usn/news/human_needs_index/; and https://humanneedsindex.org/wp-content/uploads/2017/09/Updated_HNI-Release-September-2017-FINAL52.pdf.
63. See https://www.salvationarmyusa.org/usn/overcome-poverty/ and the annual reports linked to https://www.salvationarmyusa.org/usn/newsroom/.
64. See, e.g., the United Way's recent annual reports (https://www.unitedway.org/the-latest/publications/) and policy agenda for Congress (https://www.unitedway.org/our-impact/work/public-policy/policy-agenda).
    It is possible that charitable organizations believe that terms such as "historically disadvantaged" and "medically underserved" carry less stigma than "poor," because they point to structural causes of poverty instead of individual failure. (I thank Stephen Howard for this point.)
65. See the 2018 Annual Report at https://www.bgca.org/about-us/annual-report.
66. See https://www.stjude.org/about-st-jude.html?sc_icid=us-mm-missionstatement#mission and https://www.stjude.org/about-st-jude/unique-operating-model.html.
67. See https://www.unitedway.org/annual-report/2018-annual-report; https://www.salvationarmyusa.org/usn/home/#whatwedo; and https://www.redcross.org/about-us/who-we-are/mission-and-values.html.
68. See https://www.redcross.org/content/dam/redcross/about-us/publications/2019-publications/Annual-Report-2019.pdf; https://www.redcross.org/content/dam/redcross/National/pdfs/annual-reports/Annual-Report-2018.pdf; and https://salvationarmyannualreport.org/pdf.
69. See https://s3.amazonaws.com/uww.assets/site/Goals_for_the_Common_Good.pdf; https://www.unitedway.org/our-impact/mission; and https://www.unitedway.org/our-impact/focus.
70. See https://www.habitat.org/housing-help/apply and https://habitatgnh.org/homeownership/requirements-for-homeownership-applicants/.

71. See https://www.bgca.org/about-us/our-mission-story and https://issuu.com/bgca/docs/2018_national_youth_outcomes_report?e=2043661/68936998.
72. See https://www.salvationarmyusa.org/usn/pathway/; https://www.salvationarmyusa.org/usn/overcome-poverty/; https://www.salvationarmyusa.org/usn/provide-shelter/; and https://www.salvationarmyusa.org/usn/assist-the-unemployed/.
73. See https://www.feedingamerica.org/hunger-in-america and https://www.feedingamerica.org/sites/default/files/2020-01/FA_2019_AnnReport_d7_updated1_14_20.pdf.
74. See https://www.salvationarmyusa.org/usn/the-lgbtq-community-and-the-salvation-army/; https://www.redcross.org/about-us/who-we-are/mission-and-values.html; and https://www.habitatindiana.org/top-10-myths-about-habitat.
75. See the 2018 Annual Report at https://www.bgca.org/about-us/annual-report..
76. See https://www.feedingamerica.org/research/hunger-in-america.
77. See https://www.census.gov/quickfacts/fact/table/US/PST045219.
78. Smaller charities do not always follow this pattern. Examples include 100 Black Men of America and the National Alliance for Hispanic Health.
79. See, e.g., https://www.feedingamerica.org/hunger-in-america/child-hunger-facts and https://www.feedingamerica.org/research/teen-hunger-research.
80. See https://www.feedingamerica.org/research/senior-hunger-research/senior and https://www.salvationarmyusa.org/usn/love-the-elderly/.
81. See https://sojo.net/about-us/news/circle-protection-leaders-speak-out-regarding-passage-tax-bill (December 20, 2017). Note: Catholic Charities USA also belongs to the Circle of Protection.
82. Quotation from page 7 of the 2015 Annual Report (https://www.feedingamerica.org/sites/default/files/about-us/financials/2015-feeding-america-annual-report.pdf).
83. See the United Way's Policy Agenda for the 116th Congress (https://s3.amazonaws.com/uww.assets/site/policy/PP-1018_Public_Policy_Agenda_for_16th_Congress.pdf).
84. In case readers sense a pattern among medical charities, keep in mind that the American Cancer Society and the American Heart Association have supported Medicaid expansion, and they are among the 25 largest charities in the country. https://www.fightcancer.org/what-we-do/increased-access-medicaid and http://www.heart.org/HEARTORG/Advoc ate/Medicaid-Expansion_UCM_480430_SubHomePage.jsp.
85. See https://www.bgca.org/get-involved/advocacy/federal-priorities/USDA-meal-progr ams; https://salvationarmyannualreport.org/financials/; https://www.stjude.org/media-resources/news-releases/2015-medicine-science-news/st-jude-to-receive-nih-grants.html; https://www.unitedway.org/the-latest/press/anti-poverty-advocates-earn-victory-for-low-income-families-through-permane (June 13, 2019); https://www.feedingamerica.org/sites/default/files/2020-01/FA_2019_AnnReport_d7_updated1_14_20.pdf.
86. See https://s3.amazonaws.com/uww.assets/site/policy/PP-1018_Public_Policy_Agenda_for_16th_Congress.pdf, p. 2.
87. See https://www.feedingamerica.org/about-us/press-room/feeding-america-statement-final-usda-rule-will-cut-snap-680000-people (December 4, 2019).
88. See https://www.habitat.org/multimedia/annual-report-2019/; https://www.unitedway.org/our-partners#corporate; https://www.bgca.org/about-us/annual-report; and https://www.feeding america.org/sites/default/files/2020-01/FA_2019_AnnReport_d7_updated1_14_20.pdf.
89. See https://www.forbes.com/top-charities/list/#tab:rank.
90. In the Jewish tradition, the highest form of charity "is to help sustain people before they be- come impoverished by offering a substantial gift in a dignified manner, or by extending a suit- able loan, or by helping them find employment or establish themselves in business so as to make it unnecessary for them to become dependent on others" (Ellis 2018: 167).
91. See http://www.usccb.org/beliefs-and-teachings/what-we-believe/catholic-social-teach ing/two-feet-of-love-in-action.cfm and the documents linked to that page.
92. See https://www.myjewishlearning.com/article/jewish-attitudes-toward-poverty/ and https://reformjudaism.org/node/2457. Note: this approach is more evident in Reform Judaism.
93. See https://www.poorpeoplescampaign.org/about/; https://www.poorpeoplescampaign.org/about/our-principles/; https://www.poorpeoplescampaign.org/about/our-demands/; and https://www.usnews.com/news/politics/articles/2019-09-09/poor-peoples-campa ign-to-register-voters-on-20-state-tour.

Chapter 4

1. See https://obamawhitehouse.archives.gov/the-press-office/2014/01/08/statement-presid ent-50th-anniversary-war-poverty.
2. See Matthews 2015 and Page 2014. The congressional hearings were identified through the Proquest Congressional database.
3. E.g., 50 speeches, 50 days, 50th anniversary.
4. *Annual Message to Congress* (January 4, 1935), available at https://www.presidency.ucsb. edu/documents/annual-message-congress-3.
5. *Remarks Upon Signing the Economic Opportunity Act* (August 20, 1964), available at https:// www.presidency.ucsb.edu/documents/remarks-upon-signing-the-economic-opportun ity-act.
6. Likewise, whether ordinary citizens read these platforms and base their votes on them is an interesting question, but not relevant to this study.
7. These platforms were accessed from The American Presidency Project (https://www.preside ncy.ucsb.edu/).
8. In her analysis of "poor" and "poverty" in party platforms between 1960 and 2016, Miler (2018) calculated a higher number of mentions per platform. My figures indicate that the averages were higher before 2000 than afterwards.
9. Similar to public opinion (Chapter 1), public officials' attention to "poverty," "poor," and "low income" did not increase when the economy was in trouble. The Democrats' platforms mentioned those terms less often in 2008 and 2012, during and right after the Great Recession, than in 2016. The Republican platform of 2008 barely mentioned those terms at all.
10. Farmers are supposed to need a safety net because of natural disasters and fluctuating crop prices.
11. See https://www.comparativeagendas.net/.
12. The CAP data might overstate the level of attention paid to specific issues. When Republicans said, "We want to expand opportunity instead of government" (2000 platform), that was coded as social welfare. When Republicans said, "The public demands constructive action, and we will provide it" (2008), that too was coded as social welfare. The same is true when Democrats promised, "We are committed to exploring alternatives that could better and more equitably serve seniors" (2016).
13. Notable exceptions were the Democrats' 2004 and 2012 platforms, which mentioned the middle class more often. It appears that party platforms between 1960 and 1996 consistently mentioned the poor more often than the middle class (Miler 2018).
14. Because Miler (2018) covers some of this same ground, let me clarify how my analysis differs: by including only party platforms since 2000; by describing the substance of each party's statements regarding poverty and the poor; by comparing poverty to other issues such as terrorism and inflation; and by including references to workers, not just the middle class. These differences also apply to our analysis of State of the Union speeches.

      Miler finds it impressive that the poor have been mentioned more often than the middle class since 1960. I find it impressive that working families and hard-working Americans were mentioned more often than the poor or the middle class since 2000. The language of work has been more prominent than the language of class.

      Full disclosure: I taught Miler when she was an undergraduate at the College of William & Mary, and I really admire her 2018 book.
15. Democrats have also called for more spending on jobs and education to help keep people out of jail (2016 platform).
16. Note: Republicans favor greater school choice for all parents, not just those with low incomes. Vouchers and charter schools are two of the better-known examples.
17. Most of these problems have also been associated in the public mind with racial minorities (e.g., Gilens 1999; Soss, Fording, and Schram 2011; Sparks 2003).
18. In their 2008 party platform, Democrats did encourage fathers to take more responsibility for their children.
19. I also searched through the platforms for attention to urban versus rural problems. Rural/ small-town might be interpreted as White, and urban/inner cities as Black or Hispanic.

Neither party mentioned one type of place more than the other. Interestingly, Democrats made more reference to "rural" than Republicans did.

20. These addresses were accessed from The American Presidency Project.

21. Bush I and II refer to President George W. Bush, not his father, President George H. W. Bush.

22. Haines, Mendelberg, and Butler (2019) performed a similar analysis of SOTU speeches. They searched with a longer list of keywords to indicate poverty, including some (e.g., debt, illiterate, paycheck) that strike me as questionable. More importantly, they classified any mention of workers, working Americans, or working families as references to the middle class. My interpretation is that references to working people are frequent and powerful because they cut across class lines. These terms are designed to unite many of the poor, near poor, and middle classes. As we will see in Chapter 5, many of the poor are employed in low-wage or part-time jobs.

23. For similar findings, see Haines, Mendelberg, and Butler 2019.

24. To supplement these results, I analyzed how often presidents discussed poverty in their weekly radio addresses. These addresses are typically short (1–2 pages) and have a much smaller audience than the State of the Union speeches. Because Trump stopped giving weekly addresses soon after becoming president, I compared Bush to Obama. During his two terms in office, President Bush mentioned poverty in 27 of these addresses. During Obama's two terms, the total was 26. However, if we eliminate references to global poverty, then the tally was 9 for Bush and 21 for Obama, which is a different pattern from the SOTU speeches. Most of Obama's references to domestic poverty (17) came in his second term, and the one theme he repeated over and over was that people who work full-time should not live in poverty. Source: The American Presidency Project.

25. Although Trump called attention to more women being employed (e.g., SOTU 2020), he said nothing about marriage being a good way for women or single mothers to escape poverty.

26. In a similar vein, the Republicans' 2012 platform attributed 80 percent of health care costs to poor lifestyle choices (e.g., obesity, smoking).

27. The differences between Democrats and Republicans were more visible in their party platforms than their State of the Union addresses.

28. These speeches were accessed from The American Presidency Project (https://www.preside ncy.ucsb.edu/).

29. In addition, one might study what elected officials say during congressional hearings. Nonetheless, most of these hearings have a narrow focus, making it harder to determine where poverty ranks among the other issues that officials care about, or where the poor rank among other social groups. Because few Americans pay attention to congressional hearings, it would also be easier for officials to feign concern or make promises that would quickly be forgotten.

30. Rep. Davis's comments were accessed via the ProQuest Congressional database.

Chapter 5

1. See https://www.census.gov/topics/income-poverty/poverty.html.

2. One example: the basic formula for the poverty threshold is three times the cost of a very basic diet. That formula made sense when Americans spent one-third of their budget on food. Since the 1960s, food prices have increased more slowly than other prices, and food has become a smaller share of the average budget. The current poverty threshold should therefore be five or six times the cost of food, not three.

3. See https://today.yougov.com/topics/economy/articles-reports/2019/01/14/how-much-money-do-you-need-earn-year-be-rich. This poll was conducted in September 2018, and the results were accessed on March 20, 2020.

4. To access the United Way's methodology and state-level reports, see https://www.unitedforal ice.org/methodology and https://www.unitedforalice.org/all-reports. In my part of Virginia, the number of households under the ALICE threshold is often 3 to 4 times the number in poverty.

5. Some charities distribute income for a limited time to victims of natural disasters, such as floods and tornadoes.

6. See https://www.census.gov/data/tables/time-series/demo/income-poverty/cps-pov/pov-27.html.
7. The US Bureau of Labor Statistics (2019a) uses a somewhat more restrictive definition of "working poor": individuals who were working or looking for work at least 27 weeks out of the year, but whose incomes were below the poverty threshold. If we adopted that definition, then the number of working poor adults in 2018 would have been closer to seven million than eight million.
8. In 2018, one-third of workers whose hours varied based on their employers' needs reported that they were just getting by financially or having trouble getting by (Board of Governors of the Federal Reserve System 2019).
9. In 2018, almost 85 percent of poor adults lacked a college degree (Semega et al. 2019).
10. A related strategy involves working in the informal economy. Some of the poor will clean homes, provide child care, do yard work, or cut hair (e.g., Edin and Lein 1997; Seefeldt and Sandstrom 2015). These are essentially "gig" jobs for the self-employed.
11. Among adults between the ages of 25 and 54, health problems were the most cited reason for being out of work (Board of Governors of the Federal Reserve System 2019).
12. The four million figure comes from the Census Bureau, which asks Americans six questions about disability. A "yes" to any one of them qualifies the individual as disabled. As discussed later in this chapter, the Social Security Administration uses a more restrictive definition of disability when deciding eligibility for income assistance.
13. Although many people age 65 and older keep working, this option is more viable when one is in good health and does not need to stand all day, bend over repeatedly, or lift heavy objects. Well-paid white-collar workers can take this route more readily than many low-wage workers.
14. Many studies show that when money is tight, the poor and near poor cut back on expenses. My focus in this chapter is on how they generate income.
15. That 20 percent figure could be low. The Federal Reserve estimates than one-quarter of working-age adults have saved nothing for retirement (Board of Governors of the Federal Reserve System 2019).
16. In addition, many low-income Americans overdraw their bank accounts to pay their bills. Every time they bounce a check or withdraw more from the ATM than they have in their account, they must pay a financial penalty. This is another expensive type of small, short-term loan (Bourke and Scott 2018).
17. Some social scientists refer to this problem as "network poverty."
18. The impact of child support on poverty is small. According to the Census Bureau, income from child support reduced the overall poverty rate by only 0.24 percentage points in 2018. It reduced the child poverty rate by 0.58 percentage points (Fox 2019).
19. The block grant structure of TANF allows states to use some of this money for other social programs.
20. Illegal/undocumented immigrants have never been eligible for welfare.
21. Some states and localities offer their own earned income tax credits to help offset their income taxes. These versions are much smaller than the national EITC (Williams, Waxman, and Legendre 2020).
22. The EITC is not exactly like a wage subsidy because the benefits arrive in one lump sum each year, not in every paycheck. Paying down credit card balances is one common way of using the EITC tax refund (Edin and Shaefer 2015; Halpern-Meekin et al. 2015).
23. There are also restrictions on which legal immigrants can apply for SSI.
24. Minimum wage laws do not apply to some small businesses and some younger workers. See https://www.dol.gov/agencies/whd/minimum-wage/faq.
25. See https://www.dol.gov/agencies/whd/minimum-wage/state.
26. The official name for Social Security is Old Age and Survivors Insurance (OASI).
27. To qualify for Social Security, workers need to earn at least $1,410 per quarter year, over 40 quarters. In effect, they must earn at least $5,640 per year for ten years, which is not a high hurdle. A few occupations, mostly involving government workers, are exempt from Social Security. See https://www.ssa.gov/pubs/EN-05-10072.pdf.
28. If their Social Security benefit is low enough, recipients might qualify for a small SSI benefit as well.

29. Like Social Security, eligibility for Disability Insurance is based on the number of quarters worked, but younger workers can receive disability benefits if they have worked fewer than 40 quarters. Unlike Social Security, state governments help determine who qualifies as disabled. Those determinations can vary from state to state, in part because of the subjective nature of some disabilities (e.g., chronic pain, mental illness).

30. "Disability" is not strictly a medical concept; it also reflects the jobs available at any given time. Applications for Disability Insurance tend to decrease when the economy is healthy (Schwartz 2018).

31. See https://www.ssa.gov/OACT/STATS/table6c7.html.

32. See https://www.propublica.org/article/how-much-is-your-arm-worth-depends-where-you-work.

33. These numbers are based on the 2014 wave of the Survey of Income and Program Participation (SIPP), the most recent year available.

34. Although states vary in how much workers must earn in the previous year to be eligible for UI, steadily employed part-time workers are usually covered. See https://oui.doleta.gov/unemploy/pdf/uilawcompar/2019/monetary.pdf.

35. See Woodbury 2015 and https://oui.doleta.gov/unemploy/chartboook.asp. UI recipiency rates also vary by state.

36. See https://oui.doleta.gov/unemploy/chartboook.asp.

37. Not surprisingly, employers feel that insurers are charging them too much, while insurers insist they need a financial cushion to handle any unexpected surge in compensation claims.

38. Although some payroll taxes are paid by employers, economists believe that most of the cost is ultimately borne by workers in the form of lower wages and salaries. Workers' comp is an outlier because most of the financing comes from premiums paid to private insurers and not payroll taxes paid to a state fund.

39. See https://www.taxpolicycenter.org/briefing-book/what-kinds-tax-favored-retirement-arrangements-are-there.

40. The Child Tax Credit could be interpreted as income support or as child care, which will be discussed in Chapter 9. I include it here because the CTC is available to parents with older children who may not need close supervision, and because benefit levels are not linked to child-care expenses.

   In March 2021, the Child Tax Credit was made fully refundable and benefits were increased as part of the American Rescue Plan. Although these changes represented a major expansion for low-income families, they took effect for 2021 only. Democrats (and perhaps a few Republicans) hope to make expansion permanent in subsequent legislation. We will return to this topic in the Postscript.

41. See Semega et al. 2019 and https://www.census.gov/data/tables/time-series/demo/income-poverty/cps-pov.html.

42. To appreciate how race affects the family safety net, see Park, Wiemers, and Seltzer 2019.

43. Because Social Security benefits are based on the best 35 years of earnings, immigrants who arrived in their 30s, 40s, or 50s will have zero earnings for some of that period.

Chapter 6

1. The terms "community kitchen" or "emergency kitchen" are sometimes used instead. Some people feel that "soup kitchen" is antiquated, stigmatizing, and not an accurate reflection of the meals being served. Nevertheless, many organizations still refer to themselves as soup kitchens.

2. State governments have some latitude in setting eligibility criteria for SNAP, such as asset tests and work requirements. Some states run SNAP in conjunction with local governments and some do not. Participation rates are higher in some states than others. Overall, though, geographic variation is considerably less in SNAP than TANF. See Cronquist 2019; Wiseman 2019; and https://www.fns.usda.gov/pd/supplemental-nutrition-assistance-program-snap.

3. Countable assets usually include "cash on hand, checking and savings accounts, savings certificates, stocks and bonds, and nonrecurring lump sum payments such as insurance settlements" (Aussenberg 2018: 7).

4. See Aussenberg 2018 and https://www.fns.usda.gov/snap/work-requirements.

5. Republican officials often support tougher work requirements for public assistance programs. We have seen that in Chapter 4 and will see it again in later chapters.

6. The definition of "disability" in SNAP is similar to that used by Disability Insurance and SSI (Chapter 5).

7. See https://www.fns.usda.gov/pd/supplemental-nutrition-assistance-program-snap.

8. Lyndon B. Johnson, *Remarks Upon Signing the Food Stamp Act* (August 31, 1964), http://www.presidency.ucsb.edu/ws/?pid=26472.

9. The shift to EBT cards was intended to reduce stigma and reduce fraud. The card is replenished each month electronically.

10. In general, SNAP cannot be used at restaurants. In a few parts of the country, a waiver program allows some elderly, disabled, or homeless individuals to use SNAP at participating restaurants. After natural disasters, SNAP can sometimes be used in the affected area to buy hot foods. These exceptions are designed to help low-income people who lack access to a kitchen or cannot cook for themselves. The Papa Murphy pizza chain can also accept SNAP payments because it sells pizza that must be cooked at home.

11. WIC started as a pilot program in 1972 and was made permanent in 1975.

12. See https://www.ers.usda.gov/topics/food-nutrition-assistance/wic-program/ and https://www.fns.usda.gov/wic/about-wic.

13. This is not a tough standard to meet because most Americans eat a diet with nutritional deficiencies.

14. However, the Trump administration's hostility toward immigrants was linked to a drop in WIC enrollment. Some immigrants feared that receiving public assistance would hurt their chances of becoming naturalized citizens (Baumgaertner 2018).

15. Like Food Stamps/SNAP, the national school lunch program has roots in the New Deal era.

16. These include orphanages, homes for the disabled, juvenile detention facilities, and temporary shelters for abused children. In 2019, approximately 2,600 of these institutions participated in the school lunch program (Billings 2020).

17. See Billings 2020; https://www.ers.usda.gov/topics/food-nutrition-assistance/child-nutrition-programs/national-school-lunch-program.aspx; and https://frac.org/research/resource-library/facts-national-school-lunch-program.

18. Eating school meals is not compulsory, and millions of children each day bring their own lunches to school. Despite their broad scope, subsidized school meals are not comparable to Social Security.

19. See https://nces.ed.gov/fastfacts/display.asp?id=898.

20. See Billings 2020; Mattingly 2018; and https://www.feedingamerica.org/our-work/hunger-relief-programs/summer-food-service-program. The bookkeeping is not rigorous in some summer programs, which makes it hard to know exactly how many children benefit.

21. See Billings 2020; https://www.fns.usda.gov/csfp/csfp-fact-sheet; https://www.fns.usda.gov/tefap/tefap-fact-sheet; https://acl.gov/programs/health-wellness/nutrition-services.

22. See https://www.fns.usda.gov/snap/retailer/data.

23. For more information, see https://www.ers.usda.gov/data-products/food-access-research-atlas/ and https://www.ers.usda.gov/data-products/food-access-research-atlas/documentation/.

24. Personal communication with Professor Craig Gundersen, University of Illinois, August 4, 2018. Prof. Gundersen is a well-known expert in food security and food assistance programs, and a member of the Technical Advisory Group at Feeding America.

25. The first food bank was established in 1967 in Phoenix, Arizona, and housed in a local church. The driving force, John van Hengel, received a grant from the federal government to create more food banks in the 1970s. By the end of the decade, several food banks were connected to the Second Harvest organization. The total number of food banks grew rapidly in the 1980s, partly in response to cuts in social spending under President Reagan. The parent organization changed its name from Second Harvest to Feeding America in 2008 (Allahyari 2004; Poppendieck 1998; https://www.feedingamerica.org/about-us/our-history.

26. See https://www.feedingamerica.org/find-your-local-foodbank; https://www.houstonfoodbank.org/about-us/our-financials/; and https://www.lincolnfoodbank.org/about/publications/.

27. Before the pandemic, the Food Bank of the Rockies, based in Denver, was open to the public one Saturday morning each month (https://www.foodbankrockies.org/get-help/). The Virginia Peninsula Foodbank was open to the public for two hours every other month, and offered one-time emergency assistance during regular hours (http://hrfoodbank.org/get-help/).

28. This pattern is more evident with food banks than soup kitchens. The latter often have to purchase specific items in order to prepare a meal (Feeding America 2019).

29. Soup kitchens date back at least as far as the 19th century. Their numbers grew during hard times, such as the economic depression of the mid-1890s and the Great Depression of the 1930s. Some of the best-known examples were operated by The Salvation Army. In 1897, this organization "helped provide Christmas meals to more than 100,000 people. In 1901, the first of many mass sit-down Christmas dinners at Madison Square Garden was funded by kettle donations" (Pickert 2008; see also Bramen 2010).

30. See https://holyapostlessoupkitchen.org/ and https://www.lakeviewpantry.org/about-us/financial-information/.

31. See https://www.foodpantries.org/ci/wa-spokane and https://dilworthsoupkitchen.org/.

32. For overview, see Weinfield et al. 2014. For specific examples, see https://assumptionsyr.org/ministries/food-pantry-and-soup-kitchen/; http://www.edenton-chowanpantry.org/eligibility.php; https://foodbanklarimer.org/do-i-qualify/; https://holyapostlessoupkitchen.org/meal-service-and-outreach/; https://www.lakeviewpantry.org/get-food/requirements/; https://lssnetworkofhope.org/foodpantries/services/eligibility-for-food/; https://www.pittsburghfoodbank.org/get-help/faqs/; https://solvehungertoday.org/blog/visiting-food-pantry-myths-facts/.

33. See https://foodbankonline.org/directory/categories/mobile-pantry; https://www.cincy-caa.org/what-we-do/family-support/mobile-food-pantry.html; and https://mfbn.org/mail-a-meal/.

34. See https://www.feedingamerica.org/take-action/advocate-resource-center. The Meals on Wheels organization has also spoken out forcefully in defense of SNAP. See, e.g., https://www.mealsonwheelsamerica.org/learn-more/national/press-room/2018/04/19/meals-on-wheels-america-calls-on-congress-to-protect-our-nation-s-largest-anti-hunger-safety-net.

35. See Feeding America 2019; Weinfield et al. 2014; https://www.feedingamerica.org/take-action/advocate/federal-hunger-relief-programs/snap; https://www.feedingamerica.org/hunger-blog/community-kitchens-creating; and http://hrfoodbank.org/culinary/.

36. See Weinfield et al. 2014 and https://www.feedingamerica.org/our-work/hunger-relief-programs.

37. Food banks also generate a little revenue by charging food pantries and soup kitchens for transportation and warehousing costs.

38. See Feeding America 2019; https://www.feedingamerica.org/about-us/financials; https://www.feedingamerica.org/our-work/our-approach/reduce-food-waste. Note: the estimated value of donations from grocery stores and food producers is based on wholesale cost and not retail price.

39. These numbers do not include "informal volunteering" to help family, friends, and neighbors.

40. Unlike contributions of food or money, time and labor are not tax deductible.

41. See https://www.mealsonwheelsamerica.org/learn-more/what-we-deliver.

42. See Jaffe 2017; https://www.mealsonwheelsamerica.org/learn-more/national; and https://www.mealsonwheelsamerica.org/learn-more/what-we-deliver/meals-on-wheels-health. In particular, Meals on Wheels claims that its service lowers the chances that elderly clients will suffer a serious fall or will need to move into a nursing home.

43. See Elis 2017; Fottrell 2017; Levine 2020; https://www.mealsonwheelsamerica.org/learn-more/national/financials; https://www.mowp.org/faq/.

44. See https://www.bvfb.org/senior-outreach-program; https://chestercountyfoodbank.org/programs-education/kitchen/meals-on-wheels/; https://feedmore.org/how-we-help/; https://mealsonwheelswny.org/2019/02/28/food-bank-meals-on-wheels-combining-organizations-to-feed-more-western-new-yorkers-in-need/.

45. "'Food security' and 'food insecurity,' as defined by USDA, focus on economic and other access-related reasons associated with an individual's ability to purchase or otherwise obtain

enough to eat. They are also terms that can be objectively measured. USDA's use of these terms came out of a decades-long collaboration between federal agencies and private-sector researchers to improve the measurement of hunger in the US population. This consortium concluded that hunger, as an individual-level physiological condition, was difficult to measure through a household survey. They recommended food security and food insecurity as alternative concepts that captured the economic reasons for inadequate food and/or nutritional intake, rather than individual behaviors that may result in the physical condition of being hungry (for example, dieting or missing a meal due to illness)." Quoted in Aussenberg, Billings, and Colello 2019: 1–2).

46. In statistical analyses, the connections between these various problems and food insecurity persist, even controlling for income.

Chapter 7

1. See consumer expenditure data at https://www.bls.gov/cex/tables.htm#annual.
2. Some critics argue that the 30 percent target should be lower for families with children, who have higher expenses for food, clothing, and medical care than single adults (Airgood-Obrycki and Molinsky 2019).
3. The cost figures cited for owning and renting include utilities. The numbers in this paragraph and the next two come from the United States Census Bureau, https://data.census.gov/ced sci/?q=Housing (Selected Housing Characteristics).
4. HUD is currently developing a comprehensive measure of housing insecurity. Some pilot questions were included in the 2017 and 2019 American Housing Surveys. https://www.huduser.gov/portal/pdredge/pdr-edge-frm-asst-sec-111918.html.
5. Although a number of studies refer to "housing instability," the meaning varies. It could include some combination of homelessness, doubling up, overcrowding, frequent moves, cost burden, and the physical adequacy of the dwelling.
6. During the late 18th and early 19th centuries, most American states required voters to be property owners.
7. See https://www.census.gov/hhes/www/housing/census/historic/owner.html and https://www.census.gov/housing/hvs/index.html.
8. See https://www.census.gov/housing/hvs/index.html and https://www.nar.realtor/research-and-statistics/housing-statistics/existing-home-sales.
9. Individuals must have worked steadily for two years to qualify for an FHA-backed loan (https://www.hud.gov/program_offices/housing/sfh/handbook_4000-1.

   Affluent homeowners who receive special treatment in the tax code must have income, but it need not be from employment. It could come from stock dividends, family trusts, or rental property. Thus, the linkages between work and housing assistance are stronger for less affluent Americans.
10. Given how hard it is for many Americans to save money (Chapter 5), a modest down payment is crucial to buying a home.
11. Author's calculation based on data from https://www.mortgagecalculator.org/calcs/fha-mortgage-qualifier.php.
12. The Veterans Administration (VA) also operates a loan guarantee program. It is smaller than the FHA program, the average value of home loans is larger, and eligibility is tied to military service (Perl 2018). All these factors limit its ability to help low-income individuals buy a house.
13. For instance, some states and localities issue mortgage revenue bonds to assist first-time homebuyers. These bonds tend to help the same kind of people who benefit from FHA loan guarantees (McCarty, Perl, and Jones 2019; Schwartz 2014).
14. See, e.g., https://www.habitat.org/about/faq, https://habitatlafayette.org/about-us/sweat-equity/?doing_wp_cron=1594812338.9343268871307373046875, https://www.patuxenthabitat.org/homeownership-criteria-and-applying, and https://www.habitatoc.org/restore-orientation/.

   Note: Habitat for Humanity has Christian roots but does not impose religious tests on volunteers or recipients.

15. A few charities build homes for veterans. They tend to focus on disability rather than low income, and they build anywhere from a few dozen to a few hundred homes each year. See, e.g., https://www.hfotusa.org/mission/ and https://www.operationfinallyhome.org/.
16. Author's calculations, based on data from 2017 American Housing Survey. https://www.census.gov/programs-surveys/ahs.html.
17. For households with above-average incomes, the supply of affordable rentals exceeds the demand.
18. For state-level data, see https://reports.nlihc.org/gap.
19. See https://www.cbpp.org/research/housing/federal-rental-assistance-fact-sheets#US.
20. In most parts of the country, people who receive rental assistance pay 30 percent of their income toward rent. The Trump administration tried to raise this to 35 percent. It also called for increasing the minimum monthly rent from $50 to $150, which would hurt the poorest of the poor (Booker 2018).
21. Data from HUD's Resident Characteristics Report, https://pic.hud.gov/pic/RCRPublic/rcrmain.asp.
22. Data from HUD's Resident Characteristics Report, https://pic.hud.gov/pic/RCRPublic/rcrmain.asp.
23. As part of the Moving to Work initiative within HUD, a small number of local housing agencies (less than 3%) have been allowed to impose work requirements on some recipients of public housing and rental vouchers. Most recipients are exempt (Levy, Edmonds, and Simington 2018).
24. Data from HUD's Resident Characteristics Report, https://pic.hud.gov/pic/RCRPublic/rcrmain.asp.
25. Data from HUD's Resident Characteristics Report, https://pic.hud.gov/pic/RCRPublic/rcrmain.asp and Center on Budget and Policy Priorities, *Federal Rental Assistance Fact Sheets* (December 10, 2019). https://www.cbpp.org/research/housing/federal-rental-assistance-fact-sheets#US.
26. Data from HUD's Resident Characteristics Report, https://pic.hud.gov/pic/RCRPublic/rcrmain.asp.
27. Both the HOME program and the LIHTC require that a certain fraction of the monies go to nonprofit housing organizations (Schwartz 2014). HOME is short for the HOME Investment Partnerships Program.
28. See https://www.nmhc.org/research-insight/analysis-and-guidance/rent-control-laws-by-state/.
29. Some places distinguish between rent control and rent stabilization. The former caps the monthly rent at a certain amount, while the latter caps the rate of increase.
30. Data from the American Housing Survey (AHS) Table Creator, available at https://www.census.gov/programs-surveys/ahs.html.
31. Though used widely, the term "workforce housing" is controversial. The term might imply that low-income housing does not serve workers, even though it does.
32. Recently, large companies such as Apple, Google, and Microsoft have promised to spend millions of dollars on affordable housing in the communities where they operate. It is too soon to tell how much of that housing will benefit low-income individuals and how much will benefit those companies' workers, many of whom are well-paid.
33. See https://dhcd.dc.gov/publication/2019-inclusionary-zoning-maximum-income-rent-and-purchase-price-schedule.
34. See https://evictionlab.org/. These numbers do not include many cases where eviction occurred without a formal court order. Sometimes the threat of legal action is enough to drive tenants away. The true size of the eviction problem could be twice as large (Desmond 2016; Maciag 2018).
35. See Hatch 2017 and https://evictionlab.org/covid-policy-scorecard/. Because eviction rates vary within states as well, state laws cannot be the sole cause of differences among states.
36. See https://www.nahma.org/about/affordable-100/ and https://www.nahma.org/grassroots-advocacy/urgent-issues/.
37. The growth in shared households is one reason why the average size of American households has been growing in recent years, for the first time in well over a century (Fry 2019).

38. Author's calculations based on data from the American Housing Survey Table Creator. https://www.census.gov/programs-surveys/ahs/data/interactive/ahstablecreator.html?s_areas=00000&s_year=2017&s_tablename=TABLE1&s_bygroup1=1&s_bygroup2=1&s_filtergroup1=1&s_filtergroup2=1.
39. See https://endhomelessness.org/homelessness-in-america/homelessness-statistics/state-of-homelessness-2020/.
40. These shelters have also become a lucrative business for some companies that contract with government (Kotch and Bragman 2019).
41. See https://avaloncenter.org/about-us.
42. See, e.g., https://avaloncenter.org/sites/default/files/avalon_fy18_audit.pdf; https://www.bangorareashelter.org/wp-content/uploads/2019/02/BAHS-Annual-Report-2018.pdf; https://homelesssolutions.org/about/annual-report/; and https://www.stjohncenter.org/annual-report/.

    A few years ago, billionaire Jeff Bezos pledged $1 billion to a new Day 1 Families Fund, devoted to helping homeless families. The Fund made grants worth almost $100 million in 2018 and distributed slightly larger amounts in 2019 and 2020. The recipients have been established organizations located all over the country. The individual awards are usually for $1–5 million. That money is being used to provide temporary shelter as well as food and social services. Critics have pointed out certain inconsistencies between Bezos's charitable efforts and his company Amazon's record on affordable housing (Del Valle 2018; Feuer 2019; Vengattil and Dastin 2018).
43. Based on evidence from several countries, including the United States, Ansell (2014) found that greater wealth from housing is associated with lower public support for redistribution and social insurance.
44. The number of homeless people has declined since the Great Recession (US Department of Housing and Urban Development 2020b).
45. See US Department of Housing and Urban Development 2020b; National Alliance to End Homelessness 2020; and https://files.hudexchange.info/reports/published/CoC_Pop Sub_NatlTerrDC_2019.pdf.
46. Two smaller groups, Native Americans and Pacific Islanders, also have significantly higher chances of being homeless.
47. Data from HUD's Resident Characteristics Report, https://pic.hud.gov/pic/RCRPublic/rcrmain.asp.
48. For the exact definitions, see https://www2.census.gov/programs-surveys/ahs/2017/2017%20AHS%20Definitions.pdf?#.
49. Author's calculations, based on data from 2017 American Housing Survey. https://www.census.gov/programs-surveys/ahs.html.
50. One reason is that racial minorities are more likely to live in deep poverty.

Chapter 8

1. However, the uninsured will often be charged higher prices.
2. For more detailed statistics regarding medical costs, see the Agency for Healthcare Research and Quality, Hospital Cost and Utilization Project (https://www.hcup-us.ahrq.gov/reports/statbriefs/sb_costs.jsp) and the Health Care Cost Institute (https://healthcostinstitute.org/data).
3. Moreover, it is in our collective interest to ensure that everyone, no matter how poor, has access to medical care in order to prevent the spread of infectious diseases like whooping cough and Covid-19.
4. To pay these charges, some people rely on their credit cards, which carry high interest rates (Olen 2017; see also Chapter 5).
5. These averages conceal substantial variation. Some employers pay the entire insurance premium; others pay less than half (Claxton et al. 2019). Nevertheless, economists believe that workers ultimately foot most of the bill. Whatever employers spend on health insurance is money that could have gone to higher wages.

6. Individual policies are more expensive because insurers fear adverse selection: the people seeking health insurance might be prone to higher-than-average medical bills, for reasons known to them but not the insurer.

7. Some companies, however, are permitted to offer short-term health policies that do not conform to the ACA. They can deny coverage to people with pre-existing conditions, and they can refuse to pay for certain treatments that traditional insurance policies will cover. Such policies are appealing because they are cheaper, but they are known as "junk plans" for a reason (Andrews 2020).

8. See https://www.kff.org/infographic/employer-responsibility-under-the-affordable-care-act/.

9. As a result, the massive tax breaks for job-based health insurance mainly benefit middle-class and upper-middle class workers.

10. See https://www.census.gov/data/tables/time-series/demo/health-insurance/historical-series/hic.html.

11. After two years on Disability Insurance, individuals become eligible for Medicare. For peculiar historical reasons, Medicare also covers people with end-stage renal disease (i.e., kidney failure).

12. For data concerning Medicare beneficiaries, see https://www.cms.gov/research-statistics-data-systems/cms-program-statistics/2018-medicare-enrollment-section#Total and https://www.kff.org/state-category/health-coverage-uninsured/medicare-coverage/.

13. Medicare spent approximately $45 billion on skilled nursing facilities and home health care in 2018, which was a small fraction of the total (see https://www.cms.gov/files/document/2018-report.pdf. These types of care will be discussed more in Chapter 9.

14. See Medicare's 2020 Annual Report at https://www.cms.gov/files/document/2020-medicare-trustees-report.pdf.

15. Part C of Medicare is also optional. It delivers the services covered by Parts A, B, and D through a managed care model rather than traditional fee-for-service medicine.

16. The national government pays for most of Parts B and D, while state governments pay a small share of Part D (Kaiser Family Foundation 2019).

17. See https://www.cms.gov/Research-Statistics-Data-and-Systems/Statistics-Trends-and-Reports/NationalHealthExpendData/NHE-Fact-Sheet.

18. People who retire after the age of 65 might have Medicare and job-based health insurance.

19. Medicaid and Medicare were both enacted in 1965.

20. However, many legal immigrants cannot qualify for Medicaid until they have resided in the United States for five years. Undocumented immigrants are not eligible at all.

21. This figure reflects enrollment in Medicaid and CHIP. No more than one million of these Medicaid recipients would have been living in nursing homes. See https://www.kff.org/infographic/medicaids-role-in-nursing-home-care/.

    Note: states have the option to extend eligibility to people whose incomes are above 138 percent of the poverty line, and some states do, especially for children. Most Medicaid recipients, however, are poor or near poor.

22. See Colello 2020; https://www.cms.gov/Research-Statistics-Data-and-Systems/Statistics-Trends-and-Reports/NationalHealthExpendData/NHE-Fact-Sheet and https://www.cms.gov/files/document/2018-report.pdf.

23. See https://itep.org/fairness-matters-a-chart-book-on-who-pays-state-and-local-taxes-2019/#2.

24. One reason that children are such a large share of the Medicaid population is that many states cover young children up to 200 percent of the federal poverty line, and older children up to 150 percent. The thresholds vary considerably from state to state.

25. At best, Medicaid work requirements are symbolic gestures. It is unrealistic to think that many adults on Medicaid could find or afford health insurance in the private sector if they really tried. Alternatively, these requirements could have nothing to do with medical care; the main point is to force more adults to work in low-wage or part-time jobs.

26. For enrollment data, see https://www.kff.org/state-category/health-coverage-uninsured/.

27. As of 2018, Medicaid was paying for 38 percent of all non-elderly adults receiving treatment for opioid use disorder. https://www.kff.org/infographic/medicaids-role-in-addressing-opioid-epidemic/ (June 3, 2019).

28. See https://www.medicaid.gov/medicaid/cost-sharing/index.html. For evidence that Medicaid recipients are aware of large differences in coverage from state to state, see Michener 2018.

29. See https://www.medicaid.gov/medicaid/national-medicaid-chip-program-information/ medicaid-childrens-health-insurance-program-basic-health-program-eligibility-levels/ index.html; https://www.kff.org/medicaid/issue-brief/status-of-state-medicaid-expans ion-decisions-interactive-map/; https://www.kff.org/statedata/collection/medicaid-beh avioral-health-services/; and https://www.kff.org/state-category/medicaid-chip/medic aid-benefits/.

30. See Mitchell et al. 2021 and https://www.medicaid.gov/state-overviews/scorecard/how-much-states-spend-per-medicaid-enrollee/index.html.

31. The government also plays crucial roles in public health and medical research. I consider those to be related but distinct from medical care.

32. Medical care for the military is paid by the national government out of general revenues. Once again, the rich and corporations are footing most of the bill.

33. For more details, see https://www.tricare.mil/Plans/Eligibility. Note: members of the armed services are not well cared for in all respects. In recent years the media have called attention to military families having to use food pantries.

34. In some circumstances, the VA will pay for veterans to be treated in the private sector.

35. See https://www.va.gov/healthbenefits/apps/explorer/AnnualIncomeLimits/LegacyV AThresholds?FiscalYear=2019.

36. See https://www.va.gov/vetdata/Utilization.asp. Some veterans with service-related disabilities could also be low income.
    Throughout the VA system, the gender gap is enormous: almost 90 percent of veterans who receive benefits are men. That disparity reflects historical patterns of enlistment in the military.

37. See https://www.ihs.gov/newsroom/factsheets/quicklook/ and https://www.ihs.gov/ newsroom/factsheets/ihsprofile/.

38. See America's Essential Hospitals 2020; https://www.kff.org/state-category/providers-service-use/hospital-utilization/; https://jacksonhealth.org/about-us/; https://www.dhs. pa.gov/Services/Assistance/Pages/State-Hospitals.aspx. My thanks to Jennifer Mellor for helping me find data about public hospitals.

39. The number of public hospitals varies widely across the country, from zero in a few states to 103 in Texas (as of 2018). See https://www.kff.org/state-category/providers-service-use/ hospitals/.

40. See https://www.advisory.com/daily-briefing/2018/12/04/philanthropic-gifts; https:// www.beckershospitalreview.com/finance/25-largest-gifts-to-healthcare-organizations-in-2018.html; and https://www.beckershospitalreview.com/finance/top-26-gifts-to-healthc are-organizations-in-2019.html.

41. Likewise, money donated for a new hospital wing or the latest CAT-scan equipment might benefit a variety of people, as long as they lived nearby.

42. See https://ripmedicaldebt.org/wp-content/uploads/2019/12/RIP_MEDICAL_DEBT_ 990_2019.pdf and https://www.prnewswire.com/news-releases/rip-medical-debt-receives-transformative-gift-from-philanthropist-mackenzie-scott-301193393.html.

43. These donors' motivations could range widely, from civic duty to guilt to fear of legal action.

44. The founder of one crowdfunding site once explained the need for his business this way: "Our health care system is shit and it's trending shittier" (quoted in Olen 2017).

45. Free and charitable clinics are not always the most durable organizations. The exact number will fluctuate from year to year as clinics open and close. My thanks to Caroline Brickley for helping me find information about free and charitable clinics.

46. For example, the Olde Towne Medical Clinic, not far from my office, uses a sliding scale. Patients pay between $10 and $70 per visit, depending on their income. A free clinic in our area recommends but does not require that individuals contribute $20 for each appointment and $3 for each prescription. See https://www.oldetownemedicalcenter.org/how-much-will-i-pay and https://lackeyclinic.org/en/policies/.

47. For more details, see https://www.nafcclinics.org/.

48. See https://www.nafcclinics.org/sites/default/files/NAFC%202019%20Infographic.pdf.

49. See https://www.nafcclinics.org/find-clinic and https://capitalcityrescuemission.org/how-we-help/homeless-services/health-clinic/. Note: a small fraction of clinics operate mobile clinics to serve a wider area.

50. See the RAM fact sheet at https://www.ramusa.org/media-resources/.

51. Public charities are still obligated to pay Social Security and Medicare taxes for their employees.

52. See https://data.worldbank.org/indicator/NY.GDP.MKTP.CD?most_recent_value_desc= true. What the United States spends on prescription drugs is comparable to the entire GDP of Denmark or South Africa.

53. The employment data come from the US Bureau of Labor Statistics. See https://www.bls. gov/iag/tgs/iag62.htm#workforce; https://www.bls.gov/oes/2018/may/naics4_325400. htm; and https://www.bls.gov/iag/tgs/iag446.htm#about.

54. See https://www.usatoday.com/picture-gallery/money/2019/03/22/this-is-the-largest-employer-in-every-state/39237263/.

55. See detailed table of National Health Expenditures, 1960-2019, available at https://www. cms.gov/Research-Statistics-Data-and-Systems/Statistics-Trends-and-Reports/NationalH ealthExpendData/NationalHealthAccountsHistorical.

56. These also vary geographically. As of 2018, some states (e.g., Minnesota, New York) had no for-profit hospitals. In Florida and Texas, over half the hospitals were for-profit. See https://www.kff.org/state-category/providers-service-use/hospitals/.

57. Doctors also complain about administrative burdens in Medicaid, and patients who fail to show up for appointments (Lee 2017).

58. Hospitals have different standards for what qualifies as low income.

59. Based on Medicare cost reports from 2018, Bruch and Bellamy (2020) found no statistically significant difference between the level of charity care offered by for-profit and nonprofit hospitals. This result raises the question of whether nonprofits are doing too little.

60. "Corporate charity" includes nonprofit hospitals and clinics, which legally are nonprofit corporations.

61. Looking at Table 8.1, some readers might wonder how so many part-time workers and unemployed people can have private health insurance. Many of them are covered by the policy of a family member who is employed full-time.

62. For health insurance coverage of men and women, see https://www.census.gov/data/tables/ time-series/demo/health-insurance/historical-series/hic.html, Table HHI-01.

63. See https://www.census.gov/data/tables/time-series/demo/health-insurance/historical-series/hic.html, Table HHI-01.

64. "The definition does not include other dimensions of someone's health plan that might leave them potentially exposed to costs, such as copayments or uncovered services. It therefore provides a conservative measure of underinsurance in the United States" (Collins, Bhupal, and Doty 2019: 2).

65. When it comes to coverage gaps and underinsurance, the differences between men and women are small (Collins, Bhupal, and Doty 2019).

66. Many grocery stores and pharmacies have machines that will check blood pressure for free, though doctors recommend this be done in person on a regular basis.

Chapter 9

1. In the context of long-term services and supports, most recipients are adults. Children with special needs, such as intellectual and developmental disabilities, are also included.

2. See https://www.multivu.com/players/English/8625551-8625551-genworth-cost-of-care-survey-2019/ and https://www.payingforseniorcare.com/nursing-homes#cost-table#cost-table.

3. There is no single age when all children become able to function independently. Government child-care subsidies are usually targeted at children under the age of 13.

4. See https://www.childcareaware.org/our-issues/research/the-us-and-the-high-price-of-child-care-2019/. Note: the price of child care varies considerably from state to state.

5. Residents of nursing homes and similar facilities are therefore excluded from this count.

6. However, because racial minorities have shorter life expectancies, the lifetime probability of needing long-term care is similar among Whites, Blacks, and Hispanics who reach the age of 65. Because women live longer than men, their lifetime probability of needing long-term care is greater and the gender gap widens over time (Johnson 2019).

7. See https://www.census.gov/data/tables/2017/demo/popproj/2017-summary-tables. html, Table 2, and https://www.cdc.gov/nchs/hus/contents2019.htm?search=Life_exp ectancy, Table 004. By 2040, the United States will have more people over the age of 65 than under the age of 18.

8. These private policies usually pay some but not all costs of long-term care. In 2019, the state of Washington approved a new long-term care benefit. It will be financed out of payroll taxes, making it a form of social insurance. Beneficiaries will receive $100 per day for up to a year, and that money can be used to reimburse family caregivers. This benefit is supposed to take effect in 2025 (Lieber 2019).

9. In 2018, private insurance accounted for less than 10 percent of all spending on long-term services and supports (Colello 2019).

10. The survey estimated that at least three million children played a similar caregiving role.

11. As they try to reduce costs, hospitals have increasingly transferred medical responsibilities to family caregivers (Reinhard et al. 2019b). The line separating medical care and daily care is becoming fuzzier.

12. A different survey, based solely on Medicare beneficiaries, found that Black recipients of unpaid care were almost three times more likely than White recipients to be living in poverty, and almost four times more likely to be eligible for Medicaid (Fabius, Wolff, and Kasper 2020).

13. The Veterans Administration and the Children's Health Insurance Program provide some LTSS, but the spending levels are much lower than Medicaid and Medicare (Colello 2020). Spending on long-term care through the Older Americans Act is even smaller (Colello and Napili 2020).

14. These are usually Section 1915(c) or Section 1115 waivers.

15. For more details regarding state Medicaid programs and LTSS, see https://www.medicaidpla nningassistance.org/state-specific-medicaid-eligibility/.

16. When calculating assets, states generally exclude the value of a car and a home if it is the primary residence.

17. For example, it is easier to find out about long-term care that is provided on a fee-for-service basis than by managed care.

18. See https://www.medicare.gov/coverage/home-health-services.

19. To be eligible, individuals must have recently spent at least three days in a hospital. Medicare will pay for personal care such as bathing and dressing if the individual is also receiving medical care in these facilities.

20. See https://www.medicare.gov/coverage/skilled-nursing-facility-snf-care and https://www. medicare.gov/coverage/hospice-care.

21. See https://www.cms.gov/Medicare-Medicaid-Coordination/Medicare-and-Medicaid-Coordination/Medicare-Medicaid-Coordination-Office/Downloads/MMCO_Factsheet. pdf and https://www.cms.gov/files/document/reporttocongressmmco.pdf.

22. See https://www.bls.gov/ooh/healthcare/home-health-aides-and-personal-care-aides. htm#tab-6.

23. In the process, private equity firms might saddle nursing homes with so much debt that they eventually declare bankruptcy. This happened to HCR ManorCare in 2018, which at the time was one of the largest nursing home chains in the country. It had been bought by the Carlyle Group in 2007. A decade of their involvement generated $7 billion in debts (Goldstein, Silver-Greenberg, and Gebeloff 2020).

24. See https://franchisebusinessreview.com/post/senior-care-franchises/ (October 1, 2019) and https://homehealthcarenews.com/2021/03/home-health-profit-margins-projected-to-rem ain-strong-in-2021/ (March 16, 2021).

25. See https://www.ahcancal.org/News-and-Communications/Press-Releases/Pages/Financ ial-Struggle-of-Nursing-Homes-Puts-Medicaid-Reimbursement-Rates-Back-in-the-Spotli ght.aspx and https://www.medicaidplanningassistance.org/nursing-home-costs/.

26. See https://www.ahcancal.org/Advocacy/IssueBriefs/Medicaid.pdf. Note: the adequacy of Medicaid reimbursement also affects long-term care organizations that are nonprofits.

27. One reason Medicare pays more than Medicaid is that Medicare clients often have serious medical issues related to a recent hospitalization. Medicare is willing to pay long-term care facilities more so these people will not have to be readmitted to a hospital. These higher reimbursements could give nursing homes a perverse incentive to send their Medicaid clients to a hospital so they can come back as Medicare clients (Meyer 2020).

28. Although foster care is one type of child care, it will not be discussed in this section because it is a relatively small piece of the social safety net. As of September 2019, approximately 425,000 children were in foster care. An estimated 20 percent of foster children are living in poverty (Pac, Waldfogel, and Wimer 2017). For more information, see https://www.child welfare.gov/pubPDFs/foster.pdf (March 2021).

29. In theory, the Child Tax Credit might enable parents to stay home with their kids, since eligibility does not hinge on paying for child care. As mentioned in Chapter 5, that tax break has mostly been helping families with average and above-average incomes.

30. Single-parent families were not just a little poor. It would have taken more than $10,000 apiece just to bring them up to the poverty line (Semega et al. 2019).

31. Although some companies offer on-site day care, few low-income workers are employed by those companies.

32. The tax code includes a child-care credit, but it is small ($5 billion in 2019), and most of the money goes to families with incomes over $100,000 (Joint Committee on Taxation 2019).

33. However, the government can waive or reduce the work requirements for parents who are disabled or are caring for a disabled child.

34. See https://www.acf.hhs.gov/occ/fact-sheet/characteristics-families-served-child-care-and-development-fund-ccdf-based.

35. In general, the demand for paid child care in the United States is greater than the supply. This is especially true for infants, toddlers, and children with disabilities (Child Care Aware of America 2019; Currie 2006; Jessen-Howard, Malik, and Falgout 2020).

36. For more details, see https://www.acf.hhs.gov/occ/data/fy-2019-preliminary-data-table-12; https://www.acf.hhs.gov/occ/data/fy-2019-preliminary-data-table-12a; and https://www.acf.hhs.gov/occ/data/fy-2019-preliminary-data-table-18.

37. The specific mix of providers varies by state. For details regarding for-profit and nonprofit child care providers, see https://www.census.gov/programs-surveys/nonemployer-statist ics/data/tables.html.

38. Most child-care establishments are licensed and regulated by state governments. The rules generally concern health and safety, and they are not the same in every state. See https://www.childcareaware.org/families/child-care-regulations/who-regulates-child-care/.

39. In most respects, the people working in child-care centers and family child-care homes are quite similar. One difference is that immigrants are more likely to be working in family child-care homes. See https://www.childtrends.org/publications/professional-characterist ics-of-the-early-care-and-education-workforce-descriptions-by-race-ethnicity-languages-spo ken-and-nativity-status.

40. See https://www.bls.gov/ooh/personal-care-and-service/childcare-workers.htm#tab-1.

41. See https://www.acf.hhs.gov/occ/fact-sheet/characteristics-families-served-child-care-and-development-fund-ccdf-based.

42. See https://eclkc.ohs.acf.hhs.gov/about-us/article/head-start-program-facts-fiscal-year-2019. The rest of this paragraph is based on this source and Lynch 2019b.

43. Infants and toddlers are eligible for Early Head Start.

44. See https://eclkc.ohs.acf.hhs.gov/about-us/article/head-start-program-facts-fiscal-year-2019; https://www.childrensdefense.org/policy/policy-priorities/education/early-head-start-and-head-start/; and https://www.nhsa.org/national-head-start-fact-sheets/.

45. In the Early Head Start program, some infants and toddlers are served in home-based settings.

46. See https://eclkc.ohs.acf.hhs.gov/about-us/article/head-start-program-facts-fiscal-year-2019.

47. The high cost of child care impacts middle-class families as well. They will likely devote 10 to 15 percent of their incomes to child care, not seven percent (Malik 2019).

48. For a single-parent family living in poverty, full child support might equal $4000–$5000 per year. That couldn't pay for full-time child care in most parts of the country, but it would help. In 2017, less than half a million poor, single-parent families received full child support, which was a fraction of all such families (Grall 2020).
49. See https://www.dol.gov/sites/dolgov/files/WHD/legacy/files/whdfs28.pdf. Before 1993, some employers were offering unpaid parental leave, mostly to new mothers who were working for larger companies.
50. The emphasis on "working Americans" is consistent with patterns discussed in Chapter 4.
51. See President Clinton's Statement on Signing the Family and Medical Leave Act of 1993 (February 5, 1993). https://www.presidency.ucsb.edu/documents/statement-signing-the-family-and-medical-leave-act-1993.
52. See https://www.dol.gov/sites/dolgov/files/WHD/legacy/files/whdfs28.pdf.
53. Fifteen percent of low-wage and high-wage workers were excluded from the FMLA because they were employed by small businesses (Brown, Roy, and Klerman 2020).
54. Given that most low-wage workers are not married or living with a partner (Brown, Roy, and Klerman 2020), they cannot count on living off someone else's paycheck while on unpaid leave.
55. In 2018, 31 percent of workers in the bottom decile had access to paid sick leave. See https://www.bls.gov/news.release/archives/ebs2_07202018.htm.
56. Voters in Colorado endorsed paid family and medical leave by referendum in November 2020.
57. The AARP arrived at this $470 billion figure by totaling the number of care hours (34 billion) and multiplying by an hourly wage for each state that was "the average of the state minimum wage, median home health aide wage, and median private pay cost of hiring a home health aide" (Reinhard et al. 2019a: 23). The average hourly wage for the entire country was $13.81, which ranged from $10.57 in Louisiana to $18.01 in Alaska.

    These numbers should be treated as ballpark estimates. Unpaid care, for example, does not always mean uncompensated care. Some family members might receive free room or board in exchange for taking care of an elderly relative in that relative's home, in which case the total dollar figure should be lower. These estimates could also overlook opportunity costs incurred by unpaid caregivers (i.e., paying jobs they have given up), which would make the total even larger.
58. See https://www.childwelfare.gov/topics/systemwide/laws-policies/statutes/manda/.
59. See https://www.justice.gov/elderjustice/elder-justice-statutes-0 and http://eldermistr eatment.usc.edu/wp-content/uploads/2020/09/NCEA_NAPSA_MandatedReportBrief Full_web508.pdf.
60. Regarding ways to reduce racial bias in the child welfare system, see: https://www.childwelf are.gov/topics/systemwide/cultural/disproportionality/reducing/bias/.
61. Puerto Rico and Tennessee did not report the race or ethnicity of victims (US Department of Health & Human Services 2021).
62. Nothing I have said here should be interpreted as a defense of child neglect, much less child abuse. There is a big difference between explaining patterns and excusing them. But unintended neglect should be viewed differently than deliberate acts.
63. See https://ncea.acl.gov/What-We-Do/Research/Statistics-and-Data.aspx#_edn79; https://www.cdc.gov/violenceprevention/elderabuse/fastfact.html; https://ovc.ojp.gov/sites/g/files/xyckuh226/files/media/document/2016ncvrw_6_elderabuse-508.pdf; and https://www.nursinghomeabusecenter.com/elder-abuse/statistics/.
64. For additional evidence of problems in nursing homes, see https://www.reuters.com/legal/litigation/california-underreported-nursing-home-abuse-hhs-2021-06-14/ and https://www.cnn.com/2019/03/06/health/nursing-home-abuse-senate-hearing-bn/index.html.

Conclusion

1. For example, Catholic Charities USA receives federal money to help promote adoption and foster care.
2. See https://scholarworks.iupui.edu/bitstream/handle/1805/17666/high-net-worth2018-summary.pdf. This study did not indicate how much the rich donated to specific sectors like health care or human services.

3. Not all charitable contributions are equally available. Some wealthy individuals give to donor-advised funds that may wait years to distribute monies to working charities (Hobson 2020).

4. See https://www.census.gov/newsroom/stories/volunteer-week.html and https://ame ricorps.gov/newsroom/press-releases/2018/volunteering-us-hits-record-high-worth-167-billion.

5. One exception is when government offers tax breaks to employers that offer retirement pensions. As mentioned in Chapter 5, these pensions do not benefit many of the poor and near poor.

6. There are a few exceptions to this pattern such as subsidized school meals, public housing, and VA hospitals.

7. Personal example: the Summer Meals for Kids program in our community is a joint effort between local churches and Meals on Wheels. This program helps feed children who normally receive free lunches when school is in session. As an occasional volunteer, I have delivered bagged lunches. However, I have never met the kids or their parents. I gave the lunches to motel clerks or to the managers of subsidized housing developments, and they distributed the lunches sometime after I left. Perhaps I am misguided, but I think of my actions as caregiving.

8. I cannot say much about gender, volunteers, and caregiving. Nationally, we know that women are more likely than men to volunteer in their communities. But we do not have data specific to food pantries, soup kitchens, free and medical clinics, and other places in the social safety net. One reason is that many charities and nonprofits do not keep detailed records about their volunteers. See https://americorps.gov/sites/default/files/document/Volunteering_in_A merica_Demographics_508.pdf.

9. These numbers are based on the supplemental poverty measure, which is more accurate than the official measure. The supplemental measure gives us a better idea of how much income people have after taxes and transfers.

10. Medicare benefits are not linked to past wages.

11. Many adult recipients are employed, but they could receive these benefits if they were unemployed.

12. Blacks are more likely than Hispanics to have health insurance, a reminder that racial minorities are not alike in all parts of the social safety net.

13. Asians are closer to Whites than to Blacks or Hispanics when it comes to poverty and health insurance.

14. See https://www.healio.com/news/gastroenterology/20210115/women-in-the-us-at-hig her-risk-for-food-insecurity.

15. See https://www.kff.org/womens-health-policy/fact-sheet/womens-health-insurance-coverage/.

16. See https://www.kff.org/medicaid/fact-sheet/medicaids-role-for-women/. Having the lead in long-term care is admittedly a mixed blessing.

17. See https://map.feedingamerica.org/county/2019/overall/south-dakota.

18. See https://map.feedingamerica.org/.

19. See https://www.statista.com/statistics/727847/homelessness-rate-in-the-us-by-state/.

20. State data accessed from https://oui.doleta.gov/unemploy/ui_replacement_rates.asp (July 16, 2021).

21. Spending on low-income people represented 17 percent of the federal budget in 2008. Most of the growth between 2008 and 2018 was due to health care, especially the Affordable Care Act (Lynch et al. 2020).

22. The 1996 welfare reforms replaced AFDC, a budgetary entitlement, with TANF, a block grant.

23. Author's calculations based on 2016 American National Election Studies, accessed via https://sda.berkeley.edu/.

24. See https://www.taxpolicycenter.org/statistics/historical-income-distribution-all-hou seholds.

25. See https://www.taxpolicycenter.org/publications/distributional-analysis-conference-agreement-tax-cuts-and-jobs-act/full.

26. Some of those donations probably went to medical research, for example.

27. See https://www.whitehouse.gov/omb/historical-tables/.

Postscript: The Social Safety Net and the Pandemic

1. See https://www.bls.gov/opub/ted/2020/unemployment-rate-rises-to-record-high-14-point-7-percent-in-april-2020.htm?view_full.
2. See https://www.cdc.gov/nchs/covid19/mortality-overview.htm.
3. Public health experts believe that thousands of "excess deaths" in 2020 and 2021 should also be linked to the pandemic. See https://www.cdc.gov/nchs/covid19/mortality-overview.htm and https://www.cdc.gov/nchs/nvss/vsrr/covid19/excess_deaths.htm.
4. All survey results accessed from the Roper iPoll database.
5. Quotation is from https://www.nfib.com/content/analysis/coronavirus/nfib-in-2020-a-year-of-action-and-accomplishment/. See also https://www.nfib.com/content/analysis/coronavirus/nfib-to-congress-dont-wait-on-help-for-small-business/; https://www.nfib.com/content/analysis/coronavirus/covid-19-recovery-2-0-what-small-businesses-need-to-know/; and https://www.nfib.com/content/analysis/coronavirus/new-covid-19-recovery-2-0-package-loans-grants-forgiveness-and-tax-fixes/.
6. See from https://www.nfib.com/content/analysis/coronavirus/nfib-in-2020-a-year-of-action-and-accomplishment/; https://www.nfib.com/content/analysis/economy/nfib-members-speak-out-on-job-losses-and-increased-costs/; and https://www.nfib.com/content/news/labor/minimum-wage-hike-would-decimate-small-business-sector-in-new-jersey/.
7. See, e.g., https://aflcio.org/covid-19; https://aflcio.org/about/leadership/statements/working-peoples-demands-face-covid-19-pandemic; https://aflcio.org/2020/12/18/top-10-aflcio-blog-posts-2020; and https://aflcio.org/about/leadership/statements/protecting-workers-covid-19.
8. See http://circleofprotection.us/wp-content/uploads/2021/03/letter-to-president-biden-march-19-2021.pdf and https://www.usccb.org/resources/letter-congress-regarding-moral-principles-providing-health-care-during-covid-19-pandemic.
9. See http://circleofprotection.us/wp-content/uploads/2021/05/letter-to-president-biden-and-members-of-congress-may-24-2021.pdf.
10. The 2020 Democratic party platform and Biden's Address Before a Joint Session of Congress (April 28, 2021) were both accessed from the American Presidency Project. https://www.presidency.ucsb.edu/.
11. Middle-income workers who lost their health insurance could get help from the ACA marketplaces.
12. See https://www.fns.usda.gov/sites/default/files/resource-files/34SNAPmonthly-7.pdf and https://www.cbpp.org/research/food-assistance/states-are-using-much-needed-temporary-flexibility-in-snap-to-respond-to.
13. The first relief package was worth almost $200 billion and enacted on March 18, 2020. Another package aimed largely at small businesses was enacted in April 2020 with a price tag close to $500 billion. https://www.pgpf.org/blog/2021/03/heres-everything-congress-has-done-to-respond-to-the-coronavirus-so-far.
14. For evidence that small business loans did not benefit low-income communities as much as expected, see https://publicintegrity.org/inequality-poverty-opportunity/covid-divide/ppp-loans-did-not-prioritize-low-income-areas-small-businesses-pandemic/.
15. See https://www.pgpf.org/blog/2021/03/heres-everything-congress-has-done-to-respond-to-the-coronavirus-so-far and https://www.cnbc.com/2021/03/11/biden-1point9-trillion-covid-relief-package-thursday-afternoon.html.
16. See https://www.pgpf.org/blog/2021/03/heres-everything-congress-has-done-to-respond-to-the-coronavirus-so-far and https://www.npr.org/2020/03/26/821457551/whats-inside-the-senate-s-2-trillion-coronavirus-aid-package.
17. See https://www.pgpf.org/blog/2021/03/heres-everything-congress-has-done-to-respond-to-the-coronavirus-so-far and https://www.pgpf.org/blog/2021/05/how-did-americans-spend-their-stimulus-checks-and-how-did-it-affect-the-economy.
18. See https://www.whitehouse.gov/briefing-room/statements-releases/2021/06/24/fact-sheet-biden-harris-administration-announces-initiatives-to-promote-housing-stability-by-supporting-vulnerable-tenants-and-preventing-foreclosures/ and https://www.cbsnews.com/news/emergency-rental-assistance-program-distribution-evection-moratorium/.

19. With virtual learning the norm, parents also took on more responsibility for their kids' education.
20. See https://www.feedingamerica.org/hunger-blog/food-bank-response-covid-numbers.
21. See https://covidtracking.com/analysis-updates/what-we-know-about-the-impact-of-the-pandemic-on-our-most-vulnerable-community.
22. See https://data.cms.gov/covid-19/covid-19-nursing-home-data.
23. Author's calculations based on https://www.census.gov/data/tables/2021/demo/hhp/hhp33.html, Food Table 2, Health Table 3, Household Spending Table 4, and Housing Table 1b.
24. The decline in life expectancy was greater for men (1.8 years) than women (1.2), further evidence that gender gaps do not always favor men.
25. Moreover, Covid-19 death rates in nursing homes increased as the proportion of non-White residents increased (Gorges and Konetzka 2021).
26. Author's calculations based on https://www.census.gov/data/tables/2021/demo/hhp/hhp33.html, Food Table 2, Health Table 3, and Housing Table 1b.
27. For more details, see https://www.whitehouse.gov/build-back-better/.
28. See, e.g., https://www.whitehouse.gov/build-back-better/; https://www.speaker.gov/newsroom/12121-4; and https://www.majorityleader.gov/content/what-they're-reading-build-back-better-act-will-help-build-better-lives-american-workers-and.

    Labor unions have used similar language to describe the virtues of Build Back Better (e.g., https://www.ufcw.org/press-releases/ufcw-build-back-better-framework-puts-workers-first-by-creating-millions-of-good-paying-jobs-providing-tax-cuts-for-working-families-and-strengthening-middle-class/.
29. See https://www.whitehouse.gov/build-back-better/.
30. A poll conducted by the Associated Press in March 2021 found that 60 percent of Americans would favor a long-term care insurance program similar to Medicare. Accessed from the Roper iPoll database.
31. The Affordable Care Act did this by raising the Medicare payroll tax rate on affluent workers. Opinion polls show that most Americans favor lifting the cap on income taxed by Social Security, which would make that tax less regressive.
32. There would likely be a cap so that someone spending, for example, half their income to live in a million-dollar home would not qualify as needy.
33. These results came from a Politico/Harvard Public Health Poll, accessed from the Roper iPoll database. See also https://hartresearch.com/new-poll-shows-huge-support-for-investment-in-early-care-and-education-in-build-back-better/.

BIBLIOGRAPHY

AARP and National Alliance of Caregiving. 2020. *Caregiving in the United States 2020.* Washington, DC: AARP. https://www.aarp.org/ppi/info-2020/caregiving-in-the-united-states.html.

Abad-Santos, Alex. 2020. "How US Schools Are (and aren't) Providing Meals to Children in the Covid-19 Crisis," *Vox* (March 28). https://www.vox.com/2020/3/28/21197965/coronavi rus-school-shutdown-free-meals.

Abelson, Reed. 2019. "Hospitals Stand to Lose Billions Under 'Medicare for All,'" *New York Times* (April 21). https://www.nytimes.com/2019/04/21/health/medicare-for-all-hospit als.html.

Abelson, Reed. 2021. "High Staff Turnover at U.S. Nursing Homes Poses Risks for Residents' Care," *New York Times* (March 1). https://www.nytimes.com/2021/03/01/health/covid-nursing-homes-staff-turnover.html.

Abramovitz, Mimi. 1988. *Regulating the Lives of Women: Social Welfare Policy from Colonial Times to the Present.* Boston, MA: South End Press.

Abramowitz, Alan I. 2010. *The Disappearing Center: Engaged Citizens, Polarization, and American Democracy.* New Haven, CT: Yale University Press.

Abramsky, Sasha. 2013. *The American Way of Poverty: How the Other Half Still Lives.* New York: Nation Books.

Airgood-Obrycki, Whitney, and Jennifer Molinsky. 2019. "Estimating the Gap in Affordable and Available Rental Units for Families" (April 2). Cambridge, MA: Joint Center for Housing Studies of Harvard University. https://www.jchs.harvard.edu/research-areas/working-pap ers/estimating-gap-affordable-and-available-rental-units-families.

Allahyari, Rebecca. 2004. "Food Banks." In *Poverty in the United States: An Encyclopedia of History, Politics, and Policy,* vol. 1, edited by Gwendolyn Mink and Alice O'Connor, pp. 321–24. Santa Barbara, CA: ABC-CLIO.

Allheedan, Abdullah. 2016. "Poverty and Wealth in Islam's Sacred Texts." In *Poverty and Wealth in Judaism, Christianity, and Islam,* edited by Nathan R. Kollar and Muhammad Shafiq, pp. 263–74. New York: Palgrave Macmillan.

American Enterprise Institute (AEI) and *Los Angeles Times.* 2016. "2016 Poverty Survey: Attitudes toward the Poor, Poverty, and Welfare in the United States" (August 18). https://www.aei. org/research-products/report/2016-poverty-survey/.

American Hospital Association. 2020a. "Fact Sheet: Uncompensated Hospital Care Cost" (January). https://www.aha.org/fact-sheets/2020-01-06-fact-sheet-uncompensated-hospi tal-care-cost.

American Hospital Association. 2020b. "Fact Sheet: Underpayment by Medicare and Medicaid" (January). https://www.aha.org/fact-sheets/2020-01-07-fact-sheet-underpayment-medic are-and-medicaid.

American Medical Association. 2020. *Summary of Research: Medicaid Physician Payment and Access to Care.* https://www.ama-assn.org/system/files/2020-10/research-summary-medic aid-physician-payment.pdf.

American National Election Studies (ANES). 2012. Conducted by Stanford University and University of Michigan. Accessed from https://sda.berkeley.edu/.

American National Election Studies (ANES). 2016. Conducted by Stanford University and University of Michigan. Accessed from https://sda.berkeley.edu/.

America's Essential Hospitals. 2020. "Essential Data: Our Hospitals, Our Patients" (May). https:// essentialhospitals.org/wp-content/uploads/2020/05/Essential-Data-2020_spreads.pdf.

Ammerman, Nancy Tatom. 2005. *Pillars of Faith: American Congregations and Their Partners.* Berkeley: University of California Press.

Andrews, Michelle. 2020. "Think Your Health Care Is Covered? Beware of the 'Junk' Insurance Plan," *Kaiser Health News* (December 4). https://khn.org/news/junk-insurance-plans-hea lth-consumers-beware/.

Annenberg Public Policy Center. 2017. "Americans Are Poorly Informed About Basic Constitutional Provisions" (September 12). https://www.annenbergpublicpolicycenter. org/americans-are-poorly-informed-about-basic-constitutional-provisions/.

Ansell, Ben. 2014. "The Political Economy of Ownership: Housing Markets and the Welfare State," *American Political Science Review* 108, 2 (May): 383–402.

Appelrouth, Scott. 2019. *Envisioning America and the American Self: Republican and Democratic Party Platforms, 1840–2016.* New York: Routledge.

Applebaum, Binyamin, and Damon Winter. 2019. "One Job Is Better Than Two," *New York Times* (September 1). https://www.nytimes.com/2019/09/01/opinion/working-two-jobs.html.

Arias, Elizabeth, Betzaida Tejada-Vera, Farida Ahmad, and Kenneth D. Kochanek. 2021. "Provisional Life Expectancy Estimates for 2020, Report No. 015" (July). Atlanta, GA: Centers for Disease Control and Prevention. https://www.cdc.gov/nchs/nvss/vsrr/ reports.htm.

Aussenberg, Randy Alison. 2018. "Supplemental Nutrition Assistance Program (SNAP): A Primer on Eligibility and Benefits," *Congressional Research Service Report* R42505 (April 11). Accessed from the ProQuest Congressional database.

Aussenberg, Randy Allison, Kara Clifford Billings, and Kirsten J. Colello. 2019. "Domestic Food Assistance: Summary of Programs," *Congressional Research Service Report* R42343 (August 27). Accessed from ProQuest Congressional database.

Badger, Doug, and Jamie Bryan Hall. 2019. "What You Should Know About the Uninsured" (October 29). Washington, DC: Heritage Foundation. https://www.heritage.org/health-care-reform/commentary/what-you-should-know-about-the-uninsured.

Badger, Emily, and Quoctrung Bui. 2019. "Cities Start to Question an American Ideal: A House With a Yard on Every Lot," *New York Times* (June 18). https://www.nytimes.com/interact ive/2019/06/18/upshot/cities-across-america-question-single-family-zoning.html.

Baradaran, Mehrsa. 2015. *How the Other Half Banks: Exclusion, Exploitation, and the Threat to Democracy.* Cambridge, MA: Harvard University Press.

Barbanel, Josh, and Will Parker. 2019. "Landlords Challenge New York's Rent-Control Law in Federal Court," *Wall Street Journal* (July 16). https://www.wsj.com/articles/landlords-challenge-new-yorks-rent-control-law-in-federal-court-11563274921.

Barber, William J., II, and Liz Theoharis. 2020. "What Biden and Harris Owe the Poor," *New York Times* (December 25). https://www.nytimes.com/2020/12/25/opinion/biden-harris-age nda-poverty.html.

Barnes, Marian. 2012. *Care in Everyday Life: An Ethic of Care in Practice.* Bristol, UK: Policy Press.

Bartel, Ann P., Soohyun Kim, Jaehyun Nam, Maya Rossin-Slater, Christopher Ruhm, and Jane Waldfogel. 2019. "Racial and Ethnic Disparities in Access to and Use of Paid Family and Medical Leave: Evidence from Four Nationally Representative Datasets," *Monthly Labor Review* (January), pp. 1–29. https://doi.org/10.21916/mlr.2019.2.

Baumgaertner, Emily. 2018. "Spooked by Trump Proposals, Immigrants Abandon Public Nutrition Services," *New York Times* (March 6). https://www.nytimes.com/2018/03/06/us/politics/trump-immigrants-public-nutrition-services.html.

Baumgartner, Frank R., and Bryan D. Jones. 2005. *The Politics of Attention: How Government Prioritizes Problems*. Chicago: University of Chicago Press.

Beach, Scott, Richard Schulz, Heidi Donovan, and Ann-Marie Rosland. 2021. "Family Caregiving During the COVID-19 Pandemic," *Gerontologist* 61, 5 (August): 650–60.

Béland, Daniel. 2005. *Social Security: History and Politics from the New Deal to the Privatization Debate*. Lawrence: University Press of Kansas.

Bennett, Jeannette N. 2019. "Fast Cash and Payday Loans" (April). St. Louis, MO: Federal Reserve Bank of St. Louis. https://research.stlouisfed.org/publications/page1-econ/2019/04/10/fast-cash-and-payday-loans.

Berkowitz, Edward D., and Larry DeWitt. 2013. *The Other Welfare: Supplemental Security Income and U.S. Social Policy*. Ithaca, NY: Cornell University Press.

Berliner, Lauren S., and Nora J. Kenworthy. 2017. "Producing a Worthy Illness: Personal Crowdfunding amidst Financial Crisis," *Social Science & Medicine* 187 (August): 233–42.

Bernstein, Sara, Charles Bush, Nikki Aikens, Emily Moiduddin, Jessica F. Harding, Lizabeth Malone, Louisa Tarullo, Judy Cannon, Kai Filipczak, and Serge Lukashanets. 2019. "A Portrait of Head Start Classrooms and Programs: FACES Spring 2017 Data Tables and Study Design" (March). Washington, DC: U.S. Department of Health and Human Services. https://www.acf.hhs.gov/opre/report/portrait-head-start-classrooms-and-programs-faces-spring-2017-data-tables-and-study.

Bertram, Eva. 2015. *The Workfare State: Public Assistance Politics from the New Deal to the New Democrats*. Philadelphia: University of Pennsylvania Press.

Billings, Kara Clifford. 2020. "School Meals and Other Child Nutrition Programs: Background and Funding," *Congressional Research Service Report* R46234 (February 13). Accessed from the ProQuest Congressional Database.

Billings, Kara Clifford, and Randy Alison Aussenberg. 2019. "School Meals Programs and Other USDA Child Nutrition Programs: A Primer," *Congressional Research Service Report* R43783 (February 11). Accessed from the ProQuest Congressional database.

Bitler, Marianne, Hilary Hoynes, and Elira Kuka. 2017. "Child Poverty, the Great Recession, and the Social Safety Net in the United States," *Journal of Policy Analysis and Management* 36, 2 (Spring): 358–89.

Bittman, Mark. 2013. "Welfare for the Wealthy," *New York Times* (June 4). https://opinionator.blogs.nytimes.com/2013/06/04/welfare-for-the-wealthy/?_r=0.

Black, Rachel, and Aleta Sprague. 2016. "The Rise and Reign of the Welfare Queen," *New America Weekly* 135 (September 22). https://www.newamerica.org/weekly/edition-135/rise-and-reign-welfare-queen/.

Blank, Rebecca M. 2008. "Presidential Address: How to Improve Poverty Measurement in the United States," *Journal of Policy Analysis and Management* 27, 2 (Spring): 233–54.

Block, Jason P., and S. V. Subramanian. 2015. "Moving Beyond 'Food Deserts': Reorienting United States Policies to Reduce Disparities in Diet Quality," *PLOS Medicine* 12, 12 (December): e1001914.

Board of Governors of the Federal Reserve System. 2019. "Report on the Economic Well-Being of U.S. Households in 2018" (May). https://www.federalreserve.gov/publications/report-economic-well-being-us-households.htm.

Board of Governors of the Federal Reserve System. 2021. "Report on the Economic Well-Being of U.S. Households in 2020" (May). https://www.federalreserve.gov/publications/files/2020-report-economic-well-being-us-households-202105.pdf.

Boden, Leslie I., and Emily A. Spieler. 2015. "Workers' Compensation." In *The Oxford Handbook of U.S. Social Policy*, edited by Daniel Béland, Christopher Howard, and Kimberly J. Morgan, pp. 451–68. New York: Oxford University Press.

Bolton, Alexander. 2021. "Biden's Build Back Better Bill Suddenly in Serious Danger," *The Hill* (December 16). https://thehill.com/homenews/senate/586147-bidens-build-back-better-bill-suddenly-in-serious-danger.

Bond-Taylor, Sue. 2017. "Tracing an Ethic of Care in the Policy and Practice of the Troubled Families Programme," *Social Policy & Society* 16, 1 (January): 131–41.

Bonner, Michael. 2005. "Poverty and Economics in the Qu'ran," *Journal of Interdisciplinary History* 35, 3 (Winter): 391–406.

Booker, Brakkton. 2018. "HUD Unveils Plan To Increase Rent On Millions Receiving Federal Housing Assistance," National Public Radio (April 25). https://www.npr.org/2018/04/25/605900171/hud-unveils-plan-to-increase-rent-on-millions-receiving-federal-housing-assistan.

Boris, Eileen, and Jennifer Klein. 2012. *Caring for America: Home Health Workers in the Shadow of the Welfare State*. New York: Oxford University Press.

Boris, Eileen T., and C. Eugene Steuerle (eds.). 2017. *Nonprofits and Government: Collaboration and Conflict*. Lanham, MD and Washington, DC: Rowman & Littlefield and Urban Institute Press.

Botella, Elena. 2019. "I Worked at Capital One for Five Years. This Is How We Justified Piling Debt on Poor Customers," *The New Republic* (October 2). https://newrepublic.com/article/155212/worked-capital-one-five-years-justified-piling-debt-poor-customers.

Bourke, Nick, and Andrew Scott. 2018. "Millions Use Bank Overdrafts as Credit" (March 21). Washington, DC: Pew Charitable Trusts. https://www.pewtrusts.org/en/research-and-analysis/articles/2018/03/21/millions-use-bank-overdrafts-as-credit.

Bowler, Kate. 2013. *Blessed: A History of the American Prosperity Gospel*. New York: Oxford University Press.

Brackney, William H., and Rupen Das (eds.). 2018. *Poverty and the Poor in the World's Religious Traditions: Religious Responses to the Problem of Poverty*. Santa Barbara, CA: Praeger.

Bramen, Lisa. 2010. "Count Rumford and the History of the Soup Kitchen," *Smithsonian* (December 29). https://www.smithsonianmag.com/arts-culture/count-rumford-and-the-history-of-the-soup-kitchen-26785526/.

Broaddus, Matt, and Aviva Aron-Dine. 2020. "Uninsured Rate Rose Again in 2019, Further Eroding Earlier Progress" (September 15). Washington, DC: Center on Budget and Policy Priorities. https://www.cbpp.org/research/health/uninsured-rate-rose-again-in-2019-further-eroding-earlier-progress.

Broockman, David E. 2012. "The 'Problem of Preferences': Medicare and Business Support for the Welfare State," *Studies in American Political Development* 26, 2 (October): 83–106.

Brooks, Arthur C. 2006. *Who Really Cares: The Surprising Truth about Compassionate Conservatism*. New York: Basic Books.

Brown, Scott, Radha Roy, and Jacob Alex Klerman. 2020. "Leave Experiences of Low-Wage Workers" (November). Produced for the U.S. Department of Labor, Chief Evaluation Office. Rockville, MD: Abt Associates. https://www.dol.gov/sites/dolgov/files/OASP/evaluation/pdf/WHD_FMLA_LowWageWorkers_January2021.pdf.

Brown-Iannuzzi, Jazmin L., Ron Dotsch, Erin Cooley, and B. Keith Payne. 2017. "The Relationship Between Mental Representations of Welfare Recipients and Attitudes Toward Welfare," *Psychological Science* 28, 1 (January): 92–103.

Bruch, Joseph D., and David Bellamy. 2020. "Charity Care: Do Nonprofit Hospitals Give More than For-Profit Hospitals?" *Journal of General Internal Medicine* (September 1). https://doi-org.proxy.wm.edu/10.1007/s11606-020-06147-9.

Bruch, Sarah K., Marcia K. Meyers, and Janet C. Gornick. 2018. "The Consequences of Decentralization: Inequality in Safety Net Provision in the Post-Welfare Reform Era," *Social Service Review* 92, 1 (March): 3–35.

Buch, Elana D. 2018. *Inequalities of Aging: Paradoxes of Independence in American Home Care*. New York: New York University Press.

Budge, Ian, and Richard Hofferbert. 1990. "Mandates and Policy Outputs: US Party Platforms and Federal Expenditures," *American Political Science Review* 84, 1 (March): 111–31.

Burnside, Ashley, and Liz Schott. 2020. "States Should Invest More of Their TANF Dollars in Basic Assistance for Families" (February 25). Washington, DC: Center on Budget and Policy Priorities. https://www.cbpp.org/research/family-income-support/states-should-invest-more-of-their-tanf-dollars-in-basic-assistance.

Burton, Tara Isabella. 2017. "The Prosperity Gospel, Explained: Why Joel Osteen Believes that Prayer Can Make You Rich," *Vox* (September 1). https://www.vox.com/identit ies/2017/9/1/15951874/prosperity-gospel-explained-why-joel-osteen-believes-pra yer-can-make-you-rich-trump.

Calello, Monique. 2018. "Health Care: 'I Can't Believe This Is the United States,'" *The News Leader* (March 8). https://www.newsleader.com/story/news/2018/03/07/health-care-cant-beli eve-united-states-remote-area-medical-virginia-buena-vista/399951002/.

Campbell, Andrea Louise. 2014. *Trapped in America's Safety Net: One Family's Struggle.* Chicago: University of Chicago Press.

Campbell, Andrea Louise, and Kimberly J. Morgan. 2005. "Financing the Welfare State: Elite Politics and the Decline of the Social Insurance Model in America," *Studies in American Political Development* 19, 2 (October): 173–95.

Cancian, Maria, and Ron Haskins. 2014. "Changes in Family Composition: Implications for Income, Poverty, and Public Policy," *Annals of the American Academy of Political and Social Science* 654 (July): 31–47.

Carlson, Steven, Robert Greenstein, and Zoë Neuberger. 2017. "WIC's Competitive Bidding Process for Infant Formula Is Highly Cost-Effective" (February 17). Washington, DC: Center on Budget and Policy Priorities. https://www.cbpp.org/research/food-assistance/wics-competitive-bidding-process-for-infant-formula-is-highly-cost.

Carlson, Steven, and Brynne Keith-Jennings. 2018. "SNAP is Linked with Improved Nutritional Outcomes and Lower Health Care Costs" (January 17). Washington, DC: Center on Budget and Policy Priorities. https://www.cbpp.org/research/food-assistance/snap-is-linked-with-improved-nutritional-outcomes-and-lower-health-care.

Carman, Tim. 2019. "Spray Cheese, Beef Jerky and Stuffed Olives to Be Counted as Staples under Trump Administration Food Stamp Proposal," *Washington Post* (May 30). https://www.was hingtonpost.com/news/food/wp/2019/05/30/spray-cheese-beef-jerky-and-stuffed-oli ves-to-be-counted-as-staples-under-trump-administration-food-stamp-proposal/?utm_t erm=.69a67f8dfd9e.

Center on Budget and Policy Priorities. 2017. "Policy Basics: Special Supplemental Nutrition Program for Women, Infants, and Children" (April 26). https://www.cbpp.org/research/food-assistance/policy-basics-special-supplemental-nutrition-program-for-women-infants-and.

Center on Budget and Policy Priorities. 2019a. "A Quick Guide to SNAP Eligibility and Benefits" (November 1). https://www.cbpp.org/research/food-assistance/a-quick-guide-to-snap-eligibility-and-benefits.

Center on Budget and Policy Priorities. 2019b. "Policy Basics: The Earned Income Tax Credit" (December 10). https://www.cbpp.org/research/federal-tax/policy-basics-the-earned-inc ome-tax-credit.

Center on Budget and Policy Priorities. 2019c. "Policy Basics: The Supplemental Nutrition Assistance Program (SNAP)" (June 25). https://www.cbpp.org/research/food-assistance/ policy-basics-the-supplemental-nutrition-assistance-program-snap.

Center on Budget and Policy Priorities. 2020a. "Policy Basics: Supplemental Security Income" (February 6). https://www.cbpp.org/research/social-security/policy-basics-supplemental-security-income.

Center on Budget and Policy Priorities. 2020b. "Policy Basics: Temporary Assistance for Needy Families" (February 6). https://www.cbpp.org/research/family-income-support/tempor ary-assistance-for-needy-families.

Center on Budget and Policy Priorities. 2020c. "Policy Basics: Unemployment Insurance" (April 1). https://www.cbpp.org/research/economy/policy-basics-unemployment-insurance.

Center on Budget and Policy Priorities. 2020d. "Policy Basics: Introduction to Medicaid" (April 14). https://www.cbpp.org/research/health/policy-basics-introduction-to-medicaid.

Centers for Disease Control and Prevention. 2021. "Risk for COVID-19 Infection, Hospitalization, and Death by Race/Ethnicity" (July 16). https://www.cdc.gov/coronavirus/2019-ncov/covid-data/investigations-discovery/hospitalization-death-by-race-ethnicity.html.

Centers for Medicare & Medicaid Services. 2020. "Medicaid and CHIP Beneficiary Profile: Characteristics, Health Status, Access, Utilization, Expenditures, and Experience" (February). https://www.medicaid.gov/medicaid/quality-of-care/downloads/beneficiary-profile.pdf.

Cenziper, Debbie, Joel Jacobs, Alice Crites, and Will Englund. 2020. "Profit and Pain: How California's Largest Nursing Home Chain Amassed Millions as Scrutiny Mounted," *Washington Post* (December 31). https://www.washingtonpost.com/business/2020/12/31/brius-nursing-home/.

Chappell, Marisa. 2010. *The War on Welfare: Family, Poverty, and Politics in Modern America.* Philadelphia, PA: University of Pennsylvania Press.

Chatterjee, Rhitu. 2021. "Unpaid Caregivers Were Already Struggling. It's Only Gotten Worse During The Pandemic," *National Public Radio* (June 17). https://www.npr.org/sections/health-shots/2021/06/17/1007579073/unpaid-caregivers-were-already-struggling-its-only-gotten-worse-during-the-pande.

Cherlin, Andrew J., and Judith A. Seltzer. 2014. "Family Complexity, the Family Safety Net, and Public Policy," *Annals of the American Academy of Political and Social Science* 654 (July): 231–39.

Chien, Nina. 2020. "Factsheet: Estimates of Child Care Eligibility & Receipt for Fiscal Year 2017," U.S. Department of Health and Human Services (November). https://aspe.hhs.gov/pdf-report/child-care-eligibility-and-receipt-2017.

Child Care Aware of America. 2019. "The US and the High Price of Child Care: An Examination of a Broken System." https://www.childcareaware.org/our-issues/research/the-us-and-the-high-price-of-child-care-2019/.

Children's Defense Fund. 2021. "State of America's Children 2021." https://www.childrensdefense.org/wp-content/uploads/2021/04/The-State-of-Americas-Children-2021.pdf.

Claxton, Gary, Matthew Rae, Anthony Damico, Gregory Young, Daniel McDermott, and Heidi Whitmore. 2019. "Employer Health Benefits: 2019 Annual Survey." San Francisco, CA: Henry J. Kaiser Family Foundation. https://www.kff.org/health-costs/report/2019-employer-health-benefits-survey/.

Clement, Scott, Cece Pascual, and Monica Ulmanu. 2021. "Stress on the Front Lines of Covid-19," *Washington Post* (April 6). https://www.washingtonpost.com/health/2021/04/06/stress-front-lines-health-care-workers-share-hardest-parts-working-during-pandemic/.

Cnaan, Ram A. 1999. *The Newer Deal: Social Work and Religion in Partnership.* New York: Columbia University Press.

Cnaan, Ram A. 2002. *The Invisible Caring Hand: American Congregations and the Provision of Welfare.* New York: New York University Press.

Cochrane, Emily, and Jonathan Weisman. 2021. "House Narrowly Passes Biden's Social Safety Net and Climate Bill," *New York Times* (November 19). https://www.nytimes.com/2021/11/19/us/politics/house-passes-reconciliation-bill.html.

Cohen, Patricia, and Sydney Ember. 2021. "Federal Unemployment Aid Is Now a Political Lightning Rod," *New York Times* (June 5). https://www.nytimes.com/2021/06/05/business/economy/unemployment-benefits-cutoff.html.

Colello, Kirsten J. 2019. "Overview of Long-Term Services and Supports," Congressional Research Service CRS In Focus (December 30). Accessed via ProQuest Congressional database.

Colello, Kirsten J. 2020. "Who Pays for Long-Term Services and Supports?," Congressional Research Service CRS In Focus (March 20). Accessed via ProQuest Congressional database.

Colello, Kirsten J., and Angela Napili. 2020. "Older Americans Act: Overview and Funding," Congressional Research Service Report R43414 (April 22). Accessed via ProQuest Congressional database.

Coleman, John A. 2003. "American Catholicism, Catholic Charities USA, and Welfare Reform." In Hugh Heclo and Wilfred M. McClay (eds.), *Religion Returns to the Public Square*, pp. 229–67. Washington, DC and Baltimore, MD: Woodrow Wilson Center Press and Johns Hopkins University Press.

Coleman-Jensen, Alisha, Matthew Rabbitt, Christian A. Gregory, and Anita Singh. 2019. *Household Food Security in the United States in 2018*. Washington, DC: U.S. Department of Agriculture. https://www.ers.usda.gov/webdocs/publications/94849/err-270.pdf?v=963.1.

Collins, Jane L., and Victoria Mayer. 2010. *Both Hands Tied: Welfare Reform and the Race to the Bottom in the Low-Wage Labor Market*. Chicago: University of Chicago Press.

Collins, Sara R., Herman K. Bhupal, and Michelle M. Doty. 2019. "Health Insurance Coverage Eight Years After the ACA: Fewer Uninsured Americans and Shorter Coverage Gaps, But More Underinsured" (February 7). New York: Commonwealth Fund. https://www.commonwealthfund.org/publications/issue-briefs/2019/feb/health-insurance-coverage-eight-years-after-aca.

Collinson, Robert, Ingrid Gould Ellen, and Jens Ludwig. 2021. "Reforming Housing Assistance to Better Respond to Recipient Needs," *IRP Focus on Poverty* 37, 1 (June): 11–18.

Committee for Economic Development. 2019. "Child Care in State Economies: 2019 Update." https://www.ced.org/childcareimpact.

Cook, Fay Lomax, and Edith J. Barrett. 1992. *Support for the American Welfare State: The Views of Congress and the Public*. New York: Columbia University Press.

Cooney, Patrick, and H. Luke Shaefer. 2021. "Material Hardship and Mental Health Following the COVID-19 Relief Bill and American Rescue Plan Act" (May). Ann Arbor, MI: Poverty Solutions, University of Michigan. http://sites.fordschool.umich.edu/poverty2021/files/2021/05/PovertySolutions-Hardship-After-COVID-19-Relief-Bill-PolicyBrief-r1.pdf.

Cooper, David. 2019. "Raising the Federal Minimum Wage to $15 by 2024 Would Lift Pay for Nearly 40 Million Workers" (February 5). Washington, DC: Economic Policy Institute. https://www.epi.org/publication/raising-the-federal-minimum-wage-to-15-by-2024-would-lift-pay-for-nearly-40-million-workers/.

Cooper, David, and Teresa Kroeger. 2017. "Employers Steal Billions from Workers' Paychecks Each Year" (May 10). Washington, DC: Economic Policy Institute. https://www.epi.org/publication/employers-steal-billions-from-workers-paychecks-each-year/.

Corallo, Bradley. 2022. "Analysis of Recent National Trends in Medicaid and CHIP Enrollment" (January 10). Washington, DC: Kaiser Family Foundation. https://www.kff.org/coronavirus-covid-19/issue-brief/analysis-of-recent-national-trends-in-medicaid-and-chip-enrollment/.

Coughlin, Teresa A., John Holahan, Kyle Caswell, and Megan McGrath. 2014. "Uncompensated Care for the Uninsured in 2013: A Detailed Examination" (May 30). Washington, DC: Kaiser Family Foundation. https://www.kff.org/uninsured/report/uncompensated-care-for-the-uninsured-in-2013-a-detailed-examination/.

Cozzarelli, Catherine, Anna V. Wilkinson, and Michael J. Tagler. 2001. "Attitudes Toward the Poor and Attributions for Poverty," *Journal of Social Issues* 57, 2 (Summer): 207–27.

Craig, Lee A. 2015. "Pension and Health Benefits for Public-Sector Workers." In *The Oxford Handbook of U.S. Social Policy*, edited by Daniel Béland, Christopher Howard, and Kimberly J. Morgan, pp. 549–64. New York: Oxford University Press.

Creamer, John. 2020. "Inequalities Persist Despite Decline in Poverty for All Major Race and Hispanic Origin Groups" (September 15). Washington, DC: U.S. Census Bureau. https://www.census.gov/library/stories/2020/09/poverty-rates-for-blacks-and-hispanics-reached-historic-lows-in-2019.html.

Cronquist, Kathryn. 2019. "Characteristics of Supplemental Assistance Nutrition Program Households: Fiscal Year 2018, U.S. Department of Agriculture," Food and Nutrition Service Report No. SNAP-19-CHAR. Washington, DC: U.S. Department of Agriculture. https://www.fns.usda.gov/snap/characteristics-supplemental-nutrition-assistance-program-households-fiscal-year-2018.

Cross-Call, Jesse. 2020. "Medicaid Expansion Has Helped Narrow Racial Disparities in Health Coverage and Access to Health Care" (October 21). Washington, DC: Center on Budget and Policy Priorities. https://www.cbpp.org/research/health/medicaid-expansion-has-hel ped-narrow-racial-disparities-in-health-coverage-and.

Currie, Janet M. 2006. *The Invisible Safety Net: Protecting the Nation's Poor Children and Families.* Princeton, NJ: Princeton University Press.

Dallas, Mary Elizabeth. 2019. "The Ten Most Common Surgeries in the U.S.," Healthgrades (August 28). https://www.healthgrades.com/right-care/tests-and-procedures/the-10-most-common-surgeries-in-the-u-s.

Darnell, Julie, and Lindsay O'Brien. 2015. "2015 National Survey of Free & Charitable Clinics: Preliminary Results." Presented at the 2015 NAFC Charitable Health Care Symposium, Rancho Mirage, CA (October 26). https://drive.google.com/file/d/0B2AQ m4TgBJF_Q3ZkUmR3blVGeTA/view.

Davies, Gareth. 1996. *From Opportunity to Entitlement: The Transformation and Decline of Great Society Liberalism.* Lawrence: University Press of Kansas.

Davis, Patricia A. 2020. "Medicare Part B: Enrollment and Premiums," Congressional Research Service Report R40082 (May 6). Available from ProQuest Congressional database.

Davis, Patricia A., Cliff Binder, Jim Hahn, Suzanne M. Kirchhoff, Paulette C. Morgan, Marco A. Villagrana, and Phoenix Voorhees. 2020. "Medicare Primer," Congressional Research Service Report R40425 (May 21). Available from ProQuest Congressional database.

Delaney, Arthur, and Ariel Edwards-Levy. 2018. "Americans Are Mistaken About Who Gets Welfare," *HuffPost* (February 5). https://www.huffingtonpost.com/entry/americans-welf are-perceptions-survey_us_5a7880cde4b0d3df1d13f60b.

Delli Carpini, Michael X., and Scott Keeter. 1996. *What Americans Know About Politics and Why It Matters.* New Haven, CT: Yale University Press.

DeLuca, Stefanie, Susan Clampet-Lundquist, and Kathryn Edin. 2016. *Coming of Age in the Other America.* New York: Russell Sage Foundation.

Del Valle, Gaby. 2018. "Jeff Bezos's Philanthropic Projects Aren't as Generous as They Seem," *Vox* (November 29). https://www.vox.com/the-goods/2018/11/29/18116720/jeff-bezos-day-1-fund-homelessness.

Del Valle, Gaby. 2019. "Federally Funded School Lunches Are About to Get a Lot Less Healthy," *Vox* (January 10). https://www.vox.com/the-goods/2019/1/10/18177099/school-lunch-sonny-perdue-healthy-hunger-free-kids.

DeNavas-Walt, Carmen, Bernadette D. Proctor, and Jessica C. Smith. 2010. *Income, Poverty, and Health Insurance Coverage in the United States: 2009,* U.S. Census Bureau, Current Population Reports P60-238. Washington, DC: Government Printing Office.

DeParle, Jason. 2004. *American Dream: Three Women, Ten Kids, and a Nation's Drive to End Welfare.* New York: Viking.

DeParle, Jason. 2019. "The Tax Break for Children, Except the Ones Who Need It Most," *New York Times* (December 16). https://www.nytimes.com/2019/12/16/us/politics/child-tax-cre dit.html.

DeParle, Jason. 2021. "Pandemic Aid Programs Spur a Record Drop in Poverty," *New York Times* (July 28). https://www.nytimes.com/2021/07/28/us/politics/covid-poverty-aid-progr ams.html.

Desmond, Matthew. 2012. "Disposable Ties and the Urban Poor," *American Journal of Sociology* 117, 5 (March): 1295–1335.

Desmond, Matthew. 2015a. "Severe Deprivation in America: An Introduction," *RSF: The Russell Sage Foundation Journal of the Social Sciences* 1, 2 (November): 1–11.

Desmond, Matthew. 2015b. "Unaffordable America: Poverty, Housing, and Eviction," *Fast Focus* No. 22-2015 (March). Madison, WI: Institute for Research on Poverty. https://www.irp. wisc.edu/resource_type/fast-focus/page/4/.

Desmond, Matthew. 2016. *Evicted: Poverty and Profit in the American City.* New York: Broadway Books.

Desmond, Matthew. 2017. "How Homeownership Became the Engine of American Inequality," *New York Times Magazine* (May 9). https://www.nytimes.com/2017/05/09/magazine/how-homeownership-became-the-engine-of-american-inequality.html.

Desmond, Matthew. 2018. "Americans Want to Believe Jobs Are the Solution to Poverty. They're Not," *New York Times Magazine* (September 11). https://www.nytimes.com/2018/09/11/magazine/americans-jobs-poverty-homeless.html.

Desmond, Matthew. 2020. "The Looming Eviction Crisis," *Democracy: A Journal of Ideas* (August 3). https://democracyjournal.org/voices-of-the-virus/the-looming-eviction-crisis/.

Desmond, Matthew, and Nathan Wilmers. 2019. "Do the Poor Pay More for Housing? Exploitation, Profit, and Risk in Rental Markets," *American Journal of Sociology* 124, 4 (January): 1090–1124.

Dewey, Caitlin. 2017. "GOP Lawmaker: The Bible says 'if a man will not work, he shall not eat,'" *Washington Post* (March 31). https://www.washingtonpost.com/news/wonk/wp/2017/03/31/gop-lawmaker-the-bible-says-the-unemployed-shall-not-eat/.

Dickens, William T., Robert K. Triest, and Rachel B. Sederberg. 2017. "The Changing Consequences of Unemployment for Household Finances," *RSF: The Russell Sage Foundation Journal of the Social Sciences* 3, 3 (April): 202–21.

Dilworth, Kelly. 2020. "Average Credit Card Interest Rates: Week of March 25, 2020," *CreditCards.com* (March 25). https://www.creditcards.com/credit-card-news/rate-report.php.

Dixon, Amanda. 2018. "Adding It Up: Here's How Much Americans Spend on Financial Vices," Bankrate.com (September 12). https://www.bankrate.com/personal-finance/smart-money/financial-vices-september-2018/.

Dixon, Amanda. 2019. "Survey: 21% of Working Americans Aren't Saving Anything At All," Bankrate.com (March 14). https://www.bankrate.com/banking/savings/financial-security-march-2019/.

Donovan, Sarah A. 2020. "Paid Family and Medical Leave in the United States," Congressional Research Service Report R44835 (February 19). Accessed from the ProQuest Congressional database.

Dougherty, Conor. 2021. "Pandemic's Toll on Housing: Falling Behind, Doubling Up," *New York Times* (February 6). https://www.nytimes.com/2021/02/06/business/economy/housing-insecurity.html.

Dreier, Peter, and Alex Schwartz. 2015. "Homeownership Policy." In *The Oxford Handbook of U.S. Social Policy*, edited by Daniel Béland, Christopher Howard, and Kimberly J. Morgan, pp. 510–29. New York: Oxford University Press.

Duffy, Mignon. 2011. *Making Care Count: A Century of Gender, Race, and Paid Care Work*. New Brunswick, NJ: Rutgers University Press.

Duggan, Juanita D. 2019. "Small Business Needs Permanent Tax Cuts," Fox News Network (April 14). https://www.foxbusiness.com/small-business/small-business-needs-permanent-tax-cuts.

Dunn, Amina. 2018. "Partisans Are Divided over the Fairness of the U.S. Economy—and Why People Are Rich or Poor" (October 4). Washington, DC: Pew Research Center. https://www.pewresearch.org/fact-tank/2018/10/04/partisans-are-divided-over-the-fairness-of-the-u-s-economy-and-why-people-are-rich-or-poor/.

Dushi, Irena, Howard K. Iams, and Brad Trenkamp. 2017. "The Importance of Social Security Benefits to the Income of the Aged Population," *Social Security Bulletin* 77, 2 (May): 1–12.

Dyck, Joshua J., and Laura S. Hussey. 2008. "The End of Welfare As We Know It? Durable Attitudes in a Changing Information Environment," *Public Opinion Quarterly* 72, 4 (Winter): 589–618.

Ebbs, Stephanie. 2020. "Farmers and Food Banks Grapple with Broken Food Supply Chain," ABC News (April 15). https://abcnews.go.com/Politics/farmers-food-banks-grapple-broken-food-supply-chain/story?id=70137720.

Edelman, Peter. 2012. *So Rich, So Poor: Why It's So Hard to End Poverty in America*. New York: The New Press.

Edin, Kathryn, and Laura Lein. 1997. *Making Ends Meet: How Single Mothers Survive Welfare and Low-Wage Work*. New York: Russell Sage Foundation.

Edin, Kathryn, Melody Boyd, James Mabli, Jim Ohls, Julie Worthington, Sara Greene, Nicholas Redel, and Swetha Sridharan. 2013. "SNAP Food Security In-Depth Interview Study" (March). Princeton, NJ: Mathematica. https://www.mathematica.org/our-publications-and-findings/publications/snap-food-security-indepth-interview-study.

Edin, Kathryn J., and H. Luke Shaefer. 2015. *$2.00 A Day: Living on Almost Nothing in America*. Boston: Mariner Books.

Egan, Patrick J. 2013. *Partisan Priorities: How Issue Ownership Drives and Distorts American Politics*. New York: Cambridge University Press.

Egan, Patrick. 2014. "To Understand GOP's Poverty Challenge, Start with Republican Voters," *Washington Post* (January 10). https://www.washingtonpost.com/news/monkey-cage/wp/2014/01/10/to-understand-gops-poverty-challenge-start-with-republican-voters/.

Ehrenreich, Barbara. 2011. *Nickel and Dimed: On (Not) Getting By in America*. New York: Picador.

Eiken, Steve, Kate Sredl, Brian Burwell, and Angie Amos. 2018. "Medicaid Expenditures for Long-Term Services and Supports in FY 2016" (May). Cambridge, MA: IBM Watson Health. http://www.advancingstates.org/hcbs/article/medicaid-expenditures-long-term-services-and-supports-fy-2016.

Ekins, Emily. 2019. "What Americans Think about Poverty, Wealth, and Work." Washington, DC: Cato Institute. https://www.cato.org/sites/cato.org/files/2019-09/Cato2019WelfareWorkWealthSurveyReport%20%281%29.pdf..

Elis, Niv. 2017. "Funding Confusion Complicates Meals on Wheels Budget Fight," *The Hill* (May 27). https://thehill.com/policy/finance/335368-funding-confusion-complicates-meals-on-wheels-budget-fight.

Ellis, Rabbi David. 2018. "Poverty and the Poor in the Jewish Tradition." In *Poverty and the Poor in the World's Religious Traditions: Religious Responses to the Problem of Poverty*, edited by William H. Brackney and Rupen Das, pp. 149–86. Santa Barbara, CA: Praeger.

Erkulwater, Jennifer L. 2006. *Disability Rights and the American Social Safety Net*. Ithaca, NY: Cornell University Press.

Ewing-Nelson, Claire. 2020. "One in Five Child Care Jobs Have Been Lost Since February, and Women Are Paying the Price" (August). Washington, DC: National Women's Law Center https://nwlc.org/wp-content/uploads/2020/08/ChildCareWorkersFS.pdf.

Fabius, Chanee D., Jennifer L. Wolff, and Judith D. Kasper. 2020. "Race Differences in Characteristics and Experiences of Black and White Caregivers of Older Americans," *The Gerontologist* 60, 7 (October): 1244–53.

Fadulu, Lola. 2020. "Trump Backs Off Tougher Food Stamp Work Rules for Now," *New York Times* (April 10). https://www.nytimes.com/2020/04/10/us/politics/trump-food-stamps-delay.html.

Fahmy, Dalia. 2018. "Americans Are Far More Religious than Adults in Other Wealthy Nations" (July 31). Washington, DC: Pew Research Center. https://www.pewresearch.org/fact-tank/2018/07/31/americans-are-far-more-religious-than-adults-in-other-wealthy-nations/.

Falk, Gene, and Patrick A. Landers. 2019. "The Temporary Assistance for Needy Families (TANF) Black Grant: Responses to Frequently Asked Questions," Congressional Research Service Report RL32760 (December 30). Accessed from ProQuest Congressional database.

Feeding America. 2019. *2019 Annual Report*. https://www.feedingamerica.org/about-us/financials.

Feldman, Stanley, Leonie Huddy, Julie Wronski, and Patrick Lown. 2020. "The Interplay of Empathy and Individualism in Support for Social Welfare Policies," *Political Psychology* 41, 2 (April): 343–62.

Feldman, Stanley, and Marco R. Steenbergen. 2001. "The Humanitarian Foundation of Public Support for Social Welfare," *American Journal of Political Science* 45, 3 (July): 658–77.

Fender, Elizabeth. 2017. "Poll: Vast Majority Support Four Simple Fixes to Welfare System" (December 7). Washington, DC: Heritage Foundation. https://www.heritage.org/public-opinion/report/poll-vast-majority-support-four-simple-fixes-welfare-system.

Feuer, Will. 2019. "Jeff Bezos' Day One Fund Gives $98.5 Million to 32 Groups Helping the Homeless," CNBC (November 21). https://www.cnbc.com/2019/11/21/bezos-day-one-fund-gives-98point5-million-to-groups-helping-the-homeless.html.

Finegold, Kenneth. 1988. "Agriculture and the Politics of US Social Provision: Social Insurance and Food Stamps." In *The Politics of Social Policy in the United States*, edited by Margaret Weir, Ann Shola Orloff, and Theda Skocpol, pp. 199–234. Princeton, NJ: Princeton University Press.

Fiorina, Morris P., with Samuel J. Adams and Jeremy C. Pope. 2010. *Culture War? The Myth of a Polarized America*, 3rd ed. New York: Longman.

Fischer, Will. 2018. "Trump Plan to Condition Rental Assistance on Work Will Hurt Families, Not Support Work" (February 7). Washington, DC: Center on Budget and Policy Priorities. https://www.cbpp.org/blog/trump-plan-to-condition-rental-assistance-on-work-will-hurt-families-not-support-work.

Fischer, Will. 2019. "Rental Assistance Cuts Homelessness and Poverty, But Doesn't Reach Most Who Need It" (December 5). Washington, DC: Center on Budget and Policy Priorities. https://www.cbpp.org/blog/rental-assistance-cuts-homelessness-and-poverty-but-doesnt-reach-most-who-need-it.

Fisher, Berenice, and Joan C. Tronto. 1990. "Toward a Feminist Theory of Care." In *Circles of Care: Work and Identity in Women's Lives*, edited by Emily K. Abel and Margaret K. Nelson, pp. 36–54. Albany, NY: SUNY Press.

Fisher, Gordon M. 1992. "The Development and History of the Poverty Thresholds," *Social Security Bulletin* 55, 4 (Winter): 3–14.

Fiske, Susan T. 1998. "Stereotyping, Prejudice, and Discrimination." In *The Handbook of Social Psychology*, 4th ed., edited by Daniel Todd Gilbert, Susan T. Fiske, and Gardner Lindzey, pp. 357–411. Boston, MA: McGraw-Hill.

Fiske, Susan T., Amy J. C. Cuddy, and Peter Glick. 2007. "Universal Dimensions of Social Cognition: Warmth and Competence," *Trends in Cognitive Sciences* 11, 2 (February): 77–83.

Fiske, Susan T., Jun Xu, Amy C. Cuddy, and Peter Glick. 1999. "(Dis)repecting versus (Dis)liking: Status and Interdependence Predict Ambivalent Stereotypes of Competence and Warmth," *Journal of Social Issues* 55, 3 (Fall): 473–89.

FitzGerald, Frances. 2017. *The Evangelicals: The Struggle to Shape America*. New York: Simon & Schuster.

Flavin, Patrick, and William W. Franko. 2017. "Government's Unequal Attentiveness to Citizens' Political Priorities," *Policy Studies Journal* 45, 4 (November): 659–87.

Flinn, Brian. 2020. "Nursing Home Closures and Trends, June 2015–June 2019," *Leading Age* (February). https://leadingage.org/sites/default/files/Nursing%20Home%20Closures%20and%20Trends%202020.pdf.

Floyd, Ife. 2018. "Despite Recent TANF Benefit Boosts, Black Families Left Behind" (October 25). Washington, DC: Center on Budget and Policy Priorities. https://www.cbpp.org/blog/despite-recent-tanf-benefit-boosts-black-families-left-behind.

Floyd, Ife. 2020. "Cash Assistance Should Reach Millions More Families" (March 4). Washington, DC: Center on Budget and Policy Priorities. https://www.cbpp.org/research/family-income-support/cash-assistance-should-reach-millions-more-families.

Fong, Kelley. 2020. "Getting Eyes in the Home: Child Protective Services Investigations and State Surveillance of Family Life," *American Sociological Review* 85, 4 (August): 610–38.

Food Research & Action Center. 2012. "Replacing the Thrifty Food Plan in Order to Provide Adequate Allotments for SNAP Beneficiaries" (December). https://frac.org/research/resource-library/replacing-thrifty-food-plan-order-provide-adequate-allotments-snap-beneficiaries.

Ford, Tiffany, and Jenny Schuetz. 2019. "Workforce Housing and Middle-Income Housing Subsidies: A Primer" (October 29). Washington, DC: Brookings Institution. https://www.brookings.edu/blog/up-front/2019/10/29/workforce-housing-and-middle-income-housing-subsidies-a-primer/.

Foster, Carly Hayden. 2008. "The Welfare Queen: Race, Gender, Class, and Public Opinion," *Race, Gender & Class* 15, 3/4: 162–79.

Fottrell, Quentin. 2017. "This Is How Much It Costs 'Meals on Wheels' to Feed One Elderly Person for a Year," MarketWatch (March 19). https://www.marketwatch.com/story/this-is-how-much-it-costs-meals-on-wheels-to-feed-one-elderly-person-for-a-year-2017-03-16..

Fox, Cybelle. 2012. *Three Worlds of Relief: Race, Immigration, and the American Welfare State from the Progressive Era to the New Deal.* Princeton, NJ: Princeton University Press.

Fox, Liana. 2019. "The Supplemental Poverty Measure: 2018," Current Population Reports P60-268 (RV) (October). Washington, DC: U.S. Census Bureau. https://www.census.gov/content/dam/Census/library/publications/2019/demo/p60-268.pdf.

Fox, Liana, and Kalee Burns. 2021. "The Supplemental Poverty Measure: 2020," Current Population Reports P60-275 (September). Washington, DC: U.S. Census Bureau. https://www.census.gov/library/publications/2021/demo/p60-275.html.

Frazier, Mya. 2021. "When No Landlord Will Rent to You, Where Do You Go?" *New York Times Magazine* (May 20). https://www.nytimes.com/2021/05/20/magazine/extended-stay-hotels.html.

Fremstad, Shawn. 2016. "The Federal Poverty Line Is Too Damn Low," *The Nation* (September 14). https://www.thenation.com/article/archive/the-federal-poverty-line-is-too-damn-low/.

Friedman, Milton. 1962. *Capitalism and Freedom.* Chicago: University of Chicago Press.

Fry, Richard. 2018. "More Adults Now Share Their Living Space, Driven In Part by Parents Living with Their Adult Children" (January 31). Washington, DC: Pew Research Center. https://www.pewresearch.org/fact-tank/2018/01/31/more-adults-now-share-their-living-space-driven-in-part-by-parents-living-with-their-adult-children/.

Fry, Richard. 2019. "The Number of People in the Average U.S. Household Is Going Up for the First Time in Over 160 Years" (October 1). Washington, DC: Pew Research Center. https://www.pewresearch.org/fact-tank/2019/10/01/the-number-of-people-in-the-average-u-s-household-is-going-up-for-the-first-time-in-over-160-years/.

Frymer, Paul. 1999. *Uneasy Alliances: Race and Party Competition in America.* Princeton, NJ: Princeton University Press.

Galewitz, Phil. 2014. "Business Groups Split on Medicaid Expansion," *Kaiser Health News* (March 10). https://khn.org/news/business-groups-split-on-medicaid-expansion/.

Galewitz, Phil. 2015. "Why Urban Hospitals Are Leaving Cities for Fancy Suburbs," *Governing* (April 14). https://www.governing.com/archive/why-urban-hospitals-are-leaving-cities-for-fancy-suburbs.html.

Gandhi, Ashvin, Huizi Yu, and David C. Grabowski. 2021. "High Nursing Staff Turnover in Nursing Homes Offers Important Quality Information," *Health Affairs* 40, 3 (March): 384–91.

Garcia, Adrian D. 2019. "Survey: Most Americans Wouldn't Cover a $1K Emergency with Savings," Bankrate.com (January 16). https://www.bankrate.com/banking/savings/financial-security-january-2019/.

Garcia, Tonya. 2018. "Amazon's $15 Minimum Wage Could Put Pressure on Other Retailers to Raise Pay," *MarketWatch.com* (October 4). https://www.marketwatch.com/story/amazons-15-minimum-wage-could-put-pressure-on-other-retailers-to-raise-pay-2018-10-03.

Garfield, Rachel, Kendal Orgera, and Anthony Damico. 2019. "The Uninsured and the ACA: A Primer" (January). Washington, DC: Kaiser Family Foundation. https://www.kff.org/uninsured/report/the-uninsured-and-the-aca-a-primer-key-facts-about-health-insurance-and-the-uninsured-amidst-changes-to-the-affordable-care-act/.

Garfield, Rachel, Robin Rudowitz, Kendal Orgera, and Anthony Damico. 2019. "Understanding the Intersection of Medicaid and Work: What Does the Data Say?" (August 8). Washington, DC: Kaiser Family Foundation. https://www.kff.org/medicaid/issue-brief/understanding-the-intersection-of-medicaid-and-work-what-does-the-data-say/.

Gaunt, Angelike. 2020. "ADLs and IADLs: An Essential Guide for Seniors," *A Place for Mom* (April 26). https://www.aplaceformom.com/caregiver-resources/articles/adls-iadls.

Gee, Emily. 2019. "The High Price of Hospital Care" (June 26). Washington, DC: Center for American Progress. https://www.americanprogress.org/issues/healthcare/reports/2019/06/26/471464/high-price-hospital-care/.

Gelles, David, and David Yaffe-Bellany. 2019. "Shareholder Value Is No Longer Everything, Top C.E.O.s Say," *New York Times* (August 19). https://www.nytimes.com/2019/08/19/business/business-roundtable-ceos-corporations.html.

General Social Survey (GSS). 2016. Conducted by NORC of the University of Chicago. Accessed from https://sda.berkeley.edu/.

Gerring, John. 1998. *Party Ideologies in America, 1828–1996.* New York: Cambridge University Press.

Getter, Darryl E. 2017. *Short-Term, Small-Dollar Lending: Policy Issues and Implications* (June 14). Washington, DC: Congressional Research Service. Accessed from ProQuest Congressional database.

Ghilarducci, Teresa. 2015. "Private Pensions." In *The Oxford Handbook of U.S. Social Policy*, edited by Daniel Béland, Christopher Howard, and Kimberly J. Morgan, pp. 279–95. New York: Oxford University Press.

Giannarelli, Linda, Laura Wheaton, and Katie Shantz. 2021. "2021 Poverty Projections" (February 16). Washington, DC: Urban Institute. https://www.urban.org/research/publication/2021-poverty-projections.

Gilens, Martin. 1999. *Why Americans Hate Welfare: Race, Media, and the Politics of Antipoverty Policy.* Chicago: University of Chicago Press.

Gilligan, Adrienne M., David S. Alberts, Denise J. Roe, and Grant H. Skrepnek. 2018. "Death or Debt? National Estimates of Financial Toxicity in Persons with Newly-Diagnosed Cancer," *American Journal of Medicine* 131, 10 (October): 1187–99.

Gitterman, Daniel P. 2010. *Boosting Paychecks: The Politics of Supporting America's Working Poor.* Washington, DC: Brookings Institution Press.

Giving USA Foundation. 2019. *Giving USA: The Annual Report on Philanthropy for the Year 2018.* Chicago, IL: Giving USA Foundation.

Gleckman, Howard. 2020a. "Why Are So Many Nursing Homes Shutting Down?" *Forbes* (March 2). https://www.forbes.com/sites/howardgleckman/2020/03/02/why-are-so-many-nursing-homes-shutting-down/?sh=20f138ac1712.

Gleckman, Howard. 2020b. "How Will We Pay For All the Coronavirus Relief?" (April 23). Washington, DC: Tax Policy Center. https://www.taxpolicycenter.org/taxvox/how-will-we-pay-all-coronavirus-relief/

Glenn, Evelyn Nakano. 2010. *Forced to Care: Coercion and Caregiving in America.* Cambridge, MA: Harvard University Press.

Goehring, Benjamin, Christine Heffernan, Sarah Minton, and Linda Giannarelli. 2019. "Welfare Rules Databook: State TANF Policies as of July 2018" (August). Washington, DC: Urban Institute. https://www.urban.org/research/publication/welfare-rules-databook-state-tanf-policies-july-2018/view/full_report.

Gogoi, Pallavi. 2020. "Stuck-At-Home Moms: The Pandemic's Devastating Toll on Women," *National Public Radio* (October 28). https://www.npr.org/2020/10/28/928253674/stuck-at-home-moms-the-pandemics-devastating-toll-on-women.

Golden, Tim. 1996. "If Immigrants Lose U.S. Aid, Local Budgets May Feel Pain," *New York Times* (July 29): A1.

Goldstein, Matthew, Jessica Silver-Greenberg, and Robert Gebeloff. 2020. "Push for Profits Left Nursing Homes Struggling to Provide Care," *New York Times* (May 7). https://www.nytimes.com/2020/05/07/business/coronavirus-nursing-homes.html.

Goldstone, Brian. 2019. "The New American Homeless," *The New Republic* (August 21). https://newrepublic.com/article/154618/new-american-homeless-housing-insecurity-richest-cities.

Gollan, Rachel. 2019. "'The Rats Sensed She Was Going to Pass Away': Elderly Often Face Neglect in California Care Homes that Exploit Workers," *Reveal* (September 18). https://revealnews.org/article/elderly-often-face-neglect-in-california-care-homes-that-exploit-workers/.

Gonyea, Judith G. 2014. "The Policy Challenges of a Larger and More Diverse Oldest-Old Population." In *The New Politics of Old-Age Policy*, 3rd ed., edited by Robert B. Hudson, pp. 155–80. Baltimore, MD: Johns Hopkins University Press.

Goodman, Peter S. 2020. "Big Business Pledged Gentler Capitalism. It's Not Happening in a Pandemic," *New York Times* (April 13). https://www.nytimes.com/2020/04/13/business/business-roundtable-coronavirus.html.

Gordon, Linda. 1994. *Pitied but Not Entitled: Single Mothers and the History of Welfare*. Cambridge, MA: Harvard University Press.

Gorges, Rebecca J., and R. Tamara Konetzka. 2021. "Factors Associated with Racial Differences in Deaths Among Nursing Homes Residents With COVID-19 Infection in the United States," *JAMA Network Open* 4, 2: e2037431. https://jamanetwork.com/journals/jamanetworkopen/fullarticle/2776102.

Gottschalk, Marie. 2000. *The Shadow Welfare State: Labor, Business, and the Politics of Health Care in the United States*. Ithaca, NY: Cornell University Press.

Gould, Elise. 2015. "Child Care Workers Aren't Paid Enough to Make Ends Meet" (November 5). Washington, DC: Economic Policy Institute. https://www.epi.org/publication/child-care-workers-arent-paid-enough-to-make-ends-meet/.

Gould-Werth, Alix, and H. Luke Shaefer. 2012. "Unemployment Insurance Participation by Education and by Race and Ethnicity," *Monthly Labor Review* 135, 10 (October): 28–41.

Graham, Judith. 2021. "What's In Biden's $400 Billion Plan To Support Families' Long-Term Health Needs," *National Public Radio* (April 9). https://www.npr.org/sections/health-shots/2021/04/09/985567929/whats-in-bidens-400-billion-plan-to-support-families-long-term-health-needs.

Grall, Timothy. 2020. "Custodial Mothers and Fathers and Their Child Support: 2017," Current Population Reports P60-269 (May). Washington, DC: U.S. Census Bureau. https://www.census.gov/library/publications/2020/demo/p60-269.html.

Green, Emma. 2019. "Evangelicalism's Silent Majority," *The Atlantic* (December 25). https://www.theatlantic.com/politics/archive/2019/12/leith-anderson-silence-moderate-evangelicals/604120/.

Greenhouse, Steven. 2019. *Beaten Down, Worked Up: The Past, Present, and Future of American Labor*. New York: Alfred A. Knopf.

Greenstein, Robert. 2016. "Welfare Reform and the Safety Net: Evidence Contradicts Likely Assumptions Behind Forthcoming GOP Poverty Plan" (June 6). Washington, DC: Center on Budget and Policy Priorities. https://www.cbpp.org/sites/default/files/atoms/files/6-6-16pov2.pdf.

Grogan, Colleen M., and Christina M. Andrews. 2015. "Medicaid." In *The Oxford Handbook of U.S. Social Policy*, edited by Daniel Béland, Christopher Howard, and Kimberly J. Morgan, pp. 337–54. New York: Oxford University Press.

Gross, Kimberly, and Julie Wronski. 2021. "Helping the Homeless: The Role of Empathy, Race and Deservingness in Motivating Policy Support and Charitable Giving," *Political Behavior* 43, 2 (June): 585–613.

Gundersen, Craig. 2015. "Food Assistance Programs and Food Security." In *The Oxford Handbook of U.S. Social Policy*, edited by Daniel Béland, Christopher Howard, and Kimberly J. Morgan, pp. 393–412. New York: Oxford University Press.

Gundersen, Craig, Emily Engelhard, and Monica Hake. 2017. "The Determinants of Food Insecurity among Food Bank Clients in the United States," *Journal of Consumer Affairs* 51, 3 (Fall): 501–18.

Gundersen, Craig, and James P. Ziliak. 2015. "Food Insecurity and Health Outcomes," *Health Affairs* 34, 11: 1830–39.

Guth, Madeline, Robin Rudowitz, and Rachel Garfield. 2021. "Federal Medicaid Outlays During the COVID-19 Pandemic" (April 27). Washington, DC: Kaiser Family Foundation. https://www.kff.org/coronavirus-covid-19/issue-brief/federal-medicaid-outlays-during-the-covid-19-pandemic/.

Habitat for Humanity International. 2019. *Annual Report FY2019.* https://www.habitat.org/about/annual-reports-990s.

Hacker, Jacob S. 2002. *The Divided Welfare State: The Battle over Public and Private Social Benefits in the United States.* New York: Cambridge University Press.

Hacker, Jacob S., and Paul Pierson. 2002. "Business Power and Social Policy: Employers and the Formation of the American Welfare State," *Politics & Society* 30, 2 (June): 277–325.

Hacker, Jacob S., and Paul Pierson. 2010. *Winner-Take-All Politics: How Washington Made the Rich Richer—and Turned Its Back on the Middle Class.* New York: Simon & Schuster.

Haddon, Heather, and Jesse Newman. 2018. "Food Stamp Cuts Would Hit Grocery Chains," *Wall Street Journal* (April 7): B1.

Hado, Edem, and Harriet Komisar. 2019. "Long-Term Services and Supports" (August). Washington, DC: AARP Public Policy Institute. https://www.aarp.org/ppi/info-2017/long-term-services-and-supports.html.

Hahn, Heather, Lauren Adon, Cary Lou, Eleanor Pratt, and Adaeze Okoli. 2017. "Why Does Cash Welfare Depend on Where You Live? How and Why State TANF Programs Vary" (June). Washington, DC: Urban Institute. https://www.urban.org/sites/default/files/publication/90761/tanf_cash_welfare_0.pdf.

Haines, Pavielle E., Tali Mendelberg, and Bennett Butler. 2019. "'I'm Not the President of Black America': Rhetorical versus Policy Representation," *Perspectives on Politics* 17, 4 (December): 1038–58.

Half in Ten Education Fund and the Center for American Progress. 2014. "50 Years After LBJ's War on Poverty: A Study of American Attitudes About Work, Economic Opportunity, and the Social Safety Net" (January). Washington, DC: Center for American Progress. https://cdn.americanprogress.org/wp-content/uploads/2014/01/WOP-PollReport2.pdf.

Halpern-Meekin, Sarah. 2019. *Social Poverty: Low-Income Parents and the Struggle for Family and Community Ties.* New York: New York University Press.

Halpern-Meekin, Sarah, Kathryn Edin, Laura Tach, and Jennifer Sykes. 2015. *It's Not Like I'm Poor: How Working Families Make Ends Meet in a Post-Welfare World.* Oakland: University of California Press.

Hamel, Liz, Mira Norton, Karen Pollitz, Larry Levitt, Gary Claxton, and Mollyann Brodie. 2016. "The Burden of Medical Debt: Results from the Kaiser Family Foundation/New York Times Medical Bills Survey" (January). Washington, DC: Kaiser Family Foundation. https://www.kff.org/wp-content/uploads/2016/01/8806-the-burden-of-medical-debt-results-from-the-kaiser-family-foundation-new-york-times-medical-bills-survey.pdf.

Han, Jeehoon, Bruce D. Meyer, and James X. Sullivan. 2021. "Real-time Poverty Estimates During the COVID-19 Pandemic through June 2021," Povertymeasurement.org (July 15). http://povertymeasurement.org/wp-content/uploads/2021/07/Real-time-Poverty-Estimates-through-June-2021-Updated-July-15-2021.pdf.

Hancock, Ange-Marie. 2004. *The Politics of Disgust: The Public Identity of the Welfare Queen.* New York: New York University Press.

Hancock, Jay, and Elizabeth Lucas. 2019. "'UVA Has Ruined Us': Health System Sues Thousands of Patients, Seizing Paychecks and Claiming Homes," *Kaiser Health News* (September 9). https://khn.org/news/uva-health-system-sues-patients-virginia-courts-garnishment-liens-bankruptcy/.

Handler, Joel F., and Yeheskel Hasenfeld. 1991. *The Moral Construction of Poverty: Welfare Reform in America.* Newbury Park, CA: Sage Publications.

Hankivsky, Olena. 2004. *Social Policy and the Ethic of Care.* Vancouver, Canada: UBC Press.

Hankivsky, Olena. 2014. "Rethinking Care Ethics: On the Promise and Potential of an Intersectional Analysis," *American Political Science Review* 108, 2 (May): 252–64.

Harrell, Allison, Stuart Soroka, and Shanto Iyengar. 2016. "Race, Prejudice and Attitudes Toward Redistribution: A Comparative Experimental Approach," *European Journal of Political Research* 55, 4 (November): 723–44.

Harrington, Charlene, Anne Montgomery, Terris King, David C. Grabowski, and Michael Wasserman. 2021. "These Administrative Actions Would Improve Nursing Home

Ownership and Financial Transparency in the Post COVID-19 Period," *Health Affairs* blog (February 11). https://www.healthaffairs.org/do/10.1377/hblog20210208.597573/full/.

Harrington, Charlene, Leslie Ross, Dana Mukamel, and Pauline Rosenau. 2013. "Improving the Financial Accountability of Nursing Facilities" (June). Washington, DC: Kaiser Family Foundation. https://www.kff.org/medicaid/report/improving-the-financial-accountabil ity-of-nursing-facilities/.

Harris-Kojetin, Lauren, Manisha Sengupta, Jessica Penn Lendon, Vincent Rome, Roberto Valverde, and Christine Caffrey. 2019. "Long-Term Care Providers and Services Users in the United States, 2015–2016." *National Center for Health Statistics, Vital and Health Statistics* 3, 43 (February). https://www.cdc.gov/nchs/nsltcp/nsltcp_webtables.htm.

Hart Research Associates and Chesapeake Beach Consulting. 2014. "Americans' Views on Hunger." Washington, DC: Food Research & Action Center. http://frac.org/wp-content/ uploads/frac_tyson_oct_2014_public_view_hunger_poll.pdf.

Hartline-Grafton, Heather. 2017. "The Impact of Poverty, Food Insecurity, and Poor Nutrition on Health and Well-Being" (December). Washington, DC: Food Research & Action Center. https://frac.org/research/resource-library/hunger-health-impact-poverty-food-insecurity-poor-nutrition-health-well..

Harty, Patricia. 2018. "Mary Kay Henry: A New Deal for America's Working Poor," *Irish America* (June/July). https://irishamerica.com/2018/05/mary-kay-henry-a-new-deal-for-ameri cas-working-poor/.

Haskins, Ron. 2005. "The School Lunch Lobby," *Education Next* 5, 3 (Summer): 11–17. https:// www.educationnext.org/the-school-lunch-lobby/.

Haskins, Ron. 2006. *Work over Welfare: The Inside Story of the 1996 Welfare Reform Law.* Washington, DC: Brookings Institution Press.

Hatch, Megan E. 2017. "Statutory Protection for Renters: Classification of State Landlord-Tenant Policy Approaches," *Housing Policy Debate* 27, 1 (January): 98–119.

Hays, Sharon. 2003. *Flat Broke with Children: Women in the Age of Welfare Reform.* New York: Oxford University Press.

Health Resources & Services Administration. 2020. "Health Center Program: Impact and Growth" (December). https://bphc.hrsa.gov/about/healthcenterprogram/index.html.

Helminiak, Daniel A. 2020. "Material and Spiritual Poverty: A Postmodern Psychological Perspective on a Perennial Problem," *Journal of Religion and Health* 59, 3 (June): 1458–80.

Henly, Julia. 2018. "Think Summer Child Care Is Tough? Low-Income Families Deal With That All Year," *New York Times* (July 29). https://www.nytimes.com/2018/07/29/opinion/ child-care-summer-low-income.html.

Herd, Patricia, and Donald P. Moynihan. 2018. *Administrative Burden: Policymaking By Other Means.* New York: Russell Sage Foundation.

Hernández, Kristian. 2021. "Some States Ban Evictions After National Moratorium Ends" (June 9). Washington, DC: Pew Charitable Trusts. https://www.pewtrusts.org/en/research-and-analysis/blogs/stateline/2021/06/09/some-states-ban-evictions-after-national-morator ium-ends.

Hero, Rodney E. 1998. *Faces of Inequality: Social Diversity in American Politics.* New York: Oxford University Press.

Hertel-Fernandez, Alexander, Theda Skocpol, and Daniel Lynch. 2016. "Business Associations, Conservative Networks, and the Ongoing Republican War over Medicaid Expansion," *Journal of Health Politics, Policy and Law* 41, 2 (April): 239–86.

Hetherington, Marc J., and Jonathan D. Weiler. 2009. *Authoritarianism and Polarization in American Politics.* New York: Cambridge University Press.

Hicks-Bartlett, Sharon. 2000. "Between a Rock and a Hard Place: The Labyrinth of Working and Parenting in a Poor Community." In *Coping with Poverty: The Social Contexts of Neighborhood, Work, and Family in the African-American Community,* edited by Sheldon Danziger and Ann Chih Lin, pp. 27–51. Ann Arbor: University of Michigan Press.

Hobson, Will. 2020. "Zombie Philanthropy: The Rich Have Stashed Billions in Donor Advised Charities—But It's Not Reaching Those in Need," *Washington Post* (June 24). https://www. washingtonpost.com/lifestyle/style/zombie-philanthropy-the-rich-have-stashed-billions-in-donor-advised-charities--but-its-not-reaching-those-in-need/2020/06/23/6a1b397a-af3a-11ea-856d-5054296735e5_story.html.

Hodgkinson, Stacy, Leandra Godoy, Lee Savio Beers, and Amy Lewin. 2017. "Improving Mental Health Access for Low-Income Children and Families in the Primary Care Setting," *Pediatrics* 139, 1 (January): e20151175.

Holgash, Kayla, and Martha Heberlein. 2019. "Physician Acceptance of New Medicaid Patients" (January 24). Washington, DC: Medicaid and CHIP Payment and Access Commission. http://www.macpac.gov/wp-content/uploads/2019/01/Physician-Acceptance-of-New-Medicaid-Patients.pdf.

Holpuch, Amanda. 2020. "'Biggest Thing to Happen to Renters since WWII': Why This US Eviction Expert Is Optimistic," *The Guardian* (October 29). https://www.theguardian.com/us-news/2020/oct/29/matthew-desmond-us-evictions-interview.

Hopkins, Daniel J. 2009. "Partisan Reinforcement and the Poor: The Impact of Context on Explanations for Poverty," *Social Science Quarterly* 90, 3 (September): 744–76.

Horowitz, Juliana Menasce, Ruth Igielnik, and Ramesh Kochhar. 2020. "Most Americans Say There Is Too Much Economic Inequality in the U.S., but Fewer Than Half Call It a Top Priority" (January 9). Washington, DC: Pew Research Center. https://www.pewsocialtre nds.org/2020/01/09/most-americans-say-there-is-too-much-economic-inequality-in-the-u-s-but-fewer-than-half-call-it-a-top-priority/.

Horowitz, Juliana Menasce, Kim Parker, Nikki Graf, and Grethcen Livingston. 2017. "Americans Widely Support Paid Family and Medical Leave, but Differ Over Specific Policies" (March 23). Washington, DC: Pew Research Center. https://www.pewresearch.org/social-trends/2017/03/23/americans-widely-support-paid-family-and-medical-leave-but-differ-over-specific-policies/.

Houser, Ari, Wendy Fox-Grage, and Kathleen Ujvari. 2018. "Across the States: Profiles of Long-Term Services and Supports" (August 27). Washington, DC: AARP Public Policy Institute. https://www.aarp.org/ppi/info-2018/state-long-term-services-supports.html.

Howard, Christopher. 1997. *The Hidden Welfare State: Tax Expenditures and Social Policy in the United States.* Princeton, NJ: Princeton University Press.

Howard, Christopher. 2002. "Workers' Compensation, Federalism, and the Heavy Hand of History," *Studies in American Political Development* 16, 1 (April): 28–47.

Howard, Christopher. 2007. *The Welfare State Nobody Knows: Debunking Myths about U.S. Social Policy.* Princeton, NJ: Princeton University Press.

Howard, Christopher. 2022. "Build Back Better: The Challenge of Selling a Hybrid on Capitol Hill," *The Hill* (January 26). https://thehill.com/blogs/congress-blog/politics/591486-build-back-better-the-challenge-of-selling-a-hybrid-on-capitol.

Howard, Christopher, Amirio Freeman, April Wilson, and Eboni Brown. 2017. "The Polls—Trends: Poverty," *Public Opinion Quarterly* 81, 3 (Fall): 769–89.

Hudnut-Beumler, James and Mark Silk (eds.). 2018. *The Future of Mainline Protestantism in America.* New York: Columbia University Press.

Hunt, Matthew O., and Heather E. Bullock. 2016. "Ideologies and Beliefs About Poverty." In *The Oxford Handbook of the Social Science of Poverty*, edited by David Brady and Linda M. Burton, pp. 93–116. New York: Oxford University Press.

Hurley, Lawrence. 2020. "U.S. Supreme Court Takes Up Trump Bid to Revive Medicaid Work Requirements," *Reuters* (December 4). https://www.reuters.com/article/us-usa-court-medicaid/u-s-supreme-court-takes-up-trump-bid-to-revive-medicaid-work-requirements-idUSKBN28E30P.

Iacurci, Greg. 2020. "40% of Low-Income Americans Lost their Jobs Due to the Pandemic," *CNBC* (May 14). https://www.cnbc.com/2020/05/14/40percent-of-low-income-americans-lost-their-jobs-in-march-according-to-fed.html.

Iceland, John. 2013. *Poverty in America: A Handbook*, 3rd ed. Berkeley: University of California Press.

Indiana University Lilly Family School of Philanthropy. 2019. "Changes to the Giving Landscape." https://scholarworks.iupui.edu/handle/1805/21217.

Institute of Medicine. 2009. *America's Uninsured Crisis: Consequences for Health and Health Care*. Washington, DC: National Academies Press.

Ivory, Danielle, Lauren Leatherby, and Robert Gebeloff. 2021. "Least Vaccinated U.S. Counties Have Something in Common: Trump Voters," *New York Times* (April 17). https://www.nyti mes.com/interactive/2021/04/17/us/vaccine-hesitancy-politics.html.

Iyengar, Shanto, and Masha Krupenkin. 2018. "The Strengthening of Partisan Affect," *Advances in Political Psychology* 39, S1 (February): 201–18.

Jacknowitz, Alison, and Laura Tiehen. 2009. "Transitions Into and Out Of the WIC Program: A Cause for Concern?" *Social Service Review* 83, 2 (June): 151–83.

Jackson, Anna-Louise, and John Schmidt. 2022. "2021 Stock Market Year In Review," *Forbes* (January 3). https://www.forbes.com/advisor/investing/stock-market-year-in-review-2021/.

Jacobs, Andrew. 2021. "Frontline Health Care Workers Aren't Feeling the 'Summer of Joy,'" *New York Times* (July 1). https://www.nytimes.com/2021/07/01/health/covid-nurses-doctors-burnout.html.

Jaffe, Ina. 2017. "Food Is Just One Serving of What Meals on Wheels Gives Seniors," *National Public Radio* (March 23). https://www.npr.org/sections/thesalt/2017/03/23/521103 662/food-is-just-one-serving-of-what-meals-on-wheels-gives-seniors.

Jaffe, Ina. 2020. "For-Profit Nursing Homes' Pleas for Government Money Brings Scrutiny," *National Public Radio* (October 22). https://www.gpb.org/news/2020/10/22/for-profit-nursing-homes-pleas-for-government-money-brings-scrutiny.

Jalonick, Mary Clare. 2015. "Panel Reverses, Says White Potatoes Should Be Included In WIC Benefits," *PBS News Hour* (February 3). https://www.pbs.org/newshour/politics/panel-reverses-says-white-potatoes-ok-wic-recipients.

Jalonick, Mary Clare. 2017. "Government Relaxes Nutrition Standards for School Lunches," *PBS News Hour* (May 1). https://www.pbs.org/newshour/health/government-relaxes-nutrit ion-standards-school-lunches.

Jensen, Laura S. 2015. "Social Provision Before the Twentieth Century." In *The Oxford Handbook of U.S. Social Policy*, edited by Daniel Béland, Christopher Howard, and Kimberly J. Morgan, pp. 23–40. New York: Oxford University Press.

Johnson, Anna D., and Anna J. Markowitz. 2018. "Associations Between Household Food Insecurity in Early Childhood and Children's Kindergarten Skills," *Child Development* 89, 2 (March/April): e1–e17.

Johnson, Martin. 2003. "Racial Context, Public Attitudes, and Welfare Effort in the American States." In *Race and the Politics of Welfare Reform*, edited by Sanford F. Schram, Joe Soss, and Richard C. Fording, pp. 151–67. Ann Arbor: University of Michigan Press.

Johnson, Richard W. 2019. "What Is the Lifetime Risk of Needing and Receiving Long-Term Services and Supports?" *ASPE Research Brief* (April 3). Washington, DC: U.S. Department of Health and Human Services. https://aspe.hhs.gov/reports/what-lifetime-risk-needing-receiving-long-term-services-supports.

Johnson, Sharon. 2020. "On the Front Lines: Community Health Centers Play a Vital Role in the Age of COVID-19," *The Progressive* (June 9). https://progressive.org/magazine/on-the-front-lines-johnson/.

Joint Center for Housing Studies of Harvard University. 2019a. "Housing America's Older Adults 2019." https://www.jchs.harvard.edu/housing-americas-older-adults-2019.

Joint Center for Housing Studies of Harvard University. 2019b. "The State of the Nation's Housing 2019." https://www.jchs.harvard.edu/state-nations-housing-2019.

Joint Committee on Taxation. 2015. "Estimates of Federal Tax Expenditures for Fiscal Years 2015–2019" (December 7). https://www.jct.gov/publications.html?func=select&id=5.

Joint Committee on Taxation. 2019. "Estimates of Federal Tax Expenditures for Fiscal Years 2019–2023" (December 18). https://www.jct.gov/publications.html?func=startdown&id=5238.

Jones, Katie. 2019. "FHA-Insured Home Loans: An Overview," Congressional Research Service Report RS20530 (January 16). Accessed from ProQuest Congressional database.

Jordan, Soren, Clayton McLaughlin Webb, and B. Dan Wood. 2014. "The President, Polarization, and the Party Platforms, 1944–2012," *The Forum* 12, 1 (April): 169–89.

Joyce, Kathryn. 2019. "The Crime of Parenting While Poor," *The New Republic* (February 25). https://newrepublic.com/article/153062/crime-parenting-poor-new-york-city-child-welf are-agency-reform. Accessed June 25, 2021.

Jyoti, Diana F., Edward A. Frongillo, and Sonya J. Jones. 2005. "Food Insecurity Affects Children's Academic Performance, Weight Gain, and Social Skills," *Journal of Nutrition* 135, 12 (December): 2831–39.

Kahlenberg, Richard D. 2019. "How Minneapolis Ended Single-Family Zoning" (October 24). New York: Century Foundation. https://tcf.org/content/report/minneapolis-ended-sin gle-family-zoning/.

Kaiser Family Foundation. 2013. "Summary of the Affordable Care Act" (April 25). https://www. kff.org/health-reform/fact-sheet/summary-of-the-affordable-care-act/.

Kaiser Family Foundation. 2019. "An Overview of Medicare" (February 13). https://www.kff. org/medicare/issue-brief/an-overview-of-medicare/.

Kalil, Ariel, and Rebecca M. Ryan. 2010. "Mothers' Economic Conditions and Sources of Support in Fragile Families," *The Future of Children* 20, 2 (Fall): 39–61.

Kalil, Ariel, Heidi Schweingruber, Marijata Daniel-Echols, and Ashli Breen. 2000. "Mother, Worker, Welfare Recipient: Welfare Reform and the Multiple Roles of low-Income Women." In *Coping with Poverty: The Social Contexts of Neighborhood, Work, and Family in the African-American Community,* edited by Sheldon Danziger and Ann Chih Lin, pp. 201–23. Ann Arbor: University of Michigan Press.

Kamimura, Akiko, Jennifer Tabler, Alla Chernenko, Guadeloupe Aguilera, Maziar M. Nourian, Liana Prudencio, and Jeanie Ashby. 2016. "Why Uninsured Free Clinic Patients Don't Apply for Affordable Care Act Health Insurance in a Non-expanding Medicaid State," *Journal of Community Health* 41, 1 (February): 119–26.

Karpman, Michael, and Stephen Zuckerman. 2021. "Average Decline in Material Hardship During the Pandemic Conceals Unequal Circumstances" (April 14). Washington, DC: Urban Institute. https://www.urban.org/research/publication/average-decline-material-hardship-during-pandemic-conceals-unequal-circumstances.

Kasakove, Sophie. 2021. "With Cases Piling Up, an Eviction Crisis Unfolds Step by Step," *New York Times* (November 7). https://www.nytimes.com/2021/11/07/us/evictions-cri sis-us.html.

Katz, Lawrence F., and Alan B. Krueger. 2019. "The Rise and Nature of Alternative Work Arrangements in the United States, 1995–2015," *ILR Review* 72, 2 (March): 382–416.

Katz, Michael B. 1986. *In the Shadow of the Poorhouse: A Social History of Welfare in America.* New York: Basic Books.

Katz, Michael B. 2001. *The Price of Citizenship: Redefining the American Welfare State.* New York: Henry Holt and Company.

Katz, Michael B. 2013. *The Undeserving Poor: America's Enduring Confrontation with Poverty* 2nd ed. New York: Oxford University Press.

Katznelson, Ira. 2005. *When Affirmative Action Was White: An Untold History of Racial Inequality in Twentieth-Century America.* New York: W. W. Norton.

Keisler-Starkey, Katherine, and Lisa N. Bunch. 2020. *Health Insurance Coverage in the United States: 2019,* U.S. Census Bureau, Current Population Reports P60-271. Washington, DC: Government Printing Office. https://www.census.gov/library/publications/2020/ demo/p60-271.html.

Kennedy, David M. 1999. *Freedom from Fear: The American People in Depression and War, 1929–1945.* New York: Oxford University Press.

Kenworthy, Nora, Zhihang Dong, Anne Montgomery, Emily Fuller, and Lauren Berliner. 2020. "A cross-sectional study of social inequities in medical crowdfunding campaigns in the United States," *PLOS ONE* 15, 3: e0229760. https://doi.org/10.1371/journal.pone.0229760.

Kershaw, Paul. 2005. *Carefair: Rethinking the Responsibilities and Rights of Citizenship*. Vancouver, Canada: UBC Press.

Khullar, Dhruv, and Dave A. Chokshi. 2018. "Health, Income, & Poverty: Where We Are & What Could Help," *Health Affairs Health Policy Brief* (October 4). https://www.healthaffairs.org/do/10.1377/hpb20180817.901935/full/.

Kidd, Thomas S. 2019. *Who Is An Evangelical? The History of a Movement in Crisis*. New Haven, CT: Yale University Press.

Kim, E. Tammy. 2020. "When You Are Paid 13 Hours for a 24-Hour Shift," *New York Times* (June 30). https://www.nytimes.com/2020/06/30/opinion/coronavirus-nursing-homes.html.

Kimberlin, Sara, Laura Tach, and Christopher Wimer. 2018. "A Renter's Tax Credit to Curtail the Affordable Housing Crisis," *RSF: The Russell Sage Foundation Journal of the Social Sciences* 4, 2 (February): 131–60.

Kinder, Donald R., and Cindy D. Kam. 2010. *Us Against Them: Ethnocentric Foundations of American Opinion*. Chicago: University of Chicago Press.

Kinder, Donald R., and Lynn M. Sanders. 1996. *Divided by Color: Racial Politics and Democratic Ideals*. Chicago: University of Chicago Press.

King, Ronald F. 2000. *Budgeting Entitlements: The Politics of Food Stamps*. Washington, DC: Georgetown University Press.

Kingdon, John W. 1984. *Agendas, Alternatives, and Public Policies*. Boston, MA: Little, Brown.

Kirchhoff, Suzanne M. 2020. "Medicare Part D Prescription Drug Benefit," Congressional Research Service Report R40611 (December 18). Available from ProQuest Congressional database.

Klein, Jennifer. 2003. *For All These Rights: Business, Labor, and the Shaping of America's Public-Private Welfare State*. Princeton, NJ: Princeton University Press.

Kleykamp, Meredith, and Crosby Hipes. 2015. "Social Programs for Soldiers and Veterans." In *The Oxford Handbook of U.S. Social Policy*, edited by Daniel Béland, Christopher Howard, and Kimberly J. Morgan, pp. 565–82. New York: Oxford University Press.

Koball, Heather. 2018. "How Federal and State Food Stamps Programs Affect Recent Immigrant Families in the United States" (January 29). Washington, DC: Scholars Strategy Network. https://scholars.org/brief/how-federal-and-state-food-stamps-programs-affect-recent-immigrant-families-united-states.

Kotch, Alex, and Walter Bragman. 2019. "The Business of Homelessness," *The American Prospect* (October 18). https://prospect.org/infrastructure/housing/business-of-homelessness-nyc-biggest-shelter-contractor/.

Kronebusch, Karl. 1997. "Medicaid and the Politics of Groups: Recipients, Providers, and Policy Making," *Journal of Health Politics, Policy and Law* 22, 3 (June): 839–78.

Kulish, Nicholas. 2020. "'Never Seen Anything Like It': Cars Line Up for Miles at Food Banks," *New York Times* (April 8). https://www.nytimes.com/2020/04/08/business/economy/coronavirus-food-banks.html.

Kullgren, Ian. 2019. "The New Union Label: Female, Progressive, and Very Anti-Trump," *Politico* (December 12). https://www.politico.com/news/magazine/2019/12/12/afl-cio-politics-union-flight-attendant-sara-nelson-president-trumka-082739.

Japson, Bruce. 2018. "As Hospitals Close, Medicaid Expansion Rises in Deep South," *Forbes* (September 30). https://www.forbes.com/sites/brucejapsen/2018/09/30/as-hospitals-close-medicaid-expansion-rises-in-deep-south/#33d1373c2e44.

Jensen, Carsten, and Michael Bang Petersen. 2017. "The Deservingness Heuristic and the Politics of Health Care," *American Journal of Political Science* 61, 1 (January): 68–83.

Jessen-Howard, Steven, Rasheed Malik, and MK Falgout. 2020. "Costly and Unavailable: America Lacks Sufficient Child Care Supply for Infants and Toddlers" (August 4). Washington, DC: Center for American Progress. https://www.americanprogress.org/issues/early-childh

ood/reports/2020/08/04/488642/costly-unavailable-america-lacks-sufficient-child-care-supply-infants-toddlers/.

Johnson, Lyndon B. 1964. "Annual Message to the Congress on the State of the Union." Online by Gerhard Peters and John T. Woolley, *The American Presidency Project*. Santa Barbara, CA: University of California, Santa Barbara. https://www.presidency.ucsb.edu/node/242292.

LaMantia, Jonathan. 2018. "Catholic Church Creates $3.2B Health Foundation from Fidelis Sale," *Modern Healthcare* (May 8). https://www.modernhealthcare.com/article/20180508/NEWS/180509920/catholic-church-creates-3-2b-health-foundation-from-fidelis-sale.

Lapp, Amber, and David Lapp. 2016. "Work-Family Policy in Trump's America: Insights from a Focus Group of Working-Class Millennial Parents in Ohio" (December). Charlottesville, VA: Institute for Family Studies. https://ifstudies.org/ifs-admin/resources/lapp-ohio-survey.pdf.

Lauter, David. 2016. "How Do Americans View Poverty? Many Blue-Collar Whites, Key to Trump, Criticize Poor People as Lazy and Content to Stay on Welfare," *Los Angeles Times* (August 14). https://www.latimes.com/projects/la-na-pol-poverty-poll/.

Layton, Lyndsey. 2015. "Majority of U.S. Public School Students Are in Poverty," *Washington Post* (January 16). https://www.washingtonpost.com/local/education/majority-of-us-public-school-students-are-in-poverty/2015/01/15/df7171d0-9ce9-11e4-a7ee-526210d665b4_story.html.

Lazarus, David. 2019. "CEOs Say They Care about Customers and Workers. Propaganda Experts Are Unimpressed," *Los Angeles Times* (August 21). https://www.latimes.com/business/story/2019-08-20/business-roundtable-propaganda-david-lazarus.

Lee, Don. 2021. "Women Put Careers On Hold During COVID to Care for Kids. They May Never Recover," *Los Angeles Times* (August 18). https://www.latimes.com/politics/story/2021-08-18/pandemic-pushes-moms-to-scale-back-or-quit-their-careers.

Lee, Michelle Ye Hee. 2017. "Paul Ryan's Claim that 'More and More Doctors Just Won't Take Medicaid,'" *Washington Post* (February 1). https://www.washingtonpost.com/news/fact-checker/wp/2017/02/01/paul-ryans-claim-that-more-and-more-doctors-just-wont-take-medicaid/.

Leonhardt, Megan. 2022. "16,000 childcare providers shut down in the pandemic. It's a really big deal," *Fortune* (February 9). https://fortune.com/2022/02/09/child-care-providers-shut-down-pandemic/.

Levendusky, Matthew. 2009. *The Partisan Sort: How Liberals Became Democrats and Conservatives Became Republicans*. Chicago: University of Chicago Press.

Levine, Martin. 2020. "Meals on Wheels: Antiquated Funding Structure Meets Ever-Increasing Need," *Nonprofit Quarterly* (January 29). https://nonprofitquarterly.org/meals-on-wheels-antiquated-funding-structure-meets-ever-increasing-need/.

Levine, Susan. 2008. *School Lunch Politics: The Surprising History of America's Favorite Welfare Program*. Princeton, NJ: Princeton University Press.

Levitsky, Sandra R. 2010. "Caregiving and the Construction of Political Claims for Long-Term Care Policy Reform." In *The New Politics of Old Age Policy*, 2nd ed., edited by Robert B. Hudson, pp. 208–30. Baltimore, MD: Johns Hopkins University Press.

Levitsky, Sandra R. 2014. *Caring for Our Own: Why There Is No Political Demand for New American Social Welfare Rights*. New York: Oxford University Press.

Levitsky, Steven, and Daniel Ziblatt. 2018. *How Democracies Die*. New York: Crown.

Levy, Diane K., Leiha Edmonds, and Jasmine Simington. 2018. "Work Requirements in Public Housing Authorities: Experiences to Date and Knowledge Gaps" (January). Washington, DC: Urban Institute. https://www.urban.org/research/publication/work-requirements-housing-authorities.

Lewis, Corinne, Melinda K. Abrams, and Shanoor Seervai. 2017. "Listening to Low-Income Patients: Obstacles to the Care We Need, When We Need It" (December 1). New York: Commonwealth Fund. https://www.commonwealthfund.org/blog/2017/listening-low-income-patients-obstacles-care-we-need-when-we-need-it.

Li, Zhe, and Joseph Dalaker. 2021. "Poverty Among the Population Aged 65 and Older," Congressional Research Service Report R45791 (April 14). Accessed from the ProQuest Congressional database.

Lichtenstein, Nelson. 1995. *The Most Dangerous Man in Detroit: Walter Reuther and the Fate of American Labor.* New York: Basic Books.

Lichtenstein, Nelson. 2013. *State of the Union: A Century of Organized Labor,* revised and expanded edition. Princeton, NJ: Princeton University Press.

Lieber, Ron. 2019. "New Tax Will Help Washington Residents Pay for Long-Term Care," *New York Times* (May 13). https://www.nytimes.com/2019/05/13/business/washington-long-term-care.html.

Lieberman, Robert C. 1998. *Shifting the Color Line: Race and the American Welfare State.* Cambridge, MA: Harvard University Press.

Lieberman, Robert C. 2015. "Race and Ethnicity in U.S. Social Policy." In *The Oxford Handbook of U.S. Social Policy,* edited by Daniel Béland, Christopher Howard, and Kimberly J. Morgan, pp. 222–38. New York: Oxford University Press.

Lipka, Michael. 2015. "Mainline Protestants Make Up Shrinking Number of U.S. Adults" (May 18). Washington, DC: Pew Research Center. https://www.pewresearch.org/fact-tank/2015/05/18/mainline-protestants-make-up-shrinking-number-of-u-s-adults/.

Loftus, Matthew. 2017. "'The Poor Will Always Be With Us' Is No Excuse to Cut Medicaid," *America: The Jesuit Review* (March 7). https://www.americamagazine.org/politics-society/2017/03/07/poor-will-always-be-us-no-excuse-cut-medicaid.

Lopez, Eric, Tricia Neuman, Gretchen Jacobson, and Larry Levitt. 2020. "How Much More Than Medicare Do Private Insurers Pay? A Review of the Literature" (April 15). Washington, DC: Kaiser Family Foundation. https://www.kff.org/medicare/issue-brief/how-much-more-than-medicare-do-private-insurers-pay-a-review-of-the-literature/.

Loprest, Pamela, and Demetra Nightingale. 2018. "The Nature of Work and the Social Safety Net" (July). Washington, DC: Urban Institute. https://www.urban.org/sites/default/files/publication/98812/the_nature_of_work_adn_the_social_safety_net_6.pdf.

Lowrey, Annie. 2014. "Income Gap, Meet the Longevity Gap," *New York Times* (March 15). https://www.nytimes.com/2014/03/16/business/income-gap-meet-the-longevity-gap.html.

Luhby, Tami. 2018. "Almost Half of US Families Can't Afford Basics Like Rent and Food," *Money* (May 18). http://money.cnn.com/2018/05/17/news/economy/us-middle-class-basics-study/index.html.

Luhby, Tami. 2019. "Many Union Members Really Love their Health Benefits. That's a Problem for Bernie Sanders," CNN (September 22). https://www.cnn.com/2019/09/22/politics/union-health-care-medicare-for-all/index.html.

Luhby, Tami. 2020. "Food Banks Struggle as Demand Explodes Thanks to Coronavirus Layoffs," *CNN* (April 3). https://www.cnn.com/2020/03/31/politics/food-banks-supplies-grocories-coronavirus/index.html.

Lupia, Arthur. 2015. *Uninformed: Why People Know So Little about Politics and What We Can Do about It.* New York: Oxford University Press.

Lynch, Karen E. 2019a. "Child Care Entitlement to States," Congressional Research Service In Focus (July 18). Available from the ProQuest Congressional database.

Lynch, Karen E. 2019b. "Head Start: Overview and Current Issues," Congressional Research Service In Focus (December 5). Available from the ProQuest Congressional database.

Lynch, Karen E., Gene Falk, Jessica Tollestrup, Conor F. Boyle, and Patrick A. Landers. 2020. "Federal Spending on Benefits and Services for People with Low Income: FY2008–FY2018 Update," Congressional Research Service Report R46214 (February 5). Accessed from the Congressional ProQuest database.

Maciag, Michael. 2018. "Where Evictions Are Most Common," *Governing* (June). https://www.governing.com/topics/health-human-services/gov-eviction-epidemic.html.

MacMillan, Douglas, Peter Whoriskey, and Jonathan O'Connell. 2020. "America's Biggest Companies Are Flourishing during the Pandemic and Putting Thousands of People Out of Work," *Washington Post* (December 16). https://www.washingtonpost.com/graphics/2020/business/50-biggest-companies-coronavirus-layoffs/.

Maharidge, Dale. 2016. "A Photographic Chronicle of America's Working Poor," *Smithsonian* (December). https://www.smithsonianmag.com/history/photographic-chronicle-america-working-poor-180961147/.

Maldonado, Camilo. 2019. "50% of Americans Have Maxed Out Credit Cards, Here's How To Dig Yourself Out Of Credit Card Debt," *Forbes* (March 26). https://www.forbes.com/sites/camilomaldonado/2019/03/26/americans-maxed-out-credit-cards/#d1d686d4fac1.

Malik, Rasheed. 2019. "Working Families Are Spending Big Money on Child Care" (June 20). Washington, DC: Center for American Progress. https://www.americanprogress.org/issues/early-childhood/reports/2019/06/20/471141/working-families-spending-big-money-child-care/.

Malik, Rasheed, Katie Hamm, Leila Schochet, Cristina Novoa, Simon Workman, and Steven Jessen-Howard. 2018. "America's Child Care Deserts in 2018" (December 6). Washington, DC: Center for American Progress. https://www.americanprogress.org/issues/early-childhood/reports/2018/12/06/461643/americas-child-care-deserts-2018/.

Malik, Rasheed, Katie Hamm, Won F. Lee, Elizabeth E. Davis, and Aaron Sojourner. 2020. "The Coronavirus Will Make Child Care Deserts Worse and Exacerbate Inequality" (June 22). Washington, DC: Center for American Progress. https://www.americanprogress.org/issues/early-childhood/reports/2020/06/22/486433/coronavirus-will-make-child-care-deserts-worse-exacerbate-inequality/.

Mandavilli, Apoorva, and Benjamin Mueller. 2021. "Delta Variant Widens Gulf Between 'Two Americas': Vaccinated and Unvaccinated," *New York Times* (July 15). https://www.nytimes.com/2021/07/14/health/delta-variant-uk-usa.html.

Mann, Thomas E. and Norman J. Ornstein. 2012. *It's Even Worse Than It Looks: How the American Constitutional System Collided with the New Politics of Extremism*. New York: Basic Books.

Marcos, Coral Murphy. 2021. "Charitable Giving Rose in 2020, with Civil Rights and Environmental Groups Benefiting," *New York Times* (June 15). https://www.nytimes.com/2021/06/15/business/philanthropy-2020-pandemic.html.

Martin, Anne B., Micah Hartman, David Lassman, Aaron Catlin, and The National Health Expenditure Accounts Team. 2021. "National Health Care Spending in 2019: Steady Growth for the Fourth Consecutive Year," *Health Affairs* 40, 1 (January): 14–24.

Masci, David, and Gregory A. Smith. 2018. "7 facts about American Catholics" (October 10). Washington, DC: Pew Research Center. https://www.pewresearch.org/fact-tank/2018/10/10/7-facts-about-american-catholics/.

Mason, Lilliana. 2018. *Uncivil Agreement: How Politics Became Our Identity*. Chicago: University of Chicago Press.

Mathews, Anna Wilde, and Tom McGinty. 2020. "Covid Spurs Families to Shun Nursing Homes, a Shift That Appears Long Lasting," *Wall Street Journal* (December 21). Accessed from ProQuest Central database.

Matthews, Dylan. 2013. "Only a Third of Charitable Contributions Go to the Poor," *Washington Post* (May 30). https://www.washingtonpost.com/news/wonk/wp/2013/05/30/only-a-third-of-charitable-contributions-go-the-poor/.

Matthews, Dylan. 2015. "Paul Ryan's Poverty Plan," *Vox* (October 8). https://www.vox.com/2014/7/24/18080430/paul-ryan-poverty.

Mattingly, Justin. 2018. "How Do Hungry Kids Get Food After School's Out? Summer Programs Fill the Gap in Richmond Area," *Richmond Times-Dispatch* (July 10). https://www.richmond.com/news/local/how-do-hungry-kids-get-food-after-school-s-out-summer-programs-fill-gap-in/article_77ffa5e8-ce8f-584e-ab85-447972523e2a.html.

McCarty, Maggie, and Libby Perl. 2021. "Federal Eviction Moratoriums in Response to the COVID-19 Pandemic," Congressional Research Service Insight IN11516 (March 30). Accessed from the ProQuest Congressional database.

McCarty, Maggie, Libby Perl, and Katie Jones. 2019. "Overview of Federal Housing Assistance Programs and Policy," Congressional Research Service Report RL34591 (March 27). Accessed from the ProQuest Congressional database.

McCarty, Nolan, Keith T. Poole, and Howard Rosenthal. 2016. *Polarized America: The Dance of Ideology and Unequal Riches*, 2nd ed. Cambridge, MA: MIT Press.

McGarry, Kathleen. 2013. "The Safety Net for the Elderly." In *Legacies of the War on Poverty*, edited by Martha J. Bailey and Sheldon Danziger, pp. 179–205. New York: Russell Sage Foundation.

McLanahan, Sara. 2009. "Fragile Families and the Reproduction of Poverty," *The ANNALS of the American Academy of Political and Social Science* 621, 1 (January): 111–31.

Medicaid and CHIP Payment and Access Commission (MACPAC). 2020. "Report to Congress on Medicaid and CHIP" (March). https://www.macpac.gov/publication/march-2020-rep ort-to-congress-on-medicaid-and-chip/.

Mehrotra, Ateev, Michael Chernew, David Linetsky, Hilary Hatch, David Cutler, and Eric C. Schneider. 2021. "The Impact of COVID-19 on Outpatient Visits in 2020: Visits Remained Stable, Despite a Late Surge in Cases" (February 22). New York: Commonwealth Fund. https://www.commonwealthfund.org/publications/2021/feb/impact-covid-19-outpati ent-visits-2020-visits-stable-despite-late-surge.

Mendelberg, Tali. 2001. *The Race Card: Campaign Strategy, Implicit Messages, and the Norm of Equality*. Princeton, NJ: Princeton University Press.

Mendez, Bryce H. P. 2020. "Defense Primer: Military Health System," Congressional Research Service In Focus (December 14). Accessed from the ProQuest Congressional database.

Mettler, Suzanne. 1998. *Dividing Citizens: Gender and Federalism in New Deal Public Policy*. Ithaca, NY: Cornell University Press.

Meyer, Bruce D., and Derek Wu. 2018. "The Poverty Reduction of Social Security and Means-Tested Transfers," *ILR Review* 71, 5 (October): 1106–53.

Meyer, Harris. 2016. "Why Patients Still Need EMTALA," *Modern Healthcare* (March 26). https://www.modernhealthcare.com/article/20160326/MAGAZINE/303289881/why-patients-still-need-emtala.

Meyer, Harris. 2019. "Some Hospitals Seize Patients' Tax Refunds," *Modern Healthcare* (June 15). https://www.modernhealthcare.com/finance/some-hospitals-seize-patients-tax-refunds.

Meyer, Harris. 2020. "Nursing Homes' Flawed Business Model Worsens COVID Crisis" (December 7). Washington, DC: AARP. https://www.aarp.org/caregiving/health/info-2020/covid-19-nursing-homes-failing-business-model.html.

Meyer, Madonna Harrington, and Jessica Hausauer. 2015. "Long-Term Care for the Elderly." In *The Oxford Handbook of U.S. Social Policy*, edited by Daniel Béland, Christopher Howard, and Kimberly J. Morgan, pp. 315–33. New York: Oxford University Press.

Meyer, Madonna Harrington, and J. Dalton Stevens. 2020. "Changes in Medicaid for People with Disabilities." In *Medicaid: Politics, Policy, and Key Issues*, edited by Daniel Lanford, pp. 261–300. New York: Nova Science Publishers.

Meyersohn, Nathaniel. 2019. "Walmart CEO: America's minimum wage is 'too low'," CNN (June 5). https://www.cnn.com/2019/06/05/business/walmart-shareholders-meeting-minimum-wage/index.html.

Meyerson, Collier. 2018. "For Women of Color, the Child-Welfare System Functions Like the Criminal-Justice System," *The Nation* (May 24). https://www.thenation.com/article/arch ive/for-women-of-color-the-child-welfare-system-functions-like-the-criminal-justice-system/.

Michener, Jamila. 2018. *Fragmented Democracy: Medicaid, Federalism, and Unequal Politics*. New York: Cambridge University Press.

Michener, Jamila, Mallory SoRelle, and Chloe Thurston. 2020. "From the Margins to the Center: A Bottom-Up Approach to Welfare State Scholarship," *Perspectives on Politics*. https://doi.org/10.1017/S153759272000359X.

Miler, Kristina C. 2018. *Poor Representation: Congress and the Politics of Poverty in the United States*. New York: Cambridge University Press.

Miller, Claire Cain. 2019. "How Unpredictable Work Hours Turn Families Upside Down," *New York Times* (October 16). https://www.nytimes.com/2019/10/16/upshot/unpredicta ble-job-hours.html.

Miller, Mark. 2019. "The Decade in Retirement: Wealthy Americans Moved Further Ahead," *New York Times* (December 14). https://www.nytimes.com/2019/12/14/business/retirem ent-social-security-recession.html.

Milligan, Christine. 2009. *There's No Place Like Home: Place and Care in an Ageing Society.* Surrey, UK: Ashgate.

Mink, Gwendolyn. 1995. *The Wages of Motherhood: Inequality in the Welfare State, 1917–1942.* Ithaca, NY: Cornell University Press.

Minton, Sarah, and Linda Giannarelli. 2019. "Five Things You May Not Know about the US Social Safety Net" (February 4). Washington, DC: Urban Institute. https://www.urban.org/resea rch/publication/five-things-you-may-not-know-about-us-social-safety-net.

Mitchell, Alison, Evelyne P. Baumrucker, Kirsten J. Colello, Angela Napili, Cliff Binder, and Julia A. Keyser. 2021. "Medicaid: An Overview," Congressional Research Service Report R43357 (February 22). Accessed via ProQuest Congressional database.

Mlinac, Michelle E., and Michelle C. Feng. 2016. "Assessment of Activities of Daily Living, Self-Care, and Independence," *Archives of Clinical Neuropsychology* 31, 6 (September): 506–16.

Mongeau, Lillian. 2021. "After Mass Closures and Too Little Support, Post-Pandemic Child Care Options Will Be Scarce," *USA Today* (February 16). https://www.usatoday.com/ story/news/education/2021/02/16/day-care-preschool-permanently-closed-covid/673 4968002/.

Moore, Kyle E., Daniel K. Thompson, and John J. Hisnanick. 2018. "Participation Rates and Monthly Payments From Selected Social Insurance Programs: 2014," Current Population Reports P70BR-157 (August). Washington, DC: U.S. Census Bureau. https://www.census. gov/library/publications/2018/demo/p70br-157.html.

Morduch, Jonathan, and Rachel Schneider. 2017. *The Financial Diaries: How American Families Cope in a World of Uncertainty.* Princeton, NJ: Princeton University Press.

Morgan, Kimberly J. 2006. *Working Mothers and the Welfare State: Religion and the Politics of Work-Family Policies in Western Europe and the United States.* Stanford, CA: Stanford University Press.

Morris, Andrew J. F. 2009. *The Limits of Voluntarism: Charity and Welfare from the New Deal through the Great Society.* New York: Cambridge University Press.

Morris, Caitlin. 2019. "Officials Seek to Attract Grocery Stores to 'Food Deserts'," AP News (April 1). https://apnews.com/a2b0356365db4e5dbdb9c4a077be315e.

Mudrazija, Stipica, and Jacqueline L. Angel. 2014. "Diversity and the Economic Security of Older Americans." In *The New Politics of Old-Age Policy*, 3rd ed., edited by Robert B. Hudson, pp. 138–54. Baltimore, MD: Johns Hopkins University Press.

Murphy, Griffin, Jay Patel, Elaine Weiss, and Leslie I. Boden. 2020. "Workers' Compensation: Benefits, Cost, and Coverage (2018 data)." Washington, DC: National Academy of Social Insurance. https://www.nasi.org/research/2020/report-workers'-compe nsation-benefits-costs-coverage---2018.

Murray, Alan. 2019. "America's CEOs Seek a New Purpose for the Corporation," *Fortune* (August 19). https://fortune.com/longform/business-roundtable-ceos-corporations-purpose/.

Musumeci, MaryBeth, Molly O'Malley Watts, and Priya Chidambaram. 2020. "Key State Policy Choices About Medicaid Home and Community-Based Services" (February 4). Washington, DC: Kaiser Family Foundation. https://www.kff.org/medicaid/issue-brief/ key-state-policy-choices-about-medicaid-home-and-community-based-services/.

Mykyta, Laryssa, and Suzanne Macartney. 2012. "Sharing a Household: Household Composition and Economic Well-Being: 2007–2010," Current Population Report P60-242 (June). Washington, DC: U.S. Census Bureau. https://www.census.gov/library/publications/ 2012/demo/p60-242.html.

National Academy of Social Insurance. 2019. "Social Security Benefits, Finances, and Policy Options: A Primer" (August). https://www.nasi.org/socialsecurityprimer.

National Alliance to End Homelessness. 2020. *State of Homelessness: 2020 Edition*. https://endh omelessness.org/homelessness-in-america/homelessness-statistics/state-of-homelessness-2020/.

National Association of Convenience Stores. 2020. "Supplemental Nutrition Assistance Program (SNAP)" (March 17). https://www.convenience.org/Advocacy/Issues/SNAP.

National Association of Free & Charitable Clinics. 2020. "2020 NAFC Annual Data Collection Report" (May). https://www.nafcclinics.org/sites/default/files/NAFC%20Data%20Col lection%20Report%202020%20Final.pdf.

National Immigration Forum. 2018. "Fact Sheet: Immigrants and Public Benefits" (August 21). https://immigrationforum.org/article/fact-sheet-immigrants-and-public-benefits/.

National Housing Law Project. 2021a. "Foreclosure Protection and Mortgage Payment Relief for Homeowners" (March). https://www.nhlp.org/wp-content/uploads/2020.04.10-NHLP-Homeowner-Relief-Info-Sheet-Update2.pdf.

National Housing Law Project. 2021b. "Federal Moratorium on Evictions for Nonpayment of Rent" (April). https://nlihc.org/sites/default/files/Overview-of-National-Eviction-Mor atorium.pdf.

National Partnership for Women & Families. 2019. "Paid Leave Works: Evidence from State Programs" (September). https://www.nationalpartnership.org/our-work/resources/econo mic-justice/paid-leave/paid-leave-works-in-california-new-jersey-and-rhode-island.pdf.

National Research Council. 1995. *Measuring Poverty: A New Approach*. Washington, DC: National Academies Press.

Newman, Katherine S. 1999. *No Shame in My Game: The Working Poor in the Inner City*. New York: Vintage Books and Russell Sage Foundation.

Newman, Katherine S., and Victor Tan Chen. 2007. *The Missing Class: Portraits of the Near Poor in America*. Boston, MA: Beacon Press.

Newman, Katherine S., and Elisabeth S. Jacobs. 2010. *Who Cares? Public Ambivalence and Government Activism from the New Deal to the Second Gilded Age*. Princeton, NJ: Princeton University Press.

Noddings, Nel. 2002. *Starting at Home: Caring and Social Policy*. Berkeley: University of California Press.

Norris, Pippa, and Ronald Inglehart. 2011. *Sacred and Secular: Religion and Politics Worldwide*, 2nd ed. New York: Cambridge University Press.

North, Anna. 2020. "America's Child Care Problem Is an Economic Problem," *Vox* (July 16). https://www.vox.com/2020/7/16/21324192/covid-schools-reopening-daycare-child-care-coronavirus.

O'Brien, Jack. 2018. "Hospital Bad Debt Rising as Patients Shoulder Bigger Share of Medical Bills," *Health Leaders* (June 26). https://www.healthleadersmedia.com/finance/hospital-bad-debt-rising-patients-shoulder-bigger-share-medical-bills.

Ochieng, Nancy, Priya Chidambaram, Rachel Garfield, and Tricia Neuman. 2021. "Factors Associated With COVID-19 Cases and Deaths in Long-Term Care Facilities: Findings from a Literature Review" (January 14). Washington, DC: Kaiser Family Foundation. https://www.kff.org/coronavirus-covid-19/issue-brief/factors-associated-with-covid-19-cases-and-deaths-in-long-term-care-facilities-findings-from-a-literature-review/.

O'Collins, Gerald. 2008. *Catholicism: A Very Short Introduction*. New York: Oxford University Press.

O'Collins, Gerald S. J., and Mario Farrugia. 2015. *Catholicism: The Story of Catholic Christianity* 2nd ed. New York: Oxford University Press.

O'Connell, Brian. 2019. "What's the Average U.S. Credit Card Debt by Income and Age in 2019?" *The Street* (February 16). https://www.thestreet.com/personal-finance/average-credit-card-debt-14863601.

Okoro, Catherine A., NaTasha D. Hollis, Alissa C. Cyrus, and Shannon Griffin-Blake. 2018. "Prevalence of Disabilities and Health Care Access by Disability Status and Type Among

Adults—United States, 2016," *Morbidity and Mortality Weekly Report* 67, 32 (August 17): 882–87.

O'Leary, Christopher J., and Stephen A. Wandner. 2020. "An Illustrated Case for Unemployment Insurance Reform" (January 22). Kalamazoo, MI: W.E. Upjohn Institute for Employment Research. https://research.upjohn.org/up_workingpapers/317/.

Olen, Helaine. 2017. "Even the Insured Often Can't Afford Their Medical Bills," *The Atlantic* (June 18). https://www.theatlantic.com/business/archive/2017/06/medical-bills/530679/.

Ollstein, Alice Miranda. 2019. "Some Labor Unions Split with Biden on 'Medicare for All,'" *Politico* (August 11). https://www.politico.com/story/2019/08/11/joe-biden-medicare-for-all-unions-1456179.

Olsen, Greg M. 2019. "Protective Legislation: The 'Third Pillar' of the Welfare State," *Social Policy & Administration* 53, 3 (May): 478–92.

Olson, Laura Katz. 2010. *The Politics of Medicaid*. New York: Columbia University Press.

Oppel Jr., Richard A., Robert Gebeloff, K. K. Rebecca Lai, Will Wright, and Mitch Smith. 2020. "The Fullest Look Yet at the Racial Inequality of Coronavirus," *New York Times* (July 5). https://www.nytimes.com/interactive/2020/07/05/us/coronavirus-latinos-african-americans-cdc-data.html.

Orloff, Ann Shola. 1991. "Gender in Early U.S. Social Policy," *Journal of Policy History* 3, 3 (July): 249–81.

Pac, Jessica, Jane Waldfogel, and Christopher Wimer. 2017. "Poverty Among Foster Children: Estimates Using the Supplemental Poverty Measure," *Social Service Review* 91, 1 (March): 8–40.

Page, Susan. 2014. "50 Years Later, War on Poverty Has New Battle Lines," *USA Today* (January 7). https://www.usatoday.com/story/news/politics/2014/01/06/war-on-poverty-50-years-later/4344985/.

Page, Benjamin I., and Lawrence R. Jacobs. 2009. *Class War? What Americans Really Think About Economic Inequality*. Chicago: University of Chicago Press.

Panangala, Sidath Viranga, and Jared S. Sussman. 2019. "Introduction to Veterans Health Care," *Congressional Research Service In Focus* (October 24). Accessed from the ProQuest Congressional database.

Park, Sung S., Emily E. Wiemers, and Judith A. Seltzer. 2019. "The Family Safety Net of Black and White Multigenerational Families," *Population and Development Review* 45, 3 (June): 351–78.

Parker, Kim, Rachel Minkin, and Jesse Bennett. 2020. "Economic Fallout From COVID-19 Continues To Hit Lower-Income Americans the Hardest" (September 24). Washington, DC: Pew Research Center. https://www.pewresearch.org/social-trends/2020/09/24/economic-fallout-from-covid-19-continues-to-hit-lower-income-americans-the-hardest/.

Parlow, Matthew J. 2013. "Whither Workforce Housing?" *Fordham Urban Law Journal* 60: 1645–65.

Patterson, James T. 1994. *America's Struggle Against Poverty, 1900–1994*. Cambridge, MA: Harvard University Press.

Peltz, Alon, and Arvin Garg. 2019. "Food Insecurity and Health Care Use," *Pediatrics* 144, 4 (October). https://pediatrics-aappublications-org.proxy.wm.edu/content/144/4.

Perez, Jessica Lauren. 2014. "The Cost of Seeking Shelter: How Inaccessibility Leads to Women's Underutilization of Emergency Shelter," *Journal of Poverty* 18, 3: 254–74.

Perl, Libby. 2018. "VA Housing: Guaranteed Loans, Direct Loans, and Specially Adapted Housing Grants," *Congressional Research Service Report* R42504 (October 15). Accessed from ProQuest Congressional database.

Peters, Jeremy W. 2014. "2 Parties Place Political Focus on Inequality," *New York Times* (January 8). https://www.nytimes.com/2014/01/09/us/politics/republicans-move-to-reclaim-poverty-fighting-mantle.html?auth=login-email&login=email&ref=todayspaper.

Petersen, Michael Bang. 2012. "Social Welfare as Small-Scale Help: Evolutionary Psychology and the Deservingness Heuristic," *American Journal of Political Science* 56, 1 (January): 1–16.

Peterson, Hayley. 2019. "More than 700,000 People Will Soon Lose Food-Stamps Benefits under a New Trump Administration Rule—and that's Terrible News for Walmart, Target, Kroger, and Dollar Stores," *Business Insider* (December 5). https://www.businessinsider.com/walm art-target-impact-from-trump-food-stamp-changes-2019-12.

Petrocik, John R. 1996. "Issue Ownership in Presidential Elections, with a 1980 Case Study," *American Journal of Political Science* 40, 3 (August): 825–50.

Pew Research Center. 2016. "Budget Deficit Slips as Public Priority" (January 22). https://www. people-press.org/2016/01/22/budget-deficit-slips-as-public-priority/.

Pew Research Center. 2019a. "Public's 2019 Priorities: Economy, Health Care, Education and Security All Near Top of List" (January 24.) https://www.people-press.org/2019/01/24/ publics-2019-priorities-economy-health-care-education-and-security-all-near-top-of-list/.

Pew Research Center. 2019b. "In U.S., Decline of Christianity Continues at Rapid Pace" (October 17). https://www.pewforum.org/2019/10/17/in-u-s-decline-of-christianity-continues-at-rapid-pace/.

Pew Research Center. 2020. "Most Americans Point to Circumstances, Not Work Ethic, for Why People Are Rich or Poor" (March 2). https://www.people-press.org/wp-content/uploads/ sites/4/2020/03/3-2-20-Wealth-in-America-FOR-RELEASE_FINAL-1.pdf.

Pew Research Center. 2021. "Americans See Broad Responsibilities for Government; Little Change Since 2019" (May 17). https://www.pewresearch.org/politics/2021/05/17/ americans-see-broad-responsibilities-for-government-little-change-since-2019/.

Pflum, Mary. 2021. "Nurse Burnout Remains a Serious Problem, Putting Patients in Danger, Experts Say," *NBC News* (May 6). https://www.nbcnews.com/news/us-news/nurse-burn out-remains-serious-problem-putting-patients-danger-experts-say-n1266513.

Phillips, Bruce D., and Holly Wade. 2008. "Small Business Problems & Priorities." Washington, DC: NFIB Research Foundation. https://www.nfib.com/Portals/0/ProblemsAndPriorities08.pdf.

Pickert, Kate. 2008. "A Brief History of the Salvation Army," *Time* (December 2), http://content. time.com/time/nation/article/0,8599,1863162,00.html.

Piston, Spencer. 2018. *Class Attitudes in America: Sympathy for the Poor, Resentment for the Rich, and Political Implications.* New York: Cambridge University Press.

Pomper, Gerald M., and Susan S. Lederman. 1980. *Elections in America: control and influence in democratic politics* 2nd ed. New York: Longman.

Poppendieck, Janet. 1998. *Sweet Charity? Emergency Food and the End of Entitlement.* New York: Viking.

Poppendieck, Janet. 2010. *Free for All: Fixing School Food in America.* Berkeley: University of California Press.

Porter, Eduardo. 2021. "How the American Unemployment System Failed," *New York Times* (January 21). https://www.nytimes.com/2021/01/21/business/economy/unemploym ent-insurance.html.

Prokop, Andrew. 2021. "The State of the Shrinking Build Back Better Act," *Vox* (December 13). https://www.vox.com/2021/12/13/22799436/build-back-better-senate-manchin-parl iamentarian.

Pugh, Tony. 2017. "Free and Charitable Clinics Increase amid Possible Cuts to Healthcare for the Poor," *Miami Herald* (June 14). https://www.miamiherald.com/news/health-care/artic le156072144.html.

Putnam, Robert D. 1993. *Making Democracy Work: Civic Traditions in Modern Italy.* Princeton, NJ: Princeton University Press.

Quadagno, Jill. 1994. *The Color of Welfare: How Racism Undermined the War on Poverty.* New York: Oxford University Press.

Quadagno, Jill. 2005. *One Nation Uninsured: Why the U.S. Has No National Health Insurance.* New York: Oxford University Press.

Quadagno, Jill. 2020. "Restructuring Medicaid's Long Term Care Benefit: Shifting Services from Institutions to Communities." In *Medicaid: Politics, Policy, and Key Issues,* edited by Daniel Lanford, pp. 337–63. New York: Nova Science Publishers.

Rahaman, Nael Abd El. 2018. "Poverty and the Poor in Islam." In *Poverty and the Poor in the World's Religious Traditions: Religious Responses to the Problem of Poverty*, edited by William H. Brackney and Rupen Das, pp. 228–63. Santa Barbara, CA: Praeger.

Rainey, Rebecca. 2019. "McDonald's Halts Lobbying against Minimum Wage Hikes," *Politico* (March 26). https://www.politico.com/story/2019/03/26/mcdonalds-lobbying-mini mum-wage-1238284.

Rampell, Catherine. 2014. "Big Potato Demands Taters for Tots," *Washington Post* (May 9): A19.

Ranji, Usha, Brittni Frederiksen, Alina Salganicoff, and Michelle Long. 2021. "Women, Work, and Family During COVID-19: Findings from the KFF Women's Health Survey" (March 22). Washington, DC: Kaiser Family Foundation. https://www.kff.org/womens-health-policy/ issue-brief/women-work-and-family-during-covid-19-findings-from-the-kff-womens-hea lth-survey/.

Rank, Mark Robert, Lawrence M. Eppard, and Heather E. Bullock. 2021. *Poorly Understood: What America Gets Wrong About Poverty*. New York: Oxford University Press.

Rank, Mark R., and Thomas A. Hirschl. 2015. "The Likelihood of Experiencing Relative Poverty over the Life Course," *PLOS ONE* 10, 7 (July). doi:10.1371/journal.pone.0133513.

Raphelson, Samantha. 2018. "Shelters Reach Capacity in Cold Weather as Homeless Population Rises," *National Public Radio* (January 9). https://www.npr.org/2018/01/09/576825276/ shelters-reach-capacity-in-cold-weather-as-homeless-population-rises.

Rappeport, Alan, and Maggie Haberman. 2020. "Trump Opens Door to Cuts to Medicare and Other Entitlement Programs," *New York Times* (February 10). https://www.nytimes.com/ 2020/01/22/us/politics/medicare-trump.html.

Rau, Jordan. 2018. "Care Suffers as More Nursing Homes Feed Money Into Corporate Webs," *New York Times* (January 2). https://www.nytimes.com/2018/01/02/business/nursing-homes-care-corporate.html.

Rau, Jordan. 2019. "Patients Eligible for Charity Care Instead Get Big Bills," *Kaiser Health News* (October 14). https://khn.org/news/patients-eligible-for-charity-care-instead-get-big-bills/.

Reagan, Courtney. 2017. "Retail Stands to Lose $70 Billion over 10 Years if Food Stamp Benefits Are Slashed, and Here's Who Gets Hit the Most," *CNBC* (July 7). https://www.cnbc.com/ 2017/06/29/retailers-that-take-the-hardest-hit-if-food-stamp-benefits-are-cut.html.

Reaves, Erica L., and MaryBeth Musumeci. 2015. "Medicaid and Long-Term Services and Supports: A Primer" (December). Washington, DC: Kaiser Family Foundation. https:// files.kff.org/attachment/report-medicaid-and-long-term-services-and-supports-a-primer.

Redden, Molly. 2018. "Struggling US Families Turn to Crowdfunding to Cover Childcare Costs," *The Guardian* (January 30). https://www.theguardian.com/us-news/2018/jan/30/parent ing-mothers-crowdfunding-childbirth.

Reddy, Vasu. 2018. "Raising Expectations: A State-by-State Analysis of Laws That Help Working Family Caregivers" (September). Washington, DC: National Partnership for Women & Families. Accessed via http://www.nationalpartnership.org/our-work/resources/econo mic-justice/raising-expectations-2018.pdf.

Reed, Eric. 2020. "How Much Do Uber and Lyft Drivers Make in 2020?" *The Street* (January 23). https://www.thestreet.com/personal-finance/education/how-much-do-uber-lyft-drivers-make-14804869.

Reese, Ellen, Stephanie D'Auria, and Sandra Loughrin. 2015. "Gender." In *The Oxford Handbook of U.S. Social Policy*, edited by Daniel Béland, Christopher Howard, and Kimberly J. Morgan, pp. 239–57. New York: Oxford University Press.

Reich, Rob. 2018. *Just Giving: Why Philanthropy Is Failing Democracy and How It Can Do Better*. Princeton, NJ: Princeton University Press.

Reiley, Laura. 2020. "What's for School Lunch: More Pizza, Fewer Veggies," *Washington Post* (January 18): A1.

Reinhard, Susan C., Lynn Friss Feinberg, Ari Houser, Rita Choula, and Molly Evans. 2019a. "Valuing the Invaluable: 2019 Update" (November). Washington, DC: AARP Public Policy Institute. https://www.aarp.org/ppi/info-2015/valuing-the-invaluable-2015-update.html.

Reinhard, Susan C., Heather M. Young, Carol Levine, Kathleen Kelly, Rita B. Choula, and Jean Accius. 2019b. "Home Alone Revisited: Family Caregivers Providing Complex Care" (April). Washington, DC: AARP Public Policy Institute. https://www.aarp.org/ppi/info-2018/home-alone-family-caregivers-providing-complex-chronic-care.html.

Reinhardt, Uwe E. 2009. "The Mounting Price of Health Care's Status Quo," *New York Times* (February 27). https://economix.blogs.nytimes.com/2009/02/27/health-cares-status-quo/.

Reinhardt, Uwe E. 2019. *Priced Out: The Economic and Ethical Costs of American Health Care.* Princeton, NJ: Princeton University Press.

Renwick, Matthew J., and Elias Mossialos. 2017. "Crowdfunding our health: Economic risks and benefits," *Social Science & Medicine* 191 (October): 48–56.

Rice, Douglas, Stephanie Schmit, and Hannah Matthews. 2019. "Child Care and Housing: Big Expenses with Too Little Help Available" (April 26). Washington, DC: Center on Budget and Policy Priorities. https://www.cbpp.org/research/housing/child-care-and-housing-big-expenses-with-too-little-help-available.

Rickert, James. 2012. "Do Medicare and Medicaid Payment Rates Really Threaten Physicians with Bankruptcy?" *Health Affairs* (October 2). https://www.healthaffairs.org/do/10.1377/hblog20121002.023684/full/.

Rockeman, Olivia, and Catarina Saraiva. 2021. "What to Know About Biden's Plans for U.S. Child Care," *Washington Post* (July 2). https://www.washingtonpost.com/business/what-to-know-about-bidens-plans-for-us-child-care/2021/07/02/712e204e-daf2-11eb-8c87-ad6f27918c78_story.html.

Rod, Marc. 2019. "Business Groups Slam House for Passing $15 Minimum Wage Bill," *CNBC* (July 18). https://www.cnbc.com/2019/07/18/business-groups-slam-house-for-passing-15-minimum-wage-bill.html.

Romano, Sebastian D., Anna J. Blackstock, Ethel V. Taylor, Suad El Burai Felix, Stacey Adjai, Christa-Marie Singleton, Jennifer Fuld, Beau B. Bruce, and Tegan K. Boehmer. 2021. "Trends in Racial and Ethnic Disparities in COVID-19 Hospitalizations, by Region— United States, March-December 2020," *Morbidity and Mortality Weekly Report* 70, 15 (April 16): 560–65.

Romig, Kathleen. 2020. "Social Security Lifts More Americans Above Poverty Than Any Other Program" (February 20). Washington, DC: Center on Budget and Policy Priorities. https://www.cbpp.org/research/social-security/social-security-lifts-more-americans-above-poverty-than-any-other-program.

Roof, Tracy. 2011. *American Labor, Congress, and the Welfare State, 1935-2020.* Baltimore, MD: Johns Hopkins University Press.

Roosevelt, Franklin D. 1935. *Statement on Signing the Social Security Act.* Online by Gerhard Peters and John T. Woolley, *The American Presidency Project.* Santa Barbara, CA: University of California, Santa Barbara. https://www.presidency.ucsb.edu/node/209017.

Root, Brian, and Lena Simet. 2021. "United States: Pandemic Impact on People in Poverty" (March 2). New York: Human Rights Watch. https://www.hrw.org/news/2021/03/02/united-states-pandemic-impact-people-poverty#.

Rosen, Eva. 2020. *The Voucher Promise: Section 8 and the Fate of an American Neighborhood.* Princeton, NJ: Princeton University Press.

Rosenbaum, Sara, and Timothy M. Westmoreland. 2012. "The Supreme Court's Surprising Decision on the Medicaid Expansion: How Will the Federal Government and the States Proceed?" *Health Affairs* 31, 8 (August): 1663–72.

Rosenfeld, Jake, and Jennifer Laird. 2016. "Unions and Poverty." In David Brady and Linda M. Burton (eds.), *The Oxford Handbook of the Social Science of Poverty*, pp. 800–19. New York: Oxford University Press.

Rosenthal, Elizabeth. 2017. *An American Sickness: How Healthcare Became Big Business and How You Can Take It Back.* New York: Penguin Random House.

Rossin-Slater, Maya, Christopher J. Ruhm, and Jane Waldfogel. 2013. "The Effects of California's Paid Family Leave Program on Mothers' Leave-Taking and Subsequent Labor Market Outcomes," *Journal of Policy Analysis and Management* 32, 2 (Spring): 224–45.

Rothstein, Richard. 2017. *The Color of Law: A Forgotten History of How Our Government Segregated America*. New York: Liveright.

Rudowitz, Robin, Kendal Orgera, and Elizabeth Hinton. 2019. "Medicaid Financing: The Basics" (March). Washington, DC: Kaiser Family Foundation. http://files.kff.org/attachment/Issue-Brief-Medicaid-Financing-The-Basics.

Rudowitz, Robin, Rachel Garfield, Elizabeth Hinton, and Anthony Damico. 2020. "Understanding the Intersection of Medicaid, Work, and COVID-19" (June 12). Washington, DC: Kaiser Family Foundation. https://www.kff.org/report-section/understanding-the-intersection-of-medicaid-work-and-covid-19-issue-brief/.

Sachs, Jeffrey. 2021. "Biden Is Right to Spend Big for Covid-19 Relief. But Who's Going to Pay for It?" *CNN* (February 16). https://www.cnn.com/2021/02/16/opinions/biden-covid-relief-who-will-pay-sachs/index.html.

Salamon, Lester M. (ed.). 2012. *The State of Nonprofit America* 2nd ed. Washington, DC: Brookings Institution Press.

Sanger-Katz, Margot. 2019. "In the U.S., an Angioplasty Costs $32,000. Elsewhere? Maybe $6,400," *New York Times* (December 27). https://www.nytimes.com/2019/12/27/upshot/expensive-health-care-world-comparison.html.

Sapiro, Virginia. 1986. "The Gender Basis of American Social Policy," *Political Science Quarterly* 101, 2: 221–38.

Saslow, Eli. 2013. "Food Stamps Put Rhode Island Town on Monthly Boom-and-Bust Cycle," *Washington Post* (March 16). https://www.washingtonpost.com/national/food-stamps-put-rhode-island-town-on-monthly-boom-and-bust-cycle/2013/03/16/08ace07c-8ce1-11e2-b63f-f53fb9f2fcb4_story.html.

Saslow, Eli. 2019. "'Urgent Needs from Head to Toe': This Clinic Had Two Days to Fix a Lifetime of Needs," *Washington Post* (June 22). https://www.washingtonpost.com/national/the-clinic-of-last-resort/2019/06/22/2833c8a0-92cc-11e9-aadb-74e6b2b46f6a_story.html.

Schenck-Fontaine, Anika, Anna Gassman-Pines, and Zoelene Hill. 2017. "Use of Informal Safety Nets during the Supplemental Nutrition Assistance Benefit Cycle: How Poor Families Cope with Within-Month Economic Instability," *Social Service Review* 91, 3 (September): 456–87.

Schlozman, Kay L. 2010. "Who Sings in the Heavenly Chorus? The Shape of the Organized Interest System." In L. Sandy Maisel and Jeffrey M. Berry (eds.), *The Oxford Handbook of American Political Parties and Interest Groups*, pp. 560–87. New York: Oxford University Press.

Schubel, Jessica, and Matt Broaddus. 2018. "Uncompensated Care Costs Fell in Nearly Every State as ACA's Major Coverage Provisions Took Effect" (May 23). Washington, DC: Center on Budget and Policy Priorities. https://www.cbpp.org/sites/default/files/atoms/files/5-23-18health.pdf.

Schultz, Michael A. 2019. "The Wage Mobility of Low-Wage Workers in a Changing Economy, 1968 to 2014," *RSF: The Russell Sage Foundation Journal of the Social Sciences* 5, 4 (September): 159–89.

Schwartz, Alex F. 2014. *Housing Policy in the United States* 3rd ed. New York: Routledge.

Schwartz, Nelson D. 2018. "Disability Applications Plunge as the Economy Strengthens," *New York Times* (June 19). https://www.nytimes.com/2018/06/19/business/economy/social-security-applications.html.

Schweid, Richard. 2021. *The Caring Class: Home Health Aides in Crisis*. Ithaca, NY: Cornell University Press.

Scott, Dylan. 2018. "White Evangelicals Turned Out for the GOP in Big Numbers Again," *Vox* (November 7). https://www.vox.com/policy-and-politics/2018/10/29/18015400/2018-midterm-elections-results-white-evangelical-christians-trump.

Seefeldt, Kristin S., and Heather Sandstrom. 2015. "When There Is No Welfare: The Income Packaging Strategies of Mothers Without Earnings or Cash Assistance Following an Economic Downturn," *RSF: The Russell Sage Foundation Journal of the Social Sciences* 1, 1 (November): 139–58.

Semega, Jessica, Melissa Kollar, John Creamer, and Abinash Mohanty. 2019. *Income and Poverty in the United States: 2018*, U.S. Census Bureau, Current Population Reports, P60-266. Washington, DC: Government Printing Office.

Semuels, Alana, and Malcolm Burnley. 2019. "Living on Tips," *Time* (September 2/9): 40–49.

Settembre, Jeanette. 2018. "Amazon Raises Minimum Wage to $15 – Plus 8 Other Companies that have Made Similar Moves," *MarketWatch.com* (October 2). https://www.marketwatch.com/story/amazon-raises-minimum-wage-to-15----plus-8-other-companies-that-have-made-similar-moves-2018-10-02.

Sevenhuijsen, Selma. 2003. "The Place of Care: The Relevance of the Feminist Ethic of Care for Social Policy," *Feminist Theory* 4, 2 (August): 179–97.

Shaban, Hamza, and Heather Long. 2020. "The Stock Market Is Ending 2020 at Record Highs, Even as the Virus Surges and Millions Go Hungry," *Washington Post* (December 31). https://www.washingtonpost.com/business/2020/12/31/stock-market-record-2020/.

Shaw, Greg M., and Robert Y. Shapiro. 2002. "The Polls—Trends: Poverty and Public Assistance," *Public Opinion Quarterly* 66, 1 (March): 105–28.

Sherman, Jennifer. 2009. *Those Who Work, Those Who Don't: Poverty, Morality, and Family in Rural America*. Minneapolis: University of Minnesota Press.

Shipler, David K. 2004. *The Working Poor: Invisible in America*. New York: Vintage Books.

Shrider, Emily A., Melissa Kollar, Frances Chen, and Jessica Semega. 2021. *Income and Poverty in the United States: 2020*, U.S. Census Bureau, Current Population Reports P60-273. Washington, DC: Government Printing Office.

Sides, John, and Daniel J. Hopkins (eds.). 2015. *Political Polarization in American Politics*. New York: Bloomsbury Academic.

Sifferlin, Alexandra. 2013. "Why Some Schools Are Saying 'No Thanks' to the School-Lunch Program," *Time* (August 29). https://healthland.time.com/2013/08/29/why-some-schools-are-saying-no-thanks-to-the-school-lunch-program/.

Silver-Greenberg, Jessica, and Robert Gebeloff. 2021. "Maggots, Rape, and Yet Five Stars: How U.S. Ratings of Nursing Homes Mislead the Public," *New York Times* (March 13). https://www.nytimes.com/2021/03/13/business/nursing-homes-ratings-medicare-covid.html.

Skocpol, Theda. 1991. "Targeting within Universalism: Politically Viable Policies to Combat Poverty in the United States." In *The Urban Underclass*, edited by Christopher Jencks and Paul E. Peterson, pp. 411–36. Washington, DC: Brookings Institution Press.

Skocpol, Theda. 1992. *Protecting Soldiers and Mothers: The Political Origins of Social Policy in the United States*. Cambridge, MA: Belknap Press of Harvard University Press.

Smietana, Bob. 2020. "Faith Groups Are Vital to the Social Safety Net. But Volunteers They Rely On Are Aging and Their Denominations Are Shrinking," *Washington Post* (November 20). https://www.washingtonpost.com/religion/faith-groups-are-vital-to-the-social-safety-net-but-volunteers-they-rely-on-are-aging-and-their-denominations-are-shrinking/2020/11/20/68a84638-2a9a-11eb-8fa2-06e7cbb145c0_story.html.

Smith, Rogers M. 1993. "Beyond Tocqueville, Myrdal, and Hartz: The Multiple Traditions in America," *American Political Science Review* 87, 3 (September): 549–66.

Smith, Steven R., and Michael Lipsky. 1993. *Nonprofits for Hire: The Welfare State in the Age of Contracting*. Cambridge, MA: Harvard University Press.

Smith, Tom W. 1987. "That Which We Call Welfare by Any Other Name Would Smell Sweeter: An Analysis of the Impact of Question Wording on Response Patterns," *Public Opinion Quarterly* 51, 1 (Spring): 75–83.

Snell, Kelsey. 2021. "Democrats Say Relief Programs Could Become This Generation's New Deal," *National Public Radio* (February 26). https://www.npr.org/2021/02/26/971438274/democrats-say-relief-programs-could-become-this-generations-new-deal.

Sniderman, Paul M., and Edward G. Carmines. 1997. *Reaching Beyond Race*. Cambridge, MA: Harvard University Press.

Snyder, Timothy. 2021. "The American Abyss," *New York Times Magazine* (January 9). https://www.nytimes.com/2021/01/09/magazine/trump-coup.html.

Social Security Administration. 2019a. "Annual Statistical Supplement to the Social Security Bulletin, 2019." https://www.ssa.gov/policy/docs/statcomps/supplement/2019/index.html.

Social Security Administration. 2019b. "SSI Annual Statistical Report, 2018." https://www.ssa.gov/policy/docs/statcomps/ssi_asr/.

Social Security and Medicare Boards of Trustees. 2019. *A Summary of the 2019 Annual Reports.* https://www.ssa.gov/OACT/TRSUM/index.html.

Sohn, Heeju. 2019. "Fraying Families: Demographic Divergence in the Parental Safety Net," *Demography* 56, 4 (August): 1519–40.

SoRelle, Mallory E. 2020. *Democracy Declined: The Failed Politics of Consumer Financial Protection.* Chicago: University of Chicago Press.

Soss, Joe. 2000. *Unwanted Claims: The Politics of Participation in the U.S. Welfare System.* Ann Arbor: University of Michigan Press.

Soss, Joe, Richard C. Fording, and Sanford F. Schram. 2011. *Disciplining the Poor: Neoliberal Paternalism and the Persistent Power of Race.* Chicago: University of Chicago Press.

Soss, Joe, and Sanford Schram. 2007. "A Public Transformed? Welfare Reform as Policy Feedback," *American Political Science Review* 101, 1 (February): 111–27.

Sparks, Grace, Ashley Kirzinger, and Mollyann Brodie. 2021. "KFF COVID-19 Vaccine Monitor: Profile of the Unvaccinated" (June 11). Washington, DC: Kaiser Family Foundation. https://www.kff.org/coronavirus-covid-19/poll-finding/kff-covid-19-vaccine-monitor-profile-of-the-unvaccinated/.

Sparks, Holloway. 2003. "Queens, Teens, and Model Mothers." In *Race and the Politics of Welfare Reform,* edited by Sanford F. Schram, Joe Soss, and Richard C. Fording, pp. 171–95. Ann Arbor: University of Michigan Press.

Staff of the Benjamin Rose Hospital. 1959. "Multidisciplinary Studies of Illness in Aged Persons: II. A New Classification of Functional Status in Activities of Daily Living," *Journal of Chronic Diseases* 9, 1 (January): 55–62.

Staff of the Benjamin Rose Hospital. 1960. "Multidisciplinary Studies of Illness in Aged Persons: III. Prognostic Indices in Fracture of the Hip," *Journal of Chronic Diseases* 11, 3-4 (March-April): 445–55.

Stark, Ellen. 2018. "5 Things You Should Know About Long-Term Care Insurance," *AARP Bulletin* (March 1). https://www.aarp.org/caregiving/financial-legal/info-2018/long-term-care-insurance-fd.html.

Stolberg, Sheryl Gay. 2013. "Pugnacious Builder of the Business Lobby," *New York Times* (June 1). https://www.nytimes.com/2013/06/02/business/how-tom-donohue-transformed-the-us-chamber-of-commerce.html

Stolberg, Sheryl Gay. 2020. "Millions Have Lost Health Insurance in Pandemic-Driven Recession," *New York Times* (July 13). https://www.nytimes.com/2020/07/13/us/politics/coronavirus-health-insurance-trump.html.

Stone, Chad, and William Chen. 2014. *Introduction to Unemployment Insurance* (July 30). Washington, DC: Center on Budget and Policy Priorities. https://www.cbpp.org/research/introduction-to-unemployment-insurance.

Stone, Deborah A. 1984. *The Disabled State.* Philadelphia, PA: Temple University Press.

Stone, Deborah. 2001. "Making the Poor Count," *The American Prospect* (December 19). https://prospect.org/economy/making-poor-count/.

Stone, Deborah. 2008. *The Samaritan's Dilemma: Should Government Help Your Neighbor?* New York: Nation Books.

Stone, Will. 2020. "Under Financial Strain, Community Health Centers Ramp Up Coronavirus Response," *Kaiser Health News* (March 27). https://khn.org/news/under-financial-strain-community-health-centers-ramp-up-coronavirus-response/.

Strolovitch, Dara Z. 2007. *Affirmative Advocacy: Race, Class, and Gender in Interest Group Politics.* Chicago: University of Chicago Press.

Swenson, Kendall, and Kimberly Burgess Simms. 2020. "Early Care and Education Arrangements of Children under Age Five" (July). Washington, DC: U.S. Department of Health and Human Services. Accessed via https://aspe.hhs.gov/pdf-report/changing-cost-child-care.

Tach, Laura, and Kathryn Edin. 2017. "The Social Safety Net After Welfare Reform: Recent Developments and Consequences for Household Dynamics," *Annual Review of Sociology* 43: 541–61.

Tagler, Michael J., and Catherine Cozzarelli. 2013. "Feelings Toward the Poor and Beliefs About the Causes of Poverty: The Role of Affective-Cognitive Consistency in Help-Giving," *The Journal of Psychology* 147, 6: 517–39.

Tax Policy Center. 2020. "Briefing Book." Washington, DC: Tax Policy Center. https://www.taxpolicycenter.org/briefing-book.

Taylor, Keeanga-Yamahtta. 2019. *Race for Profit: How Banks and the Real Estate Industry Undermined Black Homeownership.* Chapel Hill: University of North Carolina Press.

Teles, Steven M. 1996. *Whose Welfare? AFDC and Elite Politics.* Lawrence: University Press of Kansas.

Telford, Taylor, and Rachel Siegel. 2021. "2021 Goes Down as a Year of High Risk and High Reward for Markets," *Washington Post* (December 31). https://www.washingtonpost.com/business/2021/12/31/stocks-markets-2021-omicron-pandemic/.

Temple, Sydney. 2019. "America's 2019 Rental Market in Review: Did Renters Pay More?" Rentable blog (December 30). https://www.rentable.co/category/research/page/6/.

Tesler, Michael. 2016. *Post-Racial or Most Racial? Race and Politics in the Obama Era.* Chicago: University of Chicago Press.

Thach, Nga T., and Joshua M. Wiener. 2018. "An Overview of Long-Term Services and Supports and Medicaid: Final Report" (May). Washington, DC: U.S. Department of Health and Human Services. https://aspe.hhs.gov/pdf-report/overview-long-term-services-and-supports-and-medicaid-final-report.

Thal, Adam. 2017. "Class Isolation and Affluent Americans' Perception of Social Conditions," *Political Behavior* 39, 2 (June): 401–24.

The Salvation Army. 2019. *2019 Annual Report.* https://salvationarmyannualreport.org/pdf.

Thelen, Kathleen. 2019. "The American Precariat: U.S. Capitalism in Comparative Perspective," *Perspectives on Politics* 17, 1 (March): 5–27.

Theodos, Brett, Christina Plerhoples Stacy, and Helen Ho. 2017. "Taking Stock of the Community Development Block Grant" (April). Washington, DC: Urban Institute. https://www.urban.org/research/publication/taking-stock-community-development-block-grant.

Thorn, Betsy, Nicole Klein, Chrystine Tadler, Eric Budge, Elaine Wilcox-Cook, Jason Michaels, Michele Mendelson, Kelly Patlan, and Vinh Tran. 2018. *WIC Participant and Program Characteristics 2016: Final Report.* Washington, DC: U.S. Department of Agriculture. https://www.fns.usda.gov/wic/wic-participant-and-program-characteristics-2016.

Thorpe, Kenneth E., Kathy Ko Chin, Yanira Cruz, Marjorie A. Innocent, and Lillian Singh. 2017. "The United States Can Reduce Socioeconomic Disparities By Focusing On Chronic Diseases," *Health Affairs* (August 17). https://www.healthaffairs.org/do/10.1377/hblog20170817.061561/full/.

Thrush, Glenn. 2018. "With Markets Hot, Landlords Slam the Door on Section 8 Tenants," *New York Times* (October 12). https://www.nytimes.com/2018/10/12/us/politics/section-8-housing-vouchers-landlords.html.

Thurston, Chloe N. 2018. *At the Boundaries of Homeownership: Credit, Discrimination, and the American State.* New York: Cambridge University Press.

Tillotson, Amanda R., and Laura Lein. 2017. "The Policy Nexus: Panhandling, Social Capital and Policy Failure," *Journal of Sociology & Social Welfare* 44, 2 (June): 79–100.

Tirado, Linda. 2014. *Hand to Mouth: Living in Bootstrap America.* New York: Berkley.

Totenberg, Nina, and Chris Arnold. 2021. "The Supreme Court Leaves the CDC's Moratorium on Evictions in Place," *National Public Radio* (June 29). https://www.npr.org/2021/06/29/1003268497/the-supreme-court-leaves-the-cdcs-moratorium-on-evictions-in-place.

Trickey, Erick. 2020. "How Baltimore Is Experimenting Its Way Out of the Food Desert," *Politico* (January 23). https://www.politico.com/news/magazine/2020/01/23/baltimore-food-desert-policy-100121.

Tronto, Joan C. 1989. "Women and Caring: What Can Feminists Learn about Morality from Caring?" In *Gender/Body/Knowledge: Feminist Reconstructions of Being and Knowing*, edited by Alison M. Jaggar and Susan R. Bordo, pp. 172–87. New Brunswick, NJ: Rutgers University Press.

Tronto, Joan C. 1993. *Moral Boundaries: A Political Argument for an Ethic of Care*. New York: Routledge.

Tronto, Joan C. 2013. *Caring Democracy: Markets, Equality, and Justice*. New York: New York University Press.

Tronto, Joan C. 2015. *Who Cares? How to Reshape a Democratic Politics*. Ithaca, NY: Cornell University Press.

True, Sarah, Juliette Cubanski, Rachel Garfield, Matthew Rae, Gary Claxton, Priya Chidambaram, and Kendal Orgera. 2020. "COVID-19 and Workers at Risk: Examining the Long-Term Care Workforce" (April 23). Washington, DC: Kaiser Family Foundation. https://www.kff.org/report-section/covid-19-and-workers-at-risk-examining-the-long-term-care-workforce-issue-brief/.

Tuck, Kimberly D., and Jennifer E. Moore. 2019. "Understanding Long-Term Services and Supports in Medicaid" (October). Washington, DC: Institute for Medicaid Innovation. Accessed via https://www.medicaidinnovation.org/news/item/new-report-on-long-term-services-and-supports-in-medicaid-shows-trends-of-growing-population-and-opportunities-for-care

US Bureau of Labor Statistics. 2016. "Volunteering in the United States, 2015." https://www.bls.gov/news.release/volun.nr0.htm.

US Bureau of Labor Statistics. 2019a. "A Profile of the Working Poor, 2017" (April). https://www.bls.gov/opub/reports/working-poor/2017/home.htm.

US Bureau of Labor Statistics. 2019b. "Union Members—2018." https://www.bls.gov/news.release/pdf/union2.pdf.

US Department of Agriculture, 2020. "Official USDA Food Plans: Cost of Food at Home at Four Levels, U.S. Average, March 2020" (April). https://www.fns.usda.gov/cnpp/usda-food-plans-cost-food-reports-monthly-reports.

US Department of Health and Human Services, Administration on Aging. 2015. "A Profile of Older Americans: 2015." https://acl.gov/aging-and-disability-in-america/data-and-research/profile-older-americans.

US Department of Health & Human Services, Centers for Medicare & Medicaid Services. 2020. "Medicare & You 2021: The Official U.S. Government Medicare Handbook" (December). https://www.medicare.gov/Pubs/pdf/10050-Medicare-and-You.pdf.

US Department of Health & Human Services, Administration for Children and Families, Administration on Children, Youth, and Families, Children's Bureau. 2021. "Child Maltreatment 2019." https://www.acf.hhs.gov/cb/report/child-maltreatment-2019.

US Department of Housing and Urban Development. 2019. "Annual Report to Congress Regarding the Financial Status of the FHA Mutual Mortgage Insurance Program, Fiscal Year 2019." https://www.hud.gov/fhammifrpt.

US Department of Housing and Urban Development. 2020a. "Budget in Brief: Fiscal Year 2021." https://www.hud.gov/budget.

US Department of Housing and Urban Development. 2020b. "The 2019 Annual Homeless Assessment Report (AHAR) to Congress." https://files.hudexchange.info/resources/documents/2019-AHAR-Part-1.pdf.

US Department of Housing and Urban Development. 2020c. "Worst Case Housing Needs: 2019 Report to Congress" (June). https://www.huduser.gov/portal/publications/worst-case-housing-needs-2020.html.

324

BIBLIOGRAPHY

United States Conference of Catholic Bishops. 2015. "Forming Consciences for Faithful Citizenship: A Call to Political Responsibility from the Catholic Bishops of the United States." http://www.usccb.org/issues-and-action/faithful-citizenship/upload/forming-consciences-for-faithful-citizenship.pdf.

Valenti, Joe, and Eliza Schultz. 2016. "How Predatory Debt Traps Threaten Vulnerable Families" (October 6). Washington, DC: Center for American Progress. https://www.americanprogress.org/issues/economy/reports/2016/10/06/145629/how-predatory-debt-traps-threaten-vulnerable-families/.

Van de Water, Paul, and Kathleen Romig. 2020. "Social Security Benefits Are Modest" (January 8). Washington, DC: Center on Budget and Policy Priorities. https://www.cbpp.org/research/social-security/social-security-benefits-are-modest.

Veghte, Benjamin W., Alexandra L. Bradley, Marc Cohen, and Heidi Hartmann (eds.). 2019. *Designing Universal Family Care: State-Based Social Insurance Programs for Early Child Care and Education, Paid Family and Medical Leave, and Long-Term Services and Supports.* Washington, DC: National Academy of Social Insurance. https://www.nasi.org/research/caregiving/designing-universal-family-care-state-based-social-insurance-programs-for-early-child-care-and-education-paid-family-and-medical-leave-and-long-term-services-and-supports/.

Venkatesh, Sudhir Alladi. 2002. *American Project: The Rise and Fall of a Modern Ghetto.* Cambridge, MA: Harvard University Press.

Venkattil, Munsif, and Jeffrey Dastin. 2018. "Amazon's Jeff Bezos Commits $2 Billion to Help Homeless, Pre-schools," *Reuters* (September 13). https://www.reuters.com/article/us-bezos-philanthrophy/amazons-jeff-bezos-commits-2-billion-to-help-homeless-pre-schools-idUSKCN1LT2MN.

Vogel, David. 1983. "The Power of Business in America: A Re-appraisal," *British Journal of Political Science* 13, 1 (January): 19–43.

Wade, Holly. 2012. "Small Business Problems & Priorities." Washington, DC: National Federation of Independent Business. https://www.nfib.com/Portals/0/PDF/AllUsers/research/studies/small-business-problems-priorities-2012-nfib.pdf.

Wade, Holly. 2016. "Small Business Problems & Priorities." Washington, DC: National Federation of Independent Business. https://www.nfib.com/assets/NFIB-Problems-and-Priorities-2016.pdf.

Waldfogel, Jane. 2013. "The Safety Net for Families with Children." In *Legacies of the War on Poverty*, edited by Martha J. Bailey and Sheldon Danziger, pp. 153–78. New York: Russell Sage Foundation.

Walker, Alexis N. 2020. *Divided Unions: The Wagner Act, Federalism, and Organized Labor.* Philadelphia: University of Pennsylvania Press.

Walker, Theresa, and Jordan Graham. 2018. "What Happens When Homeless People Are Sent to Motels? Some Are Welcomed, Some Treated Warily, Some Kicked Out," *The Mercury News* (February 28). https://www.mercurynews.com/2018/02/28/what-happens-when-homeless-people-are-sent-to-motels-some-are-welcomed-some-treated-warily-some-kicked-out/.

Walzer, Michael. 1986. "Toward a Theory of Social Assignments." In *American Society: Public and Private Responsibilities*, edited by Winthrop Knowlton and Richard Zeckhauser, pp. 79–96. Cambridge, MA: Ballinger.

Ward, Deborah E. 2005. *The White Welfare State: The Racialization of U.S. Welfare Policy.* Ann Arbor: University of Michigan Press.

Warraich, Haider. 2017. *Modern Death: How Medicine Changed the End of Life.* New York: St. Martins.

Warraich, Haider J. 2021. "For-profit Nursing Homes and Hospices Are a Bad Deal for Older Americans," *STAT* (April 19). https://www.statnews.com/2021/04/19/for-profit-nursing-homes-hospices-bad-deal-older-americans/.

Waterhouse, Benjamin C. 2014. *Lobbying America: The Politics of Business from Nixon to NAFTA.* Princeton, NJ: Princeton University Press.

Watkins-Hayes, Celeste, and Elyse Kovalsky. 2016. "The Discourse of Deservingness: Morality and the Dilemmas of Poverty Relief in Debate and Practice." In *The Oxford Handbook of the Social Science of Poverty*, edited by David Brady and Linda M. Burton, pp. 193–220. New York: Oxford University Press.

Watts, Molly O'Malley, MaryBeth Musumeci, and Priya Chidambaram. 2020. "Medicaid Home and Community-Based Services Enrollment and Spending" (February 4). Washington, DC: Kaiser Family Foundation. https://www.kff.org/report-section/medicaid-home-and-community-based-services-enrollment-and-spending-issue-brief/.

Watts, Molly O'Malley, MaryBeth Musumeci, and Priya Chidambaram. 2021. "State Variation in Medicaid LTSS Policy Choices and Implications for Upcoming Policy Debates" (February 26). Washington, DC: Kaiser Family Foundation. https://www.kff.org/report-section/state-variation-in-medicaid-ltss-policy-choices-and-implications-for-upcoming-policy-deba tes-issue-brief/.

Weaver, R. Kent. 2000. *Ending Welfare As We Know It*. Washington, DC: Brookings Institution Press.

Weinfield, Nancy S., Gregory Mills, Christine Borger, Maeve Gearing, Theodore Macaluso, Jill Montaquila, and Sheila Zedlewski. 2014. "Hunger in America 2014" (August). Washington, DC: Feeding America. https://www.feedingamerica.org/research/hun ger-in-america.

Weingarten, Randi. 2018. "A Moral Imperative: Ending Poverty," Medium (May 20). https://med ium.com/@rweingarten/a-moral-imperative-ending-poverty-d4a681bda83d.

Weir, Margaret, and Jessica Schirmer. 2018. "America's Two Worlds of Welfare: Subnational Institutions and Social Assistance in Metropolitan America," *Perspectives on Politics* 16, 2 (June): 380–99.

Weiss, Elaine, Griffin Murphy, and Leslie I. Boden. 2019. "Workers' Compensation Benefits, Costs, and Coverage—2017 Data." Washington, DC: National Academy of Social Insurance. https://www.nasi.org/research/2019/report-workers'-compensation-benefits-costs-cover age---2017.

Welna, David. 2014. "The War over Poverty: A Deep Divide on How to Help," *National Public Radio* (January 11). https://www.npr.org/2014/01/11/261566403/the-war-over-poverty-a-deep-divide-on-how-to-help.

Werner, Erica. 2021. "Democrats' Messaging Shifts as They Pass Biden Stimulus Bill: From Economic Crisis Rescue to Poverty Relief," *Washington Post* (March 10). https://www.washingtonpost.com/us-policy/2021/03/10/stimulus-bill-transformation-poverty-covid-relief/.

Wetts, Rachel, and Robb Willer. 2018. "Privilege on the Precipice: Perceived Racial Status Threats Lead White Americans to Oppose Welfare Programs," *Social Forces* 97, 2 (December): 793–822.

Wheaton, Laura, Linda Giannarelli, and Ilham Dehry. 2021. "2021 Poverty Projections: Assessing the Impact of Benefits and Stimulus Measures" (July 28). Washington, DC: Urban Institute. https://www.urban.org/research/publication/2021-poverty-projections-assessing-impact-benefits-and-stimulus-measures.

White, Thomas Joseph. 2017. *The Light of Christ: An Introduction to Catholicism*. Washington, DC: Catholic University of America Press.

Whittaker, Julie M., and Katelin P. Isaacs. 2019. "Unemployment Insurance: Programs and Benefits," Congressional Research Service Report RL33362 (October 18). Accessed from ProQuest Congressional database.

Whoriskey, Peter. 2018. "'A Way of Monetizing Poor People': How Private Equity Firms Make Money Offering Loans to Cash-Strapped Americans," *Washington Post* (July 1). https://www.washingtonpost.com/business/economy/a-way-of-monetizing-poor-people-how-private-equity-firms-make-money-offering-loans-to-cash-strapped-americans/2018/07/01/5f7e2670-5dee-11e8-9ee3-49d6d4814c4c_story.html.

Wiener-Bronner, Danielle, and Chris Isidore. 2018. "Amazon Announces $15 Minimum Wage for All US Employees," *CNN* (October 3). https://www.cnn.com/2018/10/02/tech/amazon-minimum-wage/index.html.

Williams, Erica, Samantha Waxman, and Juliette Legendre. 2020. States Can Adopt or Expand Earned Income Tax Credits to Build a Stronger Future Economy (March 9). Washington, DC: Center on Budget and Policy Priorities. https://www.cbpp.org/research/state-budget-and-tax/states-can-adopt-or-expand-earned-income-tax-credits-to-build-a.

Williams, Fiona. 2001. "In and Beyond New Labour: Towards a New Political Ethics of Care," *Critical Social Policy* 21, 4 (November): 467–93.

Wilson, J. Matthew. 1999. "'Blessed Are The Poor': American Protestantism and Attitudes Toward Poverty and Welfare," *Southeastern Political Review* (September) 27, 3: 421–37.

Winter, Nicholas. 2008. *Dangerous Frames: How Ideas About Race and Gender Shape Public Opinion.* Chicago: University of Chicago Press.

Wiseman, Michael. 2019. "The Supplemental Nutrition Assistance Program." In *Strengths of the Social Safety Net in the Great Recession: Supplemental Nutrition Assistance and Unemployment Insurance,* edited by Christopher J. O'Leary, David Stevens, Stephen A. Wandner, and Michael Wiseman, pp. 93–155. Kalamazoo, MI: W.E. Upjohn Institute for Employment Research.

Witko, Christopher, Jana Morgan, Nathan J. Kelly, and Peter K. Enns. 2021. *Hijacking the Agenda: Economic Power and Political Influence.* New York: Russell Sage Foundation.

Wlezien, Christopher. 2005. "On the Salience of Political Issues: The Problem with 'Most Important Problem,'" *Electoral Studies* 24, 4 (December): 555–79.

Wogan, J. B. 2018. "Trump Budget Calls for Work Requirements for Housing Aid," *Governing* (February 12). https://www.governing.com/topics/health-human-services/gov-trump-work-requirement-housing-voucher.html.

Woodbury, Stephen A. 2015. "Unemployment Insurance." In *The Oxford Handbook of U.S. Social Policy,* edited by Daniel Béland, Christopher Howard, and Kimberly J. Morgan, pp. 471–90. New York: Oxford University Press.

Woolhandler, Steffie, and David U. Himmelstein. 2017. "The Relationship of Health Insurance and Mortality: Is Lack of Insurance Deadly?" *Annals of Internal Medicine* 167, 6 (September): 424–31.

Workman, Simon, and Steven Jessen-Howard. 2018. "Understanding the True Cost of Child Care for Infants and Toddlers" (November 15). Washington, DC: Center for American Progress. https://www.americanprogress.org/issues/early-childhood/reports/2018/11/15/460970/understanding-true-cost-child-care-infants-toddlers/.

Wuthnow, Robert. 1991. *Acts of Compassion: Caring for Others and Helping Ourselves.* Princeton, NJ: Princeton University Press.

Wuthnow, Robert. 2004. *Saving America? Faith-Based Services and the Future of Civil Society.* Princeton, NJ: Princeton University Press.

Wuthnow, Robert, and John H. Evans (eds.). 2002. *The Quiet Hand of God: Faith-Based Activism and the Role of Mainline Protestantism.* Berkeley: University of California Press.

Yan, Holly, and Madeline Holcombe. 2021. "Covid-19 Deaths and Hospitalizations Are Increasing, and the Vast Majority Were Not Vaccinated," *CNN* (July 20). https://www.cnn.com/2021/07/19/health/us-coronavirus-monday/index.html.

Zito, Salena. 2018. "How America Is Fighting Back against Predatory Lending," *New York Post* (January 13). https://nypost.com/2018/01/13/how-america-is-fighting-back-against-predatory-lending/.

INDEX

For the benefit of digital users, indexed terms that span two pages (e.g., 52–53) may, on occasion, appear on only one of those pages.